Skills for Law Students

Skills for Law Students

Helen Carr, Sarah Carter, Kirsty Horsey

OXFORD
UNIVERSITY PRESS

OXFORD
UNIVERSITY PRESS

Great Clarendon Street, Oxford OX2 6DP

Oxford University Press is a department of the University of Oxford. It furthers the University's objective of excellence in research, scholarship, and education by publishing worldwide in

Oxford New York

Auckland Cape Town Dar es Salaam Hong Kong Karachi Kuala Lumpur Madrid Melbourne Mexico City Nairobi New Delhi Shanghai Taipei Toronto

With offices in

Argentina Austria Brazil Chile Czech Republic France Greece Guatemala Hungary Italy Japan Poland Portugal Singapore South Korea Switzerland Thailand Turkey Ukraine Vietnam

Oxford is a registered trade mark of Oxford University Press in the UK and in certain other countries

Published in the United States by Oxford University Press Inc., New York

First published 2009

British Library Cataloguing in Publication Data
Data available

Library of Congress Cataloging in Publication Data
Data available

Typeset by Newgen Imaging Systems (P) Ltd, Chennai, India
Printed in Great Britain
on acid-free paper by

Ashford Colour Press Ltd., Gosport, Hampshire

ISBN 978–0–19–953219–3

10 9 8 7 6 5 4

» How to use *Skills for Law Students*

Skills for Law Students covers all of the study skills and legal skills you'll need to develop during the course of your law degree.

There are 32 chapters mirrored in this book and on the website and each chapter deals with a separate skill. Each chapter contains two key elements:

The first is the 'text': an overview of what that skill is; why it is important; and what you need to do to develop it. This text is all reproduced in this book.
The second are the 'activities': interactive tests which enable you to understand the topic better; to put the skills into practice; and to self-study and receive immediate feedback on your progress.

What is online?

Everything is online. If you prefer, you can simply use the printed resource to activate your online account and you can access 100% of the content online.

What is in the book?

The book contains all of the 'text' for each skill area, but does not contain the activities. You may find it easier or more convenient to read the text from the book and then log on to the website to complete the activities. We flag up in the book when there is a relevant activity online, so that you always know where the activities occur and what they are.

How do I access the website?

Access to the website is via a unique access code which is printed in a sealed card inside every book.

» How to access the website

Accessing the website is easy. Follow these four simple steps:

1. Tear off the strip on the activation card which is bound between the final page and the back cover of this book to reveal your unique activation code
2. Log onto your computer at https://subscriberservices.sams.oup.com/token
3. Enter your access code and activate your account
4. Fill in your details and choose a password to create your account.

Your account is now activated and you can begin studying!

Note

You will not need your activation code once your account has been set up. On subsequent log-ins you will just need your username and password.

Your account is accessible for the period stated on the access token at the back of the book. After that time your access will expire. Your access code can be redeemed once and is not transferable.

Registering your access code is very straightforward, but if you have any problems please call Customer Services on +44 (0)1865 353705.

» If I just use the book what am I missing?

Interactive activities

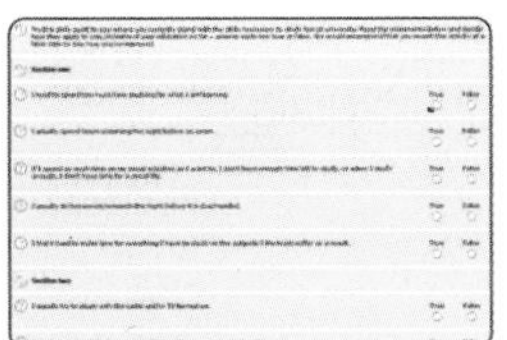

The site contains over 170 interactive activities which are designed to help you understand the topics better; to put the skills into practice; and to enable you to self-study and receive immediate feedback on your progress.

Why not get started with the 'skills audit' in the Introduction to test how much you already know about law and how law affects our day-to-day lives?

Video recordings

There are over 50 video recordings throughout the site for you to watch. These will not only add more variety and interest to your learning; they will also enable you to see good and bad practice of some of the more practical skills (such as presentation skills and mooting).

The video clips also show you current law students and legal practitioners reflecting on the skills they have developed and which have become key to their careers.

Reflective diary

At various points throughout the site you will be encouraged to reflect upon something you have just read or done. You can then click on the reflective diary icon (which appears on every page) to log your thoughts. This could then feed into your personal development plan at university.

Hyperlinked glossary

We have provided definitions for any words or phrases we think you might not be familiar with. Simply click on the word to see the definition before continuing with your reading.

Cross-references

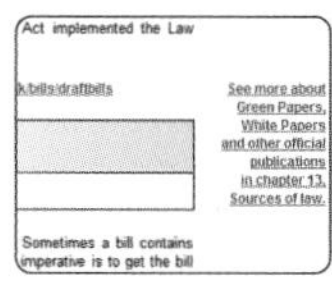

Whatever you undertake in your studies, you will realise that a combination of different skills are required for most tasks. Some skills are very closely related to others and we highlight links between topics throughout the resource with numerous hyperlinked cross-references. This will enable you to navigate your way around the site and to see how various topics interlink.

Your scores

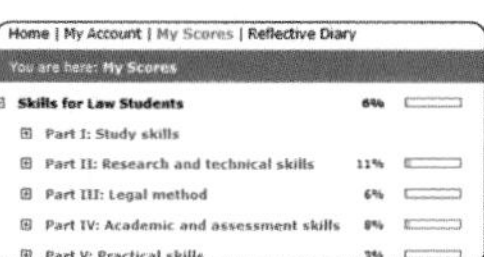

Most of the activities you undertake will provide you with immediate answers, feedback, and scoring. The feedback is specifically tailored to the answer you choose.

Your scores are recorded on the 'my scores' page. This page will be updated every time you complete an activity and you can re-take the activities as many times as you like. Why not use this page to evaluate where your strengths and weaknesses lie and which areas you may want to focus on?

» About the authors

Helen Carr

Helen studied law at university and then qualified as a solicitor. She practised for 12 years before starting a career as an academic. Her current post is as a senior lecturer with Kent Law School. Her specialism is social welfare law, particularly housing, and she teaches public law and property law to undergraduates. She has taught law to both undergraduate and postgraduate students including many non-law students and she has co-directed a Legal Practice Course. She is a part-time lawyer chair with the Residential Property Tribunal Service and she was also legal adviser to the Commissioner for the Social Fund for four years. She worked for four years at the Law Commission as a member of the public law team working on the reform of housing law. She has co-authored a variety of law books, including *Law for Social Workers* published by Oxford University Press, *Law and Supported Housing* published by Legal Action Group and a commentary on the Housing Act 2004 published by Jordans.

She recently completed an MA with the Open University on social policy and criminology so has recent experience of the horror of exams and essays.

Sarah Carter

Sarah Carter was law librarian at the University of Kent from 1985 until she retired in 2006. She has been interested in electronic legal information since its early days. Her Lawlinks website is an internationally recognised guide to web-based legal resources and has received several awards. Much of her work has involved the teaching of skills to law students, both in the classroom and online. In the course of this she designed online resources for teaching legal skills, and became interested in the concept of sharing resources with other people and institutions.

She has written extensively on the subject of law on the internet and legal databases, as well as teaching (both as part of her job and freelance) and has given a number of conference presentations.

Kirsty Horsey

Kirsty studied law at university and then decided not to go into practice. Instead, she started a research Master's degree in medical/family law – which quickly became 'too big', so was converted to a PhD. While researching for her PhD, she taught seminars to undergraduates at Kent Law School and became involved in the teaching and co-ordination of the VALUE programme for law, a scheme launched by the University of Kent to help struggling first-year students get through the year and enter confidently into the second stage of their degrees. She also took over the running of the internal mooting programme, set up, ran and taught on the Foundation in Law course, for students entering the university (usually from overseas) without the requisite qualifications to begin degree-level study, and helped students set up an in-house student mentoring scheme. She is currently a lecturer in law at Kent Law School, teaching Obligations 1 and 2 (contract and tort) to undergraduate students across all years, as well as some family law. She is co-author, with Erika Rackley, of *Tort Law* (Oxford University Press, 2009). Her main research interests still lie in the overlap of medical and family law, particularly in the area of assisted reproduction and she has co-edited a book on the review of the law in this area: *Human Fertilisation and Embryology: Reproducing Regulation* (Routledge-Cavendish, 2007).

» Preface

It would be difficult for us to present this new online resource and accompanying textbook as the culmination of a long planned endeavour. It is more the result of a series of fortuitous encounters, serendipitous conversations and shared concerns. Our drivers are twofold: first, a belief that the diversity of student experience prior to entering higher education means that lecturers cannot, if indeed they ever could, take what students know for granted; and second, the realisation that transformations in technology mean that the textbook, if it is to remain a useful tool for the student, must evolve. It needs to respond to the immediate needs of the students in a useful and purposeful manner.

We have chosen to focus on legal skills in part because they provide an opportunity for us to test our ideas and to see what can be achieved, and in part because we are all becoming so much more aware of the underpinning role of skills in ensuring academic and vocational success. However, we do think our approach could be transferred to textbooks covering substantive law areas, and we look forward to watching new projects emerge.

However innovative our writing task has been, a preface is still the proper place to deliver traditional courtesies. This book would not have been possible without the support of our colleagues and students at Kent Law School. They have been enthusiastic and generous. Particular thanks go to Nick Jackson and Rosemary Hunter for agreeing to be filmed, and to Alan Thomson and John Wightman whose shared experience and wisdom have ensured that teaching, learning and students remain as important as research in our law school agenda. Our students gave up weekends in the summer to participate in the project and we are grateful and wish them all the best in their future careers. Many of our friends in the legal profession gave up their time too. We know how busy they are and appreciate their involvement. We think their perspective is particularly valuable for students beginning their legal education. There is one person without whom this project would not have happened. Sarah Viner has been an extraordinary editor; she has enthused, organised, and cajoled us to ensure that we have given the best we could to this project. She has worked so hard to help us achieve our ambitions and we are very very grateful.

We would also like to thank each other. It's been a real joy working as a team, learning from each other, and sharing experiences which between us cover a huge range of legal education.

Helen would like to thank her family. Richard and Rowan have been more interested in this project than any other she has been involved in, and their observations and contributions have been invaluable. She would like to thank Hugh Brayne and Stephen Cottle for their patience when their projects have been delayed because the project took more time than planned. She would also like to thank two particularly gifted teachers of law, Leslie Sheinman and Mic Jeeves who taught her to take legal education seriously and whose ideas and enthusiasms she has drawn on, perhaps more than she has been aware, throughout the development of this resource.

Sarah is indebted to her colleagues in the law librarian profession who have supported her over the years, in particular Sue Pettit, Cathie Jackson and Steven Whittle, who know how much she owes them, and Guy Holborn, whose erudite and witty book on legal skills is always at her right hand. Her long association with Kent Law School, and Nick Jackson in particular, has been inspirational, and she would also like to extend thanks to all the law and technology people at Warwick University. Finally, her part of this enterprise is dedicated to her twin grand-daughters, Agnes and Molly, who arrived just in time to distract her from the work in hand, and who are therefore totally responsible for any deficiencies.

Kirsty has many people to thank, some of whom have already been mentioned, but it can be added that their teaching while she was at Kent inspired her to remain in academia and generated her passion for learning law. Erika Rackley and Karen Devine also deserve thanks – for their input and the answers they gave to various questions as this project progressed. And, last but not least, thanks go to Mike Walters, who ended up holding the baby for many weekends and much of the summer. This book is dedicated to Francis, who was conceived around the same time as the idea for this project and born during the writing of it.

Each chapter of this resource was reviewed prior to publication by a number of academics and e-learning co-ordinators, and we would particularly like to thank the following people for their constructive feedback:

Ray Arthur, University of Teesside
Simon Askey, University of London
Sheena Banks, University of Sheffield
Vanessa Bettinson, De Montfort University
Jo Boylan-Kemp, Nottingham Trent University
Deveral Capps, University of Northumbria
Sandra Clarke, University of Greenwich
Karen Counsell, University of Glamorgan
Dennis Dowding, Bournemouth University
Sam Halliday, University of Liverpool
Nicola Isaacs, University of Plymouth
Lesley Lomax, Sheffield Hallam University
Stewart Motha, University of Kent
Janette Porteous, University of Lincoln
Sue Prince, University of Exeter

Tony Wragg, University of Derby

Lucy Yeatman, University of Greenwich

We are also grateful to the following people for sharing their expertise, time, and experience in contributing to the audio and video clips which form a key part of this resource:

Hunsiye Akdogan

Tamsin Arthur

Poonam Bhari

Jill Evans

Hayley Gow

Tom Holmes

Rosemary Hunter

Nick Jackson

Ed Kirton-Darling

Stephanie Le Couteur

Viv Matthews

Sarah McCracken

Berenice Mulvanny

Mark Pritchard

Jon Viner

Pete Walters

Patrick Whetter

Bianca Wu

Finally – one further significant tradition. Despite all the help we have received, we know that mistakes remain in the text. We take full responsibility, we would be grateful if you could draw them to our attention, and we apologise if they confuse. Despite them, we hope you enjoy this resource and it provides you with a sound foundation for a stimulating legal education.

Helen Carr
Sarah Carter
Kirsty Horsey
Canterbury

» Acknowledgments

Grateful acknowledgement is made to all the authors and publishers of copyright material that appears in this online resource and accompanying textbook, and in particular to the following for permission to reprint material from the sources indicated:

Blackwell Publishing: extracts from H Reece, 'The End of Domestic Violence' (2006), 96 (5) *MLR* 770

Professor Dame Hazel Genn: PowerPoint slides written to accompany the presentation 'Mediation in England'

Guardian News & Media Ltd: article 'Privy Council overrules Lords to put judgment back on track: Ruling reverses decision on provocation: Lawyer says murder move is retrograde step', The Guardian, 30 January 2006, copyright © Guardian News & Media Ltd 2006

Tom Holmes: essay entitled 'The emergence of proportionality in judicial review has led to greater protection of human rights. However, it has also distorted the institutional balance between the judiciary, administration and Parliament.'

Oxford University Press: extract from M Lunney and K Oliphant, *Tort Law Text and Materials* (Oxford University Press, 2007)

Oxford University Press and the Faculty of Law at the University of Oxford: Oxford Journal of Legal Studies front cover

Richard Alcock: example student essay on the use of statutory interpretation in *Stevenson* v *Rogers*

Routledge: material adapted from A Franklyn-Stokes and S. E. Newstead, 'Undergraduate Cheating: Who Does What and Why' (1995), 20 (2) *Studies in Higher Education* 159

Sage Publications Ltd and the author: Erika Rackley, 'Difference in the House of Lords' (2006), 15 (2) *Social and Legal Studies* 163, copyright © Sage Publications Ltd 2006

The University of Michigan Press: exercise adapted from J. M. Swales and C. B. Feak, *Academic Writing for Graduate Students: Essential Tasks and Skills* (The University of Michigan Press, 2004)

The University of Kent Unit for Enhancement of Learning and Teaching for advice on plagiarism. www.kent.ac.uk/uelt/ai.

Every effort has been made to trace and contact copyright holders prior to publication. If notified, the publisher will undertake to rectify any errors or omissions at the earliest opportunity.

» Outline contents

» Detailed contents

Part 2. Research and technical skills

Part 3. Legal method

Part 4. Academic and assessment skills

www.oxfordinteract.com

Chapter 1

Introduction

Suddenly it hits you! After a few weeks, you realise that everything they told you is true. Life at university is not at all like school or college. It's not just the independence, and the new friends, it's the studying as well. At school or college you knew the ropes, and if you did not do what you were supposed to do, then the teachers made it pretty clear where you were going wrong. They seemed to care if you were falling behind and were always on-hand for help and advice. At university, there are plenty of people telling you things, and plenty of things you have to do, but the link between what you are being told and what you are to do is not always made very clear. And you may have a growing unease that you have not quite got what it is that is expected of law students. And whilst you are pretty clear that the only person who is going to sort it out is you, you aren't quite sure where to start.

Of course, your lecturers do care and they will help, but you will only get a lot of extra attention if you are really in difficulties. Much of what you need to know, lecturers haven't got time to tell you, and anyway, they won't 'spoon-feed' you; they expect you to take responsibility for your own learning – which is what university is really all about. Many students who start a law degree are shocked when they get their first marks and feedback. If you did well at school, you may expect to do equally well at university. And for some people, it does come naturally. For others, however, it is only by consciously acquiring the necessary skills that the results begin to show.

This online resource and accompanying textbook is designed to help you take that responsibility. University study requires you to 'step up' from the level you did things while at school – we aim to help you to be able to do that and to help you fulfil your lecturers' expectations – to deal with the gap between being told about the law and understanding it. In other words, this resource is designed to help you begin to develop the skills of a lawyer. Two points you should note here:

- We say 'begin' to develop the skills necessary for law – not because we have limited aspirations, or because this resource is shallow, but because skills training and development is something that can (and should) be continuously built on throughout your academic and working life.

» glossary

- We say 'lawyer' to include everyone who uses the law in any context, rather than simply referring to solicitors or barristers. You can be a lawyer without going into practice. Whatever your intentions are once you have completed your degree, our concern is the skills you need to succeed in your degree, as well as subsequently, whether in law or in any other career path.

We think law is special – not only because we have spent all our working lives researching law, practising law and teaching law – but also because it demands a set of specialised skills. Most degree courses require that you be able to research adequately, write and speak fluently, work in groups and alone to solve problems and handle and analyse factual information. Law requires this and more to be done in the context of a highly specific discipline. Lawyers must be able to research the law, getting up-to-date information in a rapidly changing environment; they must be able to communicate technical concepts in a persuasive and authoritative way; they must be able to employ legal reasoning to analyse and advise on complex problems in a wide range of areas; at times they need to work as part of interdisciplinary teams; at other times – for instance when judging – they must even be prepared to take sole responsibility for an individual's future. So you can see why the three years of your degree are just the beginning of the acquisition of legal skills. However, these three years do provide you with a crucial foundation for anything you choose to do in the future.

It can be very daunting starting a law degree. It will seem like there is so much you need to know, and so much you need to do – and you will mainly be concerned with getting things right. That said, one of the things we hope to show you is that there is not always a 'right' and 'wrong' when studying law – often it is the approach you take that is more vital than anything else.

We will start by sharing the 10 things that we wish we had known in our first few weeks of studying law.

- Lawyers don't say versus – they say 'and' or 'against' even though there is a 'v' between the names of the parties to a case.

» glossary

- Lecturers aren't interested in how well or how badly you did at school. Starting your degree is like a blank slate – and everyone is on a level playing field.
- Being enthusiastic about your studies is more likely to impress your lecturers than being right – at least at this stage of your degree.
- Everyone finds the first term of studying law difficult. It's just that your peers aren't cool enough to admit it, and your lecturers can't remember.
- Judges don't 'squash' decisions of administrative bodies – they 'quash' them.
- The organised tour of the law library saves a lot of embarrassment later in the term.
- The burden of proof in a criminal case is beyond reasonable doubt; in a civil case it is on the balance of probabilities.
- You have been party to a contract (even though you might not have realised it) – each time you buy a bus ticket, go to the cinema or a club, or buy a mobile phone, you have entered into a contract.
- Sometimes, for instance when you rent a house, or get arrested, or someone starts telling you about their divorce, it is better not to admit that you are studying law. It only gets you into trouble.

» glossary

- Bills are made up of clauses; Acts have sections; Schedules are attached 'to' the Act, rather than being part 'of' the Act.

Another thing you need to know is that your entry qualifications have already given you a lot of the study skills you need to succeed in law. Of course not everyone's skills levels are the same so, before we go any further, we want you to assess where **you** think you are in terms of the skills you need for your degree, using a simple activity – a 'skills audit'.

Activity 1 and 2

Now try the skills audit to see where you currently stand with the skills necessary to study law at university.

There are two versions of the skills audit, depending on whether you have or have not studied law before. If, for example, you have done A level law and think you know something about the law (note: the questions are not legal questions, they are about you!), choose activity 1A. If, however, you have never studied any law and think that you know little or nothing about law, choose activity 1B. The purpose of this audit is to identify those areas where you may lack study skills. For this reason, it might be worth carrying out the test again in 2-3 months time to check your progress.

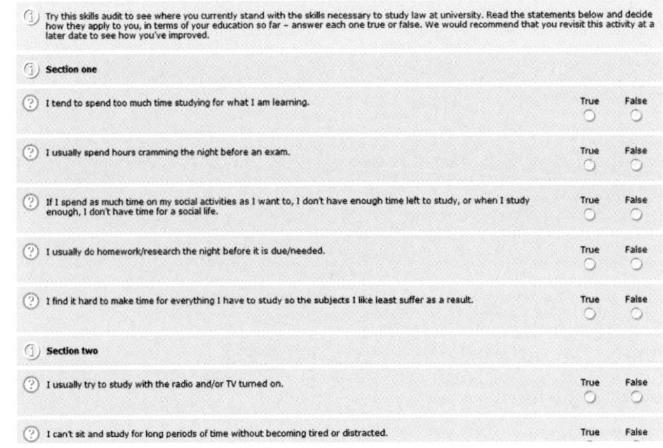

Try this skills audit to see where you currently stand with the skills necessary to study law at university. Read the statements below and decide how they apply to you, in terms of your education so far – answer each one true or false. We would recommend that you revisit this activity at a later date to see how you've improved.

Section one

Statement	True	False
I tend to spend too much time studying for what I am learning.	○	○
I usually spend hours cramming the night before an exam.	○	○
If I spend as much time on my social activities as I want to, I don't have enough time left to study, or when I study enough, I don't have time for a social life.	○	○
I usually do homework/research the night before it is due/needed.	○	○
I find it hard to make time for everything I have to study so the subjects I like least suffer as a result.	○	○

Section two

Statement	True	False
I usually try to study with the radio and/or TV turned on.	○	○
I can't sit and study for long periods of time without becoming tired or distracted.		

What skills will I need to develop?

We have given you an indication of some of the complex set of skills that lawyers require.

Activity 3

What skills do you think you, as a lawyer, will need? Write a list of the skills you think should be in the 'top ten'.

Go online to see our thoughts on this question.

There are also some things that lawyers as lawyers need to know and to know how to do. These are things that you will learn variously throughout your substantive law modules, but include any, or all, of the following:

- where law comes from
- the functions of the legal system
- the context of the law: social, economic, political, historical
- critiques of and perspectives on the law
- the law itself (e.g. 'criminal law', 'property law', 'tort law' etc.)

You will see from the list above that it is not enough simply to know what the law **is**. This comes last on our list for a reason; for it is only by understanding the history, development and context of the law that we have that we can truly understand the law itself. Many people go through life simply accepting the law for what it is: the attitude seems to be that if that is how it is then that is how it should be. Law students in particular seem to fall into this trap – although not all of them – in their desire to know all the law there is to know. There is a lot of law to learn – there are many different disciplines of law and you will have to study a fair number of them in order to obtain a law degree. But being able to recall the substance of the law should not be the end of the story – what you **do** with the law is equally, if not more, important, and to develop the skills to do something with the law requires a greater level of understanding than simply knowing the law. The best students – who will be the best lawyers – are those who think about the law, who question it and challenge it and the assumptions behind it.

Activity 4

Now watch a number of legal practitioners talking about their careers and the skills which are important to them.

What do we mean by skills?

Skills training has become one of the key parts of education, seemingly at all levels. From schooling, through university and into the workplace, 'skills' seems to be the buzz word – the implication being that you'll get further if you gain and cultivate the necessary skills.

» glossary

In this resource we deal with three 'types' of skills. The first type comprises the general and transferable academic skills that you need to develop in order to gain a degree in any humanities, arts or social sciences degree. We have called these **study skills**. The second comprises those more specific to the research and study of law. We have grouped these into parts called **research and technical skills** – or tools – that you need in order to be able to study law effectively and **legal method skills**. Once you have acquired the basic skills, you need to be able to put them to use, for example for the purposes of assessment or demonstration. With this in mind, the fourth part deals with **academic and assessment skills** and the fifth part deals with other **practical skills** that, as a lawyer, you will need to develop.

Within the five parts, all of the skills outlined in the lists above are covered, perhaps more. However, you should also remember that there is a great deal of overlap between the general and specific, as well as some overlap between the skills themselves, despite our best efforts to separate them into coherent chapters. For this reason, you may see similar ideas in some chapters, as well as a great deal of cross-referencing.

Part 1: Study skills

The chapters in this part will help you with the things you need to get on top of just to be at university – it could equally have been called 'university skills'. Essentially this is 'the basics' – but this includes many areas that a lot of students coming to university think they have already mastered, or don't need to work on. Take 'Writing good English' as an example: as a skill, this often gets 'lost' when you don't actually sit down and write on a daily, or even weekly basis. As teachers, we know that there are a lot of common mistakes made – making this chapter a necessary one for us to include and one that you will get something from, no matter how good you think your writing style already is!

Cross reference See chapter 3, Writing good English.

Other chapters in this part may be helpful simply because university life is different – managing your own time, for example, will become a lot more of a priority! And you may not have a clue about the best way to approach taking notes from your lectures. Hopefully, the help we provide in the chapters in this part will help you to master the essential skills you need for university study as a whole.

» glossary

Parts 2 and 3: Research and technical skills and legal method

These two parts move on from looking at the general tools you need for university study to looking at the more specific skills you need in order to study law. This is divided into two parts. First, we look at some of the technical legal skills you will need to master – and those that, once you have mastered them, will make the rest of your study of law a lot easier! Legal research skills, such as accessing legal databases and using legal journals are vital both as a student of law and as a practitioner. Secondly, we move on to deal with some legal method skills that tend to get a bit lost by students in their desire to get everything 'right' or to know all there is to know about a legal discipline. Included here are chapters on thinking critically and creatively.

» glossary

Parts 4 and 5: Academic and assessment skills and practical skills

The final two parts could, in a sense, be said to do with assessment and demonstration of the skills you have acquired via the previous three parts. By this we do not necessarily only mean the kind of assessments that you hand in and get marks for, but any way you might be assessed, such as giving as presentation. Of course, like the majority of the skills dealt with in this resource, mastering these skills will stand you in good stead for your professional life. Here we include writing essays and dissertations, mooting, interviewing and making presentations, split

» glossary

» glossary

into two parts – one on academic and assessment skills and the other on the more practical-based skills.

How will this online resource help me?

There are a number of skills and self-help study books on the market. This is different in that it has everything we think you need to know in one place, while also having the benefits of being online where you can work through activities and actually interact with the skills you are meant to be developing. Other benefits of this resource over others include:

- It is written by a team who understand both that law is challenging in the early stages even for the brightest of students and that all of you have the ability to do very well in the subject.
- It is designed to help you take responsibility for your own learning, yet also provides you with the necessary guidance to stop you floundering in the dark.
- It provides a huge range of interactive activities, so that you can learn by listening, by thinking and by practising.
- The activities are grounded in areas of law which are compulsory in most law degrees. Therefore, as you complete the activities you will improve your skills and increase your knowledge of the subject.

Throughout the resource we also build on important understandings about learning skills that have been proved in research by educationalists:

» glossary

- Skills are not acquired by 'magic' – you need to work on them, particularly through proper preparation for seminars – but we help you learn how to focus your preparation.
- Skills improve with practice – so we give you plenty of opportunity to practise basic skills and confidence to apply those skills in your seminars and assessments.
- We learn skills through modelling ourselves on expert performers. Listen to how your lecturers talk about the law, how they use language, and how they approach cases. We provide you with examples of academic and practising lawyers talking about the law so you can learn through listening.
- We also learn through reflection on our own past performance – so we help you to give and receive constructive criticism.
- What seems like common sense to the experienced lawyer is a mystery to the novice – so we share our common sense about learning law.

» glossary

- Technical skills such as the ability to search electronic databases, citation skills etc., don't require the intellect of a brain surgeon. However, the sooner you acquire them, the sooner you will start to enjoy your studies.

Employability and skills

The vast majority of the skills in this book are those that you will need to have in the 'real world' of work. So, the sooner you begin to develop them at university, the sooner you will master them, and many of them will become second nature to you. Remember that university is training for life – although you may go on to law school for professional training as a lawyer and will have to further develop some of the skills we talk about, these skills are the building blocks of a successful career in whatever you choose to do. Even if you don't become a lawyer, the skills we help you with here will be vital. Having these skills will help you to stand out from the crowd and beat the competition.

Also remember that in as much as these skills are transferable, you will need to continually develop them. Your skills should show progression in much the same way as your knowledge should – there is always room for improvement! And an understanding that these skills – although we have separated them into sections and chapters – all overlap or interlink will help your development even further. Having these skills is not always something that can go on your CV, but they will make you more employable. Also, don't forget the 'hidden skills': those that we can't really tell you about, you just have to think where they fit in. For example, having the skill of being able to write a dissertation or extended essay shows that you have the 'hidden skill' of being able to work alone on a project for a concentrated period of time – definitely an asset to an employer. Similarly, an understanding of plagiarism and demonstrating that you have not engaged in this will suggest that you are honest and trustworthy – again an asset that potential employers will be looking for.

Cross reference
See chapter 25, Writing essays; and chapter 26, Writing dissertations.

Cross reference
For further information on plagiarism, see chapter 7.

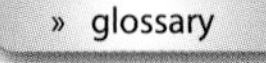

Activity 5

Now watch Viv Matthews, Head of Human Resources at Henmans LLP, talking about the skills she looks for in law graduates.

www.oxfordinteract.com

Part 1

Study skills

Chapter 2

Managing your time

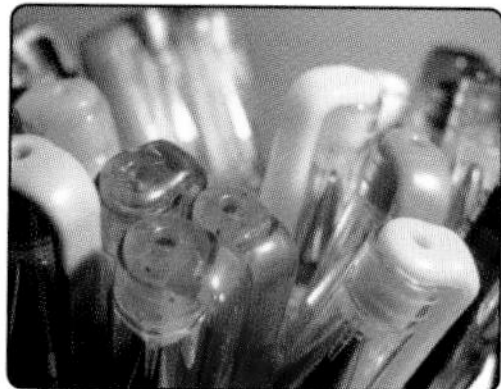

Rationale

Having good time management is essential at university. At school or college, you may have been used to a timetable whereby every day was full with lessons and other activities, but this will not be the case while studying for a degree. You will have timetabled lectures and seminars or tutorials, but these 'contact hours' will not take up the bulk of your time through the week as school hours did. A big part of doing a degree, particularly in law, is 'self-study' – which is exactly what it sounds like – that is, you are at university to **study** a subject in depth, rather than be **taught** about it in the same way you have been taught previously. The skills required for self-study are different from those required in your learning so far and you will find that you have a lot more time on your hands, which you may not at first know what to do with.

This being the case, you will need to be able to organise the bulk of your time yourself. You will need to be motivated and organised in order to be able to study effectively. Not all the information you will need to learn will come in the form of lectures – you will undoubtedly be asked to do a lot of reading and preparation and you will do best if you are ready for this. One of the absolute keys to success for capable students is **time management** and many students who find they are struggling or falling behind are able to improve by dealing with this.

This chapter is devised to:

- Explain why good time management is essential at university
- Help you to understand how much time you actually do need to spend on study
- Give you some tips about how to manage your time effectively.

» glossary

Cross reference
For further information, see chapter 15, Using law books, and chapter 6, Contributing to seminars and tutorials.

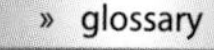

Learning to manage your time

You may think that you are quite organised and that time management is something that is quite easy to do. However, many university students find that this is not the case and that they often 'don't have time' to complete their reading or other assignments. Often they end up trying to do things the night before they need to, or spend one hour reading a chapter of a textbook or an article that should really take a couple of hours, and then not remembering any of it. Part of this is down to the complete change in the method of teaching and learning at university level – you will have much more of what will seem like 'free time' during the days. Added to that is a new independence, and while it is important to enjoy this, you must also realise that you are the one who must now be totally responsible for organising yourself. You will find that you need to learn how to manage your time.

Some of the things that you will have to make time for each week are:

- Lectures
- Seminars/tutorials
- Reading
- Preparation.

Other things that you may have to take into account are:

- Work for assessments
- Paid work

Don't panic

*Of course, you should always try and leave a bit of time for **rest** and **fun**!*

General time management

The best way to ensure that you have sufficient study time is with a **time management schedule**. Sitting down and thinking about the time you do have, and how much you can allocate to self-study per week is a valuable activity – as is drawing yourself up a proper timetable – building on the timetable of contact hours that you have.

How much time do I have?

Depending on the number of contact hours you have been timetabled per week, you should ideally aim for around 20–25 hours of independent study time per week, if you are a **full-time student**. Think about what hours are involved in a **full-time job**: about 35–40 hours (minimum – probably even more if you go into legal practice!) per week. So, say you have 12 contact hours per week, adding 25 hours of independent study to this would still only make 37 hours. Thinking in terms of Monday to Friday, this means less than 7.5 hours of 'work' (of all types, contact and independent) **per day** – which still, therefore, allows time for socialising and/or paid work in the evenings or at weekends. This is probably adequate for the amount of work you will need to do in an average week (although you may find that some weeks are harder than others, or that you need to do more when you have assessments coming up!); so if you are organised, you should have no problems getting all your preparatory work and assessments done. Of course, while you should aim to put about this much time aside for work, as students learn at different rates, you need to find out what is right for you to be able to cope with the work.

Note

Many students these days find that they need to have part-time paid work. How this fits in to your schedule is up to you but you may find that to find your 20–25 independent study hours per week, you have to jiggle your schedule a little. For example, if you have paid work during the day, you may find that some of your independent study hours have to be found in the evenings, or at the weekend.

Activity 1

The following activity is designed as a tool to enable you to visually realise how much time you spend on various activities – including those essential to day-to-day life – and, more importantly, to see how much time there is actually available for study. Many students lose sight of this, so we feel it is important to highlight it as soon as possible after starting university, as well as to keep it under review throughout your period of study.

The following activity is designed as a tool to enable you to visually realise how much time you spend on various activities – including those essential to day-to-day life – and, more importantly, to see how much time there is actually available for study. Many students lose sight of this, so we feel it is important to highlight it as soon as possible after starting university, as well as to keep it under review throughout your period of study.

Use the questions below to build up a picture of how much time you have each week. Your answers should be based on what you usually do, i.e. on your average week. You may be surprised at how much spare time you do actually have! Pay attention to the feedback, as this will help you start to organise your time better, potentially (and hopefully) increasing your effectiveness as a student.

How much time do you spend in timetabled classes (lectures, seminars, etc) per week?

- less than 10 hours
- between 10 and 20 hours
- more than 20 hours

How much do you sleep (on average) per night?

- 7 hours or less × 7 = less than 49 hours per week
- approx 8 hours × 7 = about 56 hours per week
- more than 8 hours × 7 = more than 56 hours per week

How much time do you spend on 'the necessities of life' (eating, showering, doing hair, etc) per day?

- 2 hours or less × 7 = less than 14 hours per week

Now, having done the activity, you should take a step back and think about how you organise your week. If you find you do not have 20–25 hours per week to devote to independent study, the solution is **not** to think 'I won't do as much work'; rather it is to consider which areas need to be looked at and 'cut down' to allow you to have 20–25 hours study time:

- some **cannot** be cut (e.g. travel)
- some **should not** be (e.g. sleep)
- some **could be** (e.g. socialising, but you must have 'rest' time); and
- some perhaps **should** be (e.g. paid work – the 'enemy' of good results – do some, but not too much).

What should I do in my study time?

Again, there is no real 'right' or 'wrong' answer to this – although you do actually need to be dedicating that time to study. For example, if you find yourself using a couple of hours a week to tidy up your folders, this is not 'study' time, although it is related to it. When we say study time, we are talking mainly about **reading** your textbooks and casebooks, **reading** cases, **reading** academic articles, as well as taking notes on any or all of these, or **researching** around a topic either in the library or online (using a recognised academic source). Other things that could be incorporated into this time include:

Cross reference
For more information see chapter 4, Taking notes; chapter 15, Using law books; chapter 12, Using a law library; and chapter 18, Using reference materials.

- preparing answers to seminar questions
- getting together in a group to talk about a topic you are studying
- reading some 'extra' on a subject, such as historical background, or critiques of the law
- reading broadsheet newspaper accounts of a current aspect of law.

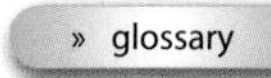

Don't just think of the reading you are set as all you have to do – it is really the minimum required for a good all-round understanding of the law. That said, there are ways to read that don't take up so much of your time, as explained in the chapter on using law books.

Cross reference
See chapter 15, Using law books.

You should think of your studies in the same way as you would think of a job. That is, **if you are a full-time student, studying should occupy as much of your time per week as a full-time job would.**

Suggested time management schedule

Now you should try and draw yourself up a **time management schedule**, using the following tips:

- You should not seek to have a **very** specific schedule for every day – this may be very difficult to keep to, and may lead to a sense of failure.

- Nor should you 'lurch' from day to day with no schedule at all.
- Don't leave things until the last minute.
- You should seek to have an overview on a **weekly basis** of your commitments, and organise your time accordingly.
- Perhaps set aside a dedicated time each week to review your schedule – maybe Sunday afternoon over a cup of tea, or first thing Monday morning.

Activity 2

The following method of organising time may be helpful.

1. Regular commitments

- Construct a schedule of your fixed commitments only – lecture and seminar contact hours, hours you typically spend at paid work, other regular activities. These could be added to your table and photocopied (or save a copy on your computer and alter the other details each week).

2. Weekly schedule

- Each week when you review your schedule you should add any major events (assessments due, for example, or even birthday parties!) to it.
- Also add the **amount of work** to be accomplished in each of your subjects/modules that week.
- These events will change from week to week and it is important to make a **new list for each week.**

3. Daily review

- Having established a weekly schedule, you should conduct a daily review (morning or evening) **adding** any new activities, deadlines or work as they arise.
- The daily review should **not** involve you crossing off something you earlier included, except in exceptional circumstances.

» glossary

Note

There is no point in doing this if you are not going to stick to it!

This is an example of the type of table you may want to be creating after completing the above activity to analyse how much time you have. The following examples will show how you can build up the table to become a completed time management schedule. Note that Saturday and Sunday are included – even though we describe full-time study as like a full-time job, an essential part of time management is to know what you will be doing (and how much of it) **outside** of your normal working (study) hours.

WEEK COMMENCING:

DAY	REGULAR ACTIVITIES	OTHER ACTIVITIES	AMOUNT OF WORK	DAILY REVIEW
Monday				
Tuesday				
Wednesday				
Thursday				
Friday				
Saturday				
Sunday				

Motivation

Everything you have done so far in this chapter is all very well if you are motivated. And you should be motivated – remember that you chose to come and study law at university – and there must be a good reason for this! There is really no reason not to enjoy your studies. University should be a fun time precisely because you are now studying what you want to study (presumably with one eye on the future) and you have that extra degree of independence. However, for many, university is the first big step into the 'adult' world and what comes with that is the need to take responsibility for your own motivation: no one else can do this for you. It is different from having a job – although you still have work to do, deadlines to meet etc., you are not getting paid for it; you have to do these things because you want to. And wanting to – being enthusiastic about your studies – is the first step towards enjoying your career in or after law, whatever that may be.

Everyone suffers from a lack of motivation at times, whether they are studying, researching, parenting or at work. As a law student you may feel, for example, somewhat overwhelmed with the amount of work you think you have to do, particularly if you have friends on other courses who seem to have less than you (although this may not actually be the case). When this happens, many students either try to ignore the work, in which case they fall behind, or they work so hard they have no opportunity for any fun, which leads to stress. If you feel either of these things happening, you should go back to your time management schedule and review once again how you spend your time – what can be cut down? Where can you find 'extra' time for study? Are you spending too much time on one thing and not another? In addition to this, try the following reflection activity, which looks at whether you use your study time well – the substance of this comes from our experiences of talking to and working with students with motivation and time management problems.

Activity 3

Do I use my study time well?

Think about everything you actually do when you are 'studying' and try to identify whether you are studying **well**, or whether you are spending a lot of **time** on study but not getting much from it. Some of the following questions might help:

- Am I attending all my lectures and seminars?
- Am I enjoying my lectures and seminars?
- Do I understand the material from lectures and seminars?
- Where (and how) do I sit in lectures and seminars?

Activity 3 (continued)

- When I prepare for seminars, do I read all that I need to in one sitting or spread it out over the week?
- Am I focused on the **aim** of the seminar? What is it trying to help me to learn?
- Does my reading seem to take forever?
- Do I enjoy reading about law?
- Where do I read? Am I easily distracted by, e.g. the radio or TV (if at home) or chatting to friends in person (if in library) or online or by text (anywhere)?
- Do I tend to leave things until the last minute?
- Do I go out (to the bar, club, shopping etc.) a lot?

Now go online to read our thoughts on this question.

Note

A lot of people find that although they are generally quite motivated, their motivation dwindles sometimes, for example in the approach to the university holidays. We find that this is especially the case in the run up to the winter vacation in first year – probably because students look forward to the end of term, there are a lot more social activities going on and possibly even Christmas shopping to do! Try not to let this spoil any good habits you have cultivated, especially as there are likely to be assessments around this time, or perhaps even exams to prepare for! One of the good things about university is how long the holidays are. Look forward to and take advantage of this – in fact, use it as a motivating **tool** to help you work hard until the end of term!

Don't panic

Add up the total number of weeks you are at university **per year**. *In most cases, this will only be about half of the year – so think how much spare time you actually do have. Now do you feel more motivated about the time you are actually studying at university?*

Help! I'm still not motivated

If after reviewing your time and other things that may mean you work less effectively than you should, poor motivation remains a consistent problem for you, the following checklist may prove helpful in identifying its source.

1. Really preferring something other than attending this university:
   - University is not what I thought it would be like
   - I would prefer not to go to university at all
   - I would rather attend another university
   - I would prefer a different kind of training.
2. University as means to ends other than learning:
   - To avoid getting a job
   - To be with friends
   - To have a good time
   - To prove self-worth.
3. Distracting personal problems:
   - I'm lonely or homesick
   - Conflict with friends
   - Conflict with boyfriend/girlfriend
   - Conflict with parents
   - I'm not getting on in halls of residence
   - I haven't met any people I like
   - I lack confidence about my abilities
   - University is so much harder than school
   - Use of drugs or alcohol.
4. Lack of interest in the study of law:
   - Studying law is not what I thought it would be like
   - I have undefined vocational goals
   - I have undefined educational goals
   - The course material is not what I think is important
   - Some of my modules are 'boring'
   - Interest in university is not the 'in' thing among my friends.

5. Other factors:
    - I'm always too tired to study
    - Paid employment takes up too much of my time
    - I have bad habits from A-Level schooling and before
    - Lack of financial resources
    - Parental pressure: 'it's what is expected'.

If you have identified any of these as applying to you, something needs to be done about it, and this can only be by you taking some action. These are 'bigger' problems than can be dealt with by altering your schedule or improving your study and research skills and, hopefully, identifying them will then allow you to take more bold steps to overcome the problem(s). Remember that you can, and should, always discuss any problems with your tutors or student advisers or mentors, if you have them, as well – that is what they are there for and even if they don't have 'the answers', they are trained to help you to find your own, or to point you in the direction of someone who might have! Take advantage of anything and everything that's offered in the way of help!

Conclusion

One of the keys to success at university is to have good time management. Without this, you may find that you fall behind in your work, making you ill-prepared for seminars and late in starting and completing assessments, for example. And this can have a deleterious effect on your motivation, which can lead to problems managing your time: a vicious circle. You will probably find that you have a lot of things that you need to juggle but this is part of 'normal' adult life, and managing your time effectively is a skill you will need to learn both for university and for any career path you choose beyond your law degree. In fact, being good at organising your time is something that employers will be looking for in the future! Hopefully this chapter has helped you to identify areas in which you could manage your time better, and give you some tips on **how** this can be achieved.

Links

Time management

http://www.kent.ac.uk/uelt/learning/learning-resources/timeman.html
Kent University's Unit for the Enhancement of Learning and Teaching provides some time management tips, including basic points to remember and a list of useful books.

Chapter 3

Writing good English

Rationale

If you are able to express your ideas clearly and accurately, you are on the way to getting good marks for your work. This means writing grammatically, watching your spelling and punctuation, and using appropriate language for the task. As well as making a real difference to how your work is judged while you are a student, it will become of crucial importance when you are working, whether in legal practice or elsewhere.

There is a tension between those who are prescriptive about grammar and insist on a set of rules, and those who see language as continuously evolving and who therefore tolerate 'bad grammar'. In practice, it is sensible to err on the side of keeping to rules: First, they help you to avoid ambiguity, and secondly, they avoid distracting the reader.

This chapter is devised to help you improve your written English as follows:

- Recognise the pitfalls and common mistakes
- Use appropriate language for different purposes
- Tips on avoiding spelling mistakes
- Tips on avoiding grammatical errors
- The use of legal terminology
- Reviewing your work.

Writing appropriately

Emails and discussion

'Text speak' is now so ubiquitous that it is creeping beyond the text message into emails, letters and other writing. It's best regarded as something you do between friends, and which should not be used for other communication. While many of your tutors may not object to being addressed in this way, don't underestimate the irritation that some feel at receiving badly drafted, misspelt emails. The same applies to discussion boards or chat rooms that are used for academic discussion.

Consider this email to a law lecturer:

> hi can u help me I need to see u urgently about my prop law assessment

You might well find that the response would be something like *Go back and write this in a proper courteous manner, then I might answer you.* Whereas if you were to write:

> Dear Dr Moran
>
> I need some help on my property law assignment. Could I make an appointment with you on Thursday?
>
> Regards
>
> Susan Smith

then you might get a more positive response.

Note

Be courteous, and write grammatically and accurately when corresponding – even in emails!

Essays

↳ **Cross reference**
For further information see chapter 25, Writing essays.

Your institution will give you guidance on essay-writing style, and we also provide more detail in the chapter on 'Writing essays'. Here, we will just emphasise some basic rules about writing:

Keep it simple! While your style in an essay should be formal, you should try to avoid an 'over-blown' style. It's often a good idea to stand back from what you have written, and ask yourself "what am I trying to say?" and then say it. You will often find that you can express your ideas more simply than you have done. And watch your spelling and punctuation! In the next section we will look at how to avoid some of the common pitfalls.

Spelling

Surely running your work through a spellcheck solves the problem of spelling, doesn't it? Well, no: while it is a useful way of identifying 'typos', it doesn't deal with some of the very common errors which people make. These fall into several distinct categories:

- Homophones (words which sound the same but are spelt differently and have different meanings)
- Americanisms
- Very common spelling errors.

One of the difficulties with these rules is that mistakes are so common you could be forgiven for thinking that the rules no longer apply. But they do, and it's worth making a real effort to get them right. To do this you need to be on the alert for problem words or phrases, so that you can check the correct usage.

To start with, let's look at homophones. These are words which sound the same, but are spelled differently and have different meanings. Some of these are in general usage, but others have very specific legal meanings, and it is essential that you get them right. Here is a list of very common spelling confusions:

Accept	Consent to receive	Except	Exclude from a general statement
Acceptance	Agreement to the terms of an offer	Exception	That which is excepted, excluded
Accede	To take office (usually of a monarch)	Exceed	To go beyond, to surpass
Access	A way of approaching or entering [a building, land] (as in Access to land)	Excess	Over the limit (as in excess baggage)
Accession	Entering upon an office (as in Accession to the throne)		
Annex	(verb) To add as a subordinate part; to append	Annexe	(noun) A separate or added building
Affect	To change or make a difference to	Effect	(n) A result; (v) to bring about a result
Breach	Breaking of or failure to observe [a law] (as in breach of contract)	Breech	The back part of a rifle or cannon
Canon	General law, rule or principle; criterion ; also a clergyman; musical piece in parts	Cannon	Large heavy gun
Council	An organisation, local authority	Counsel	(n) Barrister (v) to give advice
Councillor	A member of a council, usually elected	Counsellor	Someone who counsels
Dependant	(n) Someone who relies on another for financial support	Dependent	(adj) Relying on, influenced by
Disburse	To pay money. Expend [money]	Disperse	Distribute in different directions

Continued

Discreet	Tactful, unobtrusive	Discrete	Separate, distinct
Enquire	Ask, seek information	Inquire	Seek information, investigate (more formal than enquire)
Enquiry	Act of information-seeking	Inquiry	Formal investigation; always used for official commissions of inquiry
Ensure	To make sure something happens	Insure	To secure payment in the event of death or damage
Forward	In front, onward	Foreword	Introductory remarks at the beginning of a book
Its	Possessive, as in 'the reason for its popularity'	It's	Contraction of *It is*, as in 'it's a beautiful day'
Judgment	A legal decision, handed down by a judge	Judgement	A critical opinion; discernment
Principal	(adj.) First in rank or importance (n) Leader, head [of a school]. Original sum lent or invested	Principle	Fundamental truth as the basis of reasoning (Never an adjective)
Proceed	(v) To go forward	Precede	To come before or go before
Proceeds	(n) Profit (e.g. from a crime)	Precedence	Priority in time, order or importance
Procedure Proceedings	The formal manner in which legal proceedings are conducted	Precedent	A judgment of a court used as an authority in subsequent cases
Proscribe	Prohibit (as in proscribed organisation)	Prescribe	Advise or recommend authoritatively (as in prescribed drug)
Proscription	Prohibition	Prescription	Instructions for e.g. taking medicine
Right	Correct. Opposite to left	Write	As in write an essay
Stationary	Still, not moving (as in stationary vehicle)	Stationery	Writing materials
Tenant	A person who rents land or property from a landlord	Tenet	A doctrine or principle
Their	Belonging to them	There	In that place
		They're	They are (as in they're going out)
Whether	Introduces alternative possibiities,often interchangeable with 'if' (as in 'I don't know whether they are going to London or Paris')	Weather	The state of the climate.
		Wether	A castrated ram
Whose	Of whom, or belonging to whom, or as in 'Whose books are these?'	Who's	Contraction of *Who is*, as in 'Who's coming with me?
Your	Belonging to you (as in 'is this your book?)	You're	You are (as in 'you're going out')

Now you've absorbed this list, perhaps you will remember that there may be a problem with this or that word, even if you can't remember what the problem is. Then you can look it up, and eventually it will come naturally.

Key Point

Be aware of your potential errors, and check them if you are not sure.

Licence to practise?

There is a group of words which you will come across on a daily basis in legal literature. They also are some of the most commonly misspelt. They are:

Defence	Defense
Offence	Offense
Licence	License
Practice	Practise

Let's dispose of the first two straightaway. You'll probably recognise *offense* and *defense* as US spellings. They are both nouns (the associated verbs being *offend* and *defend*). Their usage is incorrect in UK English.

Licence; license and *Practice; practise* are more problematic, because the words are both nouns and verbs, but are used differently in UK and US English. While you are unlikely (we hope) to come across incorrect usage in a law book, you will come across it all the time in the press, in journal articles and in non-legal books.

UK English usage	US English usage
Licence as a noun	*License* as a noun
In the UK you hold a driving *licence*	In America you don't require a television *license*
License as a verb	*License* or *Licence* as a verb
In the UK you are *licensed* to practise as a conveyancer. We have pub *licensing* hours	In America you are *licensed* to practice as an attorney, but the usage *licenced* is also acceptable
Practice as a noun	*Practice* as a noun
In the UK you intend to go into *practice* as a solicitor. It's good *practice* to check your spelling when you have written an essay	In America this is normally spelt as in UK English
Practise as a verb	*Practice* as a verb
In the UK I *practise* the piano, the law, yoga etc.	In America I *practice* as an attorney, I *practice* the violin.

Because these are words which you will use frequently, you need to fix the correct usage in your mind. The one that is most commonly misspelt is *license* as a noun. This is complicated by the fact that in many cases this is the legitimate usage, because it's an American company whose *license* you agree to every time you download something on the internet. Just remember that it's not the UK English usage.

Be aware of where you may make mistakes!

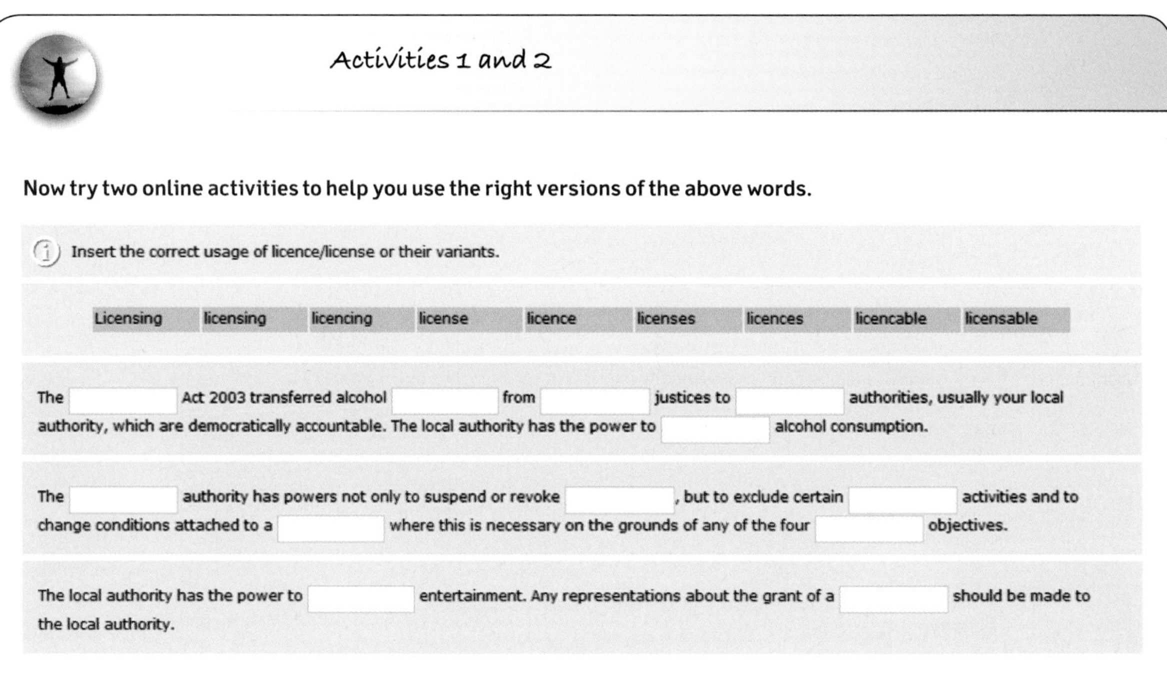

Activities 1 and 2

Now try two online activities to help you use the right versions of the above words.

Insert the correct usage of licence/license or their variants.

Licensing	licensing	licencing	license	licence	licenses	licences	licencable	licensable

The ____ Act 2003 transferred alcohol ____ from ____ justices to ____ authorities, usually your local authority, which are democratically accountable. The local authority has the power to ____ alcohol consumption.

The ____ authority has powers not only to suspend or revoke ____, but to exclude certain ____ activities and to change conditions attached to a ____ where this is necessary on the grounds of any of the four ____ objectives.

The local authority has the power to ____ entertainment. Any representations about the grant of a ____ should be made to the local authority.

Other Americanisms

There are a number of other Americanisms which you should be aware of.

- The ending –or (as in *labor, honor, color*) is American, and you should use the UK *labour, honour, colour.*
- *Gotten* is an American form and should not be used.
- In the UK use *traveller, travelled, marvellous, quarrelling* (American English uses *traveler, traveled, marvelous* and *quarreling*).

- US English truncates words ending in –og (*catalog, dialog*) whereas UK English uses *catalogue, dialogue*, although *dialog* is permissible when referring to computer programs. *Program*, which is the normal usage in the US, is always *programme* in the UK, except in computing.
- In the UK use *centre, fibre* rather than the American *center* or *fiber* (except, of course, where *Center* refers to an American institution, such as 'American Center for Law and Justice').
- There are also variant endings, both of which are permissible, such as –ise ; –ize. Americans tend to write *organization, analyze, globalization; organisation, analyse, globalisation* are more common in the UK. But there is no hard and fast rule for this, although *analyze* is regarded as incorrect in the UK. While it doesn't matter which usage you choose – as long as you are consistent throughout a piece of written work – it is something you need to bear in mind if you are carrying out an online search. In many databases you will ned to use both versions, or truncate the word, in order to find what you are looking for.

The Economist journal has a useful instruction to its writers on avoiding Americanisms which you can find at http://www.economist.com/research/styleGuide/index.cfm?page=673931

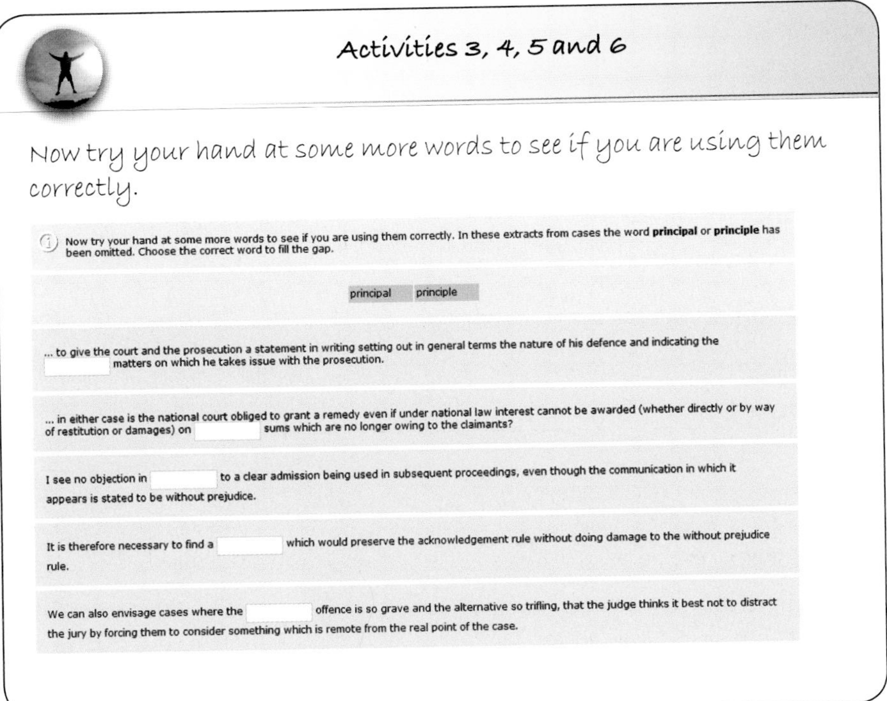

Activities 3, 4, 5 and 6
Now try your hand at some more words to see if you are using them correctly.
Now try your hand at some more words to see if you are using them correctly. In these extracts from cases the word **principal** or **principle** has been omitted. Choose the correct word to fill the gap.
principal principle
... to give the court and the prosecution a statement in writing setting out in general terms the nature of his defence and indicating the ______ matters on which he takes issue with the prosecution.
... in either case is the national court obliged to grant a remedy even if under national law interest cannot be awarded (whether directly or by way of restitution or damages) on ______ sums which are no longer owing to the claimants?
I see no objection in ______ to a clear admission being used in subsequent proceedings, even though the communication in which it appears is stated to be without prejudice.
It is therefore necessary to find a ______ which would preserve the acknowledgement rule without doing damage to the without prejudice rule.
We can also envisage cases where the ______ offence is so grave and the alternative so trifling, that the judge thinks it best not to distract the jury by forcing them to consider something which is remote from the real point of the case.

Errors so common you come across them all the time

Right	Wrong
Accommodation	Accomodation
Achieve	Acheive
Achievement	Acheivement
Acquit ; acquitted; acquittal	Aquit: aquitted; aquittal
Adviser	Advisor
Advisory	Advisery
Apparent	Apparant
Arbitrary	Arbitary
Argument	Arguement
Belief; believe	Beleif; beleive
Biased	Biassed
Caribbean	Carribean
Commitment	Committment
Comparative	Comparitive
Concede	Consede
Consensus	Concensus
Deceive	Decieve
Disappoint; disappointment	Dissapoint; dissapointment
Embarrass; embarrassment	Embarass; embarassment
Except; exception	Exept; exeption
Focus; focused; focusing	Focussed; focussing
Friend	Freind
Fulfil; fulfilment	Fulfill; fulfillment
Gauge	Guage
Government	Goverment
Guarantee; guarantor	Gaurantee; gaurantor

Harassment ▯	Harrassment ▯
Hierarchy ▯	Heirarchy ▯
Inadmissible ▯	Inadmissable ▯
Inadvertent ▯	Inadvertant ▯
Independent ▯	Independant ▯
Install; installation ▯	Instal; instalation ▯
Instalment ▯	Installment (American) ▯
Liaise; liaison ▯	Liase; liason ▯
Minuscule ▯	Miniscule ▯
Mischievous ▯	Mischievious; mischeivous; mischeivious ▯
Necessary; necessity ▯	Neccessary; neccessity ▯
Occasion ; occasionally ▯	Occassion; occassionally ▯
Occur ▯	Ocurr ▯
Occurring; Occurrence ▯	Ocurring; occuring; Ocurrence; occurence ▯
Permanent ▯	Permanant ▯
Permissible ▯	Permissable ▯
Persistent ▯	Persistant ▯
Possess; possession ▯	Posess; posession; possesion ▯
Publicly ▯	Publically ▯
Receive; receipt ▯	Recieve; reciept ▯
Responsible ▯	Responsable ▯
Seize; seizure ▯ (NB: this is an exception to the rule 'i before e except after c')	Sieze; siezure ▯
Separate ▯	Seperate ▯
Supersede ▯	Supercede ▯
Thief ▯	Theif ▯
Unenforceable ▯	Unenforcable ▯
Unforeseen ▯	Unforseen ▯
Until ▯	Untill ▯
Withhold ▯	Withold ▯

Key Point

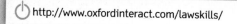

Try to note the spellings that you habitually get wrong, and learn them!

Activities 7 and 8

Now test yourself with two different activities to do with spelling.

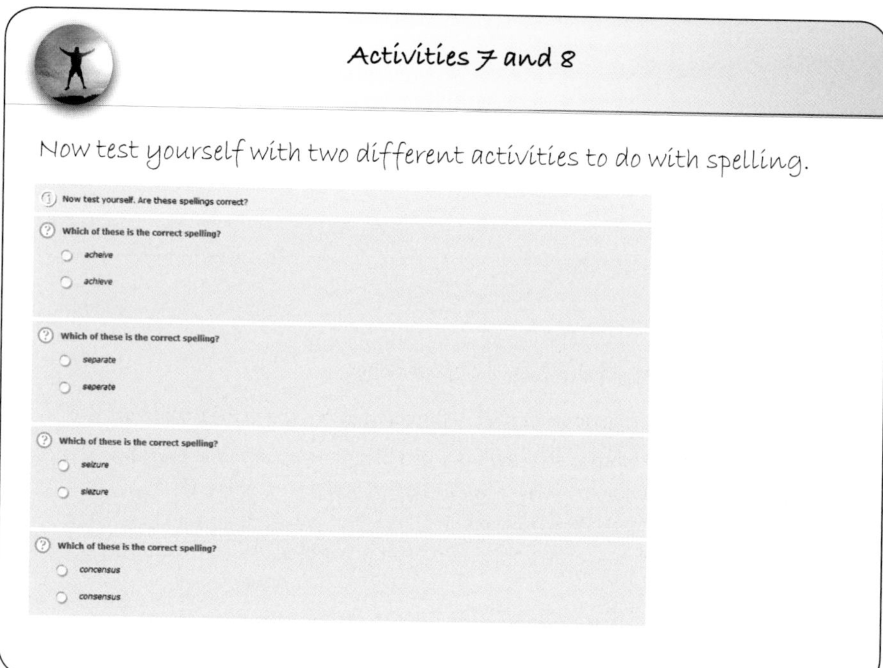

Now test yourself. Are these spellings correct?

Which of these is the correct spelling?

- acheive
- achieve

Which of these is the correct spelling?

- separate
- seperate

Which of these is the correct spelling?

- seizure
- siezure

Which of these is the correct spelling?

- concensus
- consensus

Punctuation

Punctuation causes even more problems than spelling, to which it is closely allied. And, just as with spelling mistakes, errors in punctuation are so common that you can begin to wonder what is right and what is wrong. While incorrect spelling, for the most part, doesn't affect the meaning, careless punctuation can lead to ambiguity.

Apostrophes

These cause endless problems and, if incorrectly used, can make your work seem illiterate. You probably know the rules if you think about it, but it's very easy to be lazy, especially in rapid communications such as emails. Look at this one:

> Hi everyone!
>
> The Law School is hosting a party for all law student's to celebrate it's 40th Anniversary.

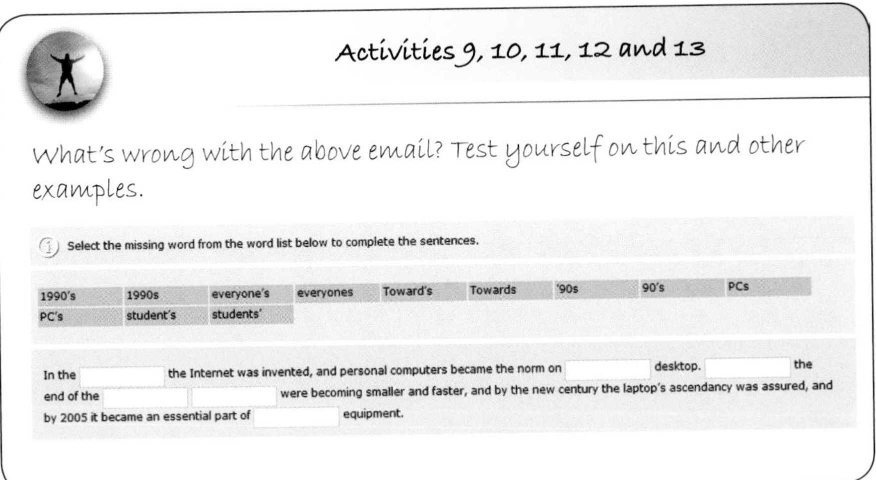

Activities 9, 10, 11, 12 and 13

What's wrong with the above email? Test yourself on this and other examples.

Select the missing word from the word list below to complete the sentences.

1990's	1990s	everyone's	everyones	Toward's	Towards	'90s	90's	PCs
PC's	student's	students'						

In the ______ the Internet was invented, and personal computers became the norm on ______ desktop. ______ the end of the ______ ______ were becoming smaller and faster, and by the new century the laptop's ascendancy was assured, and by 2005 it became an essential part of ______ equipment.

These are the main ways in which we use the apostrophe:

- In **possessives**, e.g. *Robert's coat; the cat's whiskers; the judge's opinion.*

  If, however, the word is in the plural, you place the apostrophe after the 's', e.g. *students' accommodation; lawyers' qualification; judges' opinions.* If you are unsure, you can make a mental note as follows:
  - Is it the opinion of a single judge (*judge's opinion*) or several judges (*judges' opinions*)?

  If the plural of a word doesn't end in s (women, children), then the possessive uses an apostrophe before the 's'
  - *The children's game*; *women's liberation*

  Possessive pronouns never use an apostrophe
  - *Its* (not it's); *hers* (not her's); *theirs* (not their's); *yours* (not your's)
  - *The cat chases its tail*; *this essay is yours*

  Its is the one which causes most confusion: see below.
- To **replace a letter or letters**

  These are the most common forms:
  - *It's* for 'it is', e.g. *It's time to go*
  - *Can't* for 'cannot' e.g. *I can't finish this essay*
  - *Don't* for 'do not' e.g. *Please don't block the entrance*

Key Point

If you are not sure whether to write *its* or *it's* try saying 'it is' instead. If you can use 'it is' then you should write it's. If it doesn't make sense, then it should be the possessive *its*.

The Law School is celebrating its ***[it is – NO]*** *40th anniversary.*

It's ***[it is – OK]*** *celebrating its* ***[it is – NO]*** *40th anniversary.*

Activity 14

Try another simple activity to see how to use apostrophes.

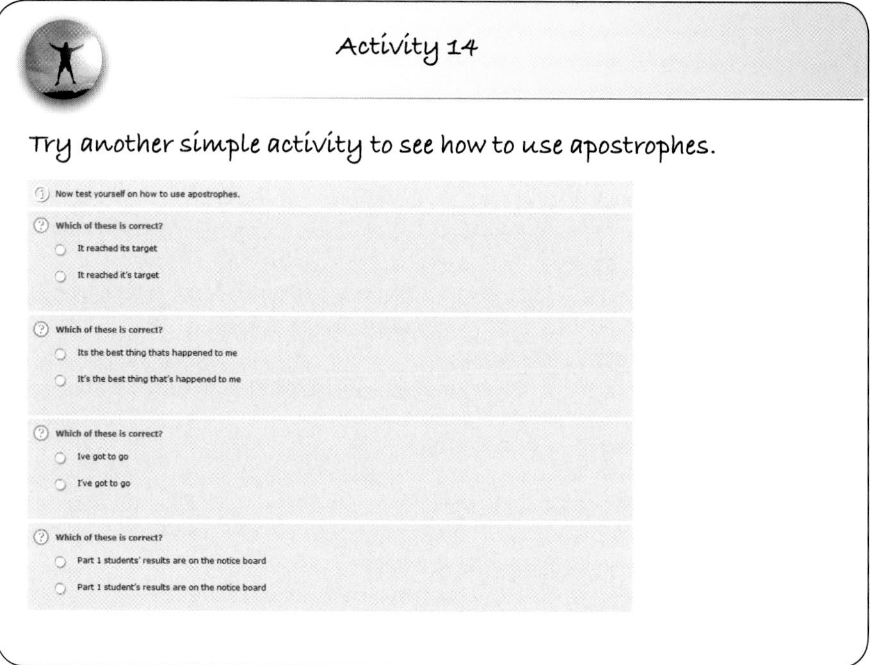

Now test yourself on how to use apostrophes.

Which of these is correct?
- It reached its target
- It reached it's target

Which of these is correct?
- Its the best thing thats happened to me
- It's the best thing that's happened to me

Which of these is correct?
- Ive got to go
- I've got to go

Which of these is correct?
- Part 1 students' results are on the notice board
- Part 1 student's results are on the notice board

- Where you **don't** use apostrophes
  - In plurals: *cats; judges; students*
  - In plurals after initials: *MPs; PCs* (not *MP's* or *PC's*)
  - After numbers: *the 1960s; the '60s* (not *the 1960's*; the *'60's*)
  - In possessive pronouns: *its; theirs; ours* etc.

Commas

Commas are used primarily to provide 'breathing space' in a sentence, and usage can vary considerably. When badly used, misplaced commas can alter the meaning of a sentence radically.

- **Commas are used to join lists of words or concepts.**
  - *The foundational subjects of law are Criminal Law, Contract, Equity, European Union Law, Land Law, Public Law, and Tort*
  - *An introductory law book has traditionally included a description of the institutions of the law, an explanation of the methods of the law, and some consideration of legal principles and rules*

  In this example, there is no comma before the final 'rules', which belongs to the consideration of legal principles rather than the contents of a law book.
  - *The three courses are Contract and Tort, Equity and Trusts, and Constitutional and Administrative Law*

  These pairs of words are separated by commas. If you change the positioning of the commas, or omit them, you are left with an ambiguous sentence:
  - *The three courses are Contract and Tort Equity and Trusts and Constitutional and Administrative Law*
  - *The three courses are Contract, and Tort, Equity, and Trusts, and Constitutional, and Administrative Law*
- **Commas are used to join two parts of a sentence** using one of the following connecting words: 'and', 'or', 'but', 'while' and 'yet'.
  - *We have a choice of six options, but we can only take two in the second year*
  - *The latest enlargement of the EU took place in 2004, when seven states joined*
  - *It is raining in the south, while the sun is shining in the north*

  You can't use a comma without the conjunction, as these are two separate sentences:
  - *We have a choice of six options, we can only take two in the second year*
  - *The latest enlargement of the EU took place in 2004, seven states joined*
  - *It is raining in the south, the sun is shining in the north*

  In these last examples you would need to separate the two sentences with a semi-colon, colon or full stop:
  - *We have a choice of six options. We can only take two in the second year*
  - *The latest enlargement of the EU took place in 2004: seven states joined*
  - *It is raining in the south; the sun is shining in the north*

  The best way to avoid this is to use your ear.

  Other connecting words such as 'however', 'therefore', 'hence', 'consequently', 'nevertheless' and 'thus' **cannot** be used with a comma:
  - *An Act of Parliament may not come into force immediately, therefore, you need to check the commencement order*

  This is **wrong.** You need to use a full stop or a semi-colon before 'therefore':
  - *An Act of Parliament may not come into force immediately. Therefore, you need to check the commencement order*

  Exception: 'However' is enclosed in commas if it is used in the middle of a sentence to qualify a statement:
  - *An exception, however, is when this is used in the middle of a sentence*
  - *The House of Commons is elected. The House of Lords, however, is mainly appointed*

- **Commas are used to separate sub-clauses in a sentence**
  - *In the latest enlargement of the EU, which took place in 2004, seven countries joined*
  - *The Human Rights Act, the flagship of the new Labour Government's legislative programme, was passed in 1998*
  - *The war in Iraq, of course, damaged Tony Blair's reputation*

  To check whether this is correct, you can remove the clause between the commas: the remainder of the sentence should still make sense:
  - *In the latest enlargement of the EU seven countries joined*
  - *The Human Rights Act was passed in 1998*
  - *The war in Iraq damaged Tony Blair's reputation*
- **Common mistakes using commas**

  The commonest misuse of commas is putting them in where they are not required.
  - *The Human Rights Act, was passed in 1998*
  - *An introductory law book, has traditionally included a description of the institutions of the law*
  - *The foundational subjects of law, form the basis of the qualifying law degree*

  None of the commas in the above sentences should be there.

Mis-use of commas is one of the most common forms of bad writing. Try to improve your use, and you will improve your writing style **and** your grades.

Some common grammatical mistakes

- **You and I**
  - *The difference between you and I…* should be *the difference between you and me…*
  - *She gave it to Helen and I* should be *she gave it to Helen and me*
  - *This gift is from Patrick and I* should be *this gift is from Patrick and me*

  This very common construction often arises from over-correction. See what it looks like if you remove the other person *The difference between I; She gave it to I, This gift is from I.* Avoid this!
- **Less/fewer**
  - *Less* means 'not as much'; *Fewer* means 'not as many'
  - *We have fewer assignments and less work*
  - *The university is admitting fewer students this year*

- **Amount/number**
  - *Amount* and *Number* are often misused
  - *There are a large number of students* (not 'amount')
  - *We have a large amount of work*

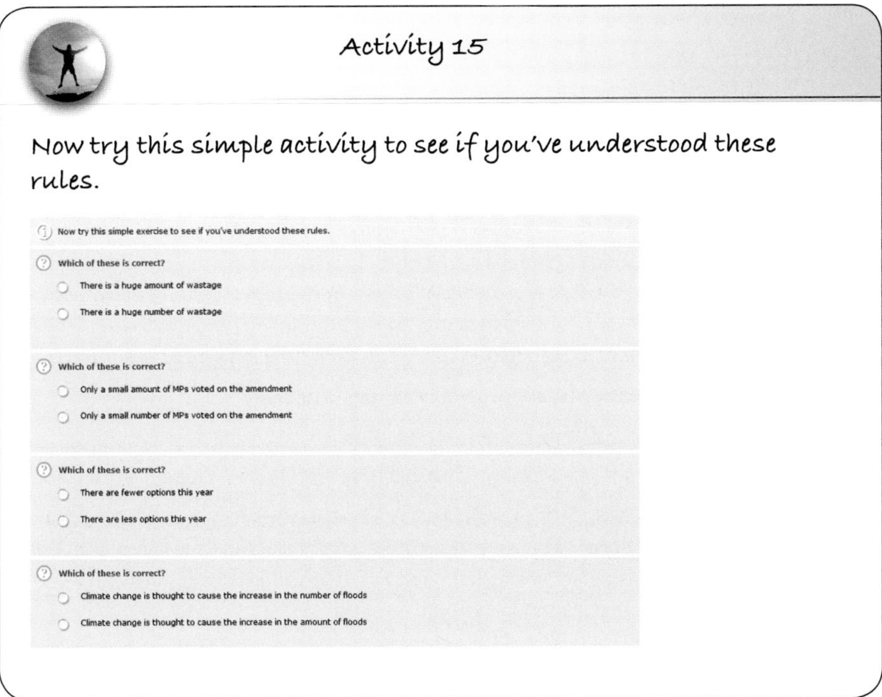

Activity 15

Now try this simple activity to see if you've understood these rules.

Now try this simple exercise to see if you've understood these rules.

Which of these is correct?
- There is a huge amount of wastage
- There is a huge number of wastage

Which of these is correct?
- Only a small amount of MPs voted on the amendment
- Only a small number of MPs voted on the amendment

Which of these is correct?
- There are fewer options this year
- There are less options this year

Which of these is correct?
- Climate change is thought to cause the increase in the number of floods
- Climate change is thought to cause the increase in the amount of floods

Getting help with grammar, punctuation and spelling

There are lots of free websites which will help you with common problems of style. www.askoxford.com will answer your questions, and also has a useful set of frequently asked questions (FAQs).

As a student you are likely to have access to a number of online subscription services such as Oxford Reference Online (which includes dictionaries and other reference books and the OED (Oxford English Dictionary). Check your library website to find these.

Lynn Truss, *Eats, Shoots and Leaves*, London: Profile Books, 2003, pp. 209, ISBN: 1861976127, is very readable, and a useful book to have at hand.

Jack Lynch's *Guide to Grammar and Style* (Rutgers University) http://andromeda.rutgers.edu/~jlynch/Writing/index.html

Larry Trask's *Guide to Punctuation* (University of Sussex) http://www.informatics.sussex.ac.uk/department/docs/punctuation/node00.html

Reviewing your work

Now you have learned (or been reminded of) some of the problems inherent in writing well, you need to be sure that you apply these in your writing. Assuming that you have taken everything on board, you must still check your work for mistakes.

Re-reading

Anyone checking over their work for submission knows that they find new errors each time they check. This is a rather depressing thought, but you can avoid presenting badly written work if you follow some simple rules:

- **Always** read your work over before you submit it.
- Try reading it aloud. This will help you to get a feel for whether it reads well. If it sounds right, there's a good chance it will read well.
- Be aware of the appropriateness of your style. Again, reading it silently and aloud will help you to develop a sense of whether the style is too informal, or whether you are saying things more elaborately than you need to.
- If you get tangled up in an explanation, imagine someone asking you 'What are you trying to say?' Then say it. This will often make you explain your ideas more clearly.

Proofreading

Whether they are 'typos' or genuine spelling mistakes, they will detract from your finished work, however good the argument.

- Beware of spellcheck! It's very useful to run your work through a spellcheck program, but if you are not careful you can easily find it chooses the wrong words for you. So after you have done this, make sure that you look carefully at the suggested changes to ensure that they make sense.
- Be aware of your own weaknesses. Everyone has some spellings that they always get wrong, or grammatical traps they fall into. If you can alert yourself to your own problem points, then you are halfway to succeeding.

Be vigilant – re-read your work – proofread for mistakes.

Conclusion

Writing good English is more than a matter of learning rules, although these can be helpful. You will have learned some of these by doing the activities in this chapter. The rules that we have outlined in this chapter are not always prescriptive. Especially when it comes to punctuation, there are often various options, each of which may be acceptable. What you must try to avoid, however, are the obvious mistakes, some of which are very common!

You must also learn to 'listen' to what you write. Read it out aloud to yourself to see if it makes sense, sounds fluent, and is consistent in style. Whenever you write, be sure that your style is appropriate to the writing activity, be it essay, report or email. Read widely and absorb good style from what you read.

Links

Economist's instruction to its writers on avoiding Americanisms
http://www.economist.com/research/styleGuide/index.cfm?page=673931

Oxford dictionaries
www.askoxford.com

Jack Lynch's *Guide to Grammar and Style* (Rutgers University)
http://andromeda.rutgers.edu/~jlynch/Writing/index.html

Larry Trask's *Guide to Punctuation* (University of Sussex)
http://www.informatics.sussex.ac.uk/department/docs/punctuation/node00.html

Chapter 4

Taking notes

Rationale

At university, you will find that the teaching style is somewhat different from that used in schools. When doing a law degree, it is likely that you will be taught by a combination of lectures and seminars as well as having periods of self-study in which you have to manage your own time and learning. In order to learn law effectively, one thing that you will need to be able to do is to take comprehensive notes.

In law, the sources of your learning will be many and varied – taking notes properly is therefore a skill that needs to be developed and, again, is probably different from what you will have been used to in your studies so far. Moreover, once into their degree course, many students find that they have notes from their lectures, notes from their reading, notes from their seminars and so on, and when it comes to needing to write assessments or to revision for exams, their notes are all over the place, with no system or order to them.

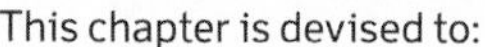

This chapter is devised to:

- Explain the purpose of notes
- Show why you don't need to write **everything** down
- Introduce systems of note taking that are both sensible and effective and that can be adapted to suit your own preferred way of studying.

Making your notes work for you

» glossary

The skill of effective note taking is an important one to develop at an early stage of your university education. It may seem surprising that something that seems so simple is described here as an essential skill. However, it is often the things that seem so straightforward that need more attention when it comes to making learning easier. Note taking is a skill that can be developed and honed to fit your particular way of learning, and finding out what works for you can be an invaluable tool, saving both time and stress at later stages.

↳ **Cross reference**
For further information see chapter 2, Managing your time.

In the study of law, you will use a wide variety of sources and so having carefully consolidated notes, rather than many different bits of pieces of paper, will be very useful when it comes to writing both assessments and exams. You may need to take notes from any or all of the following sources:

- Lectures
- Seminars
- Textbooks
- Casebooks

» glossary

» glossary

- Cases
- Academic articles
- Other reading material used on your course, including non-law sources.

The way you take and keep your notes will have an impact on your ability to go back and review topics and therefore on your overall learning. However, it is important to recognise from the outset that the skill of note taking is not set in stone: differences between modules you study may mean that you take your notes in different styles, or you may find that your note-taking style changes or develops as you progress in your studies.

Note

The most important thing is to be proactive, rather than passive in your note taking. This means that you should not just sit back and write down everything you are told or that you read, but should work to a purpose.

What should my notes look like?

You might think that there is only one way to take notes – writing across the page from left to right, perhaps with the occasional underlining or capitalisation of important key points – and, in fact, this is what most students tend to do. This is not 'wrong', but it is sometimes more helpful, especially when it comes to the end of a module, to have all your notes on a particular topic (from lectures, seminars, reading etc.) in one place – even on the same page! Furthermore, there are other ways to take notes, such as in **mind map, table** or **spider diagram** form, techniques that you may find useful for some topics, or in some modules, but not in others. The thing to remember is that the way you take notes doesn't always have to be the same.

Below you will find more information and help with effective note taking, as well as some suggestions about different things to try, particularly if you are one of those students who find that their notes are hard to follow when they come back to them later. We detail the purpose of taking notes from lectures and other sources and give other useful hints about, for example, using abbreviations or colour-coding to assist learning. Activities are also included to help you see the effectiveness of various ways of taking notes.

Lectures

You will probably need to make notes from your lectures, and it may be that these form the bulk of your notes while you study; therefore we focus on these first and in most detail. In order to take notes effectively, you should be aware that lectures are:

- The provision of selected information – usually the **basic outline** or **key points** of a topic, simply presented.
- Usually not interactive – although some lecturers prefer to interact with students, for example by asking questions, even in large lectures.
- Not the 'full picture', and should not be thought of as such.

Don't panic

Although lecturers won't be able to tell you everything you need to know about a topic, invariably you will be given further reading to do and be encouraged to discuss topics further, for example in seminars, in order to cover and understand a topic fully.

Cross reference
See chapter 6, Contributing to seminars and tutorials.

The purpose of a lecture is to deliver information, but, because of the limited time in which there is to do this (lectures usually last around one hour) compared to the wealth of information about law there is out there, not all the information about any topic can be delivered by lectures alone. Lectures should thus be seen as the delivery of the **key points** of a particular topic in order to provide a basis for further study and discussion.

Following from this description of lectures, it should be evident that students who rely on their lecture notes alone will not have as good a picture or understanding of the law as those who read, research, think about and discuss a topic further.

Remember *Usually, the information given in lectures is the 'skeleton' for the knowledge you need – you will need to add the 'flesh' via your own reading and work for and participation in seminars.*

Your lecture notes therefore need to reflect this and should simply be the framework upon which you build your full notes, whichever way you choose to do this.

Activity 1

This activity involves you listening to a short excerpt of a Property Law lecture and making notes on it. This is 'practice' note taking, to help you to see if you take notes effectively, in a way that will be most useful when it comes to assessments and/or revision for exams.

Note

In some universities, lectures are recorded and students have access to the recorded lecture for the whole period of their study of that module. Or, with permission from the lecturer, you may be able to record the lecture yourself. If this is the case, note taking in the lectures themselves becomes less important. Going to the lecture (or listening to the recorded version of it for the first time) could be an opportunity to just **listen** to what is said and to **think** about it. This is in fact very helpful as it helps you to **understand** what is being said, rather than panicking about getting everything written down, and note taking can then be saved for a second run-through. This also applies to the use of lecture outlines or slides (see below).

Tips for getting the best from your lectures

Note

Lectures are given prominence here as they are the main source of 'notes' that students tend to take, as well as being a new 'style' of teaching that students have to get used to. However, notes can come from other sources, such as reading from your text and casebooks, as well as from cases themselves – and there is more guidance on this in the relevant chapters.

Cross reference
See chapter 15, Using law books, and chapters 21–24, Reading cases 1–4.

Here are some practical hints for getting the best out of lectures if you are taking your own notes – none of these are new, nor are they rocket science, but sometimes it's useful to remind yourself and, if you feel that your notes are not as effective as they may be, it may be worth checking this list to see what you can improve:

- Ensure that you have **all** necessary materials with you in your lectures: any books required, lecture outline or printed out slides, paper/notebook, a pen!, or a laptop if you use one, plus a disc or memory stick.
- If you are taking your own notes rather than using an outline, listen actively – and **think** before you write – but don't lose track.
- Ask the lecturer questions if you are not sure about something, or ask them to repeat it if you did not hear or understand it fully; you could do this at the end of the lecture if it's easier.
- Develop and use your own standard method of note taking including punctuation and abbreviations (see later). As long as it is legible for you – and consistent – it is fine!
- Take and keep notes in a large notebook or A4 loose-leaf file. The only merit to a small notebook is that it takes up less space – not your highest priority.
- Leave a few spaces blank as you move from one point to the next so that you can fill in additional points later if necessary – for example from your further reading – or use columns (see later). Your objective is to take helpful notes, not to save paper.
- **Do not** try to take down everything that the lecturer says. It is both impossible and unnecessary because not everything said is of equal importance. Spend more time

listening and attempt to take down the main points – or utilise the lecture outlines or other handouts you may be given – that's what they are there for!

- Listen for cues to the main points, transition from one point to the next, repetition of points for emphasis. Lecturers will be trying to help you make accurate notes and to take down what is important.
- Similarly, listen for cues as to critiques that it might be important for you to make note of and follow up with further reading. There is often more than one way of understanding something – look out for explanations of this.
- Remember: although neatness is valuable in some respects, it does not of itself increase your learning – making your work neat may just take up time.
- Sit closer to the front of the lecture theatre – there are fewer distractions and it is usually easier to hear, see, note important material and ask questions, if necessary.

Using lecture outlines

Often, lecturers will provide a lecture outline (a breakdown of what they are going to talk about in the lecture) or use slides – e.g. in PowerPoint – to illustrate what they are talking about. These are very useful tools for you to use for your own notes, especially if they are available to you in hard copy or to download (and definitely if you use a laptop to take your notes). You can use the outline or slides as the basic structure of your notes and just add other important bits in the margins (or in the notes area format in PowerPoint) to form the skeleton of your notes on the topic.

Having an outline provided by the lecturer is very useful as it means that you have already been given the framework for the rest of your notes. In this way, they can act as a **substitute** for your own note taking in lectures – you won't need to worry about missing the key points as they will already have been given to you. You can then simply listen to the lecture and only need to make notes of any bits that seem complicated or that you know you need to read about in order to fully understand what was said. You will also be able to make clear which points the lecturer points out (if any) as being particularly important.

After the lecture

It is very helpful to set aside some time to read/review your lecture notes as soon as possible after the lecture, because:

- **It ensures that you understand the framework you have been given and have a solid foundation from which to build your further notes.** You could even rewrite your notes, or type them up, to consolidate them in a neat and organised manner, and prepare them for any notes to be added later, such as after you have read further about a topic.
- **Re-reading and thinking about what notes you have taken in a lecture will help the information sink in.** Many students find that by the time they come to go back to them,

the notes they took in a lecture mean relatively little to them, as they were so busy trying to write things down, they didn't really hear what was being said.

- While the topic is still fresh in your mind, you can fill in from memory examples/facts which you did not have time to write down during the lecture.
- You can easily recall what parts of the lecture were unclear to you so that you can consult the lecturer, a friend or your books for further information.
- Immediate review results in better retention than review after a longer period of time. Remember that reviewing becomes relearning after a period of 24 hours.

You do not need to write down absolutely everything said by the lecturer. It is more important to **listen** and try to follow and understand what you are being told. Make a note of the key points (or use any lecture outlines or slides provided) and flesh these out later, after reviewing them.

Reviewing your lecture notes

You do not want to waste your time when reviewing a lecture by simply recopying your notes. The following suggestions may be helpful:

- Underline key statements or important concepts.
- Use various punctuation or other marks to indicate importance or other things (see later).
- Use margins or blank sections for additional notes.
- Perhaps indicate relevant pages of your textbook beside the corresponding information in the notes.
- **Always** write a summary.
- Keep a **glossary** of technical terms in a separate file or notebook.

Other sources of notes

To supplement what you hear in lectures (or even before your lectures, for preparation), it is likely that you will asked to read from various sources. These could include:

- Textbooks
- Casebooks
- Statutes

Cross reference
See chapter 15, Using law books.

» glossary

Cross reference
See chapters 21–24, Reading cases 1–4.

See chapter 16, Using legal journals.

- Cases
- Academic articles
- Other sources such as newspapers
- Non-law texts and sources used.

Again, you may need to take notes from these sources, but to maximise the effectiveness of your notes it would be useful to see this type of notes as some of the 'flesh' that you are putting on your skeleton of lecture notes. However, it is absolutely **unnecessary** to make notes on absolutely everything you read, particularly if it is from your own textbooks etc.

The books will still be there at a later date, so why duplicate what they say?!

What is more useful than taking complex notes from your books and other sources of reading is making a note of **where** exactly the 'flesh' to put on the 'bones' of your notes can be found.

Example 1

Notes from lecture/handout/slide	Adding extra 'flesh' from a book
Rule: Performance of an existing duty cannot be consideration for a fresh promise (e.g. of extra money) ➢ Stilk v Myrick	Sailors case – captain didn't have to give extra money he'd promised as they did nothing extra – see casebook page xxx
Rule later modified by ➢ Williams v Roffey – concept of 'practical benefit'	Carpenter – was offered more money – no extra work but 'practical benefit' found to amount to consideration at CA – see casebook page xxx and textbook page xxx. Case highlighted at xxx.

Other useful hints

As already mentioned, there are various methods that you can use to take your notes, and you have to work out what works best for you. However, what follows are some techniques that you could incorporate into your usual way of note taking that might make it even more effective for you:

Use abbreviations/symbols in your notes

Work out (and stick to!) abbreviations that suit you. Some examples of commonly used abbreviations are listed below, but you can obviously include as many others as you need to – dev yr own system!

↳ Cross reference
There is a list of abbreviations at the end of this resource.

Legal abbreviations

CA	Court of Appeal
HL	House of Lords
Parl	Parliament
Gov	Government

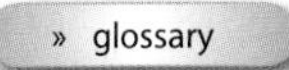

General abbreviations

Dev	Development/Developed
Ref	Reference/Referred
e.g.	For example
i.e.	That is

Symbols

∴	Therefore
∵	Because
>	The

Remember Don't make your shorthand such shorthand that it's later impossible to work out what you were writing! Be sensible and consistent with abbreviations and symbols and you will soon find you write/read them as second nature.

Use punctuation symbols as memory aids

Certain points that you note may be of high importance, or you may make notes in a lecture or from your reading that you wish to expand upon or find out more about later. Or, for example, there may be something a lecturer says that you are not sure about, and so need to ask a question about it in order that you understand it. Again, as long as you are consistent, using punctuation symbols can be very helpful. These can be placed in the margin against the particular note they refer to. Common examples might include the following:

!	Important point
!!	Very important point
*	This also relates to something else
>*	See later at *
?	Need to check this by reading or asking a question
?!	I might disagree with this point
@	Look this up on internet

Use colour coding

As well as using the framework and/or column system as described above, colour coding may help you to make sense of your notes when you come later to refer to them again. Using the same example as used when looking at 'other sources of notes', the following example illustrates how effective colour coding can be.

Example 2

Notes from lecture/handout/ slide	Adding extra 'flesh' from a book and using a colour code
Rule: Performance of an existing duty cannot be consideration for a fresh promise (e.g. of extra money) ➤ Stilk v Myrick	Sailors case – captain didn't have to give extra money he'd promised as they did nothing extra – details at page xxx
Rule later modified by ➤ Williams v Roffey – concept of 'practical benefit'	Carpenter – 'practical benefit' found to amount to consideration at CA page xxx – ratio explained page xxx – this said to 'modify' but not overrule the rule from Stilk page xxx

In this example, references in the 'flesh' section are colour coded, using the following key:

- Notes in red refer to a helpful passage or explanation in the casebook
- Notes in green refer to the textbook
- Notes in blue refer to a passage from the actual case.

In this way, the note can **mean** something: for example, the passage in red above directs you instantly back to the page of the casebook where the details of the first case and the ratio of the second case can be found and are explained. The note in green tells us how the writer of the textbook has interpreted the impact of the later case – which may be useful information to later include in an assessment or exam. And the note in blue directs you back to the original case where a passage gives you some important insight into the decision or outcome.

» glossary

You will see that there is less writing in the second column than in the earlier example. This is because these notes **direct you** to information elsewhere. You will also see that there is still quite a lot of space around the notes – this means that more can be added later!

This is not the only way your work can be colour-coded – using the same colours as in the example above (black, red, green, blue), you could use each in your notes to mean a different kind of information.

For example, notes in black could be the **main legal points** and/or basic information; in red could be the explanation of those points; in green could be application points (real-world examples and/or cases); and blue could be evaluative points (often called 'critique').

A very basic example can be used to illustrate this:

Example 3

Consideration is needed to make a contract binding

The concept of exchange or reciprocity in contracts

e.g. £1000 given for a second-hand car (executed). OR the promise of money for the promise of the car (executory).

Rules: Consideration must not be past, or the promise to perform a pre-existing obligation.

The problem with this concept is that it seems inflexible, but there have been some modifications – e.g. Williams v Roffey modifying rule from Stilk v Myrick (why? More realistic? Moving with the times?)

Use other techniques, e.g. mind maps or tables

When taking notes from books or articles, or when consolidating your lecture notes, or even when doing both at the same time, another way of recording the information is to create a mind map (spider diagram) or table. On the same topic as used in the above example (consideration in contracts), making a mind map or spider diagram conveying the same information as in the examples above might look like this:

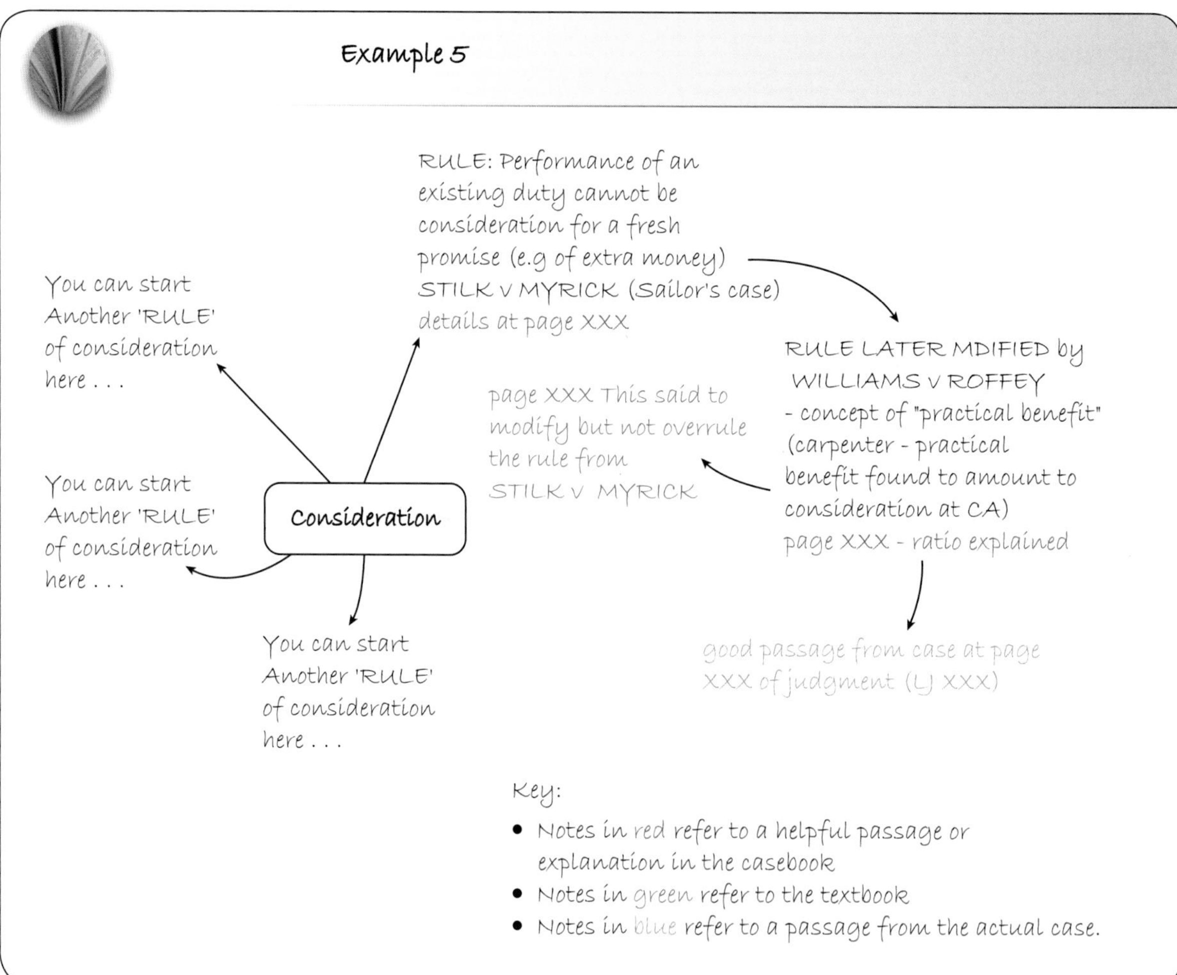

Example 5
RULE: Performance of an existing duty cannot be consideration for a fresh promise (e.g of extra money) STILK v MYRICK (Sailor's case)
details at page XXX
RULE LATER MDIFIED by WILLIAMS v ROFFEY - concept of "practical benefit" (carpenter - practical benefit found to amount to consideration at CA)
page XXX - ratio explained
page XXX This said to modify but not overrule the rule from STILK v MYRICK
good passage from case at page XXX of judgment (LJ XXX)
You can start Another 'RULE' of consideration here . . .
You can start Another 'RULE' of consideration here . . .
You can start Another 'RULE' of consideration here . . .
Consideration
Key:
• Notes in red refer to a helpful passage or explanation in the casebook
• Notes in green refer to the textbook
• Notes in blue refer to a passage from the actual case.

The best way to create a mind map is to read the whole passage through first (or listen to the whole section of a lecture). Then go back and select the main points from the passage – these would be the headings or substance of each 'leg' of the spider. As a general rule, you might expect that each new paragraph or section of writing under a subheading will contain a new point of substance. Within that paragraph or section, there will often be a number of smaller points, fleshing out the main point. Even in a mind map, headings – as well as any other techniques you have chosen to adopt (colour coding, abbreviations, symbols etc.) – work well.

Similarly, in table format, the information might be built up like this:

Example 5

Consideration

Rule	Cases etc	Detail	Extra info
Performance of an existing duty cannot be consideration for a fresh promise (e.g. of extra money)	Stilk v Myrick	Sailors case – captain didn't have to give extra money he'd promised as they did nothing extra	details at page xxx
Rule later modified by concept of 'practical benefit'	Williams v Roffey	Carpenter – 'practical benefit' found to amount to consideration at CA	page xxx – ratio explained page xxx – this said to 'modify' but not overrule the rule from Stilk page xxx

Activity 2

This activity involves you listening to short excerpt of a Property Law lecture and making notes on it, including making use of some or all of the extra tips above. Hopefully this activity can be used to 'bring it all together'.

Conclusion

Making efficient and accurate notes from lectures and further reading are vital to your success. This chapter has given you some suggestions for how to achieve this, but in the end, the way you take notes is up to you. You must find (and stick to) a system that suits the way that you learn – and this won't be the same for everyone. Remember to be prepared, organised and consistent and you should reap the benefits.

Links

http://www.support4learning.org.uk/education/index.cfm
The Support4Learning education pages, which contain information on education, training and learning, from finding a course to general details on exams, further and higher education and useful links for those interested in brushing up their study or presentation skills.

http://www.brunel.ac.uk/~mastmmg/ssguide/sshome.htm
Study Skills Online – An electronic guide to some of the best ways to study, compiled by a lecturer from Brunel University. Some good tips here!

Chapter 5

Working in groups

Rationale

Most of your recent educational experience will have involved individual effort and assessment. GCSEs, AS levels and A levels are essentially tests of your individual knowledge, skills and industry. However, group work is an equally important form of educational experience. It replicates the way people work outside the academic world; for instance, both the domestic world and the world of employment rely on teams of workers to achieve their objectives. Moreover, many educational experts would claim that group learning is more effective and more challenging than the traditional idea of lone scholarship. Group work requires additional skills; not only do you have to be competent; you also have to work with others to achieve a shared outcome. In this chapter we begin by thinking about what it means to work in teams and then we concentrate on some techniques to help you succeed at group work. We do this first by suggesting ways you can manage a formal requirement of your LLB to work in groups which is to be assessed and secondly by considering how you can set up a successful informal study group.

This chapter is devised to:

- Help you reflect on your experience of working in teams
- Highlight the different roles necessary to the success of a team
- Introduce you to some theoretical work on teams
- Set out the organisational requirements for a successful team project
- Provide some strategies for solving problems when working in teams
- Suggest a model for a successful informal study group.

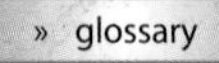

Thinking about working in teams

Most job applications, even for temporary low skilled work, require you to demonstrate your experience of teamwork. Lawyers are no exception to the requirement for teamwork.

Activity 1

We often think about the lawyer as some sort of lone hero working for his or her client – someone like Atticus Finch from Harper Lee's *To Kill a Mocking Bird* who stands up against the crowd to defend an innocent victim of prejudice. In real life, however, lawyers, like everyone else, work in teams. Give five examples of teams that lawyers are involved in.

Go online to read our thoughts on this question.

Most lawyers' firms require that applicants for traineeships demonstrate experience of teamworking.

Example

Freshfields, a leading City practice, explains on its website that it is looking for teamworking/interpersonal skills. The information states:

> Plenty of activities require teamwork, and it means far more than simply appearing on a sports pitch or turning up at a committee meeting. You need to provide examples of how you have approached and interacted with others, as you will need to get on with a huge range of colleagues and clients http://www.freshfields.com/uktrainees/meetusjoinus/what

Nor should you assume that teamwork becomes less important as your career develops. One of the criteria for appointment to judicial office involves teamwork. Applicants are required to demonstrate 'an ability to work constructively with others (including leadership and managerial skills where appropriate)' (www.judicialappointments.gov.uk). We fully expect that many of you will become judges at some time in your career. Working effectively in a team requires practice, like all skills, and it is important that you start developing these skills early in your legal career.

The ability to demonstrate teamwork skills is just as important if you decide not to pursue a legal career. It is difficult to think of many jobs where teamwork is not an essential requirement. However, you are not starting from a blank sheet. Everyone has had some experience of working in a team.

Activity 2

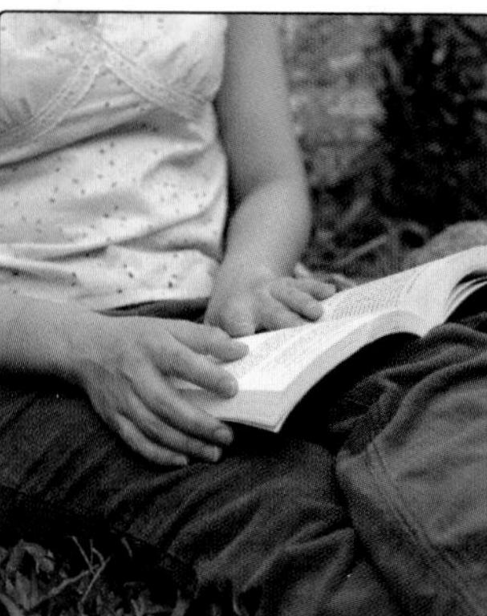

Now try an activity which asks you to reflect upon the teams you have been part of.

Team roles

Leadership is not the only role which is essential for a successful team. There are a range of roles which can be divided into task roles and team maintenance roles which have to be fulfilled if the team is to be successful. These roles are not necessarily formal roles but they are necessary. Each team member is likely to fill more than one role and the roles will be shared among team members. Roles are also likely to change as the team progresses. We set out the necessary roles in the key point boxes below.

Key Point

Necessary team roles

Role	Tasks	Comments
Team scribe/ secretary	Records the major points, actions, and decisions of the team during its meetings.	This role should be rotated amongst members.
Timekeeper	Informs and alerts the team as time passes during scheduled meetings.	This role prevents time wasting.
Information/ opinion seeker	Asks other team members for relevant information or opinions. Takes the initiative to ask others for the information or opinions that are missing.	This role ensures that the different talents that people bring to the team are fully utilised.
Clarifier/ summariser/ shaper	Listens and identifies important and cogent points raised during the discussion. Restates what has been presented to give the team the opportunity to reflect on what has been said and decide if the team is progressing.	This role is essential to effective progression.
Orienter/focus	Speaks up when it appears that the team is getting off target.	The orienter keeps the team on track and prevents people getting disillusioned about the value of meetings.
Critic/sceptic	Focuses the team on discussing the feasibility of ideas that are generated. Asks the question – will these ideas really work?	This stops the team getting too excited by its own generation of ideas.

Key Point

Necessary team roles – team maintenance roles

Role	Tasks	Comments
Harmoniser/ compromiser	Conflict is probably inevitable in teamwork and can be productive as long as it does not get out of control. The harmoniser depersonalises disagreements and tries to reconcile differences of opinion. When discussions get heated, the harmoniser is the person who intercedes.	Useful approaches include – I think that X and Y are not that far apart – X is saying this and Y is saying this . . .
Gatekeeper	The gatekeeper focuses on getting all team members involved and preventing any one team member from dominating the team's discussion to the point that others are no longer interested in participating.	There are a range of useful techniques here, such as – we have heard what X has said, but Y has been quiet for some time. . . . What do you think, Y?
Encourager	This person keeps the team working by offering praise. Comments like – that is a really helpful approach – can be invaluable to the team.	Praise can be verbal or non-verbal; a smile or an encouraging nod can be very effective.
Standard setter	This person is the role model for team behaviour, working by example to improve the quality of the team product. For instance, he or she will volunteer to put extra work into the presentation, or suggest that the product is just not yet good enough.	The purpose of teamwork is to produce a better product than an individual effort would produce. Therefore this person plays a vital role.

Different personalities are likely to be more adept at fulfilling different roles within the team. There has been a great deal of research into effective teams and the roles that people play. In particular, Dr Meredith Belbin developed a model which suggested that there were nine different types of roles that people played in teams, and that each brought particular strengths and weaknesses to a team endeavour. If you are interested in learning more about this and understanding your likely functions in a team, and how to develop your strengths we suggest you look at www.belbin.com.

The evolution of teams

Teams are not static but dynamic. They go through different stages and each stage presents different problems and different opportunities. If you are aware of these stages you are going to be able to manage your team more effectively and if you share your knowledge you will be making a valuable contribution to the success of the team. The most developed and widely known theory of teams comes from the work of Barry Tuckman who explained that teams go through four principal stages of development – forming, storming, norming and performing. He later added a fifth stage – adjourning – which involves completing the task of the team and breaking up. A brief explanation of the first four stages may help you understand what is happening to your team and how to resolve difficulties in the performance of your team.

Forming

This is the first stage of team formation. You meet as a team for the first time, go through introductions and consider the task you have been set. This is a very important time when relationships are established and roles are developed. It is important not to let bad habits develop at this stage, for bad behaviour accepted now will become the norm in the group. This can be an enjoyable and exciting time for the team. There are important skills you can bring to ensure that forming is effective and that the next, difficult, stage of teamwork is minimised. Ensure that you are inclusive – involve everyone in the group. Remember that diversity of skills is essential to a successful team, and welcome all talents. Focus on the common objectives – and make sure that you understand what those objectives are. It may be worth engaging in a team activity, perhaps an outing to play tenpin bowling, to build trust and commitment to the team.

Storming

This stage happens when the good behaviour and politeness of the initial encounters wear off. Interpersonal conflicts arise and arguments about the group and its goals will emerge. It is important to understand that conflict is inevitable at this stage, and can be productive. This stage can be resolved by ensuring that the group objectives are clear, and ensuring that the whole team is involved in discussing the resolution of conflicts. Everyone needs to feel heard and agree how the group is to resolve its differences. For many people 'storming' is a very painful process. However, there are techniques to minimise the discomfort. The most important thing is to be open to other people's ideas and concerns. Do not avoid conflict, but handle it directly and civilly. Keep focused on the purpose of the group. Avoid personal attacks. Examine biases that may be blocking progress or preventing someone from being treated fairly or from being heard.

Norming

If the team survives the storming phase it can reach a much more constructive stage when it establishes its procedures for getting work done. Team and individual expectations are clearly set out and accepted by the group. Formal and informal procedures are established in delegating tasks, reporting back to the group and other functions of the group. There are dangers, however, in this stage. The group can collapse into 'group think' which means that it stops challenging itself about its objectives. It is necessary to keep refocusing on the objectives of the group, and ensure that you are not taking individual's contributions for granted. Keep remembering that the purpose of teamwork is to produce something better than any individual could produce alone.

Performing

During this final stage of development the group is focused on its task and working effectively to accomplish its objectives. It is important that the group celebrates its achievements during this stage and that members recognise that they have learnt new skills and experienced new roles. If the group achieves what it has to achieve, it may go on to focus on a new task. Don't forget that if new members join the group, or a new objective is set for the group, the whole process of forming, storming, norming and performing begins again.

Now that we have spent some time thinking about some of the theory of groups, we turn to some practical group activities that you are likely to face during your degree, to see how this knowledge can be applied to your studies. The first group activity we consider is the compulsory group assessment.

Succeeding in group assessments

Most law degrees incorporate one or more group assessments. Our experience is that they are not popular with students who resent not being measured on their individual achievements. We would encourage you to think more constructively about the benefits of group work. You have been used to a competitive learning environment – the value of your work has been measured against the value of other people's work. Group learning is quite distinct and you must learn to treat it in quite a different way. It involves sharing skills, resources, and approaches to produce collaboratively something of value.

There are different ways of assessing group work, and you must check the assessment criteria of any group project you are set. Sometimes, for instance, the only mark which is given is for the group project as a whole; sometimes there are two marks awarded, one for individual performance and another for group performance. In some law schools student evaluations of the contributions of their team form part of the final mark awarded.

Key Point

Collaborative learning is distinct from competitive learning. It is designed to demonstrate that:

- all group members gain from each other's efforts
- the outcome for all group members will be identical
- each person's performance is mutually dependent upon oneself and one's team members.

Key Point

Cooperative learning is one particular form of collaborative learning. Whilst students work together on a group project the assessment grade is in two parts. One mark is given for each student's individual contribution to the final outcome and a mark is also given for the project as a whole.

There are three essential ground rules for effective group work which we have already explored, but are worth restating.

- Interaction within the group must be based upon mutual respect and encouragement and not competition. What this means is that the group and each individual member of the group must be willing to respect the differences within the group and to build upon them.
- Don't confuse personalities with ideas. Try to evaluate the ideas that people contribute rather than the way they behave. A group's strength lies in its ability to develop the ideas that individuals bring. In other words, you do not have to like someone to respect the value of the ideas they contribute.
- Conflict is very likely. Part of the learning process is to develop strategies to respond to conflict. The success of your group is measured not by its ability to avoid conflict but by its ability to manage it, and to respond creatively to tensions.

Whilst the first step to successful group assessment is to understand the different philosophy of group learning, the next and equally vital step is organisation. You need to break the group

↳ Cross reference
See chapter 2, Managing your time.

project down into a series of tasks and plan for the completion of those tasks. We suggest that you adapt the model set out below. You will also find it useful to refer to the chapter on time management.

Organising a group assessment

What has to be done	Who has to do it (insert names where appropriate)	How is it to be achieved	When is it to be achieved by (insert dates)
Introductions, sharing experiences and interests	Everyone		Meeting 1
Decide who will be responsible for convening the group meetings and who will record the meetings	Everyone	The decisions should be made by the whole of the group Take into account volunteers, experience, expertise, willingness to learn	Meeting 1
Decide how you are going to communicate as a group and how frequently	Everyone	Options include: face-to-face meetings (decide when and where) telephone: list numbers and convenient times email: addresses (distribution lists) web-based communications	Meeting 1
Focus on the assignment's objectives	All	Make sure you all agree what has to be achieved and by what date. If there is any confusion ask your seminar leader for advice	
Decide upon the process by which you will achieve the objectives	All	• Word processing the written part of the assignment • PowerPoint for the presentation • Divide the tasks into stages of development • Devise a timeline • Assign tasks to individuals and decide when they are to report back on those tasks	
Research		Organise library research and field research – split into tasks	
Analyse the research		Report back on research in sufficient time to respond to problems What gaps are there in the research? How can you get further help with the research?	

Continued

Plan your presentation and written report	Decide what your main argument is, what should go into the opening paragraph and what individual topics will be dealt with in the report
Write the **essay** and compile the presentation	One person should take responsibility for the first draft of each, and then others should comment
Review the essay and presentation	Meet to discuss the work as a whole – allow time for changes
Rehearse the presentation	
Do the presentation and submit the essay	
Celebrate!	

» glossary

Resolving problems

The best way to avoid problems is to anticipate them and set in place ways to resolve them. Perhaps it is best to begin by identifying your concerns about group work.

Activity 3

Now try an activity which will help you address any concerns you may have about group work.

Now try an activity that will help you address any concerns you may have about group work. You should note that there are no right or wrong answers to this question!

Which of the following most closely represents your fears of group work?

- I am a high achiever. I know how to get high marks in my assessment and I am concerned that working in a group will mean that my marks in this assignment will fall.
- I am a high achiever. I know that if I want to get a high mark in this group assessment I am going to have to do all of the work, which is not fair.
- I am really dreading working in a group. The rest of them are all very clever and any ideas I have or work I do will be ridiculed by them.
- I enjoy working in teams but the problem is that there is always someone who does not do their fair share of work and disappears if you are ever trying to rely on them. That drags down everyone's marks.

Team contracts

One possible solution to any anticipated problems is to draw up a team contract at the first meeting of the group. This should not be something that is prepared beforehand but discussed by the team in the context of anticipated problems and the solutions should be solutions agreed by the entire group.

Activity 4

Now compile a list of matters that should be considered in your team contract. You should think about what you want your meetings to achieve, how you are going to achieve mutual respect, and how you are going to ensure that conflicts are resolved.

Go online to read our thoughts on this matter.

Agendas

Agendas are also important for ensuring successful team meetings. They bring order and focus to meetings and ensure that time is spent productively. Draft your agenda before the meeting and circulate it. The agenda should include the following items:

- Date, time (including the estimated end time) and place for the meeting.
- Designated roles for the meeting – chair and secretary in particular.
- Refreshments – who is going to provide them, and when are they going to be taken (before, during or after the meeting).
- Brief statement of the primary objective of the meeting.
- Short (5 minutes maximum) individual updates on progress made since last meeting, including an outline of any difficulties that members have experienced.
- Group agreement of overall progress, with a review of the project schedule.
- Brief discussion/reflection of how the team is functioning as a unit.
- Assignment of action items to be accomplished by the next meeting, with the name of the person taking responsibility assigned and a completion date set.

Other steps

If you run your team collectively, if you are organised, if you understand something about team dynamics, if you set up a team contract and if you run your meetings in a businesslike way utilising agendas, you are likely to minimise the possibility of problems. However, if you still have difficulties, for instance, one person is not pulling their weight, or if one person is dominating meetings, then you will have to see your lecturer to see how the matter can be resolved. Before that point we suggest that you make serious attempts to meet up with the person and address the problems. Record your efforts to do this. Do not be surprised if your seminar teacher is not very sympathetic. One of the purposes of group work is to teach you how to resolve these dilemmas, and you have not succeeded if you have to turn to the authority figure of the seminar leader for help. Nonetheless these things do happen, and there are probably mechanisms available to resolve them. You might have to forfeit some marks, because your group has not functioned successfully, but there are probably ways to end the relationship of the group with its deviant member.

However, we would prefer to think that with the skills that you have brought with you to university, and your desire to work successfully with others, together with the advice that we have given you, that the group work will be a success. Perhaps you will want to continue to work in a group informally because you realise it enhances your learning. In the next section of the chapter we consider how to run an informal study group.

Running your own study group

This part of the chapter suggests how you could go about running a study group. You can adapt our suggestions to any area of law, and of course you can run your group in whatever way you want. These are just suggestions for getting your group off the ground. An important consideration in any study group is to have a basic structure that your group can depend on, but to allow for flexibility within the limits you set. That should allow your group to flourish. If the group is badly run it could be counter-productive, as it could leave people feeling that they have wasted their time or that they are actually more confused about the law. Note that there may be an unexpected benefit from running a study group – not only will it enhance your understanding and knowledge of law, it may also impress future employers as it demonstrates the ability to work in teams and to organise tasks both voluntarily and effectively.

Stage 1 – the basics

You are not going to be the only person who finds some things about learning law difficult. You are bound to have talked to others in lectures and seminars about the problems in keeping up with the reading, or knowing what it is that lecturers expect you to have understood from the reading lists they have prepared for seminars. One way to approach the challenges of studying law is to organise a group to work together on a particular aspect of learning the law. Probably

» glossary

a group of six or seven people works best. More than that number becomes difficult to manage. Fewer mean that there are fewer people to share problems and different approaches. You can ask around your seminar groups, talk to your friends and other students in lectures. What you want are people who share your aims, will be prepared to put in the necessary preparation and will participate fully in the group. Once you have found the people who want to work with you in the study group you need to:

- Gather together contact details – email addresses and mobile phone numbers are the most useful.
- Decide when and where you are going to meet – it makes sense to organise your reading group after a lecture when everyone is around. Whatever time you decide on, be sure to stick with it. Let your members plan their schedules around the study group rather than trying to fit the study group around everyone's schedule. Probably once a fortnight is about right. More than that and you will not have time to do the reading. Less than that and you might not achieve what you want to achieve. Try not to meet where there are a lot of distractions – the student bar is not a good idea, nor is someone's home unless you are all very disciplined. Try to book a seminar room or a group study room in your library.
- Decide the focus of the study group – we discuss this below.

Stage 2 – setting an agenda

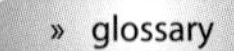

What do you want the study group to do? Perhaps you feel that you do not spend enough time in seminars talking about the cases you have read or you are not getting enough from reading the articles you have been set when you read them by yourself. Perhaps you want to spend some time going through previous exam papers and discussing how you would approach the questions, or brainstorming essay titles. Perhaps you want to concentrate on revision. You could do all or any of these things. What is important is that you decide what you want the group to achieve in advance, so that everyone involved has the opportunity to benefit from the reading you set yourselves. Reading should be done in your own time as everyone reads at a different pace; group time should be reserved to discuss problems, ask questions, share problems, have question and answer sessions, and share memory aids such as mnemonics and flow diagrams.

We are going to suggest an agenda for a public law study group which is going to concentrate on reading cases. How do you decide which cases deserve the attention of the group? Well, one place to start is to ask your lecturer. Most lecturers are going to be only too pleased to help students who are keen to help themselves. Another place is the reading lists you have been set – or you could use your text book to spot which cases are routinely referred to by the author. One useful idea is to take as a starting point those cases that you spend a lot of time on in lectures and seminars, and then see which cases are used extensively by the judges in those cases.

Our hypothetical study group is going to look at three important public law cases during the autumn term, so we are suggesting meeting every 3 weeks over a 12-week period. You will need a preliminary meeting to arrange the agendas for the study group – so there will be a total of four meetings. We suggest more specific agendas for the particular case studies below. However, your next task is to make sure that your meeting is effective and that is achieved by:

- agreeing your group objectives
- assigning particular responsibilities amongst the group.

Stage 3 – agreeing objectives

This may seem self-evident, but it is very easy for different members of a study group to have different ideas about what they want to achieve. What we suggest is that at your first meeting:

- each member of the study group independently writes down two or three main objectives for the group
- the group compares, agrees upon and records those objectives.

It may also be useful for you to talk about individual anxieties about participation in the group. If you feel that everyone else is more able or more confident than you, it is worth saying so. You will probably find that your anxieties are shared, and even if they are not, sharing them makes others aware and more understanding of how you feel. We discussed how to develop a team contract above. Even if your group is informal you may feel you will benefit from agreeing such a contract.

Stage 4 – leadership and other roles

There are a number of different tasks that have to be carried out before a study group can succeed. Once the group has decided upon the cases that you are going to concentrate on for the next meeting of your group then you need someone to email the group to say what the agenda is and remind them when and where you are going to meet. It does not matter that everyone was there when you agreed the agenda; it is always worthwhile getting it down in an email so that no one is confused. One useful tip for the agenda is to ensure that sufficient time is set aside for asking questions about what you have not understood. If you are lucky, someone will have understood the point, and you will learn from them. However, if all of you agree that you do not understand something then you should contact your lecturer for clarification.

Another task is leadership of the session. One person should take the responsibility of getting the discussion going, perhaps by introducing the case, setting out the facts and legal history, and raising some questions about the case – such as what legal point was being decided, how different judges approached the legal problem in front of them, what are the implications of the decision etc. Then others should take responsibility for different judgments perhaps, or comparing and contrasting decisions of lower courts with the decision you are considering. One person could search for case notes about the case and textbook references and summarise these for the other participants. One person should take notes of the session, summarise the conclusions and distribute them amongst the group. It is a good idea to change roles each session,

» glossary

so everyone takes a turn at leading the discussion, and taking notes and summarising the key points. However, everyone should read the decision carefully and be prepared to participate fully in the discussion. Don't forget what you read earlier about team roles. Team members are not just concerned with tasks, but also with maintaining the success of the group, so pay some attention to the different roles people play, for instance in encouraging people to participate, or by preventing people from deviating from the task in hand.

Organising the case reading study group

Here we are going to suggest agendas for four meetings of the study group which will look at three public law cases. We suggest that the following three cases would be useful to discuss.

- *Council of Civil Service Unions and others v Minister for the Civil Service* [1984] 3 All ER 935 (the GCHQ case)
- *R v North and East Devon Health Authority ex p Coughlan* [2001] QB 213
- *R (on the application of Begum) v Headteacher and Governors of Denbigh High School* [2007] 1 AC 100

Meeting 1 – setting agendas and assigning roles

You should start by agreeing amongst yourselves the objectives of the group and deciding when you will meet to discuss whether those objectives have been met and to decide whether to alter your methods of working. If you agree to a review meeting right from the beginning people will know that there will be a formal opportunity to discuss problems and are less likely to just disappear without comment.

For the purpose of this chapter we have assumed that you have agreed to read the three public law cases that we suggest, and that the agreed objectives of the group are:

- to improve your case reading skills
- to provide a supportive environment for learning law
- to consider how to use cases in essays and exams effectively.

The questions you set for yourselves and the way you operate the group should reflect your chosen objectives.

» glossary

The next step is to organise yourselves. The first role to be assigned is that of convenor.

The convenor should:

- create an email list of participants
- collate mobile phone numbers and other contact information

- organise room bookings
- distribute copies of the cases to be read in advance of the meetings
- email everyone two days before to remind them of their commitments
- chair the meeting – i.e. ensure that the agreed agenda is delivered.

Then decide on other roles. Perhaps you could draw lots with numbers on, so number 1 would be the first person on the list below, and so on. Remember to reassign roles for each case, so everyone experiences a different role. We have designed these roles for a study group of seven.

1. The person who introduces the case, explains the facts, the legal history, the legal point at issue and the decision.
2. The person who explains the legal reasoning of the judge in the leading judgment.
3. The person who takes responsibility for explaining the legal reasoning of any minority judgment, and for any decisions in the lower courts which ran counter to the majority opinion.
4. The person who summarises the views of textbook writers and case note writers for the group.
5. The person who considers the wider implications of the decision, both legally and politically. This person might want to look at Current Law to see how the case has been used.
6. The person who looks for exam questions on past papers and previously set essay questions to see how your lecturers have expected you to use the case. This person takes responsibility for ensuring that you have considered the case for assessment purposes.
7. The person who takes notes for the group and provides copies for everyone subsequently.

Once you have decided on roles for the subsequent three meetings you now need to draw up agendas for those meetings. We have adapted the agenda from the one we proposed earlier. You might decide that the agenda should be as follows:

- Date, time (including the estimated end time) and place for the meeting – we think you should spend a maximum of one and half hours discussing each case.
- Confirm the designated roles with names beside the roles.
- Refreshments – who is going to provide them, and when are they going to be taken (before, during or after the meeting).
- The convenor should restate the purpose of the meeting, to focus everyone's minds.
- Each person should report back on their role. Allow 5 minutes report back per role. If people have had difficulty in understanding anything or accessing particular information, now is the time to reveal it.

- You should then allow time for a discussion of the wider implications of the case. We have made suggestions below as to what could be discussed.
- Brief discussion/reflection of how the team is functioning as a unit and whether it is continuing to focus on its objectives (led by the convenor).
- Assignment of action items to be accomplished by the next meeting, with the name of the person taking responsibility assigned.

Meeting 2 – *Council of Civil Service Unions and others v Minister for the Civil Service* [1984] 3 All ER 935 (the GCHQ case)

The sort of things you might want to discuss are:

- What do we mean by the **Crown**? Where does its authority come from?
- What does the case tell us about the role of the Crown in the constitution?
- What do we learn about the relationship between the Crown and the courts?
- Is the case useful for explaining the limits of judicial review?

Meeting 3 – *R v North and East Devon Health Authority ex p Coughlan* [2001] QB 213

The sort of things you might want to discuss are:

- What does the case tell us about 'legitimate expectations'?
- What function does 'legitimate expectations' serve within judicial review?
- How does 'legitimate expectations' interface with proportionality?
- What sort of advice would you give to a local authority which has to cut back on service provision because of a funding crisis?
- What does this tell you about the role of the courts in the constitution?

Meeting 4 – *R (on the application of Begum) v Headteacher and Governors of Denbigh High School* [2007] 1 AC 100

The sort of things you might want to discuss are:

» glossary

- Why did the **Court of Appeal** and the **House of Lords** come to different conclusions in this case? Whose opinion do you prefer?
- How important is process and community consultation in responding to human rights challenges?
- What does the case tell us about the extent of individual autonomy in the UK constitution?

Evaluating the effectiveness of the study group meeting

If you manage to convene the group, read the three cases and have a stimulating and informative discussion you should congratulate yourselves. However, you should also ensure that you review the performance of the group. This will be particularly valuable if you are going to work again as a team. Questions you might ask include:

- What did we do well? (and why did it work?)
- Was everyone clear about what the group was trying to achieve?
- Was everyone clear about what they individually should be doing?
- Was it easy to contact other members of the team when necessary?
- Did everyone contribute equally?
- How did we respond as a group when someone did not pull their weight? Was our strategy successful?

The focus of the review is about what works, and how to improve the performance of the group in future. Do not spend much time talking about what went wrong, and whose fault it was. The lessons you learn are very valuable, they should inform any group work you do in future, and you can use them as examples in job applications and interviews. We would also like to hear about any successful study group in law; we can pass on your tips and experiences to others.

Conclusion

Group work in higher education should provide you with a different experience of working which brings different benefits from the traditional idea of the student alone with his or her book in a library. There is great value in working collaboratively rather than competitively, and the skills involved are sought after by employers. It is worthwhile thinking about what is involved in group work, and what role you can play in ensuring your group is successful. If you are required to complete a group assignment, you must be organised, manage conflict successfully and be reflective about what is happening in the group. An informal study group is a very useful way to enhance your individual learning. We have given you some suggestions about forming an informal study group in public law; however, you can develop this in a multiplicity of ways, including revising for exams and reading articles and books. Just remember that no group works smoothly all the time; they need work, reflection and honesty.

www.oxfordinteract.com

Chapter 6

Contributing to seminars and tutorials

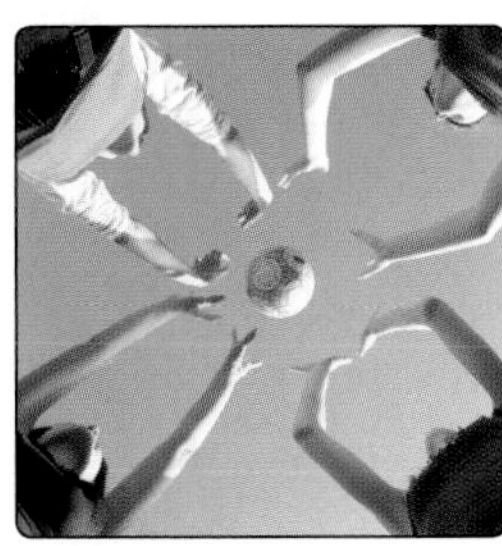

Rationale

This chapter is about seminars and/or tutorials – one of the main ways in which you will be 'taught' law. The reason, however, that 'taught' is in inverted commas, is because in many or most cases, seminars aren't actually used to 'teach' as such, but more as a forum for discussion of and engagement with the law that has been taught in lectures and supplemented by your reading.

Many students come to university unfamiliar with the seminar system and find it difficult to participate – this may partly be because they believe that they should be being taught more law, it may be because they lack confidence, or it may be because they have not understood the purpose of the use of seminar-style teaching.

This chapter is devised to:

- Explain the purpose of seminar or tutorial sessions
- Show why active participation in seminars or tutorials helps you learn better
- Help you to feel more confident about contributing to seminars.

What is a seminar?

When you came to university, or even before, you may have been told about the various teaching styles that you will encounter. Most people's degree courses are taught via a mixture of lectures and seminars or tutorials (the two terms are often interchangeable, but we will refer to seminars throughout the remainder of this chapter); it may have been explained to you that a lecture is lots of students in a big hall being talked to by a lecturer, with little or no interaction (although this varies by course and some lectures are very interactive) and that a seminar is a smaller group of students in a classroom led by a member of staff.

» glossary

» glossary

The point of seminars is to learn by discussion: by sharing ideas and asking and answering questions. Usually the member of staff actually leads the seminar, for example by going through questions on a worksheet, or talking about reading you have undertaken, but there are many different ways of running small groups, some of which may be employed in your seminars.

Students in seminars will talk about the material covered in lectures and in reading on a topic and the discussion will be led or guided by a seminar leader or tutor. This person can be a lecturer, another member of academic staff who knows the subject area, or often postgraduate research students. You will often have been given work to prepare in advance of your seminars – including (but not exclusively) reading and researching cases or statutes, reading

» glossary

» glossary

↳ Cross reference
For more information see chapters 21–24, Reading cases 1–4; chapter 19, Readings statutes and the legislative process; chapter 15, Using law books; and chapter 27, Answering problem questions.

textbooks and casebooks, reading academic articles and/or preparing answers to questions or problems.

This all sounds fairly nice and easy – but seminars can still come as a bit of a shock to some people when they arrive at university. Unlike lectures, where it is easy to imagine the shock value of seeing such a large number of students all in one place at one time, seminars can take a bit more getting used to for a lot of students. This is understandable – you are probably used to being taught in smaller groups at school or college, but these will still have been **taught** by a teacher, and it's likely that you would still be doing some work, e.g. from books or other resources, in your classes. Seminars differ in that, in most cases, you will be expected to have done the work **before** you get to the class, and the class is merely a venue for discussion of the topic and working through the work you have already prepared – some students find this a bit daunting.

Activity 1

What do you think of seminars? You may not have had any yet, or you may only just have started them – in which case this activity will help you to see what seminars might be for, and the value that you will be able to get from them. Or, if your seminars are well underway, this could be the first time you are actually really thinking about them and what they are for. Either way, complete the short series of true or false questions online to see if what you expect is right.

What do you think of seminars? You may not have had any yet, or you may only just have started them – in which case this activity will help you to see what seminars might be for, and the value that you will be able to get from them. Or, if your seminars are well underway, this could be the first time you are actually really thinking about them and what they are for. Either way, complete this short series of true or false questions to see if what you expect is right. The answers and feedback are designed to give you a picture of what seminars at university are all about.

	True	False
Seminars are where you get additional material that you didn't get in lectures.	○	○
I won't/don't have to do much work for seminars as the seminar leader will do most of the talking and all I'll need to do is take notes.	○	○
I shouldn't ask questions in seminars, only answer any that come my way.	○	○

Note

You may find that you have some modules that are seminar only, i.e. there are no lectures. This may be the case, for example, in smaller modules or the type of modules that are discussion-based, such as critical introductions to or interpretations of law. This is obviously a good way to learn, not just because of the known benefits of small-group learning but also because by working consistently in a small(er) group, you will enhance your confidence.

What kinds of activities take place in a seminar?

There is no hard and fast rule about this and you may find that your seminars vary quite considerably between modules. However, the following list shows you some of the common things you should expect to take part in during a seminar:

- Discussing a lecture – you may want to ask about points you are not clear about or to discuss what the lecturer has said about particular topics. You may wish to disagree with the lecturer too.
- Discussing what you have read – on many courses you will be given specific reading for each session, usually from casebooks and textbooks, and sometimes in the form of reading packs for the course, which may include cases and academic articles.
- Talking through the answers you have prepared to a set of questions given to you before the seminar – these will usually be linked to your reading but may require you to engage in some analysis and thought for yourself, i.e. the 'answer' might not always be in a book.
- Presentations prepared by one or more students followed by discussion – these may be in the form of notes or a mini-essay. This means that you have to put together your ideas on a subject, sometimes answering a particular question, present them to the group and get a discussion going. One way to do this is to prepare two or three questions in case the rest of the group are not sure how to start.
- Dividing into small groups to work on questions or topics which you then take back to discuss with the whole seminar group. This gives more people an opportunity to contribute.
- Asking the member of staff and other students questions.
- Listening carefully to what others say – and responding to this.

» glossary

What is a seminar for?

Once you find out what a seminar is, and how they are run in your institution, it's important to become aware of what the **purpose** of seminars is. It helps if you don't look upon them as somewhere where you will be **taught** the law (that is what lectures are for, and your reading should supplement this). The difference between school and university is that at school you are a 'pupil' and at university you are a 'student' – this should give you a hint about one of the big differences: you are at university to **study**, not necessarily to be **taught** everything you need to know. If you see seminars as somewhere where you can discuss what you have learnt, rather than somewhere where you will be taught, you will get on better.

↳ **Cross reference**
See chapter 4, Taking notes.

As explained in the chapter on how to take notes, while at university you will have a wider variety of learning environments than you did at school, including lectures, seminars or tutorials, self-study and reading etc. We have already explained how it is important to use lectures 'actively' as a forum to start taking good, helpful notes. It is even more important for your learning that you actively learn in your seminars, as this is where you will gain much of the 'flesh' of your studies to put on the skeleton information given to you in lectures. For this reason it is important that you actually do the preparation you have been given for seminars. The work will have been designed to help you to understand the law and to flesh out any areas of uncertainty.

Note

A seminar is **not** a mini-lecture, so don't expect your seminar leader or tutor to go over all the law again for you. It is your responsibility to have gathered the law from your lectures and reading.

Seminars have been described as, 'first and foremost, a conversation among people who share a common interest in expanding their understanding of an idea, a book, a painting, or some other specific topic' (Ian Johnston, 'Participating in seminars', document for Malaspina University College, December 2002). From this, you should gather that seminars are primarily forums for idea-sharing, with the idea being that all members of the group enhance and deepen their understanding of the topic being considered. The rationale for this is that it can be seen that students actually learn far more from talking and listening to each other than they do from listening passively to a lecturer. More importantly, students seem to remember what they learn in a seminar more clearly than they do lecture material.

You can also see seminars as somewhere to develop the skills of conversation, discussion and argument. These are a complex set of habits and attitudes which, in large part, determine our abilities to deal with others in a group setting – and are certainly skills you will need to develop to take forward into your chosen career, whether or not this involves going into the legal profession. Also, seminars try to gain your interest in a subject – perhaps making you want to discuss a topic further in a more informal setting outside of the classroom (in the canteen over lunch, or in the pub!).

However, 'good' seminars don't just happen. All of the participants (students and seminar leader) have to work to ensure that the seminar works and is successful. On reflection, people who have been students (of law or anything else) are likely to tell you that actively participating in seminars is better for learning than passively trying to absorb the discussions that took place in these sessions or to try and note down everything being said. With this in mind, what seminars require of you, in order for you to get the best from them, is:

- **Preparation** – you are expected to prepare for seminars. If you have been given reading to do and/or questions to prepare answers for before the seminar takes place, you should make sure you find a decent amount of time to dedicate to this. It is not fair to other students or the seminar leader if you just turn up expecting others to do all the work – this defeats the purpose of the seminar.

↳ **Cross reference**
See chapter 2, Managing your time.

- **Enthusiasm** – this helps you to participate and get the best out of seminars. It is important to take an active part in seminars. Students who do not talk lose the chance to learn through discussion. Even though you may not be enthusiastic about a particular topic, you can be enthusiastic about learning it and discussing it with your peers in a seminar setting.
- **Contribution** – seminars are based on small-group discussion and it's best if all members of the group – which could be anything from 2 to 25 students (the average size of a seminar is 12–16, but this can vary a good deal between universities, departments and even modules) – make a contribution, even if it's only to agree with someone else, or ask for a more detailed explanation of something. Even if your ideas are only half-formed, get the debate going!

Remember

Seminars exist for you to talk about **your** ideas. They are not there to test how much you know about the subject, but to help you to learn it. The best way to learn in a seminar is to make sure that you prepare well and then take an active part in it by thinking, listening, and talking.

Activity 2

The next activity is another set of true or false questions. You need to go through the questions and answer them truthfully, now that you have read what the purpose of a seminar is. See if your opinions have changed since you did the previous activity. If they have, it is time to change the way you approach seminars. If not, perhaps you should read the last section of this chapter through again.

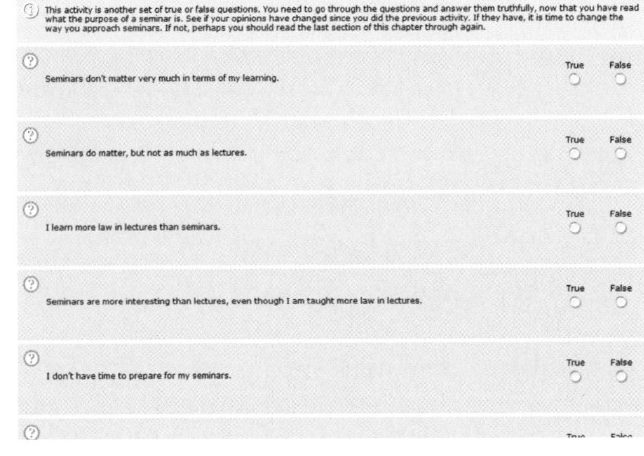

This activity is another set of true or false questions. You need to go through the questions and answer them truthfully, now that you have read what the purpose of a seminar is. See if your opinions have changed since you did the previous activity. If they have, it is time to change the way you approach seminars. If not, perhaps you should read the last section of this chapter through again.

	True	False
Seminars don't matter very much in terms of my learning.	○	○
Seminars do matter, but not as much as lectures.	○	○
I learn more law in lectures than seminars.	○	○
Seminars are more interesting than lectures, even though I am taught more law in lectures.	○	○
I don't have time to prepare for my seminars.	○	○

Contributing in seminars

Some law schools have begun to assess the oral contribution made in seminars, in order to encourage more general participation. Still others are requiring that work is handed in at each seminar which, alongside attendance, goes to make up a proportion of the coursework mark. From this, you should pick up that students not preparing for or contributing in seminars is a growing problem, and that law schools are taking steps to address this.

Why should I prepare?

You will get the most benefits from seminar discussion if you have prepared (i.e. done any required reading, possibly attempted some 'extra' reading or research, prepared answers to any questions or problems set and – importantly – **thought** about what it is the seminar is covering. Seminars are for students to question and examine the law, but if you have not thoroughly considered the material prior to the seminar, you will not know what question to ask, nor will you be able to follow the discussion or arguments. Preparation allows you to:

- check that you understand the law given to you in your lectures

- note any areas of the law (generally, or a particular case or application of a section of a statute) that you find particularly complex, so that you can ask about them
- contribute something to the seminar.

Participation is also essential – you gain nothing by sitting, burying your head, trying to avoid eye contact with the seminar leader or staring out of the window. In fact, doing this – seeming like you're not prepared to participate – may even encourage the seminar leader to try harder to get you to say something! Similarly, don't just go to a seminar with a blank sheet of paper and a pen – it won't help you.

Activity 3

Go online to see video clips of a number of law students reflecting on their experiences of contributing to seminars.

Note

Even if you go into a seminar on a topic with a list of questions, you may not have to ask them all yourself – the answers to many of them may emerge out of the group discussion and you can note them down as you go along. Of course, you can only do this if you have prepared and thought about the material covered in the seminar in advance!

Can I get away with doing nothing?

It might be possible, on occasion, for you to get away without preparing for a seminar and without having to say anything while you are there. If other students are prepared to discuss a topic, you might be able to just fade into the background. But be aware that if this happens, you are lucky – seminar leaders will be watching out for this kind of thing and are likely to ask you something precisely **because** you are not contributing. Then, if you can't answer, it will become obvious that you have done no work and more embarrassing than having tried to do the work but giving a wrong answer or an opinion others don't share.

When you don't say anything you draw attention to yourself – not just attention from the seminar leader but also from other students, who are likely to begin to resent the fact that they do all the work while you don't, and get away with it. It often looks like you are there just so your attendance record doesn't look bad (some universities have a percentage attendance policy in order for you to pass a course) and apart from this other students and the seminar leader probably won't understand why you bothered to come. When you don't prepare or participate, you can't really get anything out of a seminar – so you won't be any the wiser when you come out of it, if that's what you had hoped!

It should be noted that there are many other ways of 'not participating' in a seminar. While seminars should be informal, they should also be polite. That is, people's views should be treated with respect (which does not mean that they cannot be challenged), and the normal courtesies of polite conversation should be observed. If there is a breach of such politeness, each member of the group has the responsibility for pointing it out and helping to remedy it. It is important to remember that courtesy is not just a matter of verbal niceties. One's courtesy also manifests itself in one's tone, bodily posture, and particular activities while someone else is speaking, so that things like slouching, sitting away from the table, eating, yawning, and so on can affect the discussion for the worse (see the document, 'Participating in seminars', prepared by Ian Johnston for Malaspina University College, December 2002).

Note

On manners

- Try to ensure you turn up to your seminars on time – it is very disruptive to all concerned to have students wandering into the room at various times throughout the first 10–15 minutes. This also goes to your preparation and participation – if you are well-prepared you should **want** to be there on time.
- You should not, as a general rule, take food or drinks to seminars. There is plenty of other time in the day for you to eat and drink – and it is certainly discourteous to your seminar leader and co-students to sit there munching and slurping while they are trying to work – it may even be against the rules of your university to take food items into classrooms. It also is not good for your concentration!

What if I say the wrong thing?

Many students say that the reason they don't participate in seminars, especially those where the material being discussed is particularly difficult, is because they are scared of saying something wrong, especially in front of others. However, the answer to the question 'what if I say the wrong thing?' is 'You can't!'

Of course it is possible to give the wrong answer to a factual question (e.g. what was the case relied on?). However, even if you answer a question wrongly you'll then find out what the answer would be, as someone else will say it, or the seminar leader will point you in the right direction. Or, if you are asked 'what do you think about...?' etc., then the answer you give is only your opinion, which can't be wrong, but can only be disagreed with! In fact, in this situation, what you'll get in return is someone else's opinion – which might lead to a discussion, which is good – and you can make a note of any counter points raised and use them in essays!

Remember You are not the only one feeling reticent about contributing to seminars. There will be others in the group who feel the same way as you and are not sure they have the law 'right'. However, it is only by trying that you will know whether you have understood the law or not. What's the worst that can happen? If you are wrong in whole or in part, you will be guided towards the correct answer. Or, if you are unsure, say so!

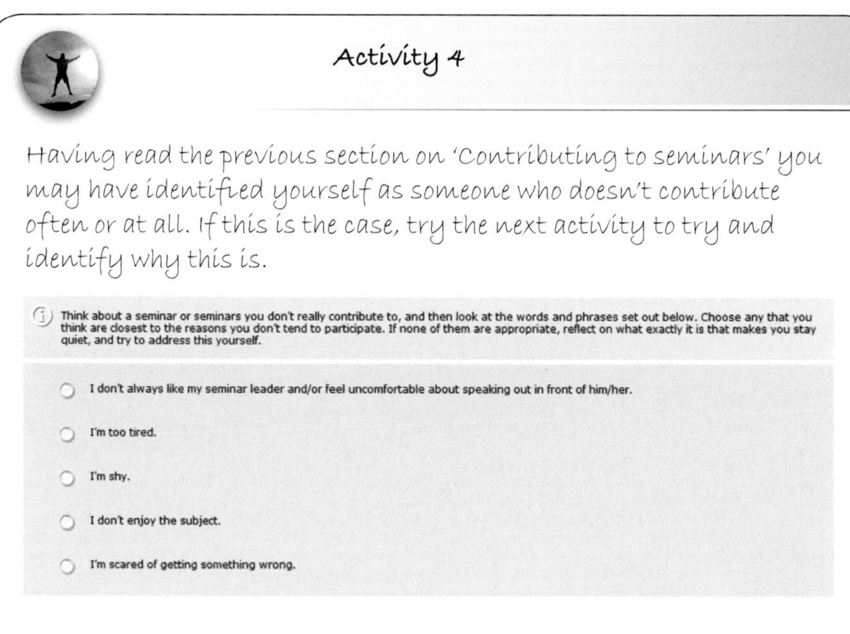

Activity 4

Having read the previous section on 'Contributing to seminars' you may have identified yourself as someone who doesn't contribute often or at all. If this is the case, try the next activity to try and identify why this is.

Think about a seminar or seminars you don't really contribute to, and then look at the words and phrases set out below. Choose any that you think are closest to the reasons you don't tend to participate. If none of them are appropriate, reflect on what exactly it is that makes you stay quiet, and try to address this yourself.

- I don't always like my seminar leader and/or feel uncomfortable about speaking out in front of him/her.
- I'm too tired.
- I'm shy.
- I don't enjoy the subject.
- I'm scared of getting something wrong.

Students who dominate

Sometimes some students don't get involved in seminars because there are other students (or just one other student) who tend to 'dominate' the discussion. If they seem to always be confident then ask yourself why. It tends to be one of three reasons: either they are really well prepared and so feel able to answer questions on most aspects of the seminar topic; or they are naturally confident, so much so they don't mind getting an answer wrong as by doing so they will learn the right answer; or it is bravado, covering up for the fact that very little work has been done and there is, in fact, little understanding.

Note

Don't be put off or intimidated by people who always seem to jump in to answer questions. Good seminar participation does not depend on the frequency, length or even accuracy of your remarks. Dominating students can be quite **disruptive** if other people feel excluded or begin to rely on one person to say something.

A seminar is meant to be a gathering of equals: everyone has an equal right to be heard and an equal responsibility for keeping the seminar working properly. While the seminar will normally have a leader, usually a member of staff, their job is really only to get the seminar started, prompt discussion or move it on, if necessary, and to bring things together at the end. Beyond that, however, the leader has no particular responsibility greater than anyone else for keeping the discussion going in a useful manner. Therefore, if you are experiencing some problems in the seminar, such as another student dominating, or you feel like your seminars are a waste of time, or boring, the first question to ask yourself is 'what can I do to help remedy the situation?' If you really can't do anything, speak to your seminar leader at the end of a seminar about the problem you are having.

Conclusion

Research into education has shown that students learn well by talking through their ideas in an exploratory way. In seminars you can do this by engaging in detailed analysis of what you have read or been taught about the law, raising aspects that you are not sure about, asking questions about fact or opinion, listening and adding to what other people say, exploring and building up an argument, re-thinking your ideas as others take them up and agree or disagree and acknowledging the worth of different viewpoints. All of these things – and more – take place in a successful seminar, and all of them are valuable to you as students. By cultivating your own participation in seminars, you will progress more smoothly through your studies. Don't be scared – remember that seminars aren't about getting things 'right' (there may not even be one right answer, especially in law!) or 'wrong'.

You are **not** being **tested** on your knowledge in a seminar, but being given an opportunity to learn more.

Links

http://www.mala.bc.ca/~johnstoi/seminars.htm

This document, which has been prepared by lecturer Ian Johnston of Malaspina University-College in Canada, describes what he believes to be good seminar participation in his Liberal Studies and English classes. However, much of what he says is equally applicable to seminars in law and the short article is worth reading to get a feel for what your seminar leaders might be expecting of you.

www.oxfordinteract.com

Chapter 7

Avoiding plagiarism

Rationale

Plagiarism is something that you should be aware of all the time. Although it has always existed, it has become much easier both to do and to detect in recent years.

At its simplest, you can think of plagiarism as stealing other people's work, and something we can presume you know to be wrong, just as you know that stealing someone else's possessions is wrong. However, it is more complicated than that, and it is easy to plagiarise without knowing you have done it.

This chapter is devised to help you know:

- What plagiarism is
- How to recognise it
- How to avoid it.

Why you need to know about plagiarism

As a law student you may not want to spend your time reading documents about plagiarism, or plodding through your university's policy on the subject. You have come to your university to study law, and that is where your energies will go. But if you are to succeed academically it is vital to be aware of what your university expects from you. This is what one organisation says:

» glossary

> Many people think of plagiarism as copying another's work, or borrowing someone else's original ideas. But terms like 'copying' and 'borrowing' can disguise the seriousness of the offence (Turnitin website, http://turnitin.com)

So the first activity is to find out your university's policy, what it offers in the way of guidance, and how it can help you maintain your own honesty and integrity.

Activity 1

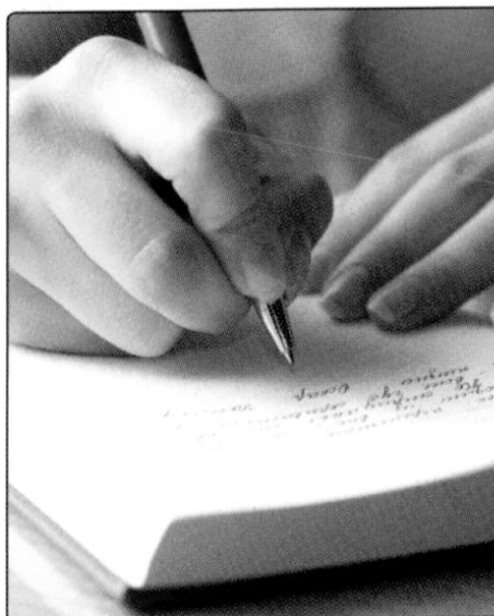

Log in to your university website and identify your university's policy on plagiarism.

Remember *In your future career, whether as a lawyer or in any other employment, you will be expected to be absolutely trustworthy. What may feel like a legitimate or insignificant device to save you time, or to help boost your marks, can turn out to compromise your integrity.*

What is plagiarism?

The Oxford Advanced Learner's Dictionary (5th edition, 1995) defines 'plagiarise' as follows: 'to take somebody else's ideas or words, and use them as if they were one's own'.

These are the ways in which you can plagiarise:

- Copying from other students
- Copying from books, online resources and internet sites
- Submitting previously submitted or assessed work of your own without attribution
- Submitting work written by others, whether 'borrowed' or bought
- Failing to reference your sources.

While you will be well aware that you are committing an offence, if, for example, you were to get someone else to write an essay for you, other breaches may not be so obvious, so we will look at them in detail.

» glossary

Copying from other students

Unless you are specifically prohibited from doing so (as in an exam situation) it is quite legitimate to discuss work with a fellow student, and indeed, this can be a very fruitful way of exploring ideas and learning. Putting these ideas into writing should be your own work. Changing the wording of a piece of writing you have worked on together is collusion, a form of plagiarism. If two students collude in producing a piece of work, each submitting it as his/her own, it is plagiarism.

This is different from group work, where students have to work together on a project and submit the work under joint authorship.

Copying from books and internet sources

If you use someone else's work and don't acknowledge the source, this is plagiarism. This includes inserting passages which you have taken from a book, article, website or online resource, unless you reference the passage properly. It also includes using what you know to be someone else's ideas without giving the source, i.e. passing them off as your own.

Word for word quotations must be indented, or put in inverted commas and properly referenced.

If you change the wording of someone else's work, or paraphrase it, this is still plagiarism, unless you acknowledge the source properly.

Submitting previously submitted work

This should be obvious. You can't get marks for work you have already been assessed for, and if you do, you will be aware that you are cheating.

Submitting work written by others

Again, you will be well aware if you try to pass off someone else's work as your own, and you will know that this is dishonest. This includes instances where you have altered the wording, or changed the order by cutting and pasting sections.

It is plagiarism if you 'borrow' work from a friend or colleague, even with permission. Remember that borrowing something also entails returning it, which you can't do if you have submitted it as your own. It's cheating.

Similarly, if you have bought a piece of work from an essay bank, or downloaded for free from the internet, you are knowingly cheating.

Failing to reference your sources

All your sources should be properly reference and cited. However, you should also ensure that any quote from any source is properly attributed.

Cross reference
For more information on legal citation, see chapter 14, Citing legal authorities.

» glossary

Plagiarism includes the presentation of another person's **ideas** as your own, not just copying what they wrote.

How to recognise plagiarism

As we have seen, some plagiarism is quite difficult to define, and can seem confusing to students. It is so easy to cut and paste passages from an online article or other internet source that you can sometimes forget that you are using someone else's words.

While you are probably well aware when you quote a passage from an article or a book that this needs to be properly cited, if you find material on an internet site whose authority you are not sure of, you may instinctively not want to acknowledge it.

Example

If you find the text of a case or statute on a website make sure that you check that the **text** comes from an accredited source, such as BAILII or OPSI.

» glossary

» glossary

Activity 2

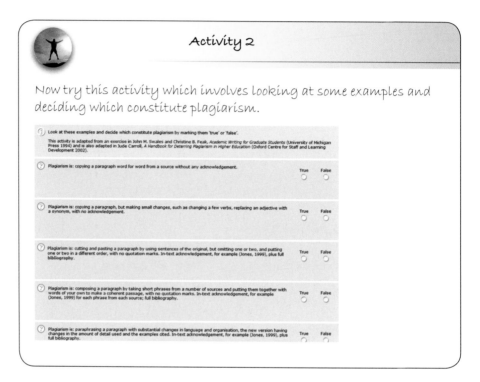

Now try this activity which involves looking at some examples and deciding which constitute plagiarism.

Look at these examples and decide which constitute plagiarism by marking them 'true' or 'false'.

This activity is adapted from an exercise in John M. Swales and Christine B. Feak, *Academic Writing for Graduate Students* (University of Michigan Press 1994) and is also adapted in Jude Carroll, *A Handbook for Deterring Plagiarism in Higher Education* (Oxford Centre for Staff and Learning Development 2002).

	True	False
Plagiarism is: copying a paragraph word for word from a source without any acknowledgement.	○	○
Plagiarism is: copying a paragraph, but making small changes, such as changing a few verbs, replacing an adjective with a synonym, with no acknowledgement.	○	○
Plagiarism is: cutting and pasting a paragraph by using sentences of the original, but omitting one or two, and putting one or two in a different order, with no quotation marks. In-text acknowledgement, for example (Jones, 1999), plus full bibliography.	○	○
Plagiarism is: composing a paragraph by taking short phrases from a number of sources and putting them together with words of your own to make a coherent passage, with no quotation marks. In-text acknowledgement, for example (Jones, 1999) for each phrase from each source; full bibliography.	○	○
Plagiarism is: paraphrasing a paragraph with substantial changes in language and organisation, the new version having changes in the amount of detail used and the examples cited. In-text acknowledgement, for example (Jones, 1999), plus full bibliography.	○	○

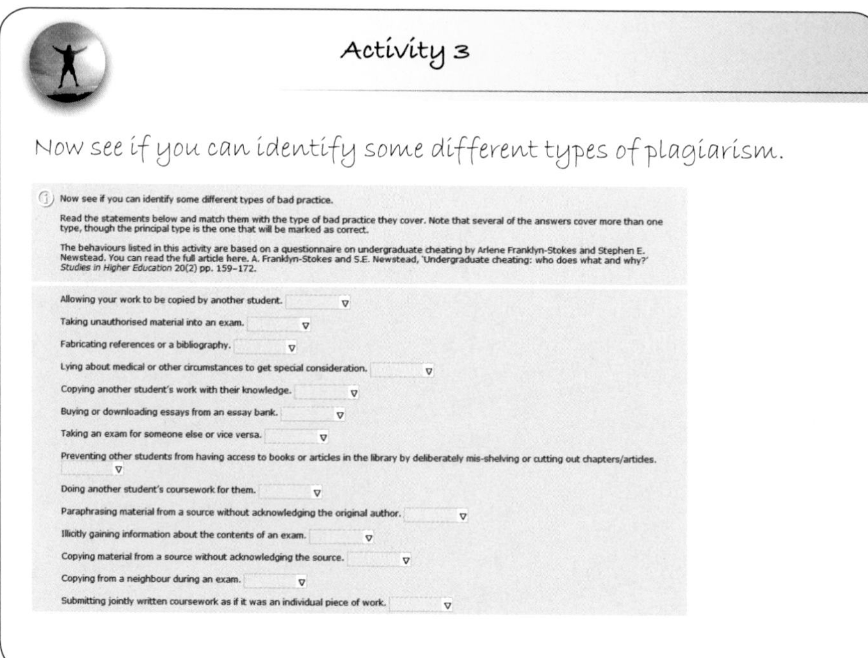

Activity 3

Now see if you can identify some different types of plagiarism.

Now see if you can identify some different types of bad practice.

Read the statements below and match them with the type of bad practice they cover. Note that several of the answers cover more than one type, though the principal type is the one that will be marked as correct.

The behaviours listed in this activity are based on a questionnaire on undergraduate cheating by Arlene Franklyn-Stokes and Stephen E. Newstead. You can read the full article here. A. Franklyn-Stokes and S.E. Newstead, 'Undergraduate cheating: who does what and why?' *Studies in Higher Education* 20(2) pp. 159–172.

Allowing your work to be copied by another student.

Taking unauthorised material into an exam.

Fabricating references or a bibliography.

Lying about medical or other circumstances to get special consideration.

Copying another student's work with their knowledge.

Buying or downloading essays from an essay bank.

Taking an exam for someone else or vice versa.

Preventing other students from having access to books or articles in the library by deliberately mis-shelving or cutting out chapters/articles.

Doing another student's coursework for them.

Paraphrasing material from a source without acknowledging the original author.

Illicitly gaining information about the contents of an exam.

Copying material from a source without acknowledging the source.

Copying from a neighbour during an exam.

Submitting jointly written coursework as if it was an individual piece of work.

Detecting plagiarism

Most UK universities have now invested in a plagiarism detection system such as Turnitin, and these are often integrated with Blackboard, WebCT or other learning environments. These have made it very difficult for students to get away with substantial plagiarising. The best way you can avoid having to defend your work against a charge of plagiarism is to be aware of what it means, and how to avoid doing it.

How to avoid plagiarism: good academic practice

You will be well aware if you are engaged in deliberately fraudulent activity, as described above. It may be that if you resort to such activity it is because you have panicked, or you feel you have not done enough work, or the **deadline** is looming and you don't have enough time to prepare.

» glossary

This resource is designed to help you to maintain good academic practice. All the practical chapters on taking notes, writing essays etc., give you advice on ways of working which will avoid the pitfalls of plagiarism.

Cross reference
See chapter 4, Taking notes; chapter 25, Writing essays; chapter 26, Writing dissertations; and chapter 27, Answering problem questions.

Ways of referring to sources

As well as the citation methods described in our chapter on citing legal authorities there are ways of ensuring that your sources are properly acknowledged. Here are some techniques to remember when you identify some text that you want to incorporate in your work. These are not absolute. The most important thing is to remember that you should make it clear that you are using and acknowledging someone else's work, and reference it properly. Good practice includes the following:

Cross reference
For more information see chapter 14, Citing legal authorities.

- A quote less than three lines long can be incorporated into your text and enclosed in single quotation marks (**OSCOLA** rules).
- A longer quote should be indented, and is not enclosed in quotation marks.
- You may paraphrase someone's ideas, and make it clear that you have done so by introducing your paraphrase with, for example 'J.C. Smith has written that...' or 'William Twining's ideas on...', but you still need to provide a reference for the source.

» glossary

Evaluating your sources

When you come across something you think might be useful **always** make a note of the source – author, publication, web address, etc. Otherwise, you may find that you are not able to attribute it properly if you want to use it later.

If you are using web-based information, evaluate it using the following checklist:

Who produced the information?	→ **Is there a named author or contact?**	→ You should be able to make contact with a named person or organisation
Is it produced by or for an organisation?	→ **If so, what kind of organisation?** - Lobby group? - Official organisation? - Law firm?	→ Check the domain name extension, which gives clues as to the origin of the site
What is the domain name extension? This can offer a clue as to the kind of information.	→ **.gov** – government **.ac.uk** – academic, UK **.edu** – academic, US **.co.uk** – UK organisation **.com, .org, .net** – commercial organisation	→ Beware taking legal information from a US site. There are many other extensions, but these ones will give you a clue as to the origin of the site
Who is it produced for?	→ **Is it for an academic audience?** The general public? A special interest group? The author's own self-promotion?	→ The information may not be suitable for an academic audience
Is it accurate?	→ **Is the information second-hand?** Does it include commentary on the law? Does it include primary materials (statutes, reports)? Is the source of these indicated?	→ Check the sources of this information Go to the original source for the accurate text
Is it up to date? Ask yourself *have there been changes in the law since this information was produced?*	→ **Can you find a date on the site?**	→ If you're not sure it is being updated, don't use it.

Activities 4, 5 and 6
Now have a go at evaluating some websites yourself.
Have a look at this website and evaluate it by filling in the boxes provided.
http://www.netlawman.co.uk
Who produced this website?
•An academic institution.
•A government body.
•A commercial organisation.
Is there a named contact?
What is the domain name extension?
• .edu
• .ac.uk
• .gov.uk
• .com
• .net
• .org
• Other
Can you tell what jurisdiction it applies to?

Disjointed writing

Because it is so easy to cut and paste information from a variety of sources, it can be a temptation to collate your written work from bits and pieces.

This is usually a way of avoiding the preparation and planning which has to go into producing your written work and is something to be avoided.

Use primary sources

Always use accredited sources for your primary materials. Never take the text of a case or a statute from a secondary source, be it a casebook or textbook, or a website.

» glossary

Don't use Google to trace documents, or if you do, make sure that you go back to the original source before quoting them.

Never use Wikipedia as a source. As it can be edited by anyone, the information is unreliable.

Prepare and plan

A considerable number of the other chapters in this resource are about giving you techniques for preparing, planning, formulating your ideas and expressing them well. If you read, absorb and follow these guidelines, this is the best way of avoiding plagiarism by following good academic practice.

Cross reference
See chapter 25, Writing essays; chapter 26, Writing dissertations; and chapter 27, Answering problem questions.

Take especially the advice given in the chapters on writing essays, problem questions and other written work to help you with this.

Try to find your own voice. As law students you will have to work with primary materials (law reports and statutes) and legal commentary, but you will need to develop your critical thinking skills so that you are not simply reproducing other people's ideas.

» glossary

Key Point

Critical thinking is your best guard against plagiarism.

Cross reference
See chapter 8, Thinking critically.

Conclusion

- Make sure you know your institution's policy and regulations on plagiarism.
- Good academic practice will help you avoid plagiarism.
- Learn from the rest of this resource to avoid plagiarising.

Links

Note: One of the problems faced when writing about plagiarism is that it is very difficult to avoid plagiarising all the excellent work that others have done. With the growing awareness of the problem in academic institutions, there has been a large amount of writing on the subject, and development of methods for identifying and preventing it. I would like, therefore, to acknowledge the help, both active and tacit, from the following:

Unit for the Enhancement of Learning and Teaching, University if Kent, whose Academic Integrity site provided a model for much of this chapter
http://www.kent.ac.uk/uelt/ai/index.html

JISC Plagiarism Advisory Service
http://www.jiscpas.ac.uk

and numerous learning and teaching materials identified through the Information Literacy website
http://www.informationliteracy.org.uk

www.oxfordinteract.com

Chapter 8

Thinking critically

Rationale

Lecturers demand that students think critically about law. Students, on the other hand, are often overwhelmed by understanding the new language of law, and the details and technical complexities of its provisions. They are often unclear what it is that lecturers require and why mastering legal provisions – knowing the law – is not in itself sufficient. They are bemused by comments on essays which suggest that the work lacked 'critical perspective' when they have worked hard to understand the law. This chapter focuses on critical thinking skills, explains their importance and what they require and provides you with ways in which you can develop your own critical perspective on law. For us, critical thinking is what marks your learning at university level. Without it, learning law is reduced to training for a profession; with it you gain the intellectual skills which define a graduate. We would also argue that critical thinking makes you a more creative and effective practitioner of law.

One important point: we talk about critical thinking skills in this chapter, but you should not think of them in isolation from everything else you do as a law student. You should employ critical thinking skills all the time, whether you are listening to lectures, reading cases and statutes, taking notes, solving legal problems, contributing to seminars, or writing essays – or even just reading a newspaper! You may find it useful to re-read this chapter at different stages of your legal education and we would certainly recommend that you do so after reading other chapters of this resource.

This chapter is devised to:

- explain what critical thinking is, and how it relates to understanding the law
- help you understand the necessity for evaluation
- clarify that critical thinking is informed by critical reading and demonstrated in critical writing
- provide some strategies to ensure that your reading is critical
- help you apply a critical perspective to your own writing.

» glossary

↳ Cross reference
See chapters 21–24, Reading cases 1–4.

See chapter 19, Reading statutes and the legislative process.

See chapter 4, Taking notes.

See chapter 27, Answering problem questions.

See chapter 6, Contributing to seminars and tutorials.

See chapter 25, Writing essays.

What is critical thinking?

Critical thinking is a **process** which involves you in thinking independently and evaluatively about law in a way which emerges from **consideration** of **evidence**. We will look carefully at the important elements of this definition, but first we should make it clear that critical thinking does **not necessarily** involve **criticising** the law. In other words, contrary to the common perception of many law students, you are not limited to thinking about what is wrong with the law. Whilst the process of critical thinking is designed to enable you to make an informed judgement, that judgement is not inevitably negative. We are not asking you to be cynical, although an element of scepticism can be valuable.

Being 'critical' does not mean 'criticise' – think of the phrase 'to cast a critical eye over something'.

Why do I want to be able to think critically?

There are a number of reasons why you should begin to train yourself to think critically, in life as well as in your law degree. And, when studying law, critical thinking and writing is especially important. Why is this?

- Because at university you are expected to do more independent reading and research; you won't have a lecturer with you in the library to interpret texts for you.
- It shows **thought** about, rather than just mere acceptance of, the law.
- It will help you to clearly articulate arguments of your own.
- It can give your writing an added dimension that helps distinguish it from others, possibly leading to a better degree classification.
- Critical thinking is a transferable skill that will prove useful no matter what you go on to do.

Understanding

Students often think that because they have worked hard to understand the law and to provide an accurate account of its provisions, they have thought sufficiently about the law. This is not correct. We do not underestimate the importance of understanding – for most law subjects it is absolutely vital that you demonstrate a technical competence in law, and many texts aiming to teach you 'legal skills', as well as much of this resource, are designed to help you acquire that competence. However, whilst understanding the law is a prerequisite to critical thinking about it, it is not the equivalent of it.

Note

A university education should be about learning **how** to think, not **what** to think.

Perhaps the best way to understand the distinction between understanding and critical thinking is to imagine a progression of intellectual skills with knowledge being the beginning of the learning process, followed by understanding and moving to application. Critical thinking then comes into play as your intellectual skills move to a higher level and you analyse, synthesise and evaluate what you are learning. This does not mean that you stop using the lower level skills of knowledge, understanding and application, but that you combine these with the higher level skills. If we think about the sort of problems you are asked to solve, for instance in the law of contract, we can see that in order to be successful you will have to know the law, to understand it and apply it, and that you are required to analyse it. If the problem then asks you to consider how the law would be relevant to a new problem which has not yet been considered by the courts, then you are required to synthesise your knowledge into a new understanding which you apply to the facts you have been given.

In the table below we provide definitions of these learning skills. Note that these definitions are simplified and will probably be contested by many readers. Nonetheless they provide a useful starting point for critical thinking.

Skill	Definition
Knowledge	An awareness of facts, feelings and experience
Understanding	The ability to make decisions based upon knowledge
Application	The use of knowledge for a particular purpose
Analysis	The breaking down of a concept into its component parts in order to examine it
Synthesis	The process of combining ideas or concepts into a complex whole
Evaluation	Assessing the value of concepts and knowledge

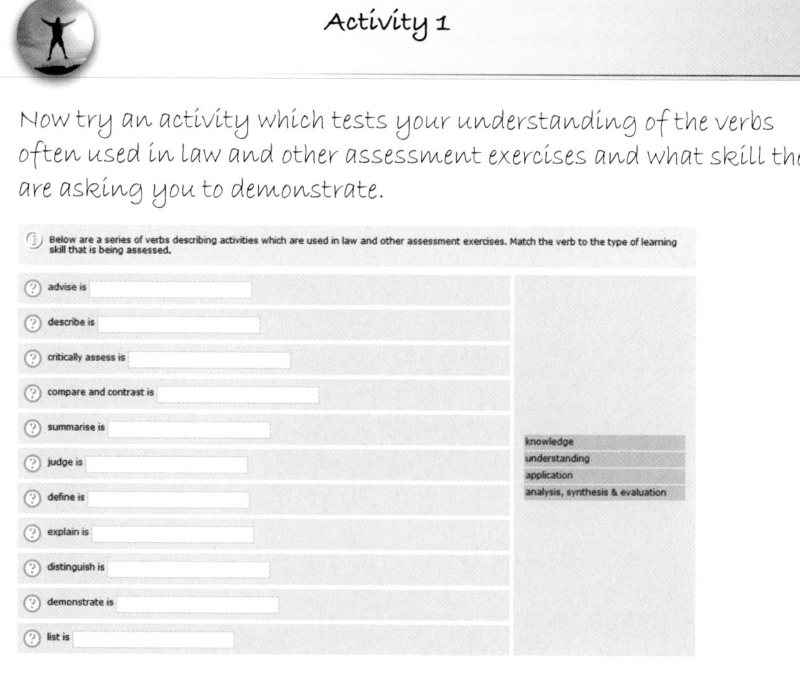

Activity 1
Now try an activity which tests your understanding of the verbs often used in law and other assessment exercises and what skill they are asking you to demonstrate.
Below are a series of verbs describing activities which are used in law and other assessment exercises. Match the verb to the type of learning skill that is being assessed.
advise is
describe is
critically assess is
compare and contrast is
summarise is
judge is
define is
explain is
distinguish is
demonstrate is
list is
knowledge
understanding
application
analysis, synthesis & evaluation

What does critical thinking require?

There are many requirements or characteristics of critical thinking – which are all intertwined, so they should be thought of as a whole – but which we have tried to outline here in a list so you can think about each element:

1. The primary requirement of critical thinking is **thinking**. Thinking requires time for reflection; don't rush through seminar preparation so that you complete it as quickly as possible. Take time to consider what you really think about the law you are learning. **Don't take it at its face value.** Consider its impact from a range of standpoints.

Most seminars are planned in a way which requires you to answer questions which ensure that you have understood, for example, the statutory provisions and the relevant cases. Those questions may then be followed by questions that ask your opinion about the law you are learning. You must devote sufficient time to formulating your answers to those questions, because **it is by evaluating the law that you develop your own critical perspective on the law.**

Cross reference
See chapter 4, Taking notes, and chapter 15, Using law books.

Note

Stimulate your thinking by asking questions as you read law and listen to your lecturers. Make your thinking progress by attempting to articulate answers to the questions you have asked.

2. The second requirement is that you **think for yourself**. It is very important to develop your own line of reasoning; that is what lecturers are looking for when they ask you to develop critical thinking skills. It is not enough, for instance, to agree or disagree with what the House of Lords states in a particular judgment. You must do more than adopt other people's arguments and you must be prepared to **explain** your own analysis. We recognise that developing your own analysis takes courage and practice – you may have to challenge, and face the challenges of, the status quo, your lecturers and/or your peers. However that is what is required.

» glossary

Don't panic

Critical thinking skills, like all skills, improve with ***practice****. If you find it difficult to formulate a reasoned opinion on the law,* ***listen*** *to the arguments of your lecturers and seminar teachers. Note their evaluations and the way that they express them. Ask yourself if you agree or disagree. Question your lecturers. Ask them* ***why*** *they think in the way that they do.*

3. **Critical thinking is a process**. What this means is that you start to think critically when you ask questions of what you have learned. Your critical thinking develops as you start to articulate answers, but that is not the end of the process; as you learn more, and understand more you ask more questions and you re-evaluate your earlier answers. Critical thinking therefore involves intellectual and personal development. You can recognise this in yourself when you think back to your previously held beliefs and now realise that you have rejected them, generally because you have acquired more knowledge and experience.

» glossary

Remember There is not necessarily a correct opinion. You don't have to agree with your lecturer, or the author of your textbook. You must constantly challenge your own conclusions. Ensure that you keep trying to **engage** with the law to work out what it is that you think about its operation, and whether your early judgements continue to be tenable. This will be made easier if you attend talks about the law, any events that your law school organises, listen to radio programmes and read good quality newspapers. All of these will raise stimulating questions which you can try to answer for yourself. The most important thing is to commit yourself to re-assess your position as your knowledge expands and your skills develop.

4. The fourth requirement is that **your argument is developed from a consideration of authoritative evidence.** The development of your argument requires that you consider what experts such as academics, judges and other commentators say about a legal issue. You then analyse and evaluate their views and decide whether, and, if so, the extent to which you agree with those views. You must consider scholarly or academic articles in order to inform your argument.

» glossary

↳ Cross reference
See chapter 4, Taking notes.

A scholarly or academic article is one in which the author demonstrates expertise, draws on other authoritative sources, and carefully evaluates those sources and the law, and then draws conclusions based on his or her analysis. Other authoritative sources you should consider are judgments of senior judges. However, you must remember to **evaluate** those authorities. It is not enough to say 'I agree with Lord Hoffmann, rather than Lord Bingham' for instance. You need to **explain why**. You should focus on the reasoning deployed in the judgment and consider whether you agree with it or not. Experts are not limited to legal academics and the judiciary. The views of policy experts and non-governmental organisations (NGOs) may also frame the development of your argument. Sometimes you may want to draw on the perspectives of, for instance, victims of crime, or users of public services in developing your analysis. Again, as long as you evaluate these opinions, they can be very useful in helping you develop critical insights into law.

Some textbooks provide authoritative evidence that you need to consider; others do not. You will have to make the judgement. One particular reason why lecturers do not like nutshell-type books is that they are unreliable and of extremely limited authority. Supporting your argument by drawing on something you read in a 'nutshell' is going to give you very little credibility.

Web pages also may not be authoritative and you must use them carefully. A particular problem is that web authors are often anonymous so the user is not able to identify their political or social location. Websites do not have to undergo the normal level of critical review prior to publication in print and therefore their integrity and authority cannot be assumed. Moreover, web authors decide themselves what links to have within their websites; some possible links are encouraged whilst others are ignored. In this way, authors can use links to justify their own perspective and ignore others.

Commonly held opinions frequently provide you with inadequate support. So, for instance, it is inadequate to argue that because most people think that a person who kills an intruder should not face criminal prosecution the law is defective. You would have to provide more authoritative evidence to support this view, and to evaluate the reasoning of the authors.

Evaluation

We have drawn your attention to the need to evaluate evidence several times. This means that you must examine sources of information and lines of reasoning to determine:

- the extent to which the source is authoritative
- the standpoint of the author and to decide how this is reflected in his or her conclusions.

In order to determine authority you should consider:

- the standing of the author
- the use of references and bibliography
- the clarity of the reasoning
- the extent to which the conclusions flow from the reasoning.

» glossary

To determine the standpoint of the source you should ask:

- What is the standpoint of the author? Consider his or her social, economic, political and historical location
- What are the article's intentions?
- What are its biases?
- What does it (or the author) gain by presenting a particular perspective?

You should ask these questions of textbooks, scholarly articles, legal judgments – indeed everything you use to frame your argument.

Activity 2

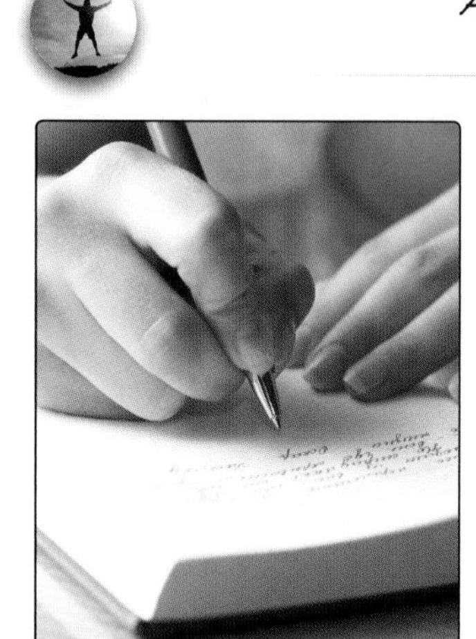

Now try an activity which asks you to reflect on what makes a piece of writing critical.

Bias

You may think that if you can detect bias in a piece of writing that this automatically invalidates the opinion of the author. This is not the case. All of us are biased although we might not always be aware of our bias. What is important is that we recognise bias and acknowledge its impact in our work. For instance, there is nothing wrong with analysing the law from a feminist perspective; it enables you to uncover practices of law that might otherwise be hidden. What is necessary, however, is to **acknowledge** that your perspective is feminist in your writing and to **explain** the value that this adds to the analysis of law.

Note

It is equally important to recognise bias **in the law** and **in commentary on law**. In particular you should be aware that most writing about law is not politically neutral but is based on a political viewpoint. No one is completely neutral! You must be sensitive to this and also acknowledge your own political leanings.

Political ideologies

Most people, to a greater or lesser extent, subscribe, consciously or subconsciously, to a political ideology. In simple terms that means that people who share political ideologies accept a particular set of ideas about how society should be organised and they share views about human nature, about history, about the importance of the individual and about the role of the state. When you read cases, articles, textbooks or commentary on law, and even newspaper articles, try to identify the ideology of the author. The table below sets out a very simplified version of the main political ideologies.

Ideology	Characteristics
Liberalism	Favours the rights of the individual in the private sphere as long as this does not cause harm to others. Liberals acknowledge the claims of society as a whole and the significance of the public sphere, but are concerned to restrain interventions by the state into private life. Civil liberties are therefore important to liberals.
Conservatism	Favours a strong state which ensures security and continuity in order to allow individuals to operate effectively. Civil liberties should not encroach upon the security of the state. Modern conservatism places greatest value on economic liberalism (free market values).
Socialism	Places great significance on society and considers that the rights of the individual are subordinate to society where wealth is distributed equally and collectively owned. Civil liberties are less important than the well-being of society as a whole.

Stereotypes

Stereotypes are more troublesome than bias. They indicate that someone has not thought very hard about their opinion, but resorted to commonly held prejudices. None of us are immune from making stereotypical assumptions. However, it can be dangerous in the law, and certainly weakens writing. One critical skill you can develop is to be alert to the use of stereotypes in texts. It is a powerful way of exposing the hidden assumptions of the author. If you are interested in thinking more about this you might like to read the following scholarly article: Didi Herman (2006) 'An Unfortunate Coincidence: Jews and Jewishness in Twentieth-century English Judicial Discourse', *Journal of Law and Society,* 33 (2) pp. 277–301. What Professor Herman does in this article is to reveal the unconscious anti-Semitism of judicial discourse.

Strategies to develop critical thinking

All strategies to develop critical thinking can be summed up in one essential requirement. **Ask questions of the law – what is it that is being said by the law or a commentator on the law in these particular circumstances?**

Don't panic

Most of us have experience of questioning authority – we challenge our parents and carers when we are young; we question what our bosses require when we are in work; we ask teachers to justify their marks. Transfer these skills to the study of law. Do not take for granted that judges or the government are right! Work it out for yourself.

» glossary

There are a range of approaches you can utilise to enhance your ability to question the law. You can:

- consider the historical and political context of judicial decisions and government proposals
- uncover any stereotypical assumptions in judgments or legislation
- consider whose interests are being served by a decision or a statute
- think about whose interests have not been represented and what debates have been silenced
- compare the legal solutions reached with those of other jurisdictions.

» glossary

You can employ these strategies in the reading that you are asked to do in preparation for seminars or when researching assessments.

» glossary

- First of all read the document quickly, noting its purpose, style and structure.
- Find the stated aims of the document and ensure that you understand them.
- Then read more slowly, pausing for reflection, asking yourself the questions we suggested above. Try to think particularly carefully about what is **not** said in the document and what is taken for granted by the author.
- Consider the text carefully – what style of writing is used, what words or phrases recur throughout the document?

Activities 3 and 4

Now try two activities where we provide you with some text and ask you to read it critically.

We have suggested that it is important to critically evaluate all writing – not just primary sources, but also commentary on those sources. This of course also applies to websites and blogs. However, you may enjoy the critical perspective of the law demonstrated by the blog 'Nearly Legal' http://nearlylegal.co.uk/blog/. Nearly Legal is a trainee **solicitor** with a legal aid franchised firm, who turned to the law as a mature career changer. Contributing to the blog would provide you with another way to enhance your critical thinking skills.

» glossary

Critical writing

A significant proportion of this chapter has been spent considering the need to read critically. However, you must also apply a critical perspective to your own writing. You must learn to **evaluate** what you write. What opinions does your writing reveal, and can you justify them? Think about the texts you draw on to make your arguments and ask yourself if they are authoritative. Say that you are questioning them, and why. Be honest about your own biases and try to eliminate assumptions from your work unless you can substantiate those assumptions. Organise your argument so that your conclusions are developed from your reasoning and try to write persuasively. The Tomkins chapter (see Activity 2) provides a useful model for scholarly and persuasive writing which is well referenced and draws on a wide range of authoritative sources.

Remember, critical writing will require you to:

- Think
- Evaluate

- Justify
- Substantiate
- Persuade.

Don't panic

As you become more adept at reading critically, you will become more skilled at writing critically and more aware of the implications and assumptions of what you write. A reflective approach to feedback will also help you develop your critical writing skills.

Cross reference
See chapter 10, Reflecting on your work.

Conclusion

Critical thinking is crucial to the study of law at university level. It is closely linked to your personal and intellectual development. If you start by asking questions about the implications of the law and the assumptions of those who comment on it, you will begin the process of critical thinking.

Remember:

- Don't take the law at face value.
- Understand the significance of the standpoint of the author.
- Try to understand the law from a range of different perspectives.
- Continue to re-evaluate your opinions as your knowledge and skills develop.

This will decrease the risk of your writing being based on a false premise and increase the likelihood of you reaching a well-justified conclusion or answer.

Links

Critical Thinking Mini-Lessons
http://skepdic.com/refuge/ctlessons.html

A classical approach to developing critical thinking skills.

www.oxfordinteract.com

Chapter 9

Thinking creatively

Rationale

When you start studying law at university it is a challenge simply to describe the law you are asked to read. You struggle to master its technicalities and your thoughts are dominated by the need to avoid legal blunders. It can seem one step too far to ask you to form authoritative and original opinions about the law. However, that is what is required. You need to move beyond description and 'think outside the box'. You need to learn how to think creatively about the law you are studying.

All thinking is creative because you are developing new thoughts from your own intellectual resources. With practice and by employing a few standard techniques you can learn to generate relevant and sustainable ideas about law and get beyond the stage where you are struggling simply to describe legal rules.

The purpose of this chapter is to provide a toolbox of techniques for creative thinking which you can refer to when you need some help in developing ideas. We begin, however, by considering what is meant by the requirement that your work demonstrates originality and by thinking about the importance of ideas.

Here we are specifically looking at creative/original thinking. We consider critical thinking in a separate chapter and a good deal of this resource focuses on developing your analytical skills. Here our focus is the generation of ideas about law. We can define what we mean by these different, but overlapping intellectual skills as follows:

- When we think analytically about a case we break the legal reasoning into its constituent parts to see how the decision is constructed and to see if it is coherent.
- When we think critically about a case we are challenging the assumptions which underpin the decision, considering for instance whose interests the decision serves, asking why the conflict between the parties has arisen, and why now and not earlier, or perhaps we consider the perspective that the judge demonstrates in the case.
- When we think creatively about a case we bring our own perspective to the problem posed by the case and the decision-making process. The chapter considers what we mean by this and what is necessary for creative thinking to be effective.

» glossary

This chapter is devised to:

- Help you understand what is meant by originality in academic work
- Enable you to consider some writing to decide whether it is 'original' in the academic sense
- Help you think about the importance of ideas in intellectual work
- Introduce you to a range of techniques to stimulate creative engagement with law.

What is originality?

» glossary

Assignments at university level – particularly essays and dissertations – require originality. This means far more than avoiding plagiarism, although you may want to refresh your understanding of plagiarism at this point. Originality in academic work is about engaging with other people's ideas/work in a creative way. It is not about promoting your own opinions if these have not been thought through properly and related to other well-informed opinions about the law, nor does it mean ranting or going off on a tangent about a subject.

Cross reference
See chapter 7, Avoiding plagiarism.

Originality has three important elements:

- You must bring your own perspective to the law, responding to questions or explaining consequences using your particular point of view, rather than adopting someone else's view.
- You must engage with other people's work or ideas. This means that you cannot just have an uninformed opinion – you cannot simply rant. You must read widely and think about what you have read. You must reference your reading in your work to demonstrate the source of your ideas.
- You must be creative with your engagement with the work of others. In other words you must produce something which is, to at least some extent new. This is what we mean by 'thinking outside the box'. At undergraduate level this need not be too daunting – applications of the reasoning of legal thinkers to a new problem would be a reasonable expectation, for instance. It is, however, useful to recognise the creativity of more senior legal thinkers.

Activity 1

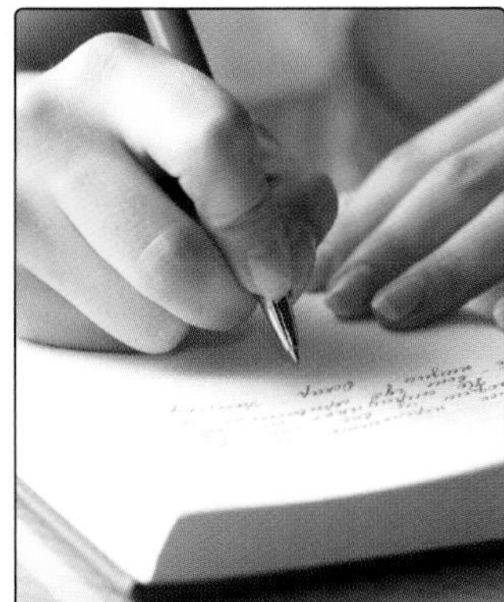

Now try an activity which asks you to consider some legal writing to decide whether it is original.

One way to understand originality is to think of it as a sort of intellectual entrepreneurship – a way in which you can think through the law to identify and exploit new opportunities and pathways for thought. It can be very exciting, even within the limits of the standard undergraduate assignment, to harness your own intellectual energies. However, the need for creative thinking is potentially daunting. Below we consider some techniques to stimulate creative thinking – but first we think about the significance of original ideas in a little more depth.

The significance of original ideas

Ideas are important – they demonstrate conceptual and creative thinking. Just as factories produce goods, universities produce ideas. No one expects undergraduates to produce big ideas or world shattering thoughts but what is expected is that you start to think creatively, produce ideas, think them through and develop them, and then communicate them coherently. Ideas do not emerge from the blue – they result from engaging with legal material and the thoughts and ideas of those who engage with the same material.

» glossary

We would like to think that during at least some of your lectures and seminars you think creatively about what you are being taught. If you have an interesting or provocative idea you must note it down. If you think of something in the course of a seminar try to articulate it – it is a very useful technique when you have a half worked out idea to ask a question in the seminar which raises your idea. At the very least, write your idea down and underline it. Go back to it when you write up your notes and see if it is useful in helping you approach essays and revision.

Some people are full of ideas. Others need help to get them started. Below we set out suggested techniques for stimulating creative thought. We have divided the techniques into two interrelated groups. The first group is intellectual techniques – ways of thinking about law in a way which could be described as top down. The second group is practical techniques – approaches which can stimulate different ways of thinking but starting from the bottom up – by thinking about the problem you are being asked to solve.

Note

One note of caution here – you must only think creatively within the constraints of the assessment you have been set. In general, in legal problem solving your creativity will be demonstrated by your developing legal reasoning in new ways or applying legal reasoning to new circumstances revealed in the set problem. There may be a broader scope for creativity within essays and dissertations. It will depend upon the essay you choose to answer. Always ensure that your creativity focuses on the task you have been set.

Intellectual techniques

Read law

We start with the most productive activity to stimulate creative thinking. You must read as much law and as much about the law as you can. Reading provides the fuel for creative thinking. It provides a model for how to think creatively, provides you with ideas to engage with, and can stimulate your own creativity. Textbooks which conform to our criteria for originality are a good place to start your reading. You are not going to get much inspiration from textbooks, such as nutshells, which simply describe the law. Read the articles suggested by your lecturers. Don't forget to look at the footnotes; writers quite often put their more interesting – because they are not fully developed – thoughts in their footnotes. These can provide you with a springboard to a creative response to the legal problem you are considering. Law reports are also worth reading. What they provide is more or less convincing demonstrations of legal reasoning and creative problem solving. Judges are accomplished advocates and writers. Their accounts can

» glossary

» glossary

be compelling and persuasive. Think about the techniques they use to convince us that they are right, and how they demonstrate creativity. Don't forget to read dissenting judgments. These may provide a fertile source for original arguments.

Ask critical questions

↳ **Cross reference**
See chapter 8, Thinking critically.

We talk elsewhere in this resource about critical thinking, and suggest that it provides the framework within which you study law at undergraduate level. Critical thinking and originality are closely linked. Our first technique of creative thinking is to ask questions of what you are learning. Question the assumptions and the standpoint of law – whether it originates from statute or cases. Consider whose interests a particular decision serves. Ask these questions of points of view promoted by textbooks and by lecturers. Can you identify and then question their biases?

However, we do not consider that critical thinking and creative thinking are necessarily synonymous. Critical thinking in simple terms is about not taking law at face value. Creative thinking is about 'thinking outside the box'. Nonetheless, if you learn to think critically then you are likely to generate original ideas which can be pursued within your work.

Find spaces for original thinking

Get into the habit of thinking about what is missing from accounts of law. Whose perspective is missing? Are the needs of minorities considered? What about victims? Or the users of law? Is law too dominated by the needs of lawyers? Once you have found a space, then make the most of it. Think through the ideas you have to their logical conclusion.

Other disciplines

You are not limited to reading law as a source for ideas about how law operates in society. Art, literature, politics and history all raise questions about rights, responsibilities, relationships and their consequences which are questions of vital importance in law. Moreover, contemporary debates are often better represented and more accessible in other disciplines, such as sociology. By reading and engaging with these ideas you will bring new and creative dimensions to your study of law. Watching films and going to the theatre may also stimulate your thinking about law. Our advice is to engage with the arts and other disciplines, and try to apply the insights they provide to the law.

Theoretical debates

↳ **Cross reference**
See chapter 26, Writing dissertations.

In our chapter on dissertations we suggest that there may be value in engaging with theoretical approaches such as feminism or regulatory theory.

Activity 2

Now try an activity which asks you to consider how theoretical approaches might stimulate creative thinking.

Practical techniques

Perhaps you do not feel comfortable with grand conceptual approaches to law at this stage of your studies. Nonetheless, there are a range of more practical techniques you can adopt to ensure that you engage with problems you are set in a creative manner.

Role play

One way you can 'think outside the box' is to imagine that you have a particular role which you are playing in the approach to the problem. One appropriate role in law is to imagine that you are a barrister arguing the case. How would a barrister analyse the strengths and weaknesses of the case? What sort of evidence would he or she emphasise? How would he or she respond to the arguments of the other side? How would a barrister seek to be authoritative, and persuasive? Your role play does not have to be limited to lawyers. Imagine yourself as the Home Secretary defending his or her decision to extend state powers. How would you present your case so that it is persuasive? What would be your overriding concerns? There are a whole range of roles you can imagine yourself playing. The point, however, is to overcome any difficulties you might have in forming an opinion about the problem to hand, and having overcome that difficulty, to stimulate your creative thinking.

» glossary

Brainstorming

Brainstorming is another very useful technique to apply to problems. There are a number of ways in which you can brainstorm a problem. You could apply these techniques to an essay question to help you develop an original approach to the question you are being asked. You take a blank sheet of paper, write down the essay question at the top, and then jot down any idea that comes to you. There is no need to evaluate your ideas at this stage – the point is just to keep thinking and generating ideas. You can do this on the computer and even use software programs such as 'Inspiration' to stimulate your thoughts. You may find it useful to work with others when you brainstorm ideas. One person's thought on a topic can lead to another person contributing a different idea and so on. The important thing when working in groups is not to question the value of anyone's idea until a later point in the process. When you are trying to think creatively all input is useful.

Current affairs

You can gain very useful ideas from reading newspapers, listening to the radio and watching television. Comment pieces, particularly about law, are very useful. They demonstrate current concerns, and are often provocative. Don't forget to ask critical questions about their standpoint and biases. Check the regular law pages in the broadsheets, and note their interests. Also find out what the specialist law programmes on BBC Radio 4 are covering. It's easy to do this on the BBC website, and there is usually the opportunity to listen to the programme for a week after broadcast via the website.

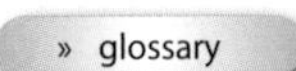

Conclusion

Whilst creative thinking about law may seem impossible at the beginning of your degree, it is absolutely necessary for your success for you to move beyond simple descriptions of law. Moreover by engaging with law on a number of different intellectual levels you add to your enjoyment of your studies, which in turn enhances your success. There are a number of techniques you can employ to ensure that you engage with the work of other legal thinkers, the most important of which is reading. We would also encourage you to engage with other disciplines, and transfer their insights to your study of law. Practical techniques, such as brainstorming, can act as very useful triggers to creative thinking. If you work with others in attempting to think through topics and problems, you are all likely to benefit from the generation of useful ideas.

www.oxfordinteract.com

Chapter 10

Reflecting on your work

Rationale

When you study at university, you may find that you need to devise your own way of learning, or include some study techniques that you may not have used before. One of these is what is called 'reflective writing' or 'self-reflection'. Some students may have been required to maintain a 'reflective' journal or submit a 'reflective assignment' while at school. These students will, therefore, be more familiar with this particular style of learning and writing.

However, even if you have not encountered this type of study before, because reflective writing is associated with higher levels of learning, it is expected that all university students (remember that this is 'higher education'!) develop skills that help them to learn from the process of reflection. Furthermore, self-reflection is a very important component of Personal Development Plans, something that you may be being asked to keep on your particular law degree.

This chapter is devised to:

- Explain why it is helpful to reflect on the work that you do
- Help you to understand how reflection can actually improve your work
- Give you some tips about how to create a reflective diary.

What does it mean to be 'reflective' and why should I do it?

» glossary

» abbreviation

Being reflective is about improving your own learning and performance – an important aspect of university study. Reflecting on your progress in writing allows you to consider more deeply what you have been doing, why you are doing it, what your goals are and how likely you are to reach them. You also gain further insights from your experiences and how these reflect the knowledge and theories that you are learning. If you go on to legal vocational training (i.e. the BVC or LPC), you will find that there is a great deal of reflection required, as with many careers, where the ability to self-reflect is regarded as one of the things that helps you to progress. This being the case, one reason why you should do it is simply to get used to it – it is probably not a familiar concept to you from your education prior to university. There is a great deal of competition for students for places in good firms and chambers, even for work experience placements, so you should practice all the necessary skills at any opportunity!

Note

On the BVC and LPC, every performance you give must be critiqued – both by others and by yourself. The idea behind this is so that you learn from it and do better next time. It's OK to make a mistake once – but it would be silly to make the same mistakes twice!

By recording your thoughts or reflections in writing as you go along you will be more easily able to explore them, to make connections between them and to come back at a later date to any unsolved questions that you might have had. Maintaining and updating a written record of your progress and achievements is also a useful source of reference and evidence that can be helpful when you fill in application forms, write your CV or prepare for an interview, so the skills needed in reflective writing are ones that you can (and should) continue to nurture and develop throughout your career.

Activity 1

Go online to watch a number of legal practitioners sharing their thoughts on the value of reflection.

In a sense, self-reflection is self-critique. Critique doesn't mean to criticise outright – to find fault – but to look at something with a view to improving it. It is an analytical evaluation of something you have done, where you ask yourself questions and try to answer them.

Example

Self-reflection on an essay you have written, handed in and had marked, would involve you re-reading your work, to see if it stirs anything in you, such as the thought that you could have improved the way you put something, or improved your conclusion. You should also read the comments on your work, thinking about each of them; what they are telling you and why. At the end of this exercise (which may only take minutes) think about what you can do **next time** – when you get your next essay title, what will you do differently, in order to improve?

The same kind of exercise can be undertaken for almost anything relating to your studies. Ask yourself, for example, the following questions:

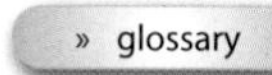

- Do I contribute much/well in seminars? If not, how can I improve my performance?

» glossary

- Do I learn anything from lectures? If not, how can I improve how much information I retain?

Critical reflection could be defined as a process of deliberation, whereby a student spends some time focusing on their own performance and thinking carefully about what caused them to act, think or write in a particular way, about how this turned out, and about what they learned (and are still learning) from doing this. The reason such an exercise might be undertaken would be to inform what they might do in the future, with a view to improvement.

What should be taken from this is that students themselves are expected to **take time** and to **learn** from the process of reflection. This is not something that anyone else can do for you, or that you can skip over, hoping to come back to later.

» glossary

There are a number of different ways in which students may write reflectively. These may include writing within a learning journal, workbook or diary, as part of either summative or formative assessments, or just to evaluate work undertaken either individually or within a group. It may also form part of the building of a personal or professional profile or CV. Similarly, there are many different reasons why this may be done. Reflecting on your own work can help you to:

- develop an idea and take it to fruition
- formulate a plan of action and take steps to put it into place
- resolve some uncertainty or make a decision that has been eluding you
- put into words your own feelings and thoughts about your development as a student (or as a lawyer)
- empower you to make further choices and decisions in the future.

Cross reference
See chapter 5, Working in groups.

Reflecting on what you have done, are doing and are going to do may well provide you with sources for further reflection, which further aids learning and understanding. It may also lead you to reflect on the process of learning itself – or even on the reasons why you are learning or choosing to learn!

Activity 2

Go online to watch a number of students sharing their experiences of when they have reflected on their studies or skills and what were the results.

How do I do it?

Reflective writing should include both description (of what you have done/are doing/will do) and analysis (why are you doing it?). This can be illustrated by a simple three-step example:

1. **Description**
   - What happened/was done and (if group work) what part did you play in it?
2. **Analysis**
   - What did you think was good/went well and why?
   - What, if anything, could/should have been improved and how would/could you do this?
3. **Reflection**
   - Your thoughts and opinions

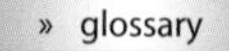

Note

Reflection should be written in the first person and should include **your** thoughts and opinions. For example:

'I thought that my essay was well written, as I had researched the topic well'

'I know I was under-prepared for the presentation – next time I will start preparing my work earlier, with more time to spare'.

Reflective writing should **not** be:

- merely a description of what happened/was done, with no analysis of this
- a chance to make excuses for yourself or others
- seen as an opportunity to blame anyone or anything else if things went badly.

But, even if something has gone badly, reflecting on this – rather than trying to forget it – helps to make it a valuable learning experience. Provided that you examine how you could have done things differently – or will do something differently in the future – an experience where everything **didn't** go according to plan can often become more valuable than if everything went well.

Reflections should be your own thoughts, not what you think others – e.g. your teachers or fellow students – think of you or your work.

Activity 3

Knowing what to do when is an important part of being able to think or write reflectively. The following activity helps you to sort out the order in which you do things when thinking or writing reflectively. If you can remember the order, the easier it will be!

In this activity, you should consider a recent situation that you have been involved in directly or indirectly. This doesn't have to have taken place within an educational context: it could be in a shop, at a club, or in the gym, as just some examples. Now complete the following flowchart by putting the descriptions of various parts of the reflective process in order.

Focus – Identify a problem
Recall any recent event/incident/encounter/situation that you were involved in and which has left you feeling, for example, anxious, confused, disturbed or unsettled.

Critical Analysis – How did you feel?
Examine all of your feelings – both positive and negative – about the thing that you have focused on, especially those feelings that you know are irrational or uncontrolled. What happened and why did it happen? Should you have challenged what was happening and what difference might this have made? How did the situation affect you and how did you affect the situation? How did others react?

Awareness – What happened?
Try to accurately describe the context, sequence of events and outcome of the event/incident/encounter/situation. Describe any negative feelings that you experienced in relation to it.

Innovation – What needs improvement?
Imagine that you find yourself in the same or a similar position again. What other options can you devise to deal with the situation?

Interpretation – What have you learned?
Try to develop a new perspective on the situation. This may involve digging deep to discover a new attitude or a different way of thinking about it.

Positive action – What shall I do about it?
Think about what kind of action you can now take to change the way you feel about similar

Reflecting on your learning

Activity 4

You should now be aware that reflection involves a consideration of your learning processes with a view to improvement. Asking similar questions to those you asked in the last activity, now apply the same consideration to something directly related to your study: for example, an essay you have written, presentation you have given, or even work you have prepared for a seminar.

Go online to read our thoughts on this issue.

You should try to reflect on the activities you do throughout your degree. One of the benefits of this is that, while what you have done is fresh in your mind, you think about ways you can improve. The pay-off is that for very little effort, you may hit upon something that then stays with you for the rest of your academic and professional career. Furthermore, it is always useful to go back and look at your reflections at a later date. If you've ever kept any kind of diary, remember how much fun it can be sometimes looking back over your thoughts and feelings of the time? This is the same, but related to your study. The types of things that you might include are:

- analyses of what went 'right' or 'wrong' in a piece of written work
- the same in relation to presentations or e.g. moot performances
- the goals you are setting yourself either generally or as a result of the above
- whether your expectations of yourself (and others) are reasonable.

Incorporating self-reflection into your study is one thing that can help you raise your level of learning from a surface stage which may consist of mere description to that which exemplifies deep learning by development of reflective skills. This theme should also be at the forefront of your reflection on your learning. Try the following two reflection activities.

Activity 5

1. **Think of something that you do well or have been successful at.**
   For example, it could be that you consistently achieve high grades in a particular module; or possibly you achieved a much higher grade in an assessment than you imagined that you might.
2. **Write a few words explaining how you became proficient in the particular area you chose.**
   For example, was there anything that specifically enhanced your learning?
3. **Now write down a few words to say how you know that you're good at this activity.**
   For example, how do you compare with other people? Has somebody told you you're good?
   Go online to read our thoughts on these questions.

Activity 6

1. **Think of something that you don't do well.**
   This could be, for example, something that you consider to have been an unsuccessful learning experience.
2. **Write a few words explaining why you think this learning experience went wrong for you.**
3. **Now write down a few words to say, honestly, whether *you* could have done anything to improve this particular learning experience.**

If you want to avoid a similar situation in the future, is there anything you would do differently?

Go online to read our thoughts on these questions.

The previous activities illustrate the various steps that we can train ourselves to go through in order to help us progress effectively in our studies. Remember, although it is essential to describe something before you can discuss or analyse it, a reflection is **not** simply an account of factual information. Rather, it is made up of your perceptions and expectations based on your experience of what has taken place. Hopefully, your reflection illustrates – or will become part of a bigger illustration of – your personal and academic growth while studying law.

What value is there in self-reflection?

Apart from what we have already said about self-reflection being an important part of professional training, in the legal profession or otherwise, there are other, more immediate benefits. Reflective writing may be more overtly encouraged on some modules, or more within some law courses compared with others. Whatever the case, or even if you are not pushed to do so, you should try and include some self-reflection as you study, as you are likely to find it valuable. In some instances, self-reflection can help us to gain more control over our thoughts, emotions, responses and behaviour and help us achieve a wider perspective on situations. It also helps us to set – and to achieve – realistic goals.

Working on your reflective skills will help you to gain a more honest perspective of yourself which, in turn, means clearer identification of your academic strengths and weaknesses, so that you will know those areas that might require a little more work on your part. Some of the key values of self-reflection are:

- analysis of your own experiences and progress enables increased learning
- critical thinking is encouraged so academic writing is improved
- independent learning is facilitated
- recognition of mistakes enhances professional competence.

↳ **Cross reference**
See chapter 8, Thinking critically, and chapter 25, Writing essays.

Most importantly, self-reflection will help you to recognise what things affect your learning and your academic performance and thus how to progress. This involves three main processes:

1. **Recognising** problems when they arise, particularly if they were unexpected.
2. **Thinking about** something you have done or a problem that has occurred and how you dealt with it.
3. **Understanding** what you need to do in order to make change, or to progress.

The first of these is about recognition and review. Realising that you have a problem is the first step in helping you to solve it. Once this has happened, you can seek help from various sources, such as:

- Your friends
- Your personal tutors
- Your seminar leaders or lecturers
- Student support services, either academic or personal.

The second of these is the more actively reflective – when you think about something that has happened in the past and review the way in which you dealt with it, you can use this as a basis for further improvement. You can also use it to detail your own qualities and skills, something that will be required of you when applying for further study in law, either professional or academic, or in applying for almost any kind of job in the future. You also need to be able to understand and talk about your own skills and to **promote** yourself – this is the third item in the list.

When you are asked to write reflectively, this could involve listing and/or appraising your current skills and attributes in order to show others (and yourself) what you can do. This comes naturally to some people, but some find it difficult to promote their finer points to others. Depending on your personality, the idea of 'selling yourself' might be contrary to your usual values. However, as a lawyer – or in many other careers – this is a skill you will need to develop!

Don't panic

You have probably undertaken this kind of exercise at least once before. Remember writing your personal statement for your UCAS application; or filling out an application for a placement or a job.

Activity 7

The following activity helps you to reflect on the skills and qualities needed to be a successful student of law.

Think of the skills, personal qualities and attributes that you think you need to have in order to sustain a successful university career in law. Now, from the following list, select the **five** skills, qualities or attributes that you think are the most important.

- Relaxed
- Hardworking
- Trustworthy
- Fast reader
- Good networker
- Gets involved
- Confident
- Intelligent
- Dogmatic
- Argumentative

The thought of appearing vain or bigheaded is unattractive. However, there is a difference between this and writing reflectively about your talents and abilities. When writing an academic essay, you are expected to refer to theories, concepts and recognised authors to substantiate the views you express. In a similar way, a reflective piece of work about you should include **evidence** to justify the statements that you make. If the evidence is there, you are not being bigheaded!

Activity 8

- Having done the last activity, now think about the specific career path you think that you want to follow and come up with a list of between five and ten talents and abilities that you will need to develop in order to be a success.
- Next give an explanation of why **each** of these skills and traits are essential.
- Now write down all of your **existing** abilities and attributes that already match those on your first list and explain **how** you know you possess them, i.e. what **evidence** do you have?
- Record this in your reflective diary or Personal Development Plan, if you have one.

» glossary

Go online to read our thoughts on this activity.

Reflective diaries

A reflective diary or journal is for you, so write about what **you** want. You may be required to keep track of certain things to do with your study, or to include some reflective work within the modules you are studying – or you may be required to create and keep a Personal Development Portfolio or Plan (PDP). That said, there should always be some space somewhere for your own reflections, undertaken as and when you feel like it. And you will probably find that the more you do it, the more you will want to do it – similarly to keeping a personal diary.

» glossary

You could include some or all of the following:

- Your feelings about particular learning experiences – from what do you think you learn the most, or the least?
- What you feel you have gained (or have not) from doing a particular piece of work, or research for it
- How you feel your current state of progress is
- What your current ambitions are – short or long term
- What you currently find challenging, and thoughts on how you might overcome those challenges
- Decisions you have made – and why you reached them
- Feelings about decisions others have made
- Your worries and hopes for the future.

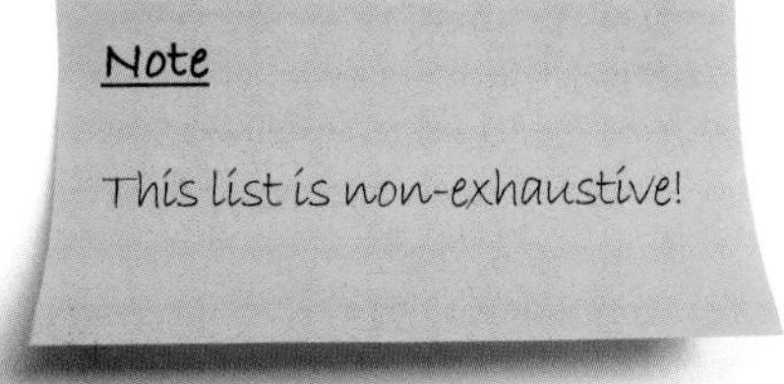
Note
This list is non-exhaustive!

Conclusion

Now that you know some of the benefits that self-reflection can bring, you should try to develop the practice of a continuous reflective cycle. This will be helpful not only in your study of law, but in 'real life' too.

You can see the cycle as:

> **ACTION** followed by **REFLECTION** followed by **ACTION** followed by **PROGRESSION** followed by **REFLECTION**…

Reflection on incidents, events and your progress on a regular basis will become habit. This helps you to develop self-awareness (and therefore often self-confidence) and to understand your own thoughts and opinions and, possibly more importantly, what has shaped these. Knowing this helps you not only in your study (you might be better at expressing opinion in an essay, for example, if you know **why** you have it), but also in life. **Remember: self-reflection is a life skill.**

» glossary

Links

http://www.goldsmiths.ac.uk/3d/tools/level1/
This site, from the excellent Goldsmiths, University of London's '3D Graduate' web pages, explains Personal Development Plans: what they are for and why they are valuable. The '3D' pages are titled such as they aim to make students more 'three-dimensional' – that is, more well rounded and with many aspects to their education. On the page you will see a link to other skills-type headings, all of which may be useful for you when studying law, including links to pages titled 'Learning through reflection' and 'Reflective writing'.

M. Pirsig, *Zen and the Art of Motorcycle Maintenance*
http://www.amazon.co.uk/Zen-Art-Motorcycle-Maintenance-Anniversary/dp/0099322617/ref=sr_1_1/026-2380819-7341235?ie=UTF8&s=books&qid=1191320857&sr=1-1

A novel written in the form of self-reflection, held up as being a modern classic. Despite not being a legal text, all law (and other) students should read it, in particular as a large section of it is reflecting on the experiences of being at (and being a teacher at) university.

www.oxfordinteract.com

» Part 2 Research and technical skills «

Part 2

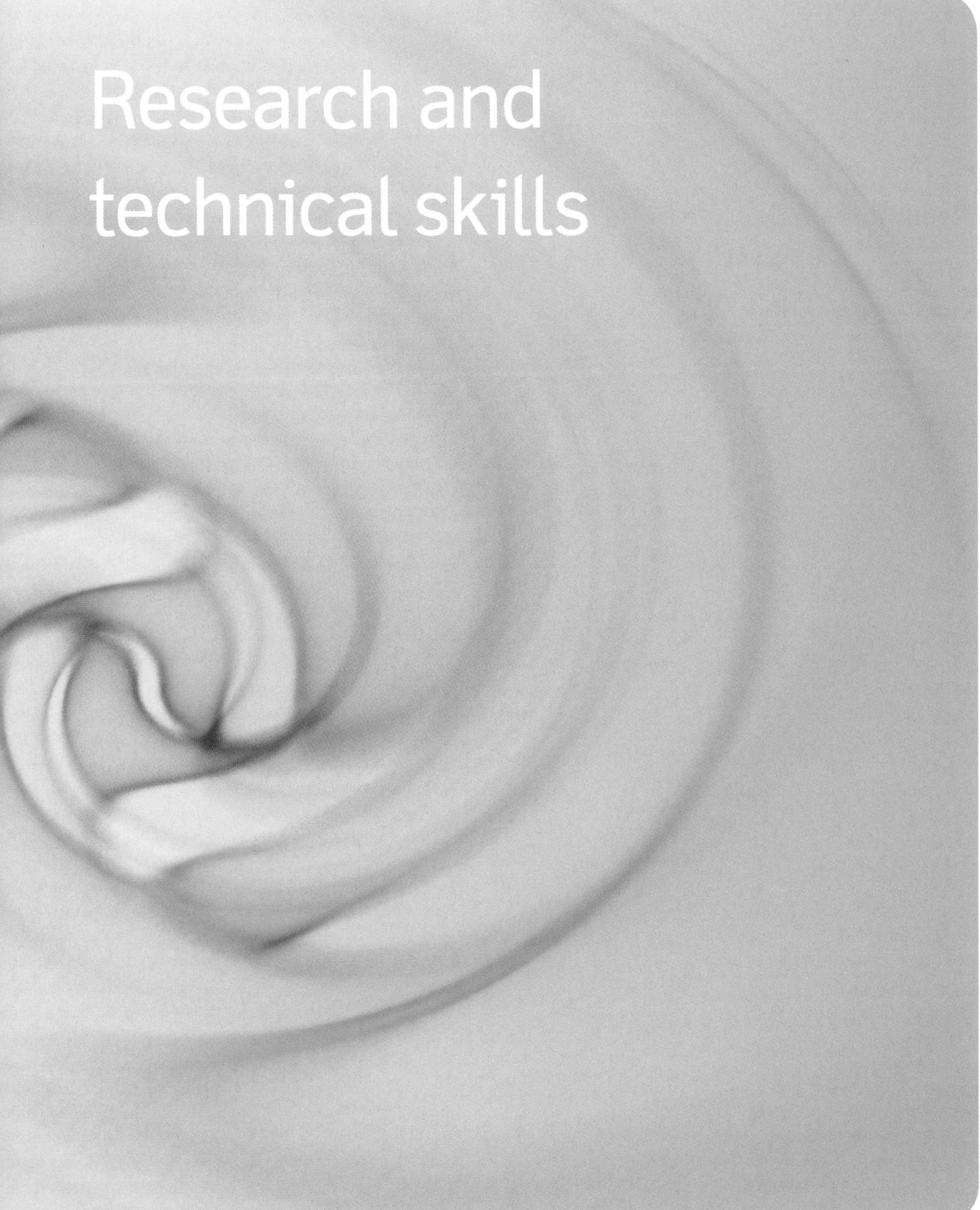

Research and technical skills

www.oxfordinteract.com

Chapter 11

Embarking on research

Rationale

It can be daunting to embark on research for an essay or dissertation. There is such a huge amount of published material that you may feel overwhelmed. You need to be able to choose your sources effectively, ensure that you don't miss any important writing, but avoid being swamped by too many articles.

Research can take time. Remember that you not only have to identify material, but you have to read it as well. Both of these activities can be time-consuming. Here we will look briefly at how to tackle the different elements of doing research. This chapter is devised to cover:

- Library research
- Books
- Articles
- Online services
- Official publications
- Internet
- Personal help.

Library research

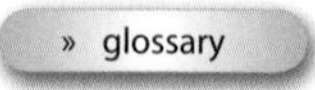

The library is your starting point for legal research. Even if you find yourself mainly using online resources, such as the major legal databases and online journals, this is still 'library-based' research.

How do I start?

Cross reference
See chapter 18, Using Reference Materials, for more details.

Your starting point depends on whether your subject is theoretical or very specific, whether it involves a precise consideration of the statutory framework and case law. One very good way to launch into a topic is to look it up in Halsbury's Laws of England (either in hard copy or online, on LexisNexis Butterworths). This will give you a narrative of the law on any topic, and lead you to the legislation and case law. Be sure to look at the latest updates on Halsbury's.

Books

» glossary

Cross reference
Books are dealt with in more detail in chapter 12, Using a law library, and chapter 15, Using law books.

Books are one obvious starting point, although you will probably not be able to find one which is concerned with the precise topic of your research. Remember that the bibliographies in books can be a valuable pointer to other materials – cases and statutes, obviously, but also other books and journal articles.

Journal articles

Articles are more up to date than books, generally speaking, but have to be used with some discrimination. Use the Legal Journals Index (on Westlaw) or the Index to Legal Periodicals to find articles on your topic. The LJI in particular, may lead you to many short articles in practitioner-oriented journals or magazines, which you should ignore as a rule: you probably won't be able to get hold of the full text articles, and in any case they tend to be ephemeral.

Cross reference
There is more detail in chapter 16, Using law journals.

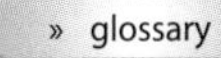

» abbreviation

Remember Books and articles will lead you to the leading cases and legislation on your topic. Use leading cases and/or statutes as search terms to find more relevant articles.

Online legal databases

Use these for your up-to-date case and statute law, and for commentary. Remember that both Westlaw and LexisNexis Butterworths contain a wealth of commentary, both on specialised subject areas, and general (Halsbury's Laws of England, described above, is the authoritative commentary on the law).

Cross reference
These online services are described in detail in chapter 17, Using legal databases.

Official publications and other reports

Your research will undoubtedly lead you to various publications of official and non-official bodies. Official publications are dealt with in the chapter on sources of law. Tracing publications from non-official bodies is usually a matter of finding their websites, and looking at their list of publications. Your library may also hold these in printed form, or have online subscriptions giving access to otherwise restricted publications. Be sure to look at the Law Commission for relevant reports.

Cross reference
See chapter 13, Sources of law.

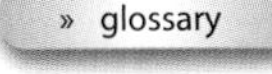

The internet

While you can often find useful material by a general internet search, you have to be very careful about the source. Wikipedia is not a reliable source for legal information! Remember that if you copy material you have found on the internet this is plagiarism, unless you fully acknowledge the source.

» glossary

Don't forget current affairs. For certain topics, especially those concerning issues with a contemporary political dimension, newspaper or BBC reports are not only valuable resources, but essential to your research.

Cross reference
See chapter 7, Avoiding plagiarism, for more details and warnings.

Getting personal help

You have two points of personal contact for getting help. Initially, your tutor can give you guidance on the reading and preparation you need to do for extended written work. But it's up to you to do the work in identifying books and articles, and you may want to get help from your library in doing this. You can get advice from your tutor about the material you have found, whether you have missed anything important, and whether you have picked up irrelevant, or less important materials.

Your law librarian, or other library staff, will usually be happy to help you. Don't expect them to drop everything if you just go in to seek help. If you are writing an essay, and more particularly if you are preparing an extended essay or dissertation, you will need to make an appointment and explain what your needs are. The librarian is not there to find material for you, but can give you pointers as to the most efficient way of searching. Most students find this one-to-one help enormously useful.

Getting materials from other libraries

If you have identified articles or books which are not available to you online or in your library, you may be able to get hold of them through your library's inter-library loan or document delivery service. This will depend on your own library's policy, but you can find out from your law librarian, or the inter-library loan department. If you do use it, remember that you have to leave time for this. Articles may be available rapidly, but books can take longer.

Remember: You can't possibly read or use everything that has been written on your topic. How much you discover will depend on the topic, but in general you should expect to read the important articles and books that you have identified.

Reference management software

There are a number of software packages to help you manage your references, and your university is likely to have access to one or more of them. Some well-known ones are **Endnote**, **Procite**, **Reference Manager**, and **RefWorks**. They may be referred to as reference management, or bibliographic management software packages. You can find out more from your library. This software will automatically format your references for you for insertion into your dissertation. You should be aware, however, that they don't always work well with legal citation conventions, and you may need to seek advice on this from your library.

» glossary

Some tips on doing research

- Keep a research trail: make a note of everything you have found, where you found it, and the date. There is nothing more frustrating than realising later that you can't remember where you found the information.
- Be sure to cite each item properly, and make a note of the citation as you are going along.
- Investigate reference management software as described above.
- Remember that the references in a key book or article will lead you to other relevant writing.

Conclusion

Follow these ground rules for doing research, leave plenty of time to do it, and use the guidelines provided in other chapters in this part of the resource.

If you want to try some activities to help you put your research skills into practice, we suggest that you look at the activities that focus on specific research skills in chapters 12–18.

www.oxfordinteract.com

Chapter 12

Using a law library

Rationale

The law library is your friend and companion throughout your degree. If you take the trouble to familiarise yourself early on with the resources and services offered by the library you will save yourself a great deal of time.

This chapter is devised to:

- Enable you to explore ways of using your library effectively
- Help you find and exploit the books, journals and online resources you need for law
- Guide you on how to move outside the strict boundaries of legal materials to expand and enhance your research
- Inform you about the kinds of services offered by libraries and how to make best use of them.

What is a law library?

You may not have a law library as such: it may be a collection within your main university library, and may be called a **learning centre** rather than a **library**. A few of the older universities have separate law libraries, usually located in or adjacent to the Law School. Others have a designated area within the main library. Whichever is the case at your institution, you should become familiar with the way it works and where to find help.

In this chapter we will use the term **law library** to cover all or any of these arrangements.

Various names for libraries

Library

Law Library

Library Services

Learning Centre

Learning Resource centre

Library and Information Services

Learning Information Resources

LIS

Information Services

Becoming familiar with the library

Get to know your library early on. Make sure you know how the catalogue works, how the books are arranged, where the main law collection is, where journals are, and so on. Be sure to familiarise yourself with restricted materials, whether on the open shelves or in a short loan collection. Find out where reference materials are kept. If you don't understand anything, ask the library staff. You will find it much easier if you have mastered the way it is organised at an early stage, before you find yourself needing to use the materials at short notice.

Libraries are inevitably full of rules and regulations about borrowing material, restrictions on use, items confined to the library, short loan collections, and (the worst of all) fines for the late return of books. It is worth remembering these rules and regulations are there to ensure the smooth running of the library and to give the best service to all students.

What you shouldn't do

You will certainly encounter examples of other students' anti-social behaviour which can seriously affect your ability to do your work. These include hanging on to books which are overdue, deliberately mis-shelving books, and at the worst, stealing books and tearing out pages. It goes without saying that these are unacceptable.

Writing in books, or highlighting text, is a form of vandalism. Not only is it extremely annoying to read someone else's comments and to find one's reading disrupted by garish highlighting, but this permanently damages the books, some of which are irreplaceable.

So, if ever you think of doing any of these things yourself, just think what it feels like when you encounter them yourself.

The library rules are there for your benefit.

Activity 1

Now try an activity which prompts you to find out a few facts about your law library.

When you have answered the questions you will have basic knowledge about your library, and know where to find further information.

What does the library contain?

The library contains a huge diversity of printed materials, including copies of all the books you will need for your studies. The following are the types of materials you are likely to encounter.

Printed materials

These are traditionally divided into the two categories of **books** and periodicals. For law, however, a third category is very important: **primary materials**, which we will look at first.

» glossary

- **Primary materials** are the printed law reports and statutes which form the backbone of any law library. You will almost certainly use online versions of these for the most part, but it is important that you also know about the printed volumes. The extent of the collection of primary materials will depend partly on the age of your institution, and the oldest institutions are likely to have a full set of older law reports and statutes while newer institutions may depend to a greater extent on online access. However, as the standard of library provision in all institutions teaching law

» glossary

is carefully monitored, you can be sure to have access to the primary resources that you need.

- **Books** line the shelves of your library. Again, the number and diversity depends largely on the size and age of your law school.
- **Journals** (often referred to as periodicals or sometimes serials) are usually accessed online. However, not all journals are available in online versions, and you may need to consult them in hard copy in your library.
- You can consult **newspapers** online, and this is valuable for looking at today's news. However, your library will take copies of the main broadsheet newspapers, which you may find useful to consult.
- **Other materials** that you will find in the library include official publications and reports of various kinds.

» glossary

» glossary

Activity 2

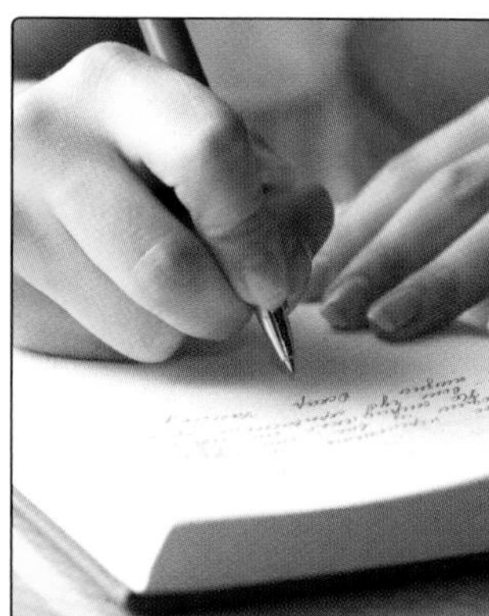

Now look in your library catalogue to find out if you have certain printed materials in the library.

Online resources

» glossary

The library is also your gateway to online resources, including the major legal databases, such as Westlaw and LexisNexis Butterworths and a large range of legal journals.

Cross reference You will find out more about using these in chapter 17, Using legal databases.

Activity 3

Now find out which of the legal databases you have access to.

Using the library off and on campus

You can use your library day and night, wherever you are. You will still need to go to the library to find the materials which are not available in online format, including most of the books you need (though e-books are a growing resource). You will also find that some journals are only available in hard copy.

It's also well worth your while becoming familiar with the printed versions of some of the great reference sources, such as Halsbury's Laws of England. Using the printed versions is a very different process from using them online, and one that you may find stands you in good stead in your future career.

» glossary

Cross reference
See chapter 18, Using reference materials.

Staff

Most libraries will have at least one dedicated law librarian, although she or he may go under another title, such as **subject specialist for law**. Larger law libraries will have several staff. It is very likely that you will meet the law librarian early on, and you will probably attend training sessions given or organised by her or him.

Activity 4

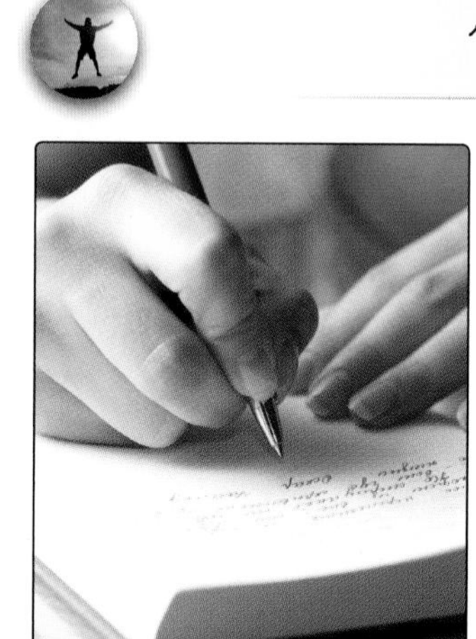

Now find out who your law librarian is.

Online help

You will almost certainly be able to access 24-hour help online by means of tutorials, guides, FAQs etc. on your library website. Look out for the specialist ones on finding and using legal materials, but also for more general ones on study skills etc.

Activity 5

Now have a look on your library website to find some guidance on using legal materials.

Using the library catalogue

The key to effective use of the library is using its catalogue. A university library is so much bigger than the one you are likely to have encountered at school that it can be overwhelming. It's no good just wandering around the shelves, you have to know exactly where the book is located.

Your library's online catalogue will tell you where the book is located, how many copies there are, and almost certainly whether it is checked out already. All librarians are familiar with the difficulties students can have using the library catalogue, and what may seem obvious once you know the system may be tricky at the beginning. Library catalogues vary, so you must use the rules of your own system. However, these tend to be the common problems:

Pitfalls

- Entering too much information – this is probably the commonest mistake. Most catalogue systems require you to enter **one** author's **surname only**.

James **Holland** and Julian Webb, ***Learning Legal Rules***, 6th edn, 2006.

- Beware, too, of trying to enter the whole title; it is better to enter one or two keywords in most library systems; that way you can avoid error.

    Loveland, I., ***Constitutional Law***, *Administrative Law and Human Rights: A Critical Introduction*, 4th edn, 2006.

Key Point

Be minimalist! The more words you enter when searching for a book, the more restrictive you will be, and the more likely you are to make mistakes.

- A characteristic of law books is that as they go through frequent editions the original author becomes part of the title, and the person who is updating the original work becomes the author.
- Law books are habitually referred to by the name of the originating author(s) only. So you may be referred to *Smith & Hogan* or *Bradley & Ewing*. Over time books can change their titles and their authors, so it may not be apparent that, for example, 'Bradley & Ewing' is an updated edition of what used to be 'Wade & Phillips'. Another characteristic is that authoritative texts become known as 'Chitty on Contracts' or 'Rayden on Divorce', and this is **sometimes** but not always reflected in the actual title of the book.

Wade & Phillips' book on Constitutional Law was first published in 1931 as

E.C.S. Wade and G.G. Phillips, ***Constitutional Law***, 1931

↓

It went through numerous editions. In 1965 the 7th edition was published, still under the authors' names, but actually written by Wade and A.W. Bradley:

E.C.S. Wade and G.G. Phillips, ***Constitutional Law***, 7th edn, 1965 by E.C.S. Wade and A.W. Bradley

↓

By the 9th edition the authors are still Wade & Phillips, but the book is 'by' Bradley (Wade is now listed as 'consulting editor'), and the title has been expanded:

E.C.S. Wade and G.G. Phillips, ***Constitutional and Administrative Law***, 9th edn, 1978 by A.W. Bradley

↓

Philips is no longer listed as author in the 10th edition and the book has become 'Wade & Bradley':

E.C.S. Wade and A.W. Bradley, ***Constitutional and Administrative Law,*** 10th edn, 1985

↓

In 1993 although it is still known as Wade and Bradley, a new author has joined:

E.C.S. Wade and A.W. Bradley, ***Constitutional and Administrative Law*** 11th edn, 1993 by A.W. Bradley and K.D. Ewing

↓

In 1999 Wade is dropped and it is now known as 'Bradley & Ewing', right up to the 14th edition, 2007:

A.W. Bradley and K.D. Ewing, ***Constitutional and Administrative Law*** 14th edn, 2007 by A.W. Bradley and K.D. Ewing

J.C. Smith's book on Criminal Law was first published in 1965 as

J.C. Smith, ***Criminal Law***, 1965

↓

By the second edition he is joined by Brian Hogan:

J.C. Smith and B. Hogan, ***Criminal Law***, 2nd edn, 1969

↓

This remains constant for the next five editions, and the book is normally referred to as ***Smith & Hogan***, but by the 8th edition J.C. Smith has acquired a knighthood, and Brian Hogan has died:

Sir John Smith and the late Brian Hogan ***Criminal Law***, 8th edn, 1996

↓

For the 9th edition, Hogan is no longer listed as author, but becomes part of the title. The book is still known as ***Smith & Hogan,*** and the catalogue entry may look something like this:

Smith, J. C. (John Cyril) ***Criminal Law***, 9th edn, 1999

[Smith & Hogan criminal law]

Some libraries may start entering the title like this:

Sir John Smith, ***Smith & Hogan Criminal Law***, 10th edn, 2002

↓

Sir John died in 2003, and the 11th edition of the book has been updated by David Ormerod, who now becomes the author:

David Ormerod, ***Smith & Hogan Criminal Law,*** 11th edn, 2005

- It is very important that you use the latest edition of a law book. Having located the title in the library catalogue be sure to note the latest edition. Depending on the catalogue system your library uses, the editions may or may not be displayed chronologically.
- Another common problem is spelling: it is easy to misspell or mistype names – this is something which everyone does from time to time. Look at the following (all taken from the Oxford University Press Law textbooks catalogue) and see how easy it would

be to make a minor spelling mistake. If you don't enter the name correctly, you won't find the book:

Beatson	Ghandhi
Birnie	Guelff
Bradley	Kealy
Bradney	Kittichaisaree
Bulloch	Mackenzie
Carrabine	McKenzie
Chrolavicius	McCorquodale
Cotterrell	Matthew
Davis	Matthews
Davies	Parpworth
Denyer	Tomkins

- As well as misspellings, be aware of legitimate alternative spellings of common words. One of the commonest is *organization*, which is also spelt *organisation*. If you look up a book on the 'World Trade Organisation' you may not retrieve it.

Cross reference There is more detail about these spelling pitfalls in chapter 3, Writing good English.

Remember If you can't find the book under the author, check the spelling, or try looking up under title only (this can be difficult with books that have generic titles such as 'constitutional law').

Advanced use of the library catalogue

Your library catalogue will present you with the simplest search form. This is likely to be a straightforward search box in which you enter keywords, or it may offer you the options of entering author, title, etc. separately. There is usually also an advanced option (a common feature on all databases).

These are the sort of advanced features which can help you to use the catalogue effectively:

- Limiting your search to the type of materials (e.g. journals, DVDs, etc.)
- Limiting your search to a particular library (especially useful in a multi-site institution)
- Using an operator to refine the search ('and', 'or', 'and not')
- Truncating words (e.g. child? To find child, children, childless, etc.) NB: the truncating character used on your system may be different – ! and * are both common)
- Using 'wildcards' to replace one or more letters in a word (e.g. wom*n to find 'woman' or women') – again your system might use a different character for this purpose.

You will have help on using the catalogue on the system, so use it!

Activity 6

Now go into your library catalogue and see if you can find a number of commonly found law books we have listed for you.

Conclusion

- This has been an introduction to the basic functions of a library. Every library is different, so you must make sure that you familiarise yourself with your own.
- Library skills are intrinsic to research skills, and you will find there is a presumption that you are using your library resources in nearly all the chapters in this resource. Some of the chapters, such as chapter 16, Using legal journals, and chapter 17, Using legal databases, are in effect an extension of this one.
- Take advantage of any induction and help you are offered. You will have help on the website, and almost certainly some tours or other guidance, and don't forget that there will be library staff whose job it is to answer your questions.

www.oxfordinteract.com

Chapter 13

Sources of law

Rationale

In this chapter we will look briefly at the sources of law, both domestic and international, which form the structure of the subject. The detailed use of these courses is covered in separate chapters. This chapter is devised to outline the key sources of law you will come across, which include:

- Primary and secondary legal literature
- Legislation and its structure
- Case law and law reports
- Official publications; parliamentary and government sources
- Sources for European law
- The law of other jurisdictions
- Treaties and other international sources
- Current awareness sources.

Primary and secondary sources

Legal literature is traditionally divided into primary and secondary sources. This is a division which you will find in all social science and humanities subjects, but in law it has a particular meaning.

- **Primary sources** comprise the main body of the law: legislation and case law.
- **Secondary sources** are the other materials: books, journals, indexes and digests for analysing the law, and reference materials such as encyclopaedias and dictionaries.

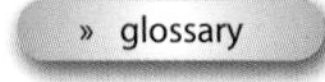

» glossary

Legislation

» glossary

Legislation consists of the body of laws passed by Parliament. Legislation itself is divided into **primary** and **subordinate** or **delegated** legislation:

» glossary

- Primary legislation: Acts of Parliament, or statutes
- Delegated legislation (often referred to as subordinate or secondary legislation) is made under the authority of an Act. Most delegated legislation is in the form of Statutory Instruments.

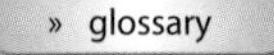

» glossary

You will learn about the detail of legislation and the legislative process in chapter 19, Reading statutes and the legislative process. In this chapter we will concentrate on where to find legislation.

Acts of Parliament

Acts of Parliament, also known as statutes, form the primary legislation of the UK. Around 50–70 Acts are passed every year.

Acts are sometimes the result of a lengthy consultation process that may take years to result in legislation. Occasionally an Act may be passed in a few days, sometimes as the result of an emergency.

Acts are published in print (the Queen's Printer copy) and simultaneously on the web, on the Acts of Parliament website.

Acts are numbered chronologically in each year. The number is known as the chapter number and is sometimes used to identify an Act.

» glossary

Acts can be amended or repealed by subsequent legislation. The skill of legal research is to be able to identify the exact status of the law in force at a particular time.

Key Point

Remember that you **must** find the latest version of a statute in order to find the law in force. This means using the research tools. Although it is important that you read the text of an Act as passed by Parliament, you should also learn how to find out all the amendments to date.

Delegated legislation

Delegated legislation, often called **subordinate** or **secondary** legislation, delegates the authority to make legally binding regulations to a non-parliamentary agency.

Statutory Instruments (SIs) are numbered sequentially within each year. They are cited by year and number, e.g.

> SI 2001 No. 2712
>
> The Greater London Magistrates' Courts Authority (Constitution) (Amendment) Regulations 2001

» glossary

Around 3,000 SIs are passed each year, and you can find them on the Office for Public Sector Information website (**OPSI**) http://www.opsi.gov.uk/legislation/about_legislation.htm

» abbreviation

Where to find legislation

↳ **Cross reference**
There is more detail on this in chapter 19, Reading statutes and the legislative process. You can also find more detail on using some of these sources in chapter 18, Using reference materials.

It is very important to understand that legislation as published (the Queen's Printer copy) is not updated on the Acts of Parliament website. As soon as it is enacted it is likely to be amended by subsequent legislation. It is crucial, therefore, that you know how to find the current version of an Act.

The following are the main sources for legislation:

Printed sources

- Acts are published in the series **Public General Acts** which you will find in your law library. The Queen's Printer copy of each Act is published as a separate document, and these cumulate into annual volumes.
- Public General Acts began in 1831. There are earlier series of Acts which you can find in your law library. It is beyond the scope of this chapter to go into detail on these, but if you need to look up older Acts you can go to your library and ask the advice of your law librarian.

- Halsbury's **Statutes of England** is the major printed research tool for tracing the current status of legislation, which you can use to find the current status of legislation. It is arranged by subject and quite complicated to use, but well worth getting to know. Halsbury's Statutes includes definitive annotations to the legislation.

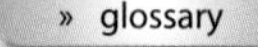

- **Current Law Statutes** is another series. This is arranged chronologically. Its great virtue is that it has very useful annotations which give the pre-legislative information on an Act, including, often, the political consensus leading to the legislation, the policy documents, Green and White Papers, and a note of the significant parliamentary debates.

Online sources

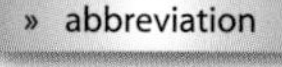

- Legislation is initially published on the Office of Public Sector Information (OPSI) website http://www.opsi.gov.uk/legislation/about_legislation.htm and also on BAILII (British and Irish Legal Information Institute), but these are the Acts and SIs as published, and do not include subsequent amendments or repeals. So, while either of these are useful for seeing the Act as passed, they can't be used for current research on legislation.
- The UK Statute Law Database http://www.statutelaw.gov.uk/ is the official revised edition of the legislation of the UK, in which you can find the later amendments to legislation as well as the published text.

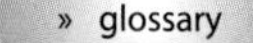

- Legislation is also included in the major legal database services. All of them have annotations, and you can use them for finding out about the current status of legislation and also a good deal of enhanced information such as cases citing the Act, articles about the Act, and annotations, depending on which database you use. More specifically:

- LexisNexis Butterworths (LNB) includes Halsbury's annotations, and you can link to them from any Act. LNB also includes a separate database, *Is It In Force?*
- Westlaw includes references to articles in legal journals.
- Justis Statutes are the only online source for repealed statutes: the database includes all Acts from 1235.

Cross reference
See chapter 17, Using legal databases.

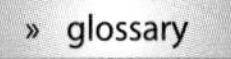

» abbreviation

Activity 1

Now test yourself on the information you've just read on statutes.

Now test yourself on statutes. Choose the correct word from the list below to fill the gaps.

Public General Acts	repealed statutes	The Queen's Printer copy	Westlaw
Justis Statutes	Halsbury's Statutes	by subject	OPSI
The Statute Law Database	LexisNexis Butterworths		

The official printing of an Act is known as ______. They are published in the series called ______. These are the Acts as passed, and do not contain any amendments. You can also find them on the ______ website.

The official revised database of statutes is called ______. You can also find revised statutes on the commercial legal databases. ______ contains links to Halsbury's annotations; ______ has links to journal articles on each Act; ______ contains all the Acts passed since 1235, and is the only online source for ______.

The major annotated series of Acts is known as ______ and is arranged ______.

Case law

Of the tens of thousands of cases heard in the courts only a small proportion are reported and published in law report series. Unlike legislation, which is published officially by the government, law reporting is primarily a commercial enterprise. The nearest we get to official series of reports are those published by the Incorporated Council of Law Reporting (ICLR).

Cross reference
You will find more about law reports and law reporting in chapter 14, Citing legal authorities. You will learn how to read and analyse a case in depth in chapters 21–24, Reading cases 1–4.

» glossary

» abbreviation

Which cases are reported?

To get an idea of which cases are reported, start off by looking at the court structure of England and Wales:

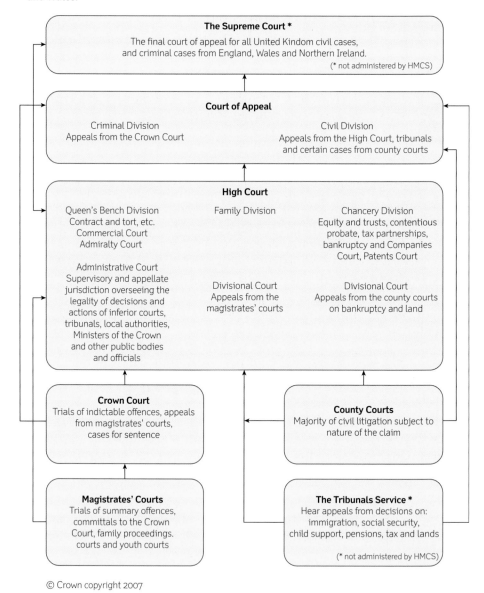

The Supreme Court *
The final court of appeal for all United Kindom civil cases, and criminal cases from England, Wales and Northern Ireland.
(* not administered by HMCS)

Court of Appeal

Criminal Division
Appeals from the Crown Court

Civil Division
Appeals from the High Court, tribunals and certain cases from county courts

High Court

Queen's Bench Division
Contract and tort, etc.
Commercial Court
Admiralty Court

Administrative Court
Supervisory and appellate jurisdiction overseeing the legality of decisions and actions of inferior courts, tribunals, local authorities, Ministers of the Crown and other public bodies and officials

Family Division

Divisional Court
Appeals from the magistrates' courts

Chancery Division
Equity and trusts, contentious probate, tax partnerships, bankruptcy and Companies Court, Patents Court

Divisional Court
Appeals from the county courts on bankruptcy and land

Crown Court
Trials of indictable offences, appeals from magistrates' courts, cases for sentence

County Courts
Majority of civil litigation subject to nature of the claim

Magistrates' Courts
Trials of summary offences, committals to the Crown Court, family proceedings. courts and youth courts

The Tribunals Service *
Hear appeals from decisions on: immigration, social security, child support, pensions, tax and lands
(* not administered by HMCS)

This diagram is taken from Her Majesty's Court Service (HMCS) website http://www.hmcourts-service.gov.uk/aboutus/structure/index.htm. You can view a PDF version of this file to print off, which you may find useful.

The higher the court, the more likely a case is to be reported. They include:

- All cases from the Supreme Court (after October 2009) and the House of Lords (until October 2009).
- Around 70 per cent of the decisions of the Court of Appeal (Civil Division), but only 10 per cent of Court of Appeal (Criminal Division) decisions.
- Between 20 and 30 per cent of decisions of the High Court, and most of these in specialised series of law reports.
- It is very rare that cases in the lower courts are reported.
- Some appeal tribunal decisions are reported, but these represent a small proportion of the cases decided. The selection is made by the Commissioners of the tribunal.

» glossary

» glossary

Unreported cases

The electronic publication of case transcripts has transformed access to unreported cases.

» glossary

- You can find a Supreme Court judgment within hours of the decision on its website http://www.supremecourt.gov.uk/index.html.
- BAILII (British and Irish Legal Information Institute) http://www.bailii.org/ publishes judgments from the Civil and Criminal Divisions of the Court of Appeal, and from the Administrative Court, selected by the judge concerned.
- Summaries of latest cases is provided by the ICLR http://www.lawreports.co.uk/ on its WLR (Weekly Law Reports) Daily and ICR (Industrial Cases Reports) Express pages.

» abbreviation

These sources are valuable for giving access to new cases before they are reported.

Where to find law reports

You will have printed copies of law reports in your library. These are likely to include the **Law Reports**, the major series published by the ICLR, **Weekly Law Reports** and **All England Law Reports**. You will also have a number of other series, such as **Criminal Appeal Reports**, though how extensive a collection of specialised reports depends on the size of your library.

Law reports are widely available on the major legal database services. Each service has a different range of law reports, but for the most part you can find a report of any case you may be looking for on Westlaw, LexisNexis Butterworths (LNB) or Justis.

» abbreviation

How to find out where cases are reported

↳ Cross reference
Use the hierarchy of reports in the section 'Which report should you use?' in chapter 14, Citing legal authorities.

Both Westlaw and LNB will give you a list of all the law reports of a case. You can therefore see if a case for which you have been given a reference in (say) a newspaper, or a specialist series, has been reported in the Law Reports.

Where to find analysis of cases

Westlaw, LNB and Justis all include detailed analysis of cases, giving the following information:

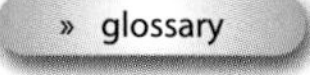

- Citations to all the reports of the case.
- Appellate history of the case (reversed or affirmed).
- The status of the judgment (whether it is still good law).
- A list of the cases considered in the judgment.
- The legislation cited in the judgment.
- Later cases which cite this judgment.
- Commentaries on the case in journals (Westlaw only).
- Summary of the judgment (Westlaw only).

More about law reports

↳ Cross reference
See the section on 'Which report should you use?' in chapter 14, Citing legal authorities.

How to read and use cases is dealt with comprehensively in chapters 21–24, Reading cases 1–4. It's worth emphasising here that there is a recognised hierarchy of law reports, and you should be aware of this when you are citing a case.

Key Point

Always cite the most authoritative report. This will be the Law Reports – AC, QB, Ch. and Fam – if it has been reported in one of these. If you are given a reference to, for example, a Times Law Report, always check to see if it has subsequently been reported in a more authoritative series.

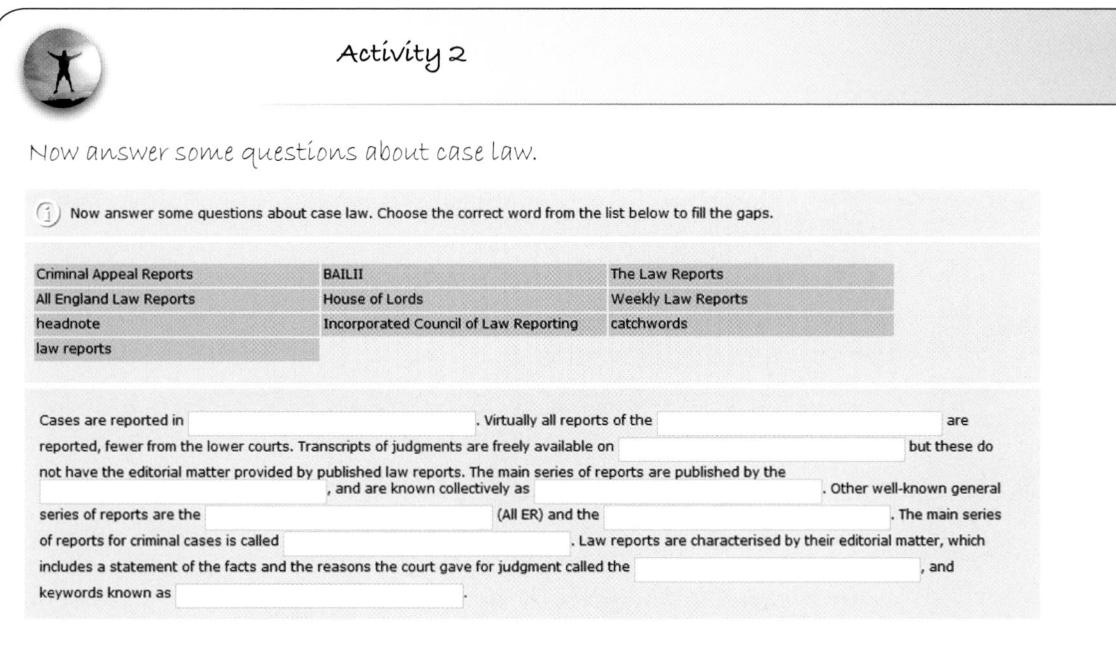

Activity 2

Now answer some questions about case law.

Now answer some questions about case law. Choose the correct word from the list below to fill the gaps.

Criminal Appeal Reports	BAILII	The Law Reports
All England Law Reports	House of Lords	Weekly Law Reports
headnote	Incorporated Council of Law Reporting	catchwords
law reports		

Cases are reported in ______. Virtually all reports of the ______ are reported, fewer from the lower courts. Transcripts of judgments are freely available on ______ but these do not have the editorial matter provided by published law reports. The main series of reports are published by the ______, and are known collectively as ______. Other well-known general series of reports are the ______ (All ER) and the ______. The main series of reports for criminal cases is called ______. Law reports are characterised by their editorial matter, which includes a statement of the facts and the reasons the court gave for judgment called the ______, and keywords known as ______.

Key Point

Always use an authoritative text for legislation or case law. Go to the primary sources, and never rely on secondary sources such as textbooks or websites. You can lay yourself open to plagiarism if you copy from sites which may themselves be using secondary sources.

» glossary

Official publications

A vast number of official publications are published by the government, its departments, and agencies. As well as the primary and secondary legislation we have already looked at, there are numerous reports of committees, research documents and informative material, falling into the following categories:

- Quasi-legislation which is not published as statutes or statutory instruments, e.g. codes of practice.

- Pre-legislative information – this includes Green Papers and White Papers, which are consultation or policy documents produced by the government or its agencies.
- Proposals for law reform.
- Reports of decision-making and regulatory bodies.
- Research carried out by public bodies, often to inform ministers or MPs. Some of this is in the form of official statistics such as Criminal Statistics and Judicial Statistics.
- Official publications can be divided broadly into Parliamentary and non-Parliamentary publications.

Parliamentary publications

Parliamentary publications cover a wide range of reports and other documents emanating from Parliament. These include Green Papers and White Papers, reports of committees, reports of inquiries, and many others. There is no single public source for these, and not all are published electronically.

» glossary

The two main categories are **Command Papers** and **House of Commons** and House of Lords Papers. Although these are distinct as categories and require different techniques for finding them, in practice there is a considerable overlap in the type of subject matter covered. Reports of government bodies may be published either as Command Papers or as House of Commons Papers, for example.

Command Papers, so-called because they are presented to Parliament **by command of Her Majesty**, include the major policy proposals (White Papers) and consultation documents (Green Papers) and also a range of other materials, such as treaties, government responses to Select Committee reports, reports of committees of inquiry and departmental reports.

Command Papers are numbered 1–9999, with a prefix indicating the different series. People sometimes get confused as to the prefix, and the chart below will show you how they match to a range of years:

1833–1869 (C 1st series)
1870–1899 (C 2nd series)
1900–1918 (Cd)
1919–1956 (Cmd)
1957–1986 (Cmnd)
1986 to the present (Cm)

If you want to know more, there is a useful House of Commons Factsheet on Command Papers at http://www.parliament.uk/documents/upload/p13.pdf

House of Commons and House of Lords Papers

These mainly consist of select committee reports, but also other material, including numerous annual reports of government agencies. Sometimes major reports of committees of inquiry are published as House of Commons Papers. An example of this is the Hutton Report: 'Report of the Inquiry into the Circumstances Surrounding the Death of Dr David Kelly', HC (2003–04) 247.

They are numbered sequentially in each parliamentary session, with the prefix HC or HL depending on whether they come from the Commons or the Lords.

Other parliamentary papers

Parliament also generates a large amount of research, done principally for ministers and MPs, but also of great interest to the law student. To get an idea of the range of research publications, have a look on the Parliamentary Publications and Records website http://www.parliament.uk/publications/research.cfm.

Parliamentary research publications often take the form of concise reports on a wide variety of topics. They include the House of Commons Library Research Papers http://www.parliament.uk/parliamentary_publications_and_archives/research_papers/research_papers.cfm. Of particular interest to law students are the papers on Parliament and Constitution Research, http://www.parliament.uk/works/notes_on_parliament_and_constitution.cfm

Key Point

Make yourself familiar with the workings of Parliament and the Parliament website. There is a mass of useful information there.

Non-parliamentary publications

Non-parliamentary publications cover the wide range of materials published by government departments and agencies.

The way to find these is to go to the department's website. There is usually a section of the site called 'Publications' where you will find all the reports and other documents produced by the department. Many of these will be presented to Parliament in the form of Command Papers.

Other material under departmental publications consists of consultations, statistics, annual reports, research and press notices. Here are two examples of the sort of material you can find on their sites:

- The Department of Constitutional Affairs (DCA), http://www.dca.gov.uk/publications.htm, for example, contains the following categories of publications:
  - Press notices

- Consultation papers
- Reports and reviews
- Research
- Speeches
- Annual reports
- Legislation
- Green Papers
- White Papers
- Forms

- The Home Office has a Science, Research and Statistics site http://www.homeoffice.gov.uk/rds/ with a huge number of reports. Have a look at their 'What's New' section to get an idea of the topics covered.

Key Point

Government departments generate lots of valuable information, including research publications that can be difficult to find elsewhere. Get to know them!

The Law Commission

» glossary

The Law Commission is the statutory body responsible for keeping the law under review, and recommending reform. All law students need to know of the work of the Law Commission, and will need to consult its publications. To find out more, have a look at its very informative website http://www.lawcom.gov.uk/

» glossary

» glossary

The Law Commission identifies areas of law in need of reform, and conducts consultations. The issues are set out in detail in published Consultation Papers (until 1990 these were known as Working Papers), with responses invited from the public and interested bodies. The Law Commission then prepares a report, for submission to the Lord Chancellor, giving its proposals for reform. A draft bill is often attached to the report.

A list on the Law Commission website shows which consultation led to which report, and the resulting legislation, if any.

Key Point

The Law Commission is an essential source for law and will give you valuable background information about areas of law on which it is working.

↳ **Cross reference** Find out how to cite official publications in chapter 14, Citing legal authorities.

Sources for European law

Detailed information on the law of the European Union is beyond the scope of this chapter, and you will learn about European institutions and the legal process in your law courses and from textbooks. The EU, however, takes its mission to explain seriously, and you will find useful information on the websites listed below.

» glossary

» abbreviation

Some universities are designated as European Documentation Centres, and if yours is one, you will have a specialist librarian and a good collection of EU materials. You will also certainly have access to detailed guides on using EU resources. Check your library website to see what is available to you.

The law of the European Union is also divided into primary and secondary legislation, but here **primary** legislation refers to the treaties which established the European Community, and the subsequent treaties, and **secondary** legislation to the Directives, Regulations and Decisions which are passed by the European Commission and the Council.

» glossary

- **Directives** do not have direct effect on national legislation, but require the member states to implement them by enacting domestic legislation.
- **Regulations** have direct effect, and do not require national implementing legislation.
- **Decisions** are binding on specific member states or organisations.

Where to find European law

- EU law is published in the Official Journal of the European Union. This daily journal publishes new legislation as well as notification of case law and other news and information from the EU. You will find links to it on the two sites mentioned below.

» glossary

- **Eur-Lex**, http://eur-lex.europa.eu/en/index.htm is the EU database for European law, including the Official Journal, treaties, recent case law, legislation in force, and legislation in preparation (COM docs). There are some informative pages on 'Process and players', http://eur-lex.europa.eu/en/droit_communautaire/droit_communautaire.htm

» glossary

which gives details of the documentary structure and the legislative procedures of the EU.

» glossary

- **Europa** http://europa.eu/ is the European Union's gateway. Here you will find documents as well as a vast amount of information about the EU, aimed at both specialists and the general public.
- Westlaw and LNB both have databases of European legislation and case law.

Cross reference
You can find information on citing European law in chapter 14, Citing legal authorities.

You will find out about the processes and structure of European law when you study the substantive subject.

The law of other jurisdictions

» glossary

You will often be called upon to find legal materials – notably case law – from other **common law** jurisdictions, especially commonwealth jurisdictions. There are excellent freely available sources for this, notably the 'Legal Information Institutes' (of which BAILII is the UK version).

This topic is also covered in chapter 17, Using legal databases, but these are some useful links:

» glossary

» glossary

» glossary

» glossary

- World Legal Information Institute (**WorldLII**) for access to worldwide law http://www.worldlii.org/
- **AustLII** for Australian law http://www.austlii.edu.au/
- **NZLII** for New Zealand Law http://www.nzlii.org/
- **CanLII** for Canadian law http://www.canlii.org/
- **LII** (Cornell Legal Information Institute) for US law http://www.law.cornell.edu/

You can find more links in gateways such as **Lawlinks** http://www.kent.ac.uk/lawlinks/otherjurisdictions.html

Westlaw and LNB both have international materials, including comprehensive coverage of US law, and case law and legislation from Commonwealth and other countries. It can be quite complicated to navigate these, so you may need to seek help from your law librarian.

Treaties and other international sources

It is beyond the scope of this chapter to go into detail on sources for international law – a huge topic in its own right. However, an important website can be mentioned:

- **EISIL** (Electronic Information System for International Law) http://www.eisil.org/ is the major source for researching international law. Using EISIL you can easily locate international legal documents arranged by broad topic. Here you will find the authentic texts of primary materials, and useful commentary and research guides.

» glossary

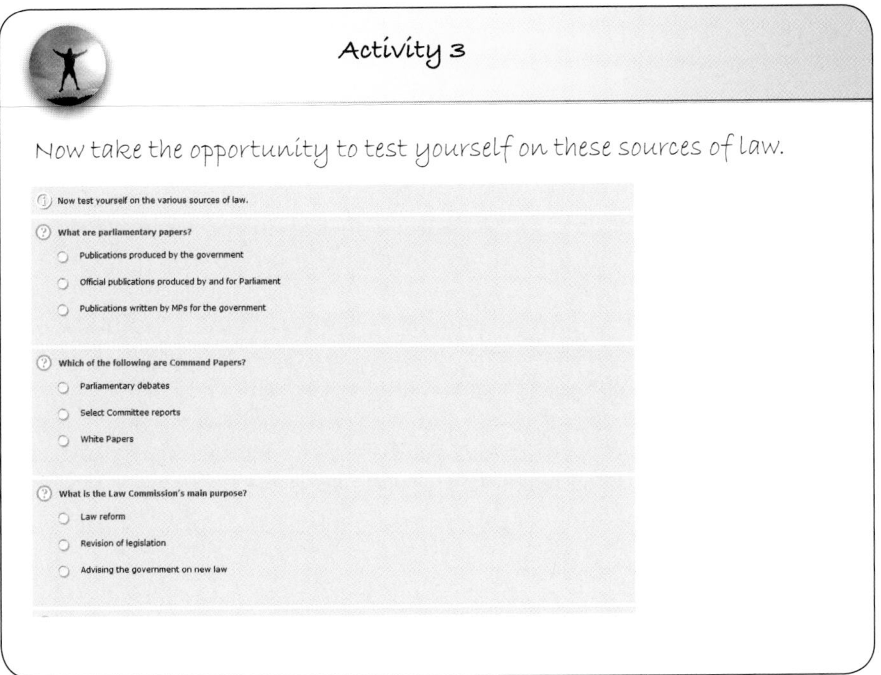

Activity 3

Now take the opportunity to test yourself on these sources of law.

Now test yourself on the various sources of law.

What are parliamentary papers?

- Publications produced by the government
- Official publications produced by and for Parliament
- Publications written by MPs for the government

Which of the following are Command Papers?

- Parliamentary debates
- Select Committee reports
- White Papers

What is the Law Commission's main purpose?

- Law reform
- Revision of legislation
- Advising the government on new law

Keeping up with the law

Keeping up with the law is a matter of ensuring you are informed about current affairs and politics as well as developments in the law. The two are interdependent. The following is some guidance on sources for this.

Newspapers

It goes without saying that you should try to read a **broadsheet** newspaper on a daily basis. *The Times*, the *Guardian* and the *Independent* are all good sources of serious news and comment. You can read them in print or follow their online editions. You can also keep track on international news using online versions of the US press, such as the *New York Times* or *Washington Post*, and the national newspapers of other countries.

» glossary

BBC

The BBC http://www.bbc.co.uk/news is a definitive source for news and comment. Listening to the news and current affairs programmes on BBC Radio 4 is a useful way of keeping yourself informed.

The BBC website also offers extensive news coverage of the world, and you can choose to look at news from different regions. The BBC World Service is an invaluable source for international current affairs.

The BBC has a number of interesting programmes with a legal focus, normally on Radio 4, of which *Law in Action* and *Unreliable Evidence* are the most informative, and well worth listening to regularly, or catching up with on the BBC website.

Official websites

The UK Parliament is a mine of information, and essential for keeping up to date with proceedings. For the devolved jurisdictions, see the websites of the Scottish Parliament, Welsh Assembly and Northern Ireland Assembly.

» glossary

Government departments and agencies also have informative websites, especially the legal ones, such as the Department of Constitutional Affairs, the Home Office and the Ministry of Justice. You will find a list of these on legal portals of which Lawlinks http://www.kent.ac.uk/lawlinks/ and **Intute** Law http://www.intute.ac.uk/socialsciences/law/ are well-known examples. **ePolitix** http://www.epolitix.com/ is a really comprehensive site with parliamentary and political information, aimed at policy-makers.

Legal journals

You can keep current with legal news in the weekly law journals. The *Lawyer* http://www.thelawyer.com/ and the *Law Gazette* http://www.lawgazette.co.uk/home.law are online versions.

Conclusion

What are **not** sources of law

It's a great temptation to bypass official sites and simply search for documents by googling them. This can be an efficient way of locating a document, but you have to be sure that the source is trustworthy and the text is authentic. Documents may not be the latest version, or may be copies which contain mistakes. Even if you identify documents from a google search, you should check them against the originating site and make sure that you have the official text.

Similarly, you should be wary of legal information that you obtain from a general web search. Although you can find useful initial information from sites such as Wikipedia you should not regard this as a serious source of legal information, and you should always use legal encyclopaedias, reference works, textbooks and databases as your principal source.

Wikipedia pages can be edited by anyone, and although the information may look authoritative, you cannot guarantee that it has not been copied from elsewhere, or contains inaccuracies. You are liable to commit inadvertent plagiarism if you copy material from Wikipedia.

Cross reference
See chapter 7, Avoiding plagiarism, for more information.

Wikipedia is not a source of law!

Links

Office for Public Sector Information (OPSI)
http://www.opsi.gov.uk/legislation/about_legislation.htm

Statute Law Database http://www.statutelaw.gov.uk/

Her Majesty's Courts Service (HMCS)
http://www.hmcourts-service.gov.uk/aboutus/structure/index.htm

House of Lords judgments
http://www.publications.parliament.uk/pa/ld/ldjudgmt.htm

Incorporated Council of Law Reporting (ICLR)
http://www.lawreports.co.uk/

House of Commons Factsheet on Command Papers
http://www.parliament.uk/documents/upload/p13.pdf

Parliamentary Publications and Records website
http://www.parliament.uk/publications/research.cfm

House of Commons Library Research Papers
http://www.parliament.uk/parliamentary_publications_and_archives/research_papers/research_papers.cfm

Parliament and Constitution Research
http://www.parliament.uk/works/notes_on_parliament_and_constitution.cfm

http://www.lawcom.gov.uk/

Eur-Lex http://eur-lex.europa.eu/en/index.htm

'Process and players'
http://eur-lex.europa.eu/en/droit_communautaire/droit_communautaire.htm

Europa http://europa.eu/

World Legal Information Institute (WorldLII) for access to worldwide law
http://www.worldlii.org/

AustLII (Australian law) http://www.austlii.edu.au/

NZLII (New Zealand law) http://www.nzlii.org/

CanLII Canadian law) http://www.canlii.org/

LII (Cornell Legal Information Institute) http://www.law.cornell.edu/

Lawlinks http://www.kent.ac.uk/lawlinks/otherjurisdictions.html

EISIL http://www.eisil.org/

BBC http://www.bbc.co.uk/news

Lawlinks http://www.kent.ac.uk/lawlinks/

Intute Law http://www.intute.ac.uk/socialsciences/law/

ePolitix http://www.epolitix.com/

The Lawyer http://www.thelawyer.com/

Law Gazette http://www.lawgazette.co.uk/

www.oxfordinteract.com

Chapter 14

Citing legal authorities

Rationale

Knowing about legal citation is a two-way process. The standard method of citing cases or other legal materials, such as statutes and journal articles, is a means to finding the source quickly and accurately. At the same time, when you make reference to a case or journal article, you need to provide the correct citation in order to identify the materials.

The conventions used in citing legal materials are unique to law. You will come across minor variations in punctuation and italicisation, but the broad structure of citation is uniform. The style of referencing used in your essays or dissertations will probably be laid down by your institution, and will follow a standardised format. Increasingly, institutions are adopting OSCOLA (Oxford Standard for the Citation of Legal Authorities). This is available online at http://www.competition-law.ox.ac.uk/published/oscola.shtml and can be referred to if you are in any doubt. You will find it particularly useful when you are writing essays or extended work, and need to make reference to materials such as official documents, reports, books and articles.

This chapter will concentrate on citing cases, because this is something you have to know about from your first day as a law student. If you can interpret the citation, you can find the case. This chapter is devised to help you:

- Know about the main forms of legal citation
- Have a source for deciphering and checking citations
- Know where to look for legal abbreviations
- Know how to check the correct citation for materials not covered in this chapter.

» glossary

» abbreviation

Note

The exercises in this chapter will use **OSCOLA** as the standard. There are many minor variants in the ways legal materials are cited, and your institution may insist on a different method. You should stick to the method which your institution recommends, and be consistent in whichever method you use.

Dealing with case citations

One of the first problems a student will face is to decipher something like this:

Donoghue v Stevenson [1932] AC 562

Khorasandjian v Bush [1993] 3 All ER 669

R v Lynch (1966) 50 Cr App R 59

Carlill v Carbolic Smoke Ball Co [1893] 1 QB 256 (CA)

R v H [2007] UKHL 7

Case citations all follow a standard format which tells you about the case and where to find it. It is usually possible to tell whether it is a civil or criminal case, at what level of the appellate system, in which court and when it was heard. The abbreviation will give you a clue as to how to find it.

Legal abbreviations

Before looking in detail at the parts of the citation, it is worth looking at legal abbreviations. They are easy to deal with when you know how.

» abbreviation

AC, QB and CA are abbreviations which will become second nature to you very quickly. Initially, however, you will need to learn how to find out what they mean.

Cross reference
See the list of abbreviations at the end of the resource.

There is a list of the most common abbreviations in this resource but the most comprehensive listing is the Cardiff Index to Legal Abbreviations http://www.legalabbrevs.cardiff.ac.uk. With this index you can find what an abbreviation stands for, or find out the correct abbreviation for a report or journal. It will also indicate the preferred abbreviation where there are variants.

» glossary

» abbreviation

An abbreviation may stand for several different publications. Usually, it is a matter of common sense to decide which is the correct one. TLR, for example, may stand for Times Law Reports, Tasmanian Law Reports, Tanzania Law Reports, Tulane Law Review among others. When in doubt, you can usually confirm the correct one by looking at the dates covered by the series, which you can find in the Cardiff Index. You will often come across variant abbreviations for the same publications. All ER is the correct abbreviation for All England Law Reports, but you will occasionally come across AER or AELR, and you should not confuse it with All ER Rep, which is the All England Law Reports Reprint of older cases. The Cardiff Index always indicates the preferred abbreviation where this is known, and you should never try to invent one of your own.

» abbreviation

Remember The Cardiff Index to Legal Abbreviations is the most comprehensive source for finding abbreviations. It covers English language legal publications, mainly law reports and periodicals.

» glossary

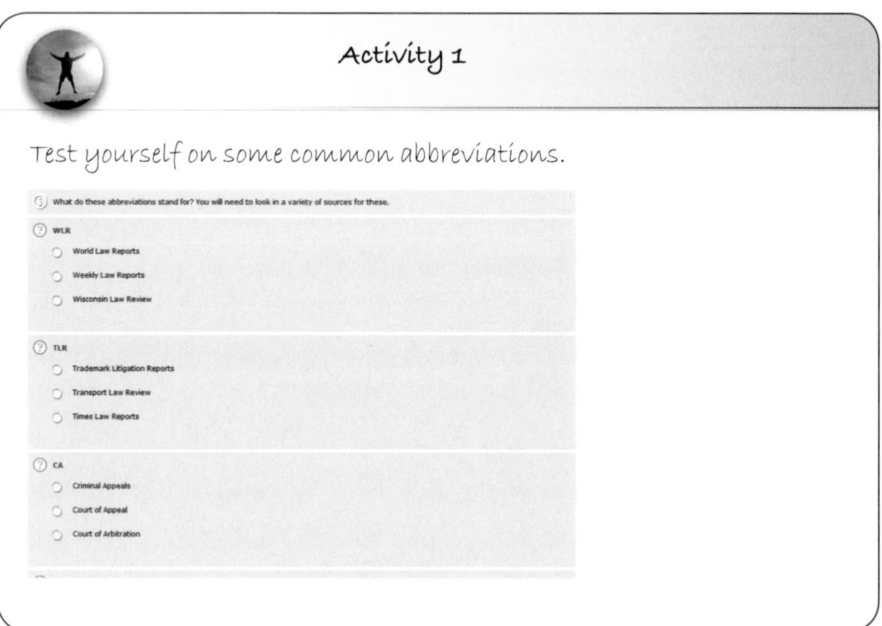

Activity 1
Test yourself on some common abbreviations.
What do these abbreviations stand for? You will need to look in a variety of sources for these.
WLR
World Law Reports
Weekly Law Reports
Wisconsin Law Review
TLR
Trademark Litigation Reports
Transport Law Review
Times Law Reports
CA
Criminal Appeals
Court of Appeal
Court of Arbitration

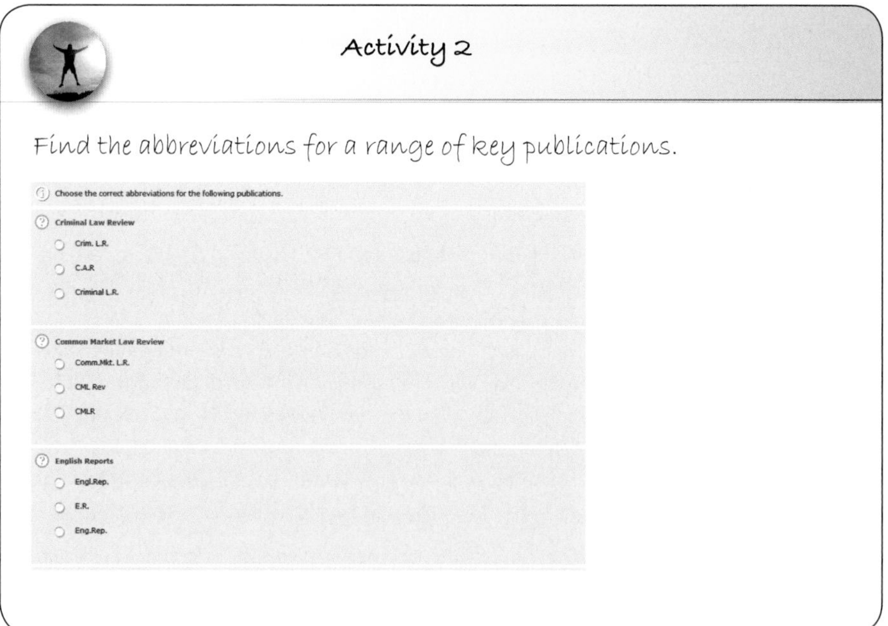

Activity 2
Find the abbreviations for a range of key publications.
Choose the correct abbreviations for the following publications.
Criminal Law Review
Crim. L.R.
C.A.R
Criminal L.R.
Common Market Law Review
Comm.Mkt. L.R.
CML Rev
CMLR
English Reports
Engl.Rep.
E.R.
Eng.Rep.

Deconstructing citations

The case citation is the standard method of referring to cases, which enables you to trace them in print or online. A citation to a case consists of various parts, which are broken down in the following table:

Names of parties	Date	Volume no. where applicable	Abbreviation of law report series (or the court for a **neutral citation**: see below)	Page no. in the law report series or case number	Sometimes the court abbreviation is added	Refers to a particular page in the report or paragraph
1. *Donoghue v Stevenson*	[1932]		AC	562	(HL)	
2. *Khorasandjian v Bush*	[1993]	3	All ER	669		675
3. *R v Lynch*	(1966)	50	Cr App R	59	(CA)	
4. *Carlill v Carbolic Smoke Ball Co*	[1893]	1	QB	256	(CA)	
5. *R v H*	[2007]		UKHL	50		[53]

You'll notice the following:

» glossary

- The names of the parties are usually in italics, or underlined.
- Square brackets round the date indicate that the year is necessary in order to find the publication on the shelves, usually because either the series has no volume numbering, or that several volumes are published in each year. Round brackets indicate that the volume number is sufficient to trace the case. This is of little importance for finding cases online, but the convention is still retained. You will note that in the example above, *R v Lynch*, Criminal Appeal Reports gave an annual; volume number. When the series reached its hundredth year of publication it split into two volumes a year, as in the *R v Benjafield* below.
- A case may be **heard** in one year but not **reported** until the following year. This is especially true of cases heard at the end of the year. Also, there is often a discrepancy in the date of different reports of the same case. It is very common to find that a report in the Law Reports (see below) is dated a year later than all the other reports. (Just occasionally, there may be a gap of several years between the decision and the report.)
- Since 2001 all law reports published by Sweet & Maxwell use sequential case numbering instead of page references to identify the cases as in *R v Benjafield* [2002] 2 Cr App R 3. This is the third case in this volume of Criminal Appeal Reports, and actually starts on p. 54.
- The abbreviation of the court in brackets is sometimes added to the citation. OSCOLA recommends this as standard practice, though you will often find it omitted.
- If you need to pinpoint a particular place in the report you can refer to the page number as in 'Lord Steyn's judgment in *R v Benjafield* [2002] 2 Cr App R 3, 72', or the paragraph number (in square brackets) in the case of a neutral citation: '... the point made by Lord Rodger in *R v H* [2007] UKHL 7 [53]'.
- For more detail on how to punctuate citations refer to OSCOLA.

Example 1 – a civil case

Johnson v Phillips... [1975] 3 All ER 682

The citation to the report itself consists of four parts: Johnson v Phillips: this is the usual form in civil cases: claimant (plaintiff) v defendant

v stands for *versus* or against, but the case is normally referred to orally as 'Johnson and Phillips'

Johnson v Phillips **[1975] 3 All ER 682**

The citation to the report itself consists of four parts:

- the date
- the volume number
- the report abbreviation
- the page number

Johnson v Phillips **[1975]** 3 All ER 682

If the data is in square brackets you need it to find the volume of law reprots, because there are several volumes in each year.

If the date is in round brackets, it is only given for added information and is not needed for finding the report, because the volumes are numbered consecutively throughtout the series.

Technically round brackets indicate the date of the judgement, and occasionally you find a disparity if the report was published some time after the judgement.

Johnson v Phillips [1975] **3** All ER 682

Many reports series have several volumes in each year, which will be numbered 1, 2, 3. In this case you need to know the date to find the report.

Some series are numbered consecutively from the beginning, in which case the date is not necessary.

Johnson v Phillips [1975] 3 **All ER** 682

There are many abbreviations to law reports, but you will come across some of them very frequently.

Johnson v Phillips [1975] 3 All ER **682**

The page number is the page within the volume of report where you will find the case.

Since 2001 some series have started using unique numbers for each case within each year. Recent reports also have paragraph numbering, so that the precise point in the case may be cited.

About case names

Full case names are sometimes lengthy, and are usually shortened. So *Hedley Byrne & Co Ltd v Heller & Partners Ltd* is usually referred to as *Hedley Byrne,* and *Central London Property Trust v High Trees House Ltd* as simply *High Trees,* with the full citation in your footnotes.

'*V*' stands for **versus**, meaning against, and is usually spoken as 'and' in civil cases. So you would refer to 'Pepper and Hart' orally. Criminal cases, however, are formally spoken of as 'The **Crown** against Brown', but are normally referred to by the name of the **defendant** only: 'Brown'. It is permissible to refer to criminal cases in this way in text, with a footnote giving the full citation to the case.

Pepper v Hart	The usual form in civil cases: **Claimant** (formerly **Plaintiff**) v Defendant, or Appellant v Respondent
R v Brown	The usual form in criminal cases: R stands for Regina or Rex, depending on whether the monarch is a queen or king, and is normally referred to as 'the Crown'. It is sometimes written in full, or abbreviated to Reg.
R v Secretary of State for the Home Department ex p Stafford	Prior to 2001, judicial review cases were cited as 'ex parte', abbreviated to 'ex p'.
R (on the application of Laporte) v Chief Constable of Gloucestershire *R (Laporte) v Chief Constable of Gloucestershire*	After 2001, cases of judicial review are named 'on the application of x' and this appears on the official **transcript**. However, these can be cited with the name of the applicant in brackets, as in the second example
R v R *Re M* *Re H (A Minor) (Care Proceedings: Child's Wishes)* *R v R (Rape: Marital exemption)*	Cases in the family court and cases of rape are generally anonymised. A term is usually added for precision, which can help to identify the case.
Re Smith *In re Smith*	'In the matter of' or 'in the estate of' Smith. This is the form usually used in probate cases.
The Aghios Nicolaos *Blue Horizon Shipping Co SA v ED&F Man Ltd (The Aghios Nicolaos) (QBD (Comm))*	The preferred way of referring to shipping cases is by the name of the ship only.
The 'Spycatcher' case *Attorney General v Guardian Newspapers Ltd (No. 1)*	Some cases become known by a popular name, and it is permissible to refer to them thus, though the full citation with the popular name in brackets should be used the first time.

About law reports

Of the 200,000 or so cases heard in the courts in England and Wales, only a small proportion are reported in published law report series, although a larger number are available in transcript form. Virtually all **House of Lords** cases are reported, some 70 per cent of Court of Appeal Civil Division decisions, but only 10 per cent of CA Criminal Division decisions. About 20–30 per cent

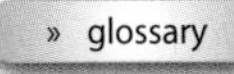

of High Court decisions are reported, but most of these are in specialist law reports. The decision as to whether a case is reported lies with the editor of the law report, not the judge. Some appeal tribunal decisions are reported, but these represent only a small proportion of the cases decided. Here, the decision to report is made by the Commissioners of the tribunal. Cases from the lower courts are rarely reported except in specialised areas such as patents (although just occasionally a lower court judgment is reported – see the landmark decision in *R v R (Rape: Marital exemption)* [1992] 1 AC 599, where the Crown Court decision, which overturned an established principle of law, was affirmed by the CA and then the HL, and was reported in [1991] 1 All ER 747).

In addition to law reports, transcripts of judgments are widely available. Many of these will be reported in due course, but by no means all.

There are more than 50 series of law reports published in England and Wales today, Most of them are specialised, in coverage, but there are three important general series.

The Law Reports

» abbreviation

The most authoritative series of reports are those published by the Incorporated Council of Law Reporting, which was set up in 1865. It publishes the series collectively known as the Law Reports, and sometimes referred to as the ICLR reports. The reports are checked by judges, and are chosen for their legal significance. The Law Reports contain counsel's argument, unlike any other series. These are the reports which should cited for preference. The Law Reports consist of several separate series, which reflect the division of the courts. The present series are the following:

» glossary

AC	Appeal Cases	Decisions of the Supreme Court, House of Lords, and the Privy Council
QB Ch Fam	Queen's Bench Division Chancery Division Family Division	There is a series for each division of the High Court. These include decisions of the Court of Appeal, which appear in the series for the division in which they originated

The Law Reports series have changed over the years.

Note

Go online to see the full list of all the series of the law reports.

The Weekly Law Reports

The Weekly Law Reports are also published by the ICLR, and started in 1954 in order to speed up the process of reporting. Volume 1 of WLR covers cases which do not merit inclusion in the Law Reports, while volume 2 contains those cases which will subsequently appear in the Law Reports with a note of counsel's argument.

All England Law Reports

The All England Law Reports started publication in 1936, and are equivalent in coverage and status to WLR. You will frequently be referred to cases reported in All ER.

Specialised series of reports

Here are some specialised series of reports which you will come across regularly.

Common Market Law Reports (CMLR)	Cases in the European Court of Justice
Criminal Appeal Reports (Cr App R)	Criminal cases – many not reported elsewhere
Environmental Law Reports (Env LR)	Cases on environmental law
Estates Gazette Law Reports (EGLR)	Cases on property
European Human Rights Reports (EHRR)	Cases from the **European Court of Human Rights**
Family Court Reports (FCR)	Family law
Fleet Street Reports (FSR)	Intellectual property cases
Industrial Relations Law Reports (IRLR)	Industrial relations
Lloyd's Reports (Lloyd's Rep)	Shipping and commercial cases
Property, Planning & Compensation Reports (P & CR)	Planning
Reports of Tax Cases (TC)	Tax

» glossary

Reports in law journals

Cases are often reported first in general law journals such as the New Law Journal, or the Solicitors' Journal. These will usually appear in one or more law report series in due course. You will also find reports cases in practitioner-oriented journals, which may sometimes be the only source in specialist areas of law.

Reports in newspapers

» glossary

All the broadsheet newspapers publish law reports, though *The Times* is generally regarded as the most authoritative. However, although these are good sources for new cases, you should always check to see that a report has been issued in a law report subsequently.

Pre-1865 reports

Prior to 1865, when the Incorporated Council of Law Reporting was founded, reports were commercially published under the names of individual law reporters, and collectively referred to as the nominate reports. These have been collected and re-published, and the series you are most likely to come across is called the English Reports, which includes cases from 1220 to 1865. The English Reports has a citation for the original report and also a running citation of its own. For example:

» glossary

> *Collier v Hicks* (1831) 2 B. & Ad. 663, 109 Eng. Rep. 1290

The nominate report citation is first, followed by the English Report citation, which is where you will find the report. OSCOLA recommends using both citations separated by a comma, though you will usually find an older case cited by its nominate report only.

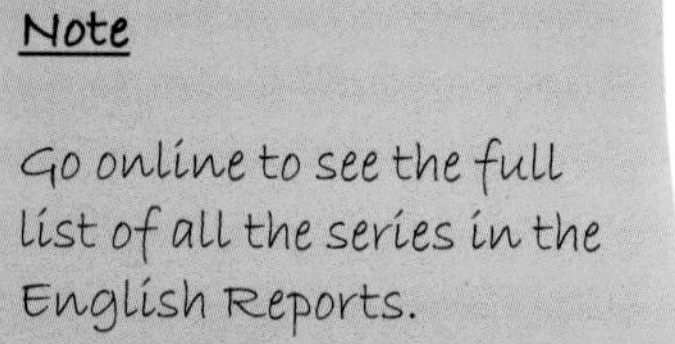

Note
Go online to see the full list of all the series in the English Reports.

Transcripts

Since the advent of electronic text, official transcripts of cases have become widely available. These are found on the electronic legal services, and are normally replaced with a report of the case when this becomes available. Transcripts should be cited with the neutral citation (see below) if it exists. Otherwise, give the name of the case, with the court and the date of the judgment.

> *R v Lowe* (CA (Crim) 31 January 1997)

Neutral citations

Since 2001 all judgments have been given a citation assigned by the court (this was introduced by the Lord Chief Justice in the *Practice Direction (Judgments: Form and Citation)* [2001] 1 WLR 194[24]). This is known as a neutral citation, as it identifies the judgment itself, and is independent of any law report. At the same time, paragraph numbering was introduced for pinpointing places in the judgment. Neutral citations allowed for the citation in court of unreported cases available in electronic transcript form only.

The neutral citation always appears first in a list of citations to a particular case, and is in the form [2006] UKHL 20. The abbreviation is to the name of the court.

When citing a case you should use the neutral citation followed by the law report citation, separated by commas:

> *Ali v Lord Grey School Governors* [2004] EWCA Civ 382, [2004] QB 1231

United Kingdom courts		**Citation format**	
UKSC	Supreme Court	[2009] UKSC 3	Paragraph no. follows if applicable [24]
UKHL	House of Lords	[2006] UKHL 20	
UKPC	Privy Council	[2007] UKPC 12	
England & Wales Court of Appeal		Citation format	
EWCA Civ	CA Civil Division	[2007] EWCA Civ 168	Paragraph no. follows if applicable [24]
EWCA Crim	CA Criminal Division	[2007] EWCA Crim 147	
England & Wales High Court		**Citation format**	
EWHC (Admin)	Administrative Court	[2007] EWHC 363 (Admin)	Paragraph no. follows if applicable [24]
EWHC (Ch)	Chancery Division	[2007] EWHC 147 (Ch)	
EWHC (QB)	Queen's Bench Division	[2007] EWHC 140 (QB)	
EWHC (Comm)	Commercial Court	[2007] EWHC 54 (Comm)	
EWHC (Admlty)	Admiralty Division	[2007] EWHC 500 (Admlty)	
EWHC (Fam)	Family Division	[2007] EWHC 1465 (Fam)	
EWHC (Pat)	Patents Court	[2007] EWHC 2333 (Pat)	
EWHC (TCC)	Technology & Construction Court	[2007] EWHC 390 (TCC)	

Which report should you use?

Cases are usually reported in several different series of law reports. You will see a list of these when you look up a case in **Westlaw** or **LexisNexis Butterworths** (**LNB**), or research it in the print Current Law. There is an accepted hierarchy of law reports, and you should cite the most authoritative. Below is a chart of the main categories of reports.

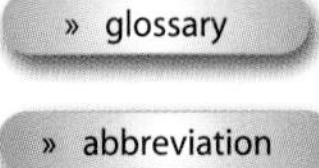

The Law Reports AC, Ch, Fam, QB and earlier series		Always cite these if available.
Weekly Law Reports If a case is reported in 2 WLR it will eventually appear in the Law Reports	**All England Law Reports**	The two general series, both equal in status.
Specialised law reports e.g. Crim LR, etc		Many cases are only reported in a specialised series
Reports in legal journals e.g. New Law Journal, Solicitor's Journal or Criminal Law Review		Check to see if they have been reported in a law report subsequently
Reports in newspapers Often cited for a very new case		Daily reports. Will nearly always appear in law reports subsequently

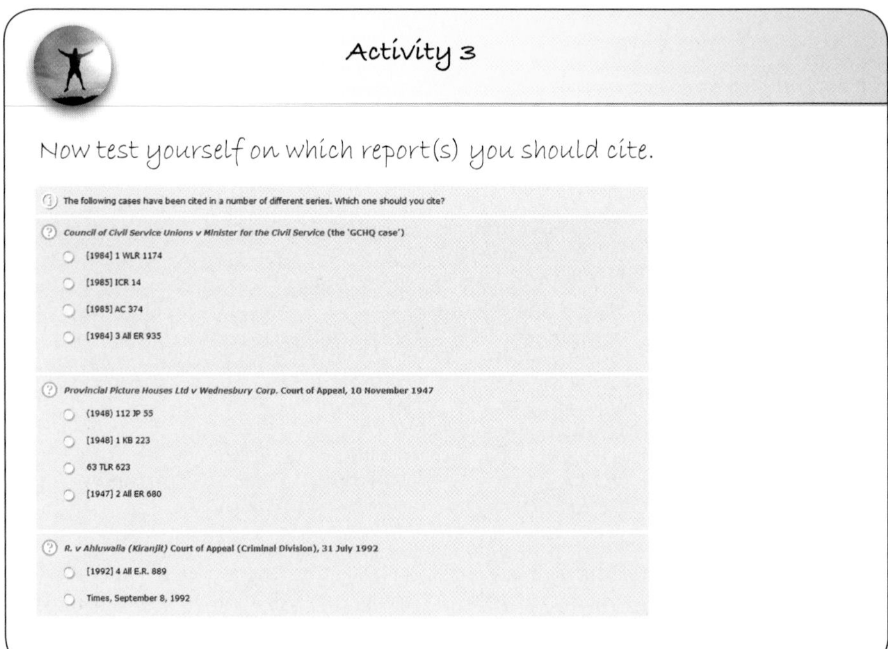

Activity 3
Now test yourself on which report(s) you should cite.
The following cases have been cited in a number of different series. Which one should you cite?
Council of Civil Service Unions v Minister for the Civil Service (the 'GCHQ case')
[1984] 1 WLR 1174
[1985] ICR 14
[1985] AC 374
[1984] 3 All ER 935
Provincial Picture Houses Ltd v Wednesbury Corp. Court of Appeal, 10 November 1947
(1948) 112 JP 55
[1948] 1 KB 223
63 TLR 623
[1947] 2 All ER 680
R. v Ahluwalia (Kiranjit) Court of Appeal (Criminal Division), 31 July 1992
[1992] 4 All E.R. 889
Times, September 8, 1992

Citing other case law

European Union cases

Cases in the European Court of Justice are cited by the case number and parties, followed by the official citation (European Court Reports: ECR) or, failing that, a series such as the Common Market Law Reports (CMLR)

Case C-434/01 *Commission v UK* [2003] ECR I-13239

Case C-177/88 *Dekker v Stichting Vormingscentrum voor Jonge Volwassenen Plus* [1990] I-03941

Case C-221/89 *R v Secretary of State for Transport ex p Factortame Ltd and Others (No. 2)* [1991] 3 CMLR 589

Case T-344/99 *Arne Mathisen AS v Council* [2002] ECR II-2905

Cases in the European Court of Justice are prefixed C-, while cases in the European Court of First Instance are prefixed T-.

European Court of Human Rights cases

Cases should be cited with their name, application number and the abbreviation for the official series (ECHR). Prior to November 1998 the reports were known as Series A. Alternatively, use the European Human Rights Report (EHRR) citation.

Handyside v UK (App no. 5493/72) (1976) Series A no 24

Handyside v UK (App no. 5493/72) (1979–80) 1 EHRR 737

Pretty v UK (App no. 2346/02) ECHR 2002-III

Pretty v UK (App no. 2346/02) (2002) 35 EHRR 1

Citing legislation

» glossary

Acts of Parliament

Acts of Parliament are cited by their short title and date: » glossary

Human Rights Act 1998

Supply of Goods (Implied Terms) Act 1973

You may also find them cited by their chapter number (1998 c.42) which is the number assigned to each Act in any calendar year. » glossary

Prior to 1963, the chapter numbers were assigned in each parliamentary session, known as the regnal year (the year of the monarch's reign), and which straddle the year, since the parliamentary session usually starts in November. Printed series of older statutes are arranged by regnal year. (Note that the only service to include all repealed statutes is Justis Statutes. Unless you have access to this, the only way of looking at a statute which has been repealed is by referring to the printed version.) It is therefore useful to include the regnal year as a finding aid, though not essential. » glossary

Example

Mutiny Act 1804 (44 Geo. 3 c.19)
This stands for the 44th year of the reign of George III, chapter 19

To refer to a specific part of an Act use the abbreviations:

s	section
ss	subsection
para	paragraph
Pt	Part
Sch	Schedule

Example

Refer to section 17, subsection 1, paragraph a of the Human Rights Act as follows:

Human Rights Act 1998, s17(1)(a)

Bills

» glossary

Bills are cited by their title, the House of Parliament in which they originated, and the parliamentary session. The number of the Bill is appended to the citation, in square brackets for a House of Commons Bill, without brackets for a House of Lords Bill.

Mental Health HL Bill (2006–7) 45

Freedom of Information (Amendment) HC Bill (2006–7) [62]

Statutory Instruments

» glossary

Statutory Instruments should be cited by their name, year, followed by the numerical reference in the form year/number. Since the year is invariably included in the title of the SI, it is repeated in the citation.

The National Health Service (Charges for Drugs and Appliances) Amendment Regulations 2007 SI 2007/543

The Land Registration Rules 1987 SI 1987/2214

Prior to 1846, the published series is known as Statutory Rules and Orders (S R & O).

Statutory Instruments do not have sections, but numbered Rules (abbreviated r and plural rr) in the case of an Order, or Regulations (abbreviated reg), according to the type of SI, which is made clear in the title. In the case of Orders the subdivisions are into paragraphs (para).

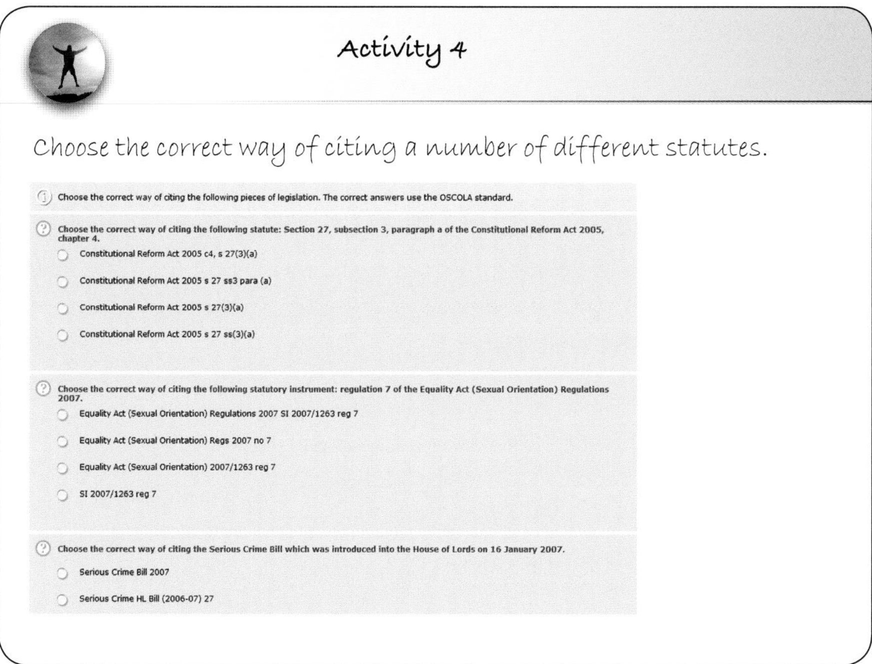

Activity 4

Choose the correct way of citing a number of different statutes.

Choose the correct way of citing the following pieces of legislation. The correct answers use the OSCOLA standard.

Choose the correct way of citing the following statute: Section 27, subsection 3, paragraph a of the Constitutional Reform Act 2005, chapter 4.

- Constitutional Reform Act 2005 c4, s 27(3)(a)
- Constitutional Reform Act 2005 s 27 ss3 para (a)
- Constitutional Reform Act 2005 s 27(3)(a)
- Constitutional Reform Act 2005 s 27 ss(3)(a)

Choose the correct way of citing the following statutory instrument: regulation 7 of the Equality Act (Sexual Orientation) Regulations 2007.

- Equality Act (Sexual Orientation) Regulations 2007 SI 2007/1263 reg 7
- Equality Act (Sexual Orientation) Regs 2007 no 7
- Equality Act (Sexual Orientation) 2007/1263 reg 7
- SI 2007/1263 reg 7

Choose the correct way of citing the Serious Crime Bill which was introduced into the House of Lords on 16 January 2007.

- Serious Crime Bill 2007
- Serious Crime HL Bill (2006-07) 27

European Union legislation

EU legislation should be cited with the legislation type (i.e. Directive, Regulation, Decision, etc.) number and title, then publication details from the Official Journal (OJ) of the EU.

» glossary

> Council Directive 76/207/EEC of 9 February 1976 on the implementation of the principle of equal treatment for men and women as regards access to employment, vocational training and promotion, and working conditions [1976] OJ L39/40
>
> Council Directive (EC) 93/104 concerning certain aspects of the organisation of working time [1993] OJ L307/18

Important directives are known by popular names, so these may be cited subsequently as the Equal Treatment Directive 76/207and the Working Time Directive 93/104.

Key Point

Always make a note of the full bibliographic details of any book or article you find and read. There is nothing more annoying than having to go back to find the correct publication details afterwards!

Citing books

Books should be cited as follows:

> Author, *Title in Italics* (series title, edition, publisher, place date)

Example

Books by one or two authors

HLA Hart, *The Concept of Law* (Clarendon Press, Oxford 1961)

Stuart Bell and Donald McGillivray, *Environmental Law* (6th edn, Oxford University Press, Oxford 2005)

Bob Fine, *Democracy and the Rule of Law:* Liberal Ideals and Marxist Critiques (Pluto Press, London 1984)

Peter Cane, *Atiyah's Accidents, Compensation and the Law* (Law in Context Series, 7th edn, Cambridge University Press, Cambridge 2006)

Note that standard law books frequently migrate from their original author and title to a version edited by someone else, and finally to that editor taking authorship, with the original name incorporated in the book title, as in the above example.

A chapter or an article from a book should be cited as follows:

> Ann Bottomley, 'Theory is a process not an end: feminist approach to the practice of theory' in J Richardson and R Sandland (eds), *Feminist Perspectives on Law and Theory* (Cavendish Press, London 2000)

Note

For publication details of a book you may need to look on the back (the verso) of the title page.

Citing journal articles

Articles should be cited as follows:

Author, 'Title in single inverted commas' [year] abbreviation

Jeffrey Jowell, 'Parliamentary Sovereignty under the New Constitutional Hypothesis' [2006] PL 562

If you want to pinpoint a page in the article, add the page number:

Walter Van Gerven, 'Bridging the Gap between Community and National Laws: Towards a Principle of Homogeneity in the Field of Legal Remedies?' (1995) 32 CML Rev 679, 692

Square brackets round the date should be used if it identifies the volume, and round brackets if a volume number is also needed.

Online journals normally have an identical citation to the print version. However, if a journal is only published online, give a full citation as above and add the website address and most recent date of access.

Citing official publications

There are numerous different kinds of official publication which you will come across including government White Papers, annual reports, reports of committees and other parliamentary papers, and a vast array of publications emanating from government departments and agencies. There can be considerable confusion between the various categories, and many have duplicate numbering schemes because they are issued in a hybrid form. You should always look out for a series number, as this will indicate which kind of publication it is. The ones you are likely to come across most often are Command Papers.

» glossary

Command Papers

This category contains most government White Papers, and numerous other publications, including government departmental reports presented to Parliament. You can get an idea of the range by looking at the Command Papers lists on the Office for Public Sector Information website, http://www.opsi.gov.uk/official-publications/index.htm

» glossary

Example

Department of Constitutional Affairs, 'House of Lords: Completing the Reform (Cm 5291, 2001)

Home Office, 'Prisons and Probation Ombudsman for England and Wales Annual Report' (Cm 6872, 2006)

Note that Command Papers have consecutive numbering within each series. The current series is prefixed Cm, and began in 1986. Previous series had different prefixes as follows:

1833–1869 (C 1st series)

1870–1899 (C 2nd series)

1900–1918 (Cd)

1919–1956 (Cmd)

1957–1986 (Cmnd)

The numbering within each series starts again at 1, and ends at 9999.

House of Commons and House of Lords papers

House of Commons papers include the reports and papers of parliamentary select committees, annual reports and accounts of various public bodies, and other reports concerning the business of the House. House of Lords papers are the reports of HL committees. The reports of joint committees of both Houses are published with both a HC and a HL number.

House of Commons and House of Lords papers are numbered sequentially in each parliamentary session. The correct citation includes the title, HC (or HL), the number of the report and the years of parliamentary session. You will find some variation in the way these are cited, but these elements should all be present.

Example

Third Report of the House of Commons Transport Committee, 'Transport for the London 2012 Olympic and Paralympic Games: The Draft Transport Plan', HC (2006–7) 199

Third report of the House of Lords Select Committee on Science and Technology, 'What on Earth? The Threat to the Science Underpinning Conservation' HL (2000–1)

7th Report of the Joint Committee on Human Rights, 'Deaths in Custody: Further Developments' HL (2006–7) 59, HC (2006–7) 364

Law Commission

The **Law Commission** publishes reports, but also consultation papers which you may need to cite. As Law Commission reports are presented to Parliament, they will also usually have a Command Paper number, or a House of Commons number, which should also be included.

» glossary

Example

Law Commission, 'Murder, Manslaughter and Infanticide' (Law Com No 303, HC 30, 2006)

Law Commission, HM Land Registry 'Land Registration for the 21st Century: a Consultative Document' (Law Com No 255, 1998)

Law Commission 'The Forfeiture Rule and the Law of Succession' (Law Com No 295, Cm 6225, 2005)

Note

Make sure you have all the details of an official publication when you find it, and remember, these are not always obvious on the document itself.

Citing websites

You will probably retrieve most of the material that you cite from internet sources, whether via an electronic service such as Westlaw and LexisNexis Butterworths, or official sources such as the Houses of Parliament and government departmental sites. Using these will ensure that you are retrieving authentic sources, and you should cite them as in the examples discussed in this chapter. However, if you simply google the title of a document you must be very careful that you are not picking up a version which is inauthentic in any way – it may be someone's own re-wording, it may be out of date, it may not be what it seems. You should always check the provenance of the site very carefully and satisfy yourself that it is trustworthy.

When citing material taken from websites you should include information to identify it, such as author and title, the URL and the date accessed. If the URL is very long it is preferable to use the main site address and indicate the pathway to the document you are citing if necessary.

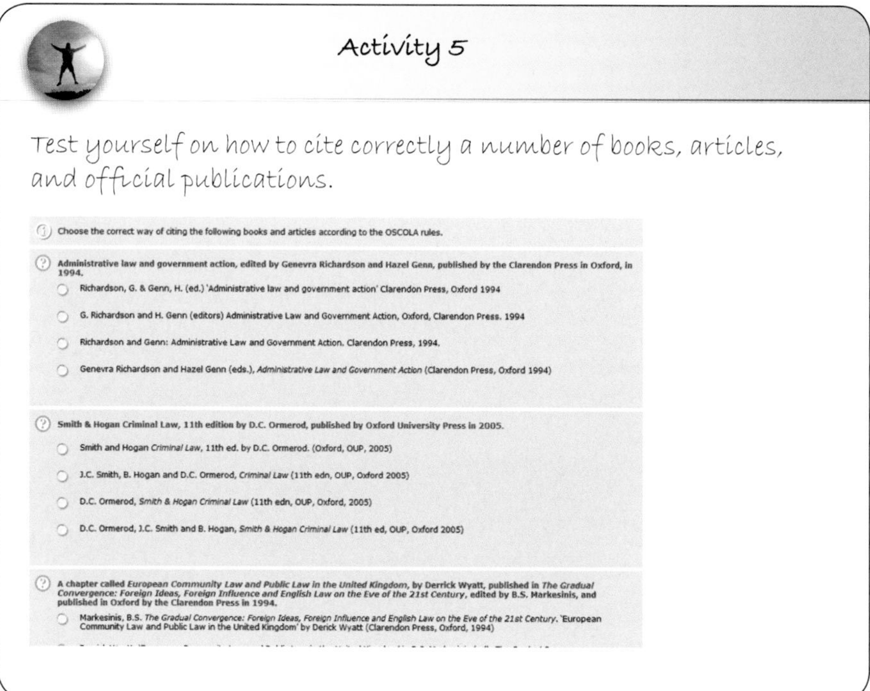

Activity 5

Test yourself on how to cite correctly a number of books, articles, and official publications.

Choose the correct way of citing the following books and articles according to the OSCOLA rules.

Administrative law and government action, edited by Genevra Richardson and Hazel Genn, published by the Clarendon Press in Oxford, in 1994.

- Richardson, G. & Genn, H. (ed.) 'Administrative law and government action' Clarendon Press, Oxford 1994
- G. Richardson and H. Genn (editors) Administrative Law and Government Action, Oxford, Clarendon Press. 1994
- Richardson and Genn: Administrative Law and Government Action. Clarendon Press, 1994.
- Genevra Richardson and Hazel Genn (eds.), *Administrative Law and Government Action* (Clarendon Press, Oxford 1994)

Smith & Hogan Criminal Law, 11th edition by D.C. Ormerod, published by Oxford University Press in 2005.

- Smith and Hogan *Criminal Law*, 11th ed. by D.C. Ormerod. (Oxford, OUP, 2005)
- J.C. Smith, B. Hogan and D.C. Ormerod, *Criminal Law* (11th edn, OUP, Oxford 2005)
- D.C. Ormerod, *Smith & Hogan Criminal Law* (11th edn, OUP, Oxford, 2005)
- D.C. Ormerod, J.C. Smith and B. Hogan, *Smith & Hogan Criminal Law* (11th ed, OUP, Oxford 2005)

A chapter called *European Community Law and Public Law in the United Kingdom*, by Derrick Wyatt, published in *The Gradual Convergence: Foreign Ideas, Foreign Influence and English Law on the Eve of the 21st Century*, edited by B.S. Markesinis, and published in Oxford by the Clarendon Press in 1994.

- Markesinis, B.S. *The Gradual Convergence: Foreign Ideas, Foreign Influence and English Law on the Eve of the 21st Century*. 'European Community Law and Public Law in the United Kingdom' by Derick Wyatt (Clarendon Press, Oxford, 1994)

Conclusion

The guidance on citation in this chapter is only the tip of the iceberg. Even the most experienced writers come across documents which they do not know how to cite correctly, and will need to refer to a style and citation manual. Make sure that you know your own institution's policy and guidelines, and when in doubt refer to an authoritative source such as OSCOLA.

You should now have some idea of how to cite, and of the structure of legal materials.

Your two authoritative sources are **OSCOLA** and the **Cardiff Index to Legal Abbreviations.**

Use them!

Links

OSCOLA
http://www.competition-law.ox.ac.uk/published/oscola.shtml

Cardiff Index to Legal Abbreviations
http://www.legalabbrevs.cardiff.ac.uk

Incorporated Council for Law Reporting (ICLR)
http://www.lawreports.co.uk

Office for Public Sector Information (OPSI)
http://www.opsi.gov.uk/official-publications/index.htm

An interesting article on the history of law reporting:
http://www.lawreports.co.uk/Publications/siforward.htm

Chapter 15

Using law books

Rationale

When doing a law degree, you will be asked to do a lot of reading. This is inevitable – there is a lot of law to learn and it can't all be covered in lectures and seminars! Reading chapters from books, academic articles and cases is probably one of the most common tasks that you will be set – and you will also be encouraged to do further reading for your own self-study. Further reading may mean reading further into your textbooks and casebooks, or it may mean reading individual case reports in full. However, it's also important not to forget there are many other valuable things that can be read that will prove useful for your studies, such as books with a historical, political or philosophical context.

Reading for information and self-learning is not necessarily something that many students have had much prior experience of, nor that they are comfortable with. However, it must be remembered that the information you gain from reading is **vital** to your studies at degree level. But there is no point in wasting your time reading in a way which means that you learn nothing. You must train your mind to learn – this will be a valuable tool if you go on to practise law, or indeed in most chosen careers post-university.

This chapter is devised to:

- Explain the differences between different types of reading material
- Explain why reading from a variety of sources – including non-law books – is both necessary and useful
- Give some ideas about how to overcome common problems that some students encounter with reading for self-study.

» glossary

Different types of reading material

You will find that you are asked to read various different types of material to enhance your studies. Although sometimes this will feel tedious – and possibly repetitive, in the sense that you may be going over information you have already been told in lectures, for example – reading is the **best way** to help you to really **absorb**, **remember** and **understand** information. In addition, it is well recognised that students who read more, and from a wide variety of sources, tend to write better, both in terms of their use of English and legal content. The more you read, for example, the better your vocabulary (including your legal vocabulary) will be.

Cross reference
See chapter 3, Writing good English, and chapter 25, Writing essays.

Some of the most common types of reading materials that you may come across are:

- textbooks
- casebooks and cases

Cross reference
See chapters 21–24, Reading cases 1–4.

» glossary

- statutes and statute books
- See chapter 19, Reading statutes and the legislative process.
- academic articles.

» glossary

Of course, this list is not exhaustive – there are many other things to read out there that may contain sources of legal information or knowledge, or contextualisation for a topic you are studying. One of the most common examples of this sort of reading is newspapers (broadsheets) – reading a good daily newspaper is a very good way to keep abreast of current affairs related to law. Interdisciplinary books with a historical, political, sociological or philosophical tangent on law are also extremely useful for good background knowledge and deepening understanding. Often, it is only by understanding the context that the law operates in that the law itself makes sense. Similarly, books that **discuss** the law, rather than just tell you what it is (i.e. textbooks and casebooks) or contain a **critique** of the law you are studying are also very useful. Expansive reading (reading from sources other than your core texts, which are designed for the purposes of mass education and can only be expected to cover the basic key elements of the law, as well as perhaps key comment on it) will greatly improve your understanding of the law and your ability to **use** the law to formulate answers to questions – or even to come up with questions of your own! Asking questions of the law you are taught is one of the best ways to learn – and shows a good level of understanding – but it is only really by reading discursive and critical texts that you will become very good at doing this.

What follows are some short explanations of each type of the main types of reading material you will come across – that is, law books – as well as an indication of why these sources may be useful for you in your studies and tips on how to use the books and articles you have got.

When studying law, you will need to read **a lot**. And this should include a wide variety of sources, not just law books. However, the pay-off is that the more you read, the more you will really **absorb**, **remember** and **understand** information, a skill essential to being a good lawyer.

Textbooks

» glossary

In most law modules, a textbook (or two!) will be the main source of your reading. You may be asked to read some given pages of your textbook(s), or a chapter or two, **before** you attend lectures or, more likely, after your lectures on a topic, in preparation for any seminar or tutorial you have on the topic or indeed to prepare for writing an assessment or sitting an exam. However, you should not feel limited by this – dipping into your textbooks now and again when you don't **have** to will help to keep you interested and help the information sink in. Reading up on a topic before you have the lecture on the subject also helps to make lectures easier to follow and even more interesting.

A textbook is exactly what it says it is – text written by an author on a particular area of law. So while you are unlikely to get any kind of comprehensive textbook on 'law' as a whole, just as you can't be lectured on 'law', you might get textbooks specific to the individual modules you study – contract law, criminal law, European law, family law etc.

Each author has an opinion and their writing will express this, whether they say this is so or not. You could read two different textbooks on the same topic and get a slightly different interpretation of the law and opinion on it. This does not mean that one author is necessarily right, or better; just that, as with many things, particularly in the study of law, interpretations and understandings of the law are different.

Another thing you should remember is that textbooks carry different 'weight' – this does not mean that some weigh more than others or have more pages (although this is true!), but refers to the content. Some textbooks, for example, could be described as **introductory** – these do exactly what the name suggests: provide an introductory outline to the topic, rather than an in-depth look at the law in that area. Of course, introductory books have their place – as introductions! But they shouldn't be relied on as **the** source of your knowledge of a subject. What you need to read in order to help you gain knowledge and understanding at the right level are the more **weighty** textbooks that go into a lot more detail, contextualisation and discussion of the law.

Legal texts are written by different authors and, as with many things, **may not always be neutral.** It is important to remember this when relying on texts for your own work. For this reason, reading **more than one text** on a particular subject (especially if it has any 'controversial' element) may be beneficial.

How to get the best from textbook reading

By **planning** for textbook study, you should be able to make the material – which is often quite difficult – more 'user friendly'. What follows are some tips for getting the best out of your textbook reading:

- Set aside a **decent amount of time** to do your textbook reading. There is no point trying to rush your reading, or seeing it as something secondary to lectures, for example – your own reading of legal texts is a **primary** source of your learning and should be built into your study time as such.

↳ **Cross reference**
See chapter 2, Managing your time.

- Make sure you look at the overall layout of the textbook and familiarise yourself with the way it works. Knowing your way round the book is one step towards more effective reading.
- Similarly, at the beginning of the module, look at the **Table of Contents** of the relevant textbook to see how the book is organised.
- When reading a particular chapter, use the Table of Contents and/or the initial chapter outline to look at an individual chapter's organisation.
- When starting your textbook assignments, develop a simple plan to proceed – and stick to it! Try not to get distracted! This is, of course, easier if you have set aside time for reading and are not just trying to squeeze in the reading you need to do around other things.

↳ **Cross reference**
See chapter 2, Managing your time.

Note

Full-time study can (and should) be treated like a **full-time job**. If you timetable yourself for five full working days per week, or 35–40 hours of work per week (your lectures and seminars combined are not likely to take up even half of this time), then you should be able to get everything you need to done.

When you are reading textbooks, in order to help what may often be quite 'dense' material sink in, the following suggestions may be helpful:

↳ **Cross reference**
See chapter 4, Taking notes.

- Read the chapter preview questions, if any, and/or go back over your lecture notes – in fact, you may want to annotate your original lecture notes from your reading.
- Make 'signposts' from the preview questions or your lecture notes – what are you going to be specifically looking out for while reading your textbook?
- Read the review questions at the end of a chapter before reading the chapter itself – and keep these in mind as you read.
- Read through the chapter at least once – you might find it helpful to read through the whole thing (or a section) quickly the first time, then go back over it some time later in a bit more detail. Plan to do both in your time management schedule.

↳ **Cross reference**
See chapter 2, Managing your time.

- Always pay attention to vocabulary words in bold or highlighted type.
- Study any illustrations (e.g. tables, graphs, photographs, charts) to clarify content; do not forget to read the captions.
- As you go along, briefly note any information that adds to or expands on what you heard in lectures. You may simply want to do this in the margins against your lecture notes, so all your notes are in one place (or e.g. in columns, tables or mind-maps if you have used these techniques).
- When you have finished reading, summarise or précis the chapter or section in your notes. Don't take detailed notes as you go along as you may end up rewriting whole chapters!
- If you do write down any passages from textbooks that you may come back to use later (such as in an essay), make sure you note down the book details and page number they came from so you can reference them correctly later.

Cross reference See chapter 4, Taking notes.

» glossary

Cross reference See chapter 7, Avoiding plagiarism.

Remember There is no real need to make written notes of absolutely **everything** you read in your textbooks – if they are your own books, they will always be there when you need to come back to them and there is no point writing down what is already written!

Activity 1

These short multiple choice questions are designed to test what you think about textbook reading – and perhaps to dispel a few myths!

Read through the questions below and select the answer you feel to be correct. Hopefully the feedback you get will help you understand better what the purpose of using a textbook is. There may be more than one 'right' answer in each question set, as there are various ways to read and use textbooks.

The way to use a textbook is...

- to read every chapter methodically in turn and make full notes on everything
- as a reference to supplement the work done in lectures and seminars/tutorials
- by always 'close reading' the text

When using your textbook, you should...

- only read the exact pages the lecturer or other teacher has suggested
- read the pages suggested in full, taking detailed notes
- dip in and out at relevant points, to supplement the information you were given in lectures

The information you read in a textbook is always...

- accurate and up to date, otherwise your lecturers wouldn't be recommending it
- the same as would be found in any other textbook on the same subject, just in more or less detail
- best supplemented by reading further around a subject

Casebooks and cases

↳ Cross reference
See chapters 21–24, Reading cases 1–4.

Some law modules require you to read, know and understand a large number of cases (see also case reports, below). Reading case reports in full is undoubtedly the best way to begin to understand and comprehend the intricacies of legal judgments. However, often, extracts of the main cases you will need to know, as well as 'commentary' on them, will be included all together, by topic, in one book called a casebook – this is a good place to start, but will not give the full depth of understanding that reading full cases will.

Note

Sometimes you may come across '**cases and materials**' books. These are like extended versions of casebooks, including not only cases and commentary on these, but other materials as well, such as extracts of articles or statutes, with commentary. There are also 'Text, cases and materials' books – a combination of a textbook and cases and materials book.

» glossary

↳ Cross reference
See chapter 17, Using legal databases, and chapters 21–24, Reading cases 1–4.

Some modules with a strong common law or case law element are best taught and learnt by using cases. You will get a strong sense of the history and development of an area of law by reading the cases relating to it – even old ones, that are not 'good law' any more – and this gives you a better overall understanding of the current law. This is why your lecturers are likely to recommend casebooks **as well as** textbooks in some modules – each serves a different purpose. However, they are also likely to recommend that you research cases yourself, by locating and reading the full reports.

Remember As with textbooks, casebooks are written by authors and, as with many things, the commentary in them **may not always be neutral**. It is important to remember this when relying on them for your own work.

Case reports

The cases you read will not always be found in casebooks. Many times you will be required to read the full text of a case you are studying and, in fact, this is the very **best** way to learn about many areas of law. You may be given the case or asked to find it for yourself, for example via one of the legal databases available – and knowing how to do this is a skill in itself.

↳ **Cross reference**
See chapter 17, Using legal databases.

Reading the **full judgment** of a case, especially a judgment from one of the higher courts, such as the Court of Appeal or House of Lords, allows you to fully understand and appreciate the legal intricacies involved in an area of law. Often, when making judgment, the judge will recap the historical development of the area of law and the points of law that have been considered throughout the case. Reading this type of thing is **invaluable**, as it is from this that you will gain the **best** account of the law, as well as continuing to learn judicial language and increasing your legal vocabulary etc. While casebooks are useful, students gain far more from reading cases in full: they learn to independently identify the ratio of a case, or what is said obiter dictum; understand how legal disputes are framed using causes of action, the court's jurisdiction, statutory frameworks and so on.

» glossary

» glossary

» glossary

↳ **Cross reference**
See chapters 21–24, Reading cases 1–4.

> **Remember** When using law textbooks or casebooks, remember that they have a **Table of Cases**. Law books generally have a table of cases at the front of the book, which you can use to identify where particular cases are discussed within the text. This is very useful if you want to dip in and out for information and discussion about a case as a reminder, rather than reading through a chapter on the relevant topic to find it!

Statutes and statute books

↳ **Cross reference**
See chapter 19, Reading statues and the legislative process.

See chapter 20, Understanding judicial interpretation of statutes.

Statutes, or Acts of Parliament, are another invaluable source of law. Some modules will require that you know and **use** statutes in your work. Where this is the case, you would be best advised to **read** the relevant statutes in full and try to understand **how** they would be used or interpreted (e.g. by a judge) where there is a legal question to answer.

Statutes are often very interesting sources of law – remember that they come from a **political** context in Parliament and, as such, reading them helps you to understand the political environment of the time the statute was passed into law. However, it is also important to remember that most

» glossary

Cross reference
See chapter 20, Understanding judicial interpretation of statutes.

statutes need, at some point, to be **interpreted** – ask yourself what the intentions of Parliament were in passing the law and whether this can easily be interpreted or misinterpreted.

Don't panic

Reading statutes may seem like hard work, or boring, but doing so often provides **the knowledge you need in order to begin to find the answers!**

While most statutes are available online or in hard copy from libraries, in some subjects they are also collated into a statute book (e.g. 'Statutes on Contract, Tort and Restitution', or 'Statutes on Property Law'). These books are generally updated annually, so all the latest pieces of legislation are included.

Statute books are very handy – all the statutes you will need should be in one place (as well as other pieces of legislation, such as Regulations, as well as (often) draft legislation if something is passing through Parliament at the current time).

When you have lectures on topics that require you to know about statutes, it is very useful to have your statute book with you in the lecture, so that you can read the sections as they are being talked about by the lecturer. You **may** also be able to use these collections of statutes in your exams – it is worth checking whether this is the case with your modules. Usually, if this is the case, the books must remain unannotated. So, while there might be excerpts of statutes in, for example, cases and materials books, or explanations of how they are used in textbooks, a statute book is a handy reference book to have alongside your other books. It also means you can have the statute open in front of you as you read about the law in your textbook – a handy cross reference tool.

Remember Unlike other types of books, statute books can contain no bias as they are not 'written' by an author as such – they are just a collation of actual Acts of Parliament and are, therefore, 'the law'.

Activity 2

Now you have read about casebooks and statute books, try this online activity which will help to cement in your mind the purpose of these different types of book and help you to remember when it might be useful for you to use them.

Now you have read about casebooks and statute books, answer the following questions. They will help to cement in your mind the purpose of these different types of book and help you to remember when it might be useful for you to use them. Read the following statements and decide whether they are true or false.

Statement	True	False
There is no point having a casebook on a module if you already have a textbook for that subject. The important cases will be in the textbook.	○	○
There is no point reading legal judgments if you already have a casebook which contains extracts of them.	○	○
Reading statutes is a skill that law students should try to develop; it is not always enough to rely on the discussion of statutes in a textbook.	○	○

Academic articles

Academic articles are specialist pieces written on particular aspects of law. For example, within a Tort Law module, there are many articles written on various individual topics such as 'causation' or 'nuisance'. Even more specifically, within the topics themselves, there are many articles on, for example, 'wrongful birth' or 'public body negligence'. Academics may also even write about a single case, if it has great significance to the area of law or, for example, contains a contentious point of law.

» glossary

What academic articles are is usually that author's interpretation about, or argument on, the chosen issue, and they will be an in-depth analysis of the finer points and legal issues raised. Like an essay, at the outset of an article, there should be an introduction explaining what the author hopes to achieve – reading this will help you to know whether reading the whole article will benefit your study.

Using academic articles when you read around a topic gives an extra dimension to your studies. And it is true to say that students who 'read around' a topic are the ones who are likely to do best. The more you read, the better your knowledge. You may be given the article, or it may be copied and available in the library, or you may be asked to find it for yourself, for example via one of the legal databases available – and knowing how to do this is also a skill in itself.

↳ **Cross reference**
See chapter 17, Using legal databases.

Many students – particularly in their first year, while they are still finding their feet at university – believe that it is enough just to listen to lectures and to read material set from textbooks and casebooks. However, as explained in the introduction to this chapter, there are many other valuable things that can – and should – be read. Academic articles come high on this list – they improve your comprehension and understanding of the law, particularly any difficult or contentious areas (of which there are many!). Article reading really brings depth to your discussion, a skill you should develop even further in years two and three.

Remember As with legal textbooks, articles are written by authors who have their own opinions and so what is said **may not always be neutral**. In fact, if an academic feels strongly enough about a topic to write a whole article on it, this is even less likely to be the case! It is important to remember this when using articles in your own work.

↳ **Cross reference**
See chapter 25, Writing essays, and chapter 26, Writing dissertations.

Remember When making notes from articles, always note the author's name, full journal reference (i.e. where the article was published), date and page number you take any quotes or phrases from, so that you can cite them accurately later if you use them in your work. Not doing this amounts to plagiarism.

» glossary

↳ **Cross reference**
See chapter 7, Avoiding plagiarism.

Getting the best from academic articles

Knowing which articles to read to help your studies is often a skill in itself, as there may be many to choose from! The following are some tips on reading and using articles in your work.

- Read your reading lists. Many lecturers will provide a reading list for their module which contains not only excerpts from textbooks etc., but lists of relevant and up-to-date articles that may be helpful when preparing your work and/or writing analytical essays.
- Build time for 'further reading' into your weekly timetable, then you won't be left needing to read everything at once, for example when you have an essay to write.
- 'Further reading', including articles, should not be looked on as a chore, but an opportunity to really understand an area of law and the arguments relating to it. Enjoy them!
- If you have your own copy of the article, use highlighters and your own annotation so that you know where the important points are and can come back to them quickly next time. If using colour coding in your notes, stick to the same colour system.

↳ **Cross reference**
See chapter 2, Managing your time.

- Make notes of the key arguments the author raises and use these in your work – even if you don't agree with them you can use them as a springboard for your own analysis. Don't forget to reference them correctly.

Articles are useful in all elements of your study, not just when writing essays and assessments. We would suggest that the best advice would be to read as many as you can – and certainly as many as are recommended to you by lecturers and seminar leaders. Using articles when preparing for lectures and seminars will give you a broader base from which to contribute and will help you to understand and be able to handle difficult material. Citing and referring to articles in your essays adds depth and context if done well, and referenced correctly. You may find that you strongly disagree with what an author of an article says – this is a good springboard for your own arguments. Articles will also be helpful in revision for examinations, and citing an article to support your answer in an exam essay will certainly impress the marker!

Cross reference
See chapter 4, Taking notes.

See chapter 7, Avoiding plagiarism.

» glossary

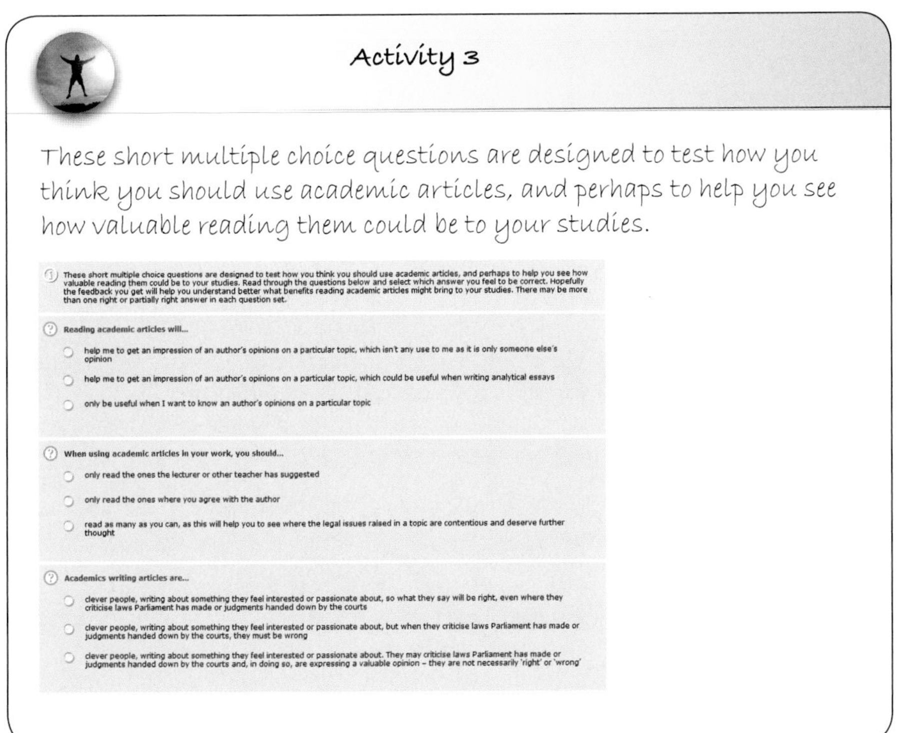

Activity 3

These short multiple choice questions are designed to test how you think you should use academic articles, and perhaps to help you see how valuable reading them could be to your studies.

These short multiple choice questions are designed to test how you think you should use academic articles, and perhaps to help you see how valuable reading them could be to your studies. Read through the questions below and select which answer you feel to be correct. Hopefully the feedback you get will help you understand better what benefits reading academic articles might bring to your studies. There may be more than one right or partially right answer in each question set.

Reading academic articles will...

- help me to get an impression of an author's opinions on a particular topic, which isn't any use to me as it is only someone else's opinion
- help me to get an impression of an author's opinions on a particular topic, which could be useful when writing analytical essays
- only be useful when I want to know an author's opinions on a particular topic

When using academic articles in your work, you should...

- only read the ones the lecturer or other teacher has suggested
- only read the ones where you agree with the author
- read as many as you can, as this will help you to see where the legal issues raised in a topic are contentious and deserve further thought

Academics writing articles are...

- clever people, writing about something they feel interested or passionate about, so what they say will be right, even where they criticise laws Parliament has made or judgments handed down by the courts
- clever people, writing about something they feel interested or passionate about, but when they criticise laws Parliament has made or judgments handed down by the courts, they must be wrong
- clever people, writing about something they feel interested or passionate about. They may criticise laws Parliament has made or judgments handed down by the courts and, in doing so, are expressing a valuable opinion – they are not necessarily 'right' or 'wrong'

Reading and note-taking skills

Much of the reading that you should do for self-study will be outlined for you by the lecturers and other teachers on your modules. You may, for example, get a reading list given to you at the beginning of a module, or even be given weekly reading assignments.

How much reading you do for each module that you study is of course up to you, but doing as much as you can is advisable. As we have already stated, it is by reading that you learn **most** and **best**, including some of the things that could be called 'learning by osmosis' – absorbing particular types of terminologies or phraseology and widening your legal (and general) vocabulary.

How to read and take notes from chapters/articles

Cross reference
See chapter 4, Taking notes.

More detail on taking notes can be found in the chapter discussing how to take notes. However, that chapter mainly covers note taking in respect of lectures, with some reference to notes from reading. What follows are some specific tips for note taking from your reading. The most important thing to realise straight away is that you will almost always have to read a piece **more than once** in order to really understand it and note the key points effectively. Ultimately, everyone develops their own reading and note-taking style, but students often need some ideas about how to start. Here are some:

Initial reading

1. Read the material once, quickly, looking for the main idea(s) (see the section below on **Types of reading**). Don't get bogged down in the details. Don't take notes. Read the abstract if there is one. If you come to an unfamiliar word, note it down but go on reading.

2. Check the meaning of unfamiliar words. If they seem to be key words, i.e. if the author uses them more than once, write a brief definition for yourself in the margin. Note all the key words separately – it may be useful later.

Making notes on the text

3. Now re-read more slowly and carefully, this time making a conscious attempt to begin to isolate the main idea(s). Take care not to confuse the main ideas (the thesis) with examples ('for instance') or narrative (the 'story'). As you are reading, doing the following may help, especially when you come to review the same material at a later date:

- There will probably be an introduction: draw a pencil line across the page after it.
- Now tackle the body of the essay. Place an asterisk or other mark whenever you come across a key idea.
- Sometimes you will find a paragraph that doesn't seem to accomplish much. Some paragraphs are purely illustrative: the 'for example' type of paragraph. Some are just comments or impressions by the author. The 'that reminds me' type. A third very common type is the 'transitional' paragraph, which just takes you rather gracefully from one point to another. When you come across a paragraph like one of these, label it in the margin.

Making notes on paper

4. When you think you have grasped the main points, write them down, either alongside your lecture notes, or on a separate sheet or page which you can file together with your lecture notes on the same topic. If you find you have several 'main points', don't panic – one or more will probably turn out to be supporting points.

5. You now have the skeleton of the author's argument. If you are still having trouble, try summarising each paragraph.

» glossary

6. Now write a **summary** or **précis** of the material. What was the author trying to put across and how did they do it? This is the most important part of the whole process as it will ensure that you have understood the main focus. It is also invariably your summaries that you will revise from.

The solution to a skill that you find difficult is to **practise** it, not avoid doing it. The more you read – and the wider you read – the easier it will become.

Activity 4

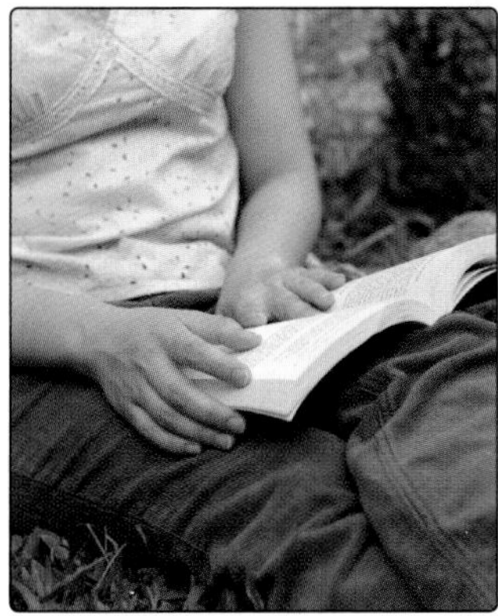

Read the article provided online by Erika Rackley, following the guidelines suggested above, and then write your own summary or précis of the main ideas and arguments contained within it - one paragraph should be enough. Also try to identify six key words for the article.

Erika Rackley, 'Difference in the House of Lords' (2006) *Social and Legal Studies* 15(2), 163–185.

Go online to read our thoughts on this activity.

Types of reading

There are three types of reading which we all use in different everyday situations. You may not realise this, but you are probably already an expert in these! Recognising this, and then knowing where to fit each reading style into your academic study, will be a great help to you. The three styles are:

1. **Scanning** the text for a specific focus. This is the technique you use, for example, when you're looking up a name in the phone book: your eye runs quickly over the page to locate specific words or phrases that are relevant to your immediate needs.

What it's useful for

When you start work, you can scan parts of texts to see if they're going to be useful to you. The following are examples of things you may wish to scan when reading your law books to prepare work for seminars, or write your essays:

» glossary

- the introduction or preface of the book or chapter, or the abstract of an academic article, or the headnote of a case
- the first and last paragraphs of chapters, articles or cases
- the concluding chapter of a book, or concluding section of an article.

2. **Skimming** the text to get the gist of something. This is the technique you use, for example, when you're reading a newspaper or magazine, or when you're trying to decide if a book in a library or bookshop is right for you: you read quickly, without focusing on every word, just to identify the main points, and skip over the bulk of the detail.

Skimming – or skim reading – is a skill that you can **develop** and **practice**. It can give you, often with surprising accuracy, a general sense of the contents of a book, or the gist of a case. It can also work for a chapter or an article. Try the following techniques:

- Look at the title page/preface and note any subtitles or other indications of the scope and aim of the piece.
- Study a Table of Contents, if there is one, to get a general sense of the structure.
- Read the opening and closing few paragraphs. Then dip into a page/section here and there, reading a paragraph or two, or sometimes several pages in a sequence. Thumb through the piece in this way, always looking for the basic pulse beat of the matter. You will eventually find those parts that are particularly useful or relevant to you and which therefore need reading in more detail.

What it's useful for

- To preview a chapter, article or case before you read it in detail.
- To refresh your understanding of a chapter, article or case when you come to review it for essays or exams.

3. **Detailed reading** for accurately extracting information. This is the type of reading you might think you have to do all the time – it's where you read every word of the text, hoping to learn from it. This, however, is a misconception, although you will need to do some detailed reading **some of the time**. However, before you do, you may find it useful to skim first, to get a general idea of what's being said, before going back to read in more detail and fill in the blanks.

The SQ3R method

An alternative approach to learning from your reading is the SQ3R method – a reading system developed by academics, particularly in the US. Research suggests that it is a very effective way of making notes, and one that students find relatively easy to master, with practice:

1. **S**urvey – making an initial overview of the text:
   - Read the title, the introduction and conclusion.
   - Read any headings and subheadings.
   - Notice any graphics. Charts, maps and diagrams are there to make a point – don't miss them.
   - Notice reading aids such as *italics*, **bold**, boxed text, chapter objectives, an abstract, or end-of-chapter questions.

   All of this will give you an idea of what the text is about.
2. **Q**uestion – a structure for your note taking:
   - Taking one section at a time, come up with as many questions as you can that will be answered in that section.
   - You may add further questions later on.
   - When your mind is actively searching for answers to questions it becomes engaged in learning.

   Having completed the question-setting, you are **ready to read**.
3. **R**ead – answer your questions:
   - Read each section (one at a time) with your questions in mind.
   - Look for the answers, and note them down.
   - Also be prepared to add new questions.

   You now need to reinforce your learning.
4. **R**ecite – testing yourself:
   - After each section, stop, recall your questions, and see if you can answer them from memory.
   - If not, look back again (as often as necessary) but don't go on to the next section until you can recite the answers. Try saying them out loud!
5. **R**eview – ensure that you have remembered everything:
   - Once you've finished the entire chapter using the preceding steps, go back over all the questions from all the headings. See if you can still answer them.
   - If not, look back and refresh your memory, then continue.

Note

This system will not work for everyone, but it is certainly worth a try!

Activity 5

This activity is designed to help you see what form of note taking works best for you when using books or other written material.

Finally: References

» glossary

As you make notes from books, articles, cases and so on, you **must** make sure that you keep a list of the texts you have consulted. This is particularly important for coursework, which will require you to use a wide variety of sources and provide a comprehensive bibliography.

↳ **Cross reference**
See chapter 14, Citing legal authorities.

See chapter 7, Avoiding plagiarism.

You should keep a note not only of title, author, publisher, date and so on, but also where you found relevant material in the book – i.e. the page or paragraph number. This will save you a great deal of time should you need to find the material again in the future and will help you to avoid plagiarism. In fact, it is recommended that you read the chapter on avoiding plagiarism before you go any further.

Conclusion

Reading as much as you can, from a variety of sources, including 'non-legal' sources, will improve your knowledge and understanding of the law. Making your reading work for you will make your study of law smoother and easier. Everyone has their own 'style' of reading, and some find it easier to understand complicated texts than others. This chapter has explained to you the difference between various types of typical reading material that you might be asked to use, and why each is important. It has also given you some suggestions for how to maximise the learning you take from your reading of these sources.

However, no one can make you read, and the amount you do is up to you – though it is undoubtedly safe to say that the more you read, and the wider variety of sources you use, the better your understanding of the law is likely to be, as well as your ability to, for example, construct arguments, develop a good writing style or even just remember things. Remember to set aside time for reading and not to see it as a chore, and it should become second nature.

It is not only law **students** who have to read a lot – if you end up practising law, your reading load will still be high – so it is better to develop the skills now!

Links

Reading Your Textbooks Effectively and Efficiently

Produced by Dartmouth College's Academic Skills Center, this US site gives some good tips on textbook use and dispels many common myths held by students about reading.
http://www.dartmouth.edu/~acskills/success/reading.html

www.oxfordinteract.com

Chapter 16

Using legal journals

Rationale

Your first encounter with legal journals may well be when you are asked to read an article. Later on, you will be required to do your own research in legal journals, to identify articles relevant to your topic. This chapter is devised to ensure that you know:

- What distinguishes a legal journal
- How to identify a journal reference
- How to find an article you have a reference to
- How to search in journal indexes to find articles on a topic.

What is a journal?

This may seem a silly question, but there is no straightforward definition. Usually it means a publication which comes out in parts on a regular basis, normally over a number of years, and which publishes several articles in each issue. You will often find journals referred to as periodicals, especially in libraries, and occasionally as serials. At the popular end of the journal spectrum are **magazines** which usually appear weekly or monthly; they may be aimed at a general or a specialist market (think of the rows of magazines in station bookshops). At the other end are serious academic journals, in which the latest research is published, and which you find in libraries.

Most journals are published regularly, with anything between 2 and 52 issues a year depending on how often they come out. In addition, there are daily publications, such as newspapers and some gazettes. Some journals are published once a year only, and these are usually referred to as yearbooks. Most journals cumulate into annual volumes.

» glossary

Types of law journals

Law journals are quite specialised, and are produced for the legal academic community and for practitioners. There is considerable overlap between the two categories. Many legal journals publish law reports as well as articles, and there is no clear distinction between journals and law reports. So, let's have a look at the different types of journals:

» glossary

Academic journals

Academic law journals form the backbone of your materials as a student. It is in these that you will find the important research in academic law. The major ones have been published for many years, but others have started more recently, and new ones are continually being launched. The following are some of the principal academic legal journals in the UK:

- Cambridge Law Journal
- International & Comparative Law Quarterly
- Journal of Law and Society
- Law Quarterly Review
- Legal Studies
- Modern Law Review
- Oxford Journal of Legal Studies
- Public Law

A significant number of academic journals are published by university law schools. This is especially true in the United States, where every law school publishes at least one journal, some of which are of great importance: the Harvard Law Review, the California Law Review and the Yale Law Journal are three of the most prestigious. In America these journals have student editors – a post of great honour given to the highest achieving students, which usually comes with a sabbatical year. Many law schools in the UK also produce their own journals, for example Edinburgh Law Review, Liverpool Law Review, Nottingham Law Journal and King's College Law Review 1997 are examples. Some universities have generated specialist journals, such as Feminist Legal Studies (University of Kent). In contrast to the US, the publication of these UK academic journals has in nearly all cases been taken over by commercial publishers.

Specialised journals

There are also many well-established specialist journals, covering a particular area of law, or a particular approach to law. These may be aimed primarily at the academic or the practitioner market, and are often hybrids, in that they are a source for reports of new cases.

- Business Law Review
- Butterworths Journal of International Banking & Financial Law
- Common Market Law Review
- Child and Family Law Quarterly
- Criminal law Review
- Family Law
- Feminist Legal Studies
- Environmental Law Review
- Environmental Law
- European Law Journal
- Human Rights Law Review

- Industrial Law Journal
- Journal of Planning & Environment Law
- Lloyd's Maritime & Commercial Law Quarterly

Practitioners' journals

As already indicated, there is no hard and fast distinction between journals aimed at the academic and practitioners' market. These are examples of journals aimed primarily at the professional market.

- Estates Gazette
- New Law Journal
- Professional Negligence
- Shipping & Trade Law
- Trademark World
- Trust Law International

In addition, there are numerous magazines, bulletins, newsletters and gazettes published by the larger commercial law firms, and usually bearing their name (e.g. *Baker & McKenzie Employment Law*), which are of marginal interest to law students.

Professional journals

These are journals or magazines published by and for the legal profession, which provide up-to-date reporting, comment, updates in various legal subject areas, reviews of new legislation and case law. Again, there is a great overlap with the specialist or practitioners' journals, and the *New Law Journal* could certainly find a place in this list as well. Among these are the following:

» glossary

- Counsel
- Lawyer
- Law Society's Gazette
- Legal Executive
- Solicitors Journal

These appear weekly, and are a valuable source for legal news. All have useful websites. They are also the journals in which professional jobs are advertised.

Campaigning journals

For want of a better word, 'campaigning' journals cover the publications of civil liberties bodies such as the Legal Action Group, which publishes the journal *Legal Action*, or Statewatch, which produces a bulletin called *Statewatch Bulletin*. The tendency is for these publications to move from paper publication to online only. These can be valuable sources for monitoring new developments in the law, especially in areas such as human rights and environmental law. The organisation websites are the starting point for finding out about these.

Newspapers

» glossary

Finally, the **broadsheet** newspapers are an important source for legal news. Some of them contain law reports, of which the ones in *The Times* are the most highly regarded. The broadsheets all include a weekly legal page. Again, *The Times* has the most comprehensive coverage, which includes a student page at http://business.timesonline.co.uk/tol/business/law/

Journal abbreviations

» glossary

↳ Cross reference
See chapter 14, Citing legal authorities.

Law journals all have abbreviations. To find out more about this look at chapter 14, Citing legal authorities, and test yourself in this activity. To do this activity you will need to use the **Cardiff Index to Legal Abbreviations** (http://www.legalabbrevs.cardiff.ac.uk) which is described in that chapter.

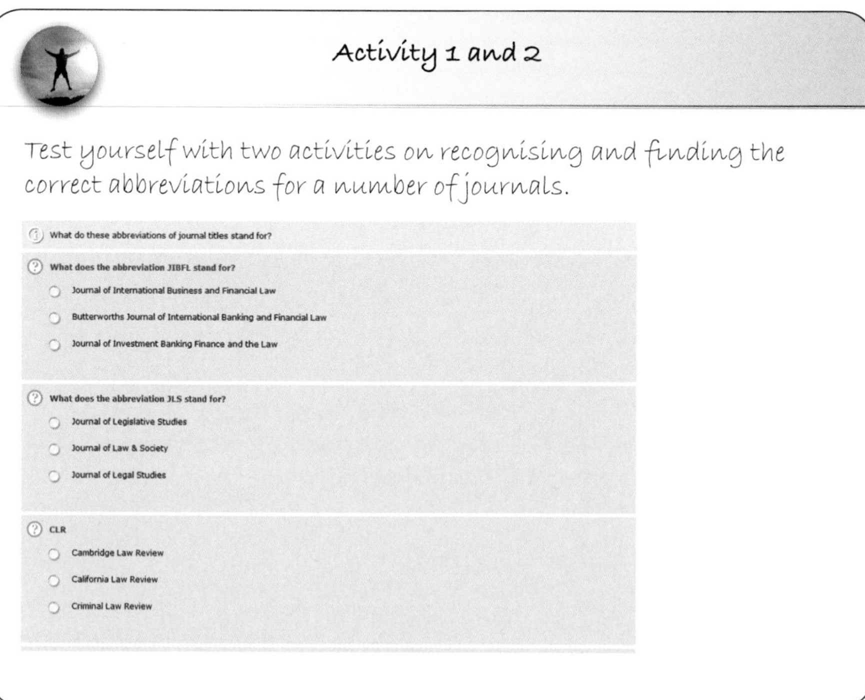

Interpreting a journal citation

At the very beginning, students sometimes get confused by journal citations, thinking that they are books. If you see a citation looking like this:

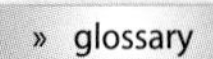

> Patricia Londono, 'Applying convention jurisprudence to the needs of women prisoners' [2007] PL 198

then it is a reference to an article in a journal ('PL', which stands for Public Law). Journal articles are normally cited with the title in single quotes, followed by the citation to the journal.

↳ Cross reference
You can find details about the forms of citation in chapter 14, Citing legal authorities.

However, it is worth looking in detail at how journals are constructed. This example is the Oxford Journal of Legal Studies, which is published four times a year.

Example

OJLS	Spring 2006	Summer 2006	Autumn 2006	Winter 2006
Volume	26	26	26	26
Issue	(1)	(2)	(3)	(4)
Pages	1-233	235-447	449-626	627-822

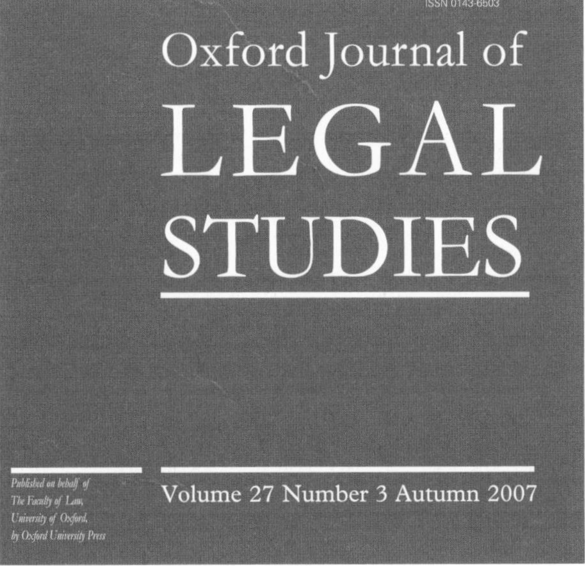

ISSN 0143-6503
Oxford Journal of
LEGAL
STUDIES
Published on behalf of
The Faculty of Law,
University of Oxford,
by Oxford University Press
Volume 27 Number 3 Autumn 2007

Pagination

The page numbering of a journal is **usually** but not always continuous throughout the year. In this example we can see that the pagination is continuous, so that the third issue (Autumn) starts with page 449.

Issues

An academic journal usually publishes between two and six issues in each year, although practitioners' journals are much more likely to be monthly (10–12 issues a year) or weekly (50–52 issues a year). The issues are not always numbered. In the OJLS example the issue number is given in brackets, although this is normally omitted in the citation to an article. In the example from Public Law above we are not given an issue number. This is because PL does not have issue numbers, but simply designates them Spring, Summer, Autumn and Winter. In any case, the issue number is not indicated in the article citation.

Volume numbering

Journals usually have journal numbers, but not always. The Cambridge Law Journal started with volume 1 in 1954, and reached volume 66 in 2007.

Journal titles

Journals are apt to change their title from time to time, which can occasionally cause confusion. The British Journal of Law and Society changed its name to Journal of Law and Society at volume 9 in 1992. The volume numbering continues from the old title. Sometimes the change of title happens in the middle of a year, or volume: The Child and Family Law Quarterly started at volume 7 (2). Until volume 7 (1) it was called the Journal of Child Law. In between, it became Tolley's Journal of Child Law when it changed publisher, although *Tolley's* was regarded as a 'cover title' only, so not the real title of the journal.

Some publishers like to give their name to a journal. Butterworths Journal of International Banking & Finance Law is also known as the Journal of International Banking & Finance Law. This does not help the user, but is something you should be aware of.

Key Point

Many journals use the symbol '&' instead of 'and' in their titles. Some systems do not recognise these as equivalents. This is particularly the case in listings of e-journals. So, if you can't find the *British Journal of Law and Society* you should also try the *British Journal of Law & Society*.

Finding journals

You may want to locate a printed copy of the journal in your library catalogue, or to trace an electronic version. While most journals are accessible electronically, this is not true of all, and it depends on what institutional subscriptions you have.

To begin with, however, you are likely to be given the name of an article to read, and this will be your first encounter with legal journals. We'll look at options for finding articles later.

Looking up journals in your library

First, you must look up the journal title in the library catalogue. Library catalogue systems vary, but most of them will allow you to limit your search to journals (or 'periodicals'). This means that when you look for a title such as Public Law you will only retrieve journals with 'public law' in their title. If you don't limit your search in this way you will also retrieve all the books with 'public law' in their title.

When you have retrieved Public Law, the catalogue entry will give you information about the library's holdings – how far back the journal run goes. You may well find that your library only holds the journal from, say, the 1990s onwards.

Activity 3

Now try an activity which asks you to look up a number of journals in your library.

Looking up online journals

You will probably do most of your searching in journals online rather than in the print copy. There are some important things to remember, however:

- Many online journals only start with more recent issues – typically from the 1990s onwards.
- Which ones you can access depends on your institutional subscriptions.
- There are many different sources for online journals – you won't find all legal journals in Westlaw or Lexis.
- You often find that a journal is available in more than one service (or 'host'). Which you use is a matter of choice, and you will probably get a preference for one or the other. But you will find differences between the holdings of the various hosts. Have a look at the various sources for the Oxford Journal of Legal Studies:

» glossary

Oxford Journals Online – from vol. 1, 1981 to the present

Hein Online – from vol. 1, 1981 to 1998

LexisNexis Butterworths – from vol. 19, 1999 to the present

Westlaw – from vol. 22, 2002 to the present

Activity 4

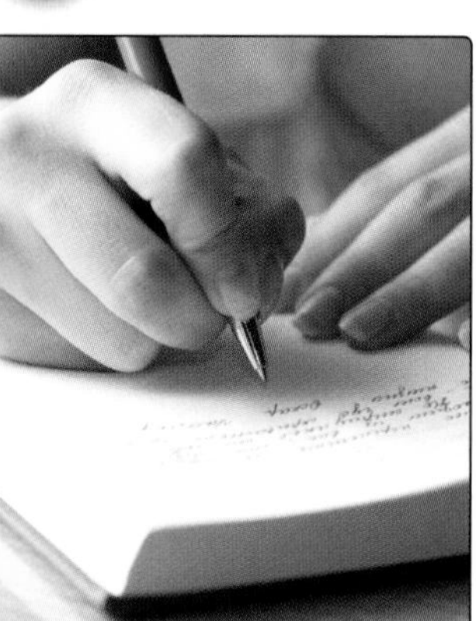

Now try an activity which asks you to find e-journals in your own library system.

Sources for online journals

Now you've done the activities, you will realise that there are several different sources for online versions of legal journals. Let's have a look at them in more detail.

First, there are the major legal services which are discussed in chapter 17, Using legal databases:

- Westlaw
- LexisNexis Butterworths.

These two are the major legal subscription services, and each contains a large number of journals. Their coverage of UK legal journals has a certain amount of overlap, but is mostly mutually exclusive. Their coverage of international journals (mainly US), is 90 per cent similar.

- Hein Online http://heinonline.org/

This is a subscription service containing a large collection of legal journals from their first volume. The run usually stops short of the latest years. This is an extremely valuable service for those institutions which subscribe, because it contains journal archives not available elsewhere. It is continually adding to its resources.

- Ingenta http://www.ingentaconnect.com/
- Wiley InterScience http://www.interscience.wiley.com/
- EBSCO http://ejournals.ebsco.com/
- SpringerLink http://www.springerlink.com/
- and many others.

These are journal hosts which include some legal journals, and which you may find are your primary source for a particular journal.

- Oxford Journals Online http://www.oxfordjournals.org/subject/law/
- Cambridge Journals http://journals.cambridge.org/
- Kluwer Law International http://www.kluwerlawonline.com/
- Hart Journals http://www.hartjournals.co.uk/

These are publishers' sites, where you will find their own publications.

Note

Access to these will depend on your institutional subscriptions, and you should always link to them from your library website, which will give you details of passwords and other information required to use them.

Finding journal articles

We've already looked at a reference to an article. Here are some others:

> Andrew Ashworth, 'Social control and "anti-social behaviour": the subversion of human rights?' [2004] LQR 263
>
> A.W.B. Simpson 'Quackery and contract law: the case of the carbolic smoke ball' (1985) 14 JLS 345
>
> Stewart Motha, 'Democracy's empire: sovereignty, law, and violence' (2007) 34 J Law & Soc. 1
>
> Nicola Lacey, 'In search of the responsible subject: history, philosophy and social sciences in criminal law theory' (2001) 64 MLR 350
>
> David Burnet, Conjoined twins, sanctity and quality of life, and invention the mother of necessity (2001) 13 CFLQ 91

In order to find these you first need to decipher the citation, using the knowledge you have already acquired from chapter 14, Citing legal authorities. The crucial element is identifying the journal from the abbreviation. Having done that, you can find the journal using the search techniques we have outlined above.

Activity 5

Now try an activity whcich asks you to look up a number of articles in your library systems and to find out whether they are available and in which service(s).

Finding articles by yourself

As you progress through your studies you will need to find articles on a topic, or perhaps by an individual author, or relating to a particular case or piece of legislation. To do this you need to use a journal index.

What is a journal index?

Journal indexes cover a range of journals and give you information about the articles in them. They don't necessarily give you access to the actual article. There are two widely used legal journal indexes with comprehensive coverage:

- Legal Journals Index
- Index to Legal Periodicals.

In addition, there is an index with much more restricted coverage on LexisNexis Butterworths, and a number of general social sciences indexes which have some limited coverage of law.

Legal Journals Index

» abbreviation

The LJI is on Westlaw, so you can only use it if you have an institutional subscription to the service. LJI indexes all the UK legal journals, as well as the most important European English language journals, such as those published in the Netherlands. It covers about 800 journals. However, it does not cover journals from America or other jurisdictions. A substantial proportion of the journals indexed are professional newsletters and bulletins, which are not of great interest to law students. Westlaw itself contains some 50 full text UK and European journals. So, you can see that by looking in the LJI you will retrieve many articles which are not in full text on the service.

Using the LJI you can search for articles in free text (i.e. by entering a word which will look in the whole of the database), by limiting the search to article title or author. The advanced search facility gives many more options, such as finding articles on cases or legislation cited or by subject keyword.

Activities 6 and 7

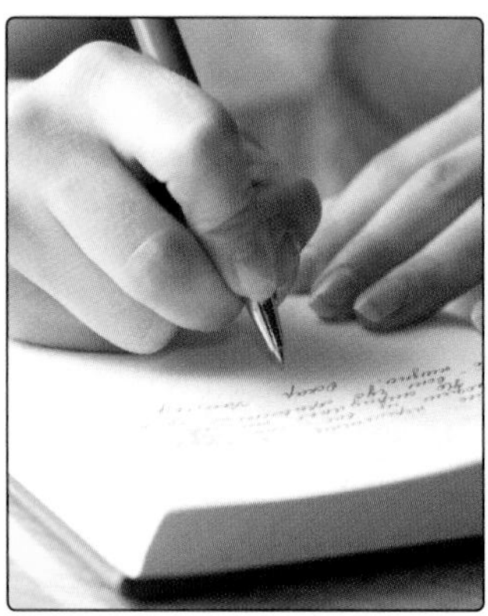

Now try these activities which ask you to find articles by yourself.

Note: To do this you need to have institutional access to Westlaw.

When you have done the exercise you will notice that some of the articles are available as an LJI abstract **only**, and some are also available in full text on Westlaw. If you want to read an article which is not in full text, you need to find a source for the journal in the way you have looked at earlier in this chapter.

Key Point

Practise using the Legal Journals Index. There are lots of features which we have not been able to touch upon. Follow the Westlaw tutorials online and use the help features. It's very easy to forget some of the tips and tricks for using Westlaw most effectively, and it's useful to get into the habit of reminding yourself.

Index to Legal Periodicals

The Index to Legal Periodicals is a stand-alone service which your institution may subscribe to. ILP is long established. It includes all the important UK and European legal journals, and also covers all American journals.

» abbreviation

If you have access to it, you may find that you get a direct link from the article to the full text.

Activity 8

Now practise using the Index to Legal Periodicals with the activity we have devised online.

Note: To do this you need to have institutional access to Index to Legal Periodicals.

Other indexes

There are a number of other indexes which you can use for more advanced research in journals, and which may become useful when you embark on extended work, such as a dissertation.

- The **Index to Foreign Legal Periodicals** indexes non Anglo-American law journals, and is valuable if you are working in the law of other jurisdictions. However, it is not so widely held as the two we have looked at above, and so you may not be able to access it.
- If you want to search for materials outside the confines of law, you may wish to use one or other of the major social science indexes such as **Social Science Citation Index**, within the over-arching service **Web of Knowledge**, or, at a more specialist level, subject-based indexes such as **Criminal Justice Abstracts.**

Your library staff can give you advice on which to use and it is worth consulting them if you have a particular research task.

Remember

Journals research can be complicated: Ask your law librarian for advice!

What if the journal isn't in your library?

You are bound to come across journal articles which you think will be essential for your work, but which are not available online in full text, or in your library. All libraries have facilities for borrowing books and articles from the British Library, or other academic libraries. This is usually known as interlibrary loan, although you may find your library names it something different, such as document delivery. There are usually restrictions on the use of this service, and you can get advice from the law librarian or your interlibrary loan service.

Conclusion

In this chapter we have looked at using legal journals and you have learned the basics of doing research to find articles. As technology advances, you may find easier direct access to articles via your library system. You need to build on your knowledge, and to remind yourself of the scope and function of the particular databases. Remember, too, that these database services are continually evolving, as are library systems, and you should keep aware of changes which are likely to happen over the course of your studies.

Links

Cardiff Index to Legal Abbreviations http://www.legalabbrevs.cardiff.ac.uk/

Hein Online http://heinonline.org/

Ingenta http://www.ingentaconnect.com/

Wiley InterScience http://www.interscience.wiley.com/

EBSCO http://ejournals.ebsco.com/

SpringerLink http://www.springerlink.com/

Oxford Journals Online http://www.oxfordjournals.org/subject/law/

Cambridge Journals http://journals.cambridge.org/

Kluwer Law International http://www.kluwerlawonline.com/

Hart Journals http://www.hartjournals.co.uk/

Chapter 17

Using legal databases

Rationale

The development of legal databases has transformed legal research over the past decade. Online searching is now the standard method of doing legal research. The major services have been in existence for many decades, but recent technological advances have vastly improved their ease of use.

From the start of your studies you will be taught about using legal databases. Most institutions subscribe to several services which give you access to a range of primary and secondary materials far greater than you could expect to find in any but the largest of university libraries. Learning how to use legal databases effectively will save you time and will be an asset in later stages of your legal education. There are several major databases which you are likely to use on a daily basis, and a number of others which you should know about.

In addition to the commercial services there are several important freely available services, and for some research these are the principal source.

This chapter is devised to cover:

- The range of databases
- The content of databases
- How to search
- Which database to use for which purpose.

Note

A note about terminology: It is more accurate to describe the major subscription databases as **Services**, since they each consist of collections of databases, organised in various different ways. The term **Database** should strictly speaking refer to one element only.

Which database?

» glossary

» abbreviation

» glossary

The two major subscription-based legal services are Westlaw and LexisNexis Butterworths (LNB). You will have access to at least one of these, and probably both. In addition there are Justis and Lawtel, and Hein Online (which for UK users operates mainly as a journals database). With all these services, there are core databases and add-on options, and depending on your institutional subscription you may have access to part or the whole of the content. In addition, your institution may subscribe to one or more of many more legal specialised databases as well as the major general services which you can use for expanding your research out of the strict boundaries of law.

Note

Online we have provided a PDF of the principal contents of the major services.

Knowing the contents

» glossary

» glossary

Many students become familiar with one service and use it all the time, so that they are sometimes surprised if they are unable to find what they need. There is a considerable overlap in the contents of Westlaw and LNB, but there are some important differences, notably in the coverage of journals and law report series. For most of the case law which you need to find there is no problem: you will find it listed in any of the main services, and Westlaw and LNB both provide a list of citations to the case. However, when it comes to looking for journal articles, you will probably need to look elsewhere. The online table shows you the principal sources for case law and legislation on the main subscription services.

Cross reference
This is treated in more detail in chapter 16, Using legal journals.

UK Legislation			
Commercial databases		**Free databases**	
LexisNexis Butterworths	Consolidated UK law in force, **statutes**, SIs	**Statute Law Database**	Official revised version of UK legislation
Westlaw	Consolidated UK law in force, statutes, SIs	Legislation on **OPSI** site	Text of all Acts and SIs from 1988: not amended
Justis	UK Statutes and SIs including all repealed legislation	**BAILII**	Text of all Acts and SIs from 1988: not amended
Lawtel	Acts back to 1984, **Bill** tracking, Statutory status tables		
UK Case Law			
LexisNexis Butterworths	The Law Reports, All ER, other series depending on subscription, Case Search (digest of cases)	BAILII	**Transcripts** of cases
Westlaw	The Law Reports, WLR, other series, Case Locators (digest of cases)		
Justis	The Law Reports, WLR, **English Reports**, other series, depending on subscription		
Lawtel	Case summaries mainly from 1980, access to transcripts.		
Hein Online	English Reports		

» glossary

» glossary

» glossary

» glossary

» glossary

Finding out about databases

Your institution will have information about the databases available to you, probably on the library website. It is really worth your while to take advantage of any database training which is offered to you. In some universities it is a compulsory part of the curriculum, while in others you need to sign up for classes. These are often provided by the services' own trainers, and students' experience is invariably positive. Details of training will be communicated to you as a student, and you can also find out from your law librarian and your library or law school website.

Your library is also likely to offer you online guides and tutorials; look on the library website to find these.

Remember Take full advantage of any training which is offered to you. It will help you to use the databases accurately and efficiently, and will give insight into all sorts of features that may not be apparent to the casual user.

Another valuable source of information is provided on the database itself. The major services all have in-context help, tutorials, downloadable leaflets and even 24-hour phone helplines to assist you. A few minutes using these can often save you a great deal of time if you are uncertain about how to proceed with your search. The online tutorials will guide you through the various functions, with examples.

You can usually get personal help from library staff, and many institutions also have LexisNexis and Westlaw student representatives who are trained to give help to fellow-students. Note that these people are not there to find the material for you, but to help you find it yourself.

Remember Five minutes spent using online help and tutorials can save you an hour of fruitless searching!

To start with, you should know which databases you have access to in your institution.

Activity 1

Find out which databases you have access to.

Search techniques

All databases have various levels of searching. At the simplest, you enter a term or terms into a search box, and retrieve all the occurrences of that term in the whole database. More advanced searching techniques include selecting the fields in which you enter a term – for example in the **title** or the **author** field. Or, you may want to choose a subset of the database, such as **legislation** or cases.

» glossary

Simple searching

Simple searching is usually fairly intuitive, and most databases nowadays allow for Google-type searching, whereby you enter a word or string of words and get results in relevance order. However, this technique is not always suitable for legal material, especially if you are searching for a specific case.

For a start, you need to know which part of the service to search in. Each of the larger services – Westlaw and LNB – consists of a collection of thousands of different databases and libraries of databases. This need not worry you, as you will be using a limited selection of the materials, and they are presented fairly simply to you when you login to the service. But at the very least you need to be aware of the different categories of material, such as cases, legislation, commentary and so on, so that you search in the right section. As you get further into your studies, you may want to explore the more specialised parts of the services, such as practitioner materials, special subject areas, and international materials.

The first thing you are likely to need legal databases for is to find a case and to do some basic research on it. We'll look at this in detail later on, but first we need to think a little more about search techniques.

More complex searching

Complex database searching, which is often flagged as **advanced search**, uses a technique of linking your search terms with AND or OR [etc.] in order to limit your search and make it more specific (technically known as Boolean searching). These linking words are sometimes called **connectors** and sometimes **operators** and are used with other techniques such as truncation of words and the use of universal characters (sometimes called **wildcards**).

» glossary

This is a diagram of how Boolean searching works:

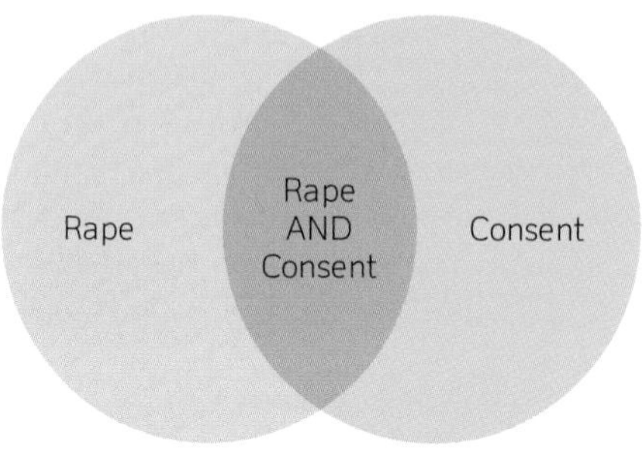

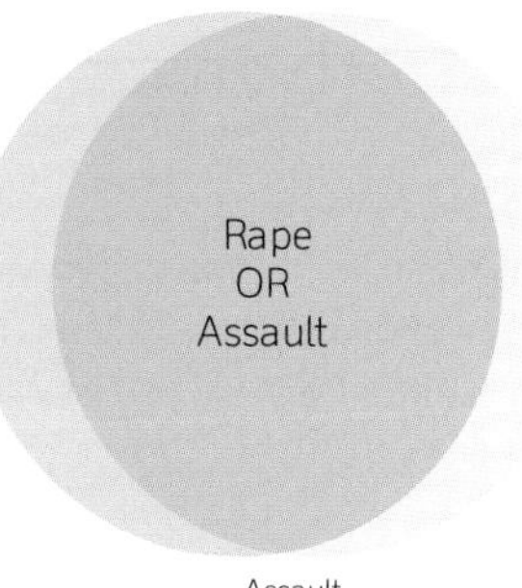

Rape AND Consent retrieves documents containing both those terms, therefore *fewer* documents than you would get using either of the terms singly.

Rape OR Assault retrieves documents containing either or both of those terms.

In practice, the dataset search interface will lead you to these techniques without your having to think too hard about them.

Key Point

Think about:

- alternative terms meaning the same thing
- different ways of combining terms
- refining your search by adding another term.

The complication is that each database uses slightly different terms and symbols to do this. Here are the most common functions and the way in which they are used in three databases. Don't worry too much about this, just remember that this table is here for reference if you should need it.

Function	Westlaw	example	LNB	example	Justis	example
AND	AND, &	Solicitor and negligence	AND	Solicitor and negligence	AND, space	Solicitor negligence
OR	OR, space	Ship vessel	OR	Ship or vessel	OR, |	Ship | vessel, ship or vessel
Proximity (within same sentence or paragraph)	/s /p	Solicitor /s negligence	w/s w/p	Solicitor w/p negligence	NEAR (terms are within 10 words)	Solicitor near negligence
Proximity (within n terms	/n	Solicitor /6 negligence	w/6	Solicitor w/6 negligence	Within 6 or w/6	Solicitor within 6 of negligence
Phrase	Enclose in " "	"fair hearing"	Phrase	Fair hearing	Enclose in " "	"fair hearing"
Universal character (wildcard)	*	Wom*n	*	Wom*n	?	Wom?n
Truncation (root expander)	!	Immigr! (finds immigrant, immigration)	!	Immigr! (finds immigrant, immigration)	*	Immigr* (finds immigrant, immigration)

There are numerous other operators which you can use for a sophisticated search, and they can be combined.

Key Point

Look at the help features and follow the online tutorials on the services to help you with the terms and symbols that they use, and to see useful examples of how to construct a search.

How to look for a case

These are the kinds of case searching you will have to do:

- Straightforward case citation e.g.
  - *Williams v Roffey Bros* [1991] 1 QB 1
  - *R v Secretary of State for Transport ex parte Factortame Limited & Others (No 2)* [1991] 3 CMLR 589
- Name of case without citation
  - *Donoghue v Stevenson*

- *Anns v Merton*

- Case with obscure citation
  - *Stilk v Myrick (1809) 2 Camp 317*
  - *Clutterbuck v Coffin (1842) 3 Man & G 842*
- Case in a non-UK jurisdiction

There is no right or wrong way of finding a case, but you should bear in mind the following:

- Many cases are known by variant names. You may be given one of these only, and therefore might fail to find it if you try entering it exactly as written.
- With complex case names it's easy to make a mistake. Therefore, the less you enter, the better.
- If you fail to find a case, it may be because the spelling of the name is wrong. In that case, try searching by a different part of the case name, or by citation.
- If one of the parties to a case has an unusual name, this is all you need to enter.
- With names of companies you can usually use one element of the name only.
- Important difference between LNB and Westlaw: in their simple search a string of words will search as a phrase on LNB, and as a set of keywords on Westlaw.

Remember If you don't find what you are looking for try a different search, for example by using different terms. Always remember that the more you enter, the less you will find!

Activity 2

This activity is designed to help you find cases on Westlaw, LexisNexis Butterworths or Justis, or indeed any of the services. Some of these cases are straightforward to find, others are more tricky. You need to enter as much of the case name as needed to find the case, but on the other hand, you want to avoid retrieving dozens of cases with similar names.

Note: the exercise assumes you are using the simple search facilities on the databases. All the services will provide advanced searching facilities as well. If you want to explore these, look at the online help provided on the service.

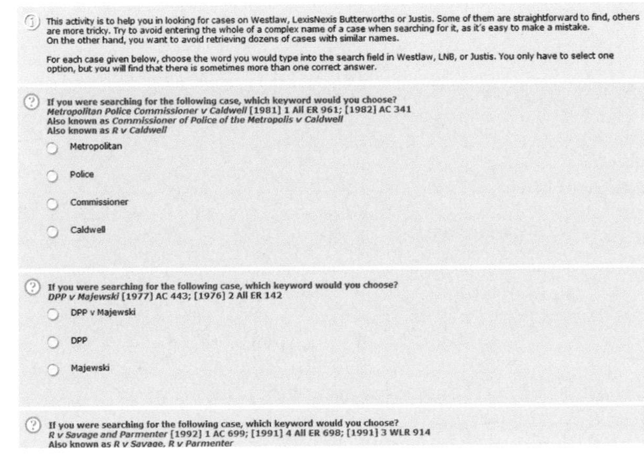

This activity is to help you in looking for cases on Westlaw, LexisNexis Butterworths or Justis. Some of them are straightforward to find, others are more tricky. Try to avoid entering the whole of a complex name of a case when searching for it, as it's easy to make a mistake.
On the other hand, you want to avoid retrieving dozens of cases with similar names.

For each case given below, choose the word you would type into the search field in Westlaw, LNB, or Justis. You only have to select one option, but you will find that there is sometimes more than one correct answer.

If you were searching for the following case, which keyword would you choose?
Metropolitan Police Commissioner v Caldwell **[1981] 1 All ER 961; [1982] AC 341**
Also known as *Commissioner of Police of the Metropolis v Caldwell*
Also known as *R v Caldwell*

- Metropolitan
- Police
- Commissioner
- Caldwell

If you were searching for the following case, which keyword would you choose?
DPP v Majewski **[1977] AC 443; [1976] 2 All ER 142**

- DPP v Majewski
- DPP
- Majewski

If you were searching for the following case, which keyword would you choose?
R v Savage and Parmenter **[1992] 1 AC 699; [1991] 4 All ER 698; [1991] 3 WLR 914**
Also known as *R v Savage, R v Parmenter*

Researching a case

As well as finding a case, you need to be able to find out additional information about it. This might include the following:

- The judicial history of the case
- Significant cases cited
- Cases which have cited the case, and how they treated the case (was it applied, considered, overruled, etc.)
- Find case commentaries in journals
- Find articles citing the case.

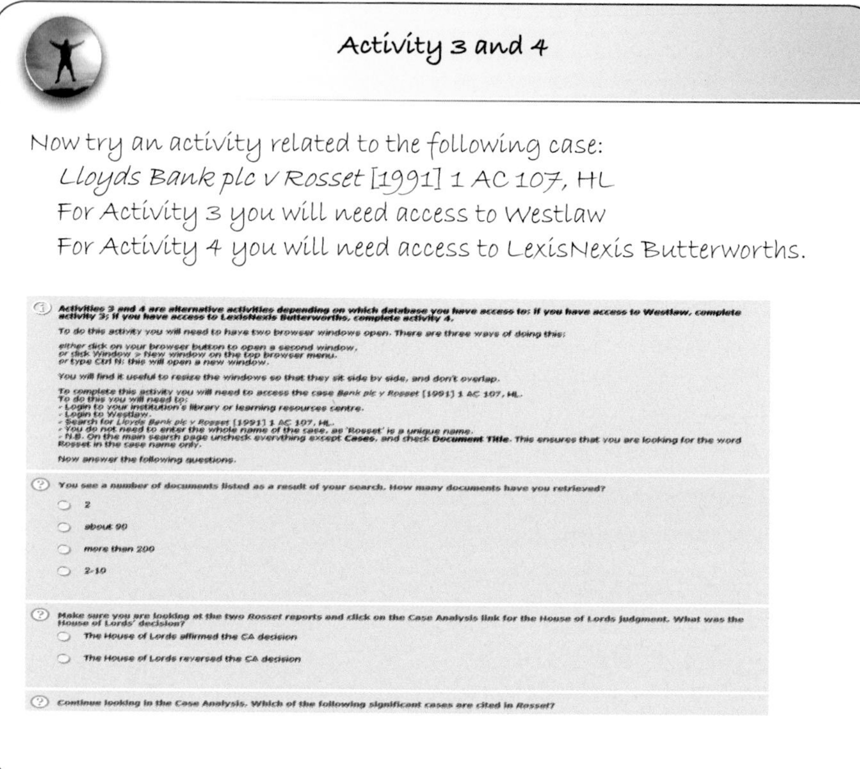

Activity 3 and 4
Now try an activity related to the following case:
Lloyds Bank plc v Rosset [1991] 1 AC 107, HL
For Activity 3 you will need access to Westlaw
For Activity 4 you will need access to LexisNexis Butterworths.
Activities 3 and 4 are alternative activities depending on which database you have access to: if you have access to Westlaw, complete activity 3; if you have access to LexisNexis Butterworths, complete activity 4.
To do this activity you will need to have two browser windows open. There are three ways of doing this:
either click on your browser button to open a second window,
or click Window > New window on the top browser menu.
or type Ctrl N: this will open a new window.
You will find it useful to resize the windows so that they sit side by side, and don't overlap.
To complete this activity you will need to access the case Bank plc v Rosset [1991] 1 AC 107, HL.
To do this you will need to:
- Login to your institution's library or learning resources centre.
- Login to Westlaw.
- Search for Lloyds Bank plc v Rosset [1991] 1 AC 107, HL.
- You do not need to enter the whole name of the case, as 'Rosset' is a unique name.
- N.B. On the main search page uncheck everything except Cases, and check Document Title. This ensures that you are looking for the word Rosset in the case name only.
Now answer the following questions.
You see a number of documents listed as a result of your search. How many documents have you retrieved?
2
about 90
more than 200
2-10
Make sure you are looking at the two Rosset reports and click on the Case Analysis link for the House of Lords judgment. What was the House of Lords' decision?
The House of Lords affirmed the CA decision
The House of Lords reversed the CA decision
Continue looking in the Case Analysis. Which of the following significant cases are cited in Rosset?

The activities give you instructions on accessing Westlaw and/or LNB, from your institution's website so that you can answer questions on *Rosset*.

↳ **Cross reference**
See chapter 23, Reading cases 3, for a discussion of *Rosset*.

By doing this activity you will have learned:

- how to formulate a search for a case using different examples of case name
- how to research the judicial history of the case
- how to find cases which have subsequently cited the case
- how to find commentaries on the case in journals.

Searching for legal materials by topic

We have concentrated on finding and researching a case, because this is the first thing you are likely to need to do.

You will also need to search for cases and journal articles by topic. In this chapter we will not go into detail on how to do this, but instead give you some pointers on how to approach the task.

1. Identify what kind of material you are looking for. Journal articles? Cases? Legislation? Commentary?

- Remember to choose the right part of the service to search in. Otherwise you may retrieve too many hits to deal with. For example, if you are looking for case law, be sure you are only searching in the cases database of the service.
- You may also want to use the advanced search facilities of the database in order to confine your search terms to the catchwords of a case, for example.

» glossary

2. Identify your topic – what are you looking for?

You may have a topic to write about, and want to find relevant cases or journal articles, or you may know about a case but not remember its name. Whatever you are looking for, you need to think about the distinguishing keywords.

- Euthanasia as a human right
- Illegal detention of suspected terrorists
- The admissibility of hearsay evidence by children
- Nuisance caused by interference with TV reception by a tall building
- Is a company liable for damages for causing pollution when it was unable to foresee the harm?
- Is a husband who has sexual intercourse with his wife against her will guilty of rape?
- ASBOs
- Is the separation of conjoined twins against the parents' wishes and leading to the inevitable death of one twin lawful?

3. Break down your topic into relevant keywords:

- **Euthanasia** as a **human right**
- **Illegal detention** of suspected **terrorists**
- **Nuisance** caused by **interference** with **TV reception** by a tall building
- Is a company liable for damages for **nuisance** caused by **pollution** when it was unable to **foresee** the harm?
- Is a **husband** who has **sexual intercourse** with his wife against her will guilty of **rape**?
- **ASBOs**
- Is the separation of **conjoined twins** against the parents' wishes and leading to the inevitable death of one twin lawful?

4. Think of alternative terms where appropriate:

- Euthanasia as a human right – **Right to die**

- Illegal detention of suspected terrorists – **Unlawful detention detainees**
- Nuisance caused by interference with TV reception by a tall building – **Television**
- Is a company liable for damages for nuisance caused by pollution when it was unable to foresee the harm? – **Foreseeability**
- Is a husband who has sexual intercourse with his wife against her will guilty of rape? – **Marital, marriage**
- ASBOs – **Anti Social Behaviour Orders**
- Is the separation of conjoined twins against the parents' wishes and leading to the inevitable death of one twin lawful? – Conjoined twins is such a specific term that you would not need to enter anything else in order to find the particular case. However, you might want to search more widely using terms such as **Right to life** or **Right to die**.

5. Consider whether you can search using a leading case.

Key Point

Searching by using a leading case is often the most efficient way of finding cases!

How to look for legislation

» glossary

Most of your research on legislation will consist of reading Acts of Parliament, and you need to be sure that you are looking at the law in force, i.e. the Acts as amended by subsequent legislation. This is the information you need to be able to find out about legislation:

- Is the Act in force? Have some sections not been brought into force yet? This requires looking at the commencement of the Act.
- Does the Act amend or repeal previous legislation? This information will be in the Schedules of the Act. (» glossary)
- Has the Act been amended by subsequent legislation?
- What subordinate legislation has been made under the authority of the Act? This will be mainly, but not invariably, in the form of Statutory Instruments. (» glossary)
- How can you find commentary on the Act?
- What cases are there which interpret the Act, or sections of the Act?
- Are there useful journal articles about the Act?

The major legal services allow you to do this research, and the activities which follow will show you how to find the information on Westlaw and LNB.

As well as the subscription services, there is a valuable free official Statute Law Database on which you can find all the details of legislation, although not cases, journal articles or commentary.

» glossary

The activities use the Human Rights Act as an example.

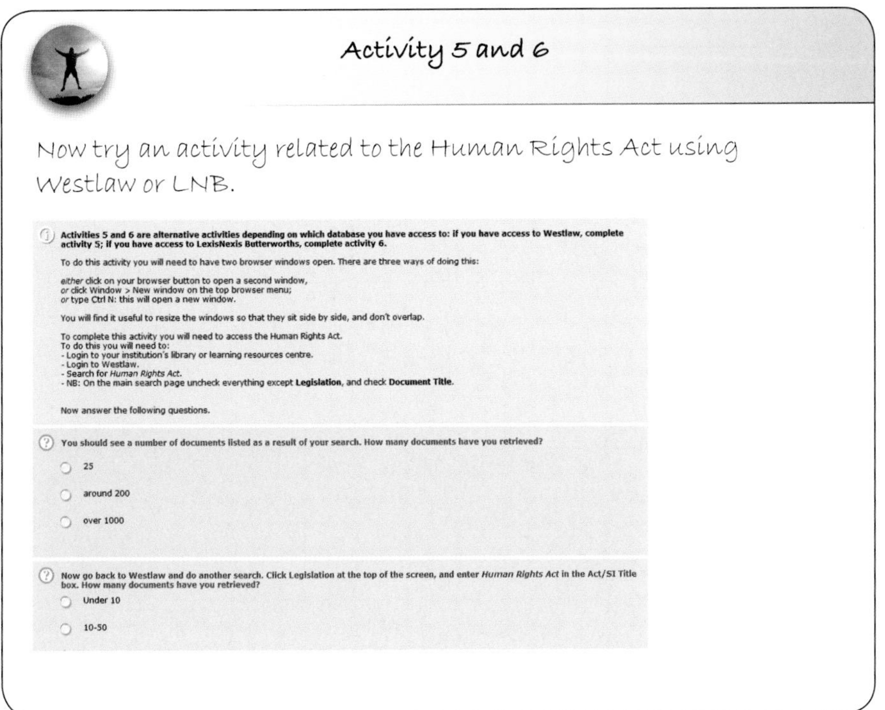

Activity 5 and 6

Now try an activity related to the Human Rights Act using Westlaw or LNB.

Activities 5 and 6 are alternative activities depending on which database you have access to: if you have access to Westlaw, complete activity 5; if you have access to LexisNexis Butterworths, complete activity 6.

To do this activity you will need to have two browser windows open. There are three ways of doing this:

either click on your browser button to open a second window,
or click Window > New window on the top browser menu;
or type Ctrl N: this will open a new window.

You will find it useful to resize the windows so that they sit side by side, and don't overlap.

To complete this activity you will need to access the Human Rights Act.
To do this you will need to:
- Login to your institution's library or learning resources centre.
- Login to Westlaw.
- Search for *Human Rights Act*.
- NB: On the main search page uncheck everything except **Legislation**, and check **Document Title**.

Now answer the following questions.

You should see a number of documents listed as a result of your search. How many documents have you retrieved?

- 25
- around 200
- over 1000

Now go back to Westlaw and do another search. Click Legislation at the top of the screen, and enter *Human Rights Act* in the Act/SI Title box. How many documents have you retrieved?

- Under 10
- 10-50

Why use databases?

It should be clear to you by now that these complex legal databases offer a range of sophisticated ways of researching the law, and that they are essential tools for your research. You should get into the habit of using them even for quite simple retrieval tasks, because they will provide you with a reliable and authentic text. Using Google or Wikipedia is no substitute for serious research on a database, as the text may be out of date, inaccurate, copied from elsewhere and unreliable.

The more you practise using databases, the more expert you will become at using them.

Conclusion

Searching on databases is a complex activity, and it is not possible in this chapter to do more than scratch the surface. Researching the *Rosset* case will have given you an idea of how to approach the most common kind of searching. Basic searching on nearly all databases is very simple, so you should have no trouble in finding materials from references you have been given.

However, as all the services vary in their content and their search protocol, it is impossible here to do more than introduce you to the concept of running more complex searches. The most useful thing you can do is to familiarise yourself with the services you have access to.

- Use the in-context help on the database
- Follow the training tutorials on the service
- Learn about the content of the databases
- Take advantage of any training offered to you
- Use your library and law school websites to find out what's on offer.

www.oxfordinteract.com

Chapter 18

Using reference materials

Rationale

Knowing how to use legal reference materials forms a backbone to your studies as a law student. There are a good many reference works which are of interest to the practitioner rather than the law student, and while mention will be made of them here, we will not go into detail, but concentrate on those which you will find useful. This chapter is devised to cover:

- Encyclopaedias
- Dictionaries
- Indexes and digests
- Practitioner resources.

Legal encyclopaedias

Encyclopaedias are essential reference works in the law, although you won't usually hear them referred to as such. They are authoritative, in that they can be used as a reputable source of the law, and cited in court.

Halsbury's Laws

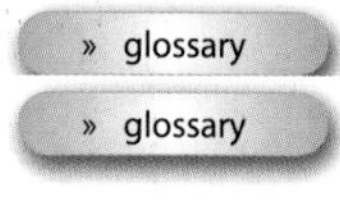

» glossary

» abbreviation

Halsbury's Laws of England is the major legal encyclopaedia, and one which you should become familiar with. It is arranged by subject in 50 volumes, each volume covering one or more of the main areas of law. Here you will find a narrative account of the law, with reference to the principal legislation and leading cases in each subject. Halsbury's Laws is the recognised starting point for research in the law.

You will find Halsbury's Laws in most law libraries, and also online on LexisNexis Butterworths (LNB). In order to use it effectively you need to know something about its structure:

- The main work consists of 50 volumes, covering 189 subjects, or 'titles'. Some subjects occupy two volumes, or in some cases three volumes. Criminal Law and Evidence occupies four volumes.
- Each subject – or title – is itself subdivided into topics, which can be looked up in the indexes. Rather than page references, Halsbury's uses **paragraphs** (based on the two-column format of the printed work).
- Volumes are reissued regularly, incorporating changes in the law, so it is important to note the date of publication for each volume.
- The main work is updated by an annual **Cumulative Supplement** arranged like a miniature version of the volumes, and a loose-leaf **Current Service**. So when you look

up a topic in the main volume, you must also check these to make sure you have the up-to-date law.

- The A–Z index to the whole work is the starting point if you are not sure which volume to look in. There is also an index in each volume.
- The online version follows the same structure as the printed work, and can be browsed or searched. The text in the online version replicates the printed version, and updates are noted at the end of each page of text.

Activity 1

Now answer some questions on Halsbury's Laws. To do this you can **either** use the online version of Halsbury's Laws **or** go to your library to consult the print version.

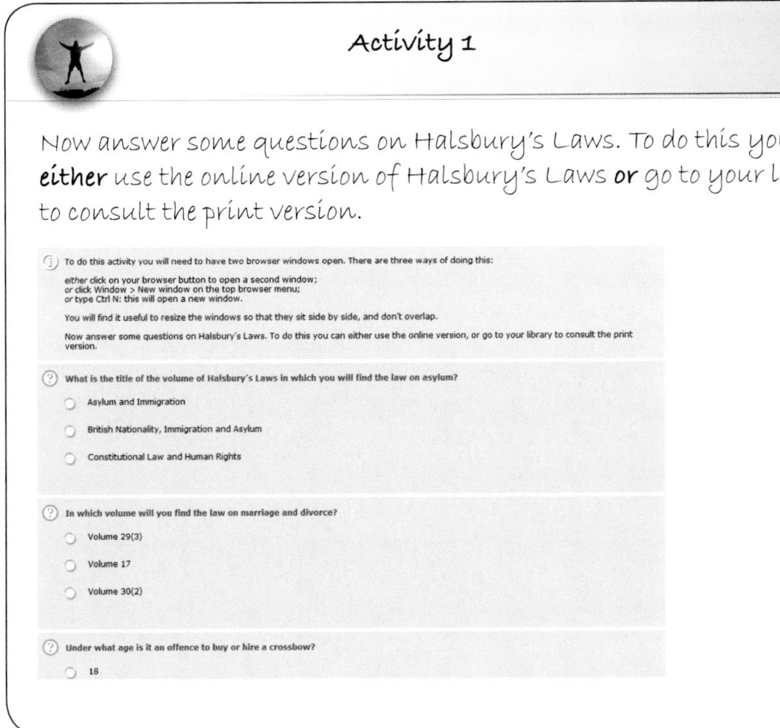

To do this activity you will need to have two browser windows open. There are three ways of doing this:

either click on your browser button to open a second window;
or click Window > New window on the top browser menu;
or type Ctrl N: this will open a new window.

You will find it useful to resize the windows so that they sit side by side, and don't overlap.

Now answer some questions on Halsbury's Laws. To do this you can either use the online version, or go to your library to consult the print version.

What is the title of the volume of Halsbury's Laws in which you will find the law on asylum?

- Asylum and Immigration
- British Nationality, Immigration and Asylum
- Constitutional Law and Human Rights

In which volume will you find the law on marriage and divorce?

- Volume 29(3)
- Volume 17
- Volume 30(2)

Under what age is it an offence to buy or hire a crossbow?

- 18

The Laws of Scotland

This is the Scottish equivalent of Halsbury's Laws, also known as the *Stair Memorial Encyclopaedia*. You will find it in any Scottish university library, and in any large English one as well.

Halsbury's Laws is the best way into the law on any topic.

Other encyclopaedias

» glossary

Encyclopaedias covering one area of the law are a distinctive form of legal publication. How many of these you have access to in print will depend on the size of your library, but some are also available in Westlaw and LNB, flagged as 'practice areas' or 'commentary'. Many of them are known familiarly by the name of the author.

Cross reference
See chapter 12, Using a Law Library, for a description of how law books are named.

There are dozens of these legal encyclopaedias, but these are a few examples:

- Harvey on Industrial Relations Law (always known as 'Harvey')
- Encyclopaedia of Planning Law
- Hill & Redman: The Law of Landlord & Tenant (always known as 'Hill & Redman')
- Woodfall – Landlord and Tenant (always known as 'Woodfall').

You will notice that we have two examples of Landlord and Tenant encyclopaedias. This is another characteristic of these works: there are nearly always two covering the same subject area. This is because historically there were two major legal publishers competing with each other.

The usefulness of these encyclopaedias is that they cover a specific area of the law and include all the legislation, important case law, and commentary on the law by experts. They are also a valuable source for regulatory information (codes of practice, etc.) which can otherwise be difficult to find.

Both Westlaw and LNB have versions of specialist encyclopaedias online, flagged as 'commentary'. What is available to you will depend on your institutional subscription.

Key Point

Legal encyclopaedias are often a short cut for finding resources in a specialist subject area, and a particularly good source for regulatory information.

Dictionaries

» glossary

A law dictionary is part of the basic equipment of any law student. In addition, it is useful to have an English dictionary at your side when you are writing essays or any other assessment. Online dictionaries can be a useful additional resource.

Law dictionaries

A law dictionary gives the specialised legal definitions of words and phrases. Because these definitions often differ from the common English language usage, you need to be sure you are using them correctly. Compare these examples from the Concise Oxford Dictionary and the Oxford Dictionary of Law.

Word	Concise Oxford Dictionary definition	Oxford Dictionary of Law definition
Possession	**Possession** *n.* **1.** the state of possessing something. • *(Law)* visible power or control, as distinct from lawful ownership. • (in soccer, rugby, and other ball games) temporary control of the ball by a player or team. **2.** a thing owned or possessed. • a territory or country controlled or governed by another. **3.** the state of being possessed by a demon, emotion, etc.	**Possession** *n.* **1.** Actual control of property combined with the intention to use it, rightly or wrongly, as one's own. In the case of land, possession may be actual, when the owner has entered onto the land, or possession in law, when he has the right to enter but has not yet done so. Possession includes receipt of rent and profits, or the right to receive them. See also **quiet possession**.
Impossibility	**Impossible** *adj.* not able to occur, exist, or be done. • very difficult to deal with. DERIVATIVES **impossibility** *n.* (pl. **impossibilities**). **impossibly** *adv.*	**Impossibility** *n.* A **general defence** that arises when compliance with the criminal law is physically impossible. This is most likely to arise in the context of crimes of omission. Thus one cannot be found guilty of failing to report a road traffic accident of which one was unaware. However, under the Criminal Attempts Act 1981 one may be convicted of attempting the impossible (see **attempt**).
Highway	**Highway** *n.* *(chiefly N. Amer.)* a main road. • (chiefly in official use) a public road.	**Highway** *n.* A road or other way over which the public may pass and repass as of right. Highways include **footpaths**, **bridleways**, **driftways**, **carriageways**, and cul-de-sacs. Navigable rivers are also highways. A highway is created either under statutory powers or by dedication (express or implied) by a landowner and acceptance (by use) by the public. Once a highway has been created, it does not cease to be a highway by reason of disuse. Obstructing a highway is a public nuisance (see also **obstruction**), and misuse of the public right to pass and repass over a highway is a trespass against the owner of the subsoil of the highway.

There are several good basic law dictionaries aimed at students, including the Oxford Dictionary of Law, Osborn's Concise Law Dictionary, and The Law Student's Dictionary.

From time to time you may want to look at one of the major multi-volume dictionaries which you will find in your library.

Multilingual dictionaries

If you are following a course in the law of another country, you may want to use a bilingual law dictionary as well as a regular bilingual dictionary.

Dictionaries of English

↳ **Cross reference**
See Chapter 3, Writing good English.

A standard dictionary of English is always useful to have at hand. In chapter 3, Writing good English, we saw how commonly words are confused, and it is useful to get into the habit of checking anything you may have doubts about, and also to check words which you come across in your reading and whose meaning you are unsure of.

The Oxford dictionaries are probably the best-known series (http://www.askoxford.com/shoponline/dicts/). Ranging from the mini to the Concise to the magisterial multi-volume OED (Oxford English Dictionary), they have always held the lead in reputation. However, there are a number of other mid-range dictionaries which are equally useful for the student user, such as the Cambridge, or Chambers dictionaries.

Online dictionaries

There are many options for using dictionaries online. There are some free sites for law dictionaries, but these should be used with caution, as the dictionaries tend to be American, and therefore the terminology will be misleading. Your university will probably have access to one or more of the online subscriptions services which include legal dictionaries, such as Oxford Reference Online (which includes the Oxford Dictionary of Law), or Cambridge Dictionaries Online. The OED comes in an online edition which your institution may subscribe to. If so, this is a wonderful resource.

Key Point

Always have a dictionary at hand and look up words and phrases if you are uncertain as to their meaning.

Judicial interpretation of words and phrases

The judicial interpretation of the law often depends on the meaning of words or phrases. There are several major dictionaries which include judicial and statutory definitions, one or more of which you will probably find in your library: Stroud's Judicial Dictionary, Words and Phrases Judicially Defined, Jowitt's Dictionary of English Law.

Halsbury's Laws also includes judicial and statutory definitions words and phrases, and you can search online for these by entering the search "words and phrases" (making sure you use the double " ").

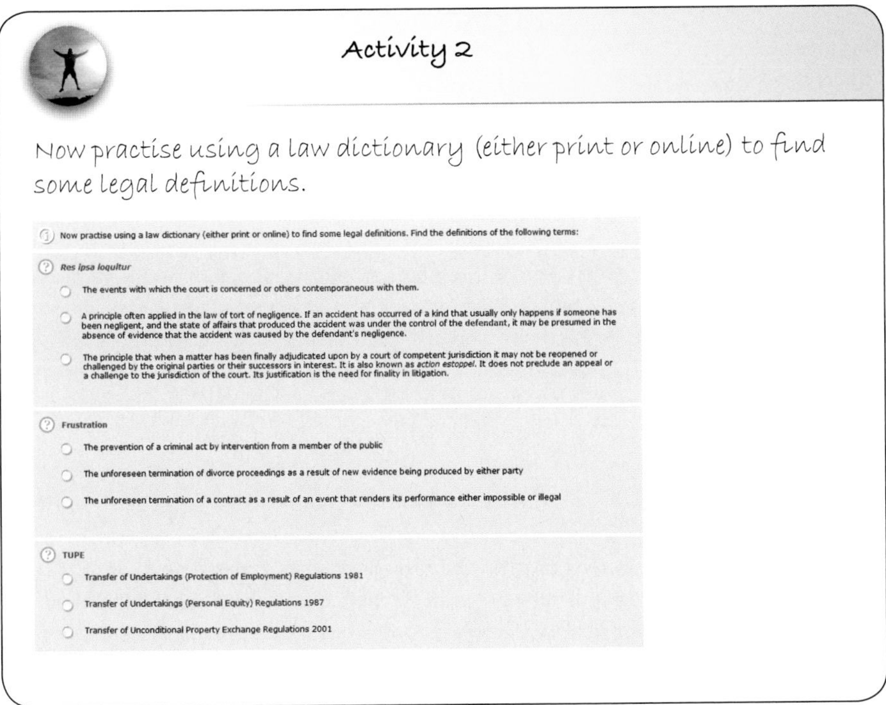

Activity 2

Now practise using a law dictionary (either print or online) to find some legal definitions.

Now practise using a law dictionary (either print or online) to find some legal definitions. Find the definitions of the following terms:

Res ipsa loquitur

- The events with which the court is concerned or others contemporaneous with them.
- A principle often applied in the law of tort of negligence. If an accident has occurred of a kind that usually only happens if someone has been negligent, and the state of affairs that produced the accident was under the control of the defendant, it may be presumed in the absence of evidence that the accident was caused by the defendant's negligence.
- The principle that when a matter has been finally adjudicated upon by a court of competent jurisdiction it may not be reopened or challenged by the original parties or their successors in interest. It is also known as *action estoppel*. It does not preclude an appeal or a challenge to the jurisdiction of the court. Its justification is the need for finality in litigation.

Frustration

- The prevention of a criminal act by intervention from a member of the public
- The unforeseen termination of divorce proceedings as a result of new evidence being produced by either party
- The unforeseen termination of a contract as a result of an event that renders its performance either impossible or illegal

TUPE

- Transfer of Undertakings (Protection of Employment) Regulations 1981
- Transfer of Undertakings (Personal Equity) Regulations 1987
- Transfer of Unconditional Property Exchange Regulations 2001

Legal indexes and digests

Printed legal indexes used to be the backbone of legal research, though they have now been largely superseded by the major online services. One peculiarity of legal reference works is that there are usually two publications doing much the same thing. As with legal encyclopaedias, this is because historically there have been two major legal publishers, and, of course, they both needed to provide the full panoply of legal reference materials. Therefore, we will look at these in pairs.

Halsbury's Statutes and Current Law Statutes

These are the two major encyclopaedias of statutes, which give you the text of legislation with annotations and commentary. Although research in legislation has been largely superseded by online services, these printed works can sometimes be a quicker and more efficient way of finding out the information.

Halsbury's Statutes is the one most often consulted. It contains the consolidated text of each Act (i.e. with repealed sections omitted and amendments inserted) with copious annotations which include judicial interpretation, leading cases and amendments and repeals in subsequent legislation. It is arranged by subject, so an Act may be divided between more than one volume (e.g. the Police and Criminal Evidence Act 1984 is spread over the volumes Criminal Law, Evidence, and Police).

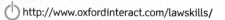

Halsbury's Statutes is updated with an annual Cumulative Supplement and a Noter-Up. Halsbury's Statutes is clearly a sister publication to Halsbury's Laws of England, described above, but the two publications should not be confused. The Halsbury's annotations are also on LexisNexis Butterworths.

» glossary

Current Law Statutes is not so commonly used. It is arranged chronologically. It has a unique feature, however, which is well worth knowing about. The annotations to each Act gives the pre-legislative information and the genesis of the Act. Here you have information about the Green Papers and White Papers which preceded the Act, Law Commission reports, the debates in Parliament, and the political process which led to the making of the Act. This analysis is not on Westlaw.

Current Law and The Digest

» glossary

'Digesting' the law is a peculiarly legal activity. The term has somewhat fallen out of use, because the work is now mostly done online rather than through an elaborate referencing system. It involves the whole process of analysing cases by finding them in the appropriate subject index, and identifying the case law and legislation cited, the history of the case, and its citation in later cases. This intricate research is carried out very easily online on the main services.

The two principal printed sources are **Current Law** and **The Digest**. The Current Law information is incorporated into Westlaw, and the Digest into LNB.

Works on civil and criminal procedure

There are numerous practitioners' works which you may well use as a student at some point, though probably not in your first year.

Forms and Precedents

» glossary

The **Encyclopaedia of Forms and Precedents** (EF & P) is a multi-volume work containing all the forms and precedents required by lawyers for drafting, arranged by subject. EF & P does not cover litigation, for which you need **Atkin's Court Forms**.

Practice books

» glossary

The Civil Procedure Rules (CPR) lay down all the rules for procedure in the civil courts. They are continually updated, and available on the Ministry of Justice website as well as in a hard copy loose-leaf format. They have replaced works known as 'the White Book' (Supreme Court

Practice) and 'the Green Book' (County Court Practice) – you may still come across references to these in your reading.

Archbold Criminal Pleading and **Blackstone's Criminal Practice** are the main works for criminal procedure. Archbold is available online on Westlaw.

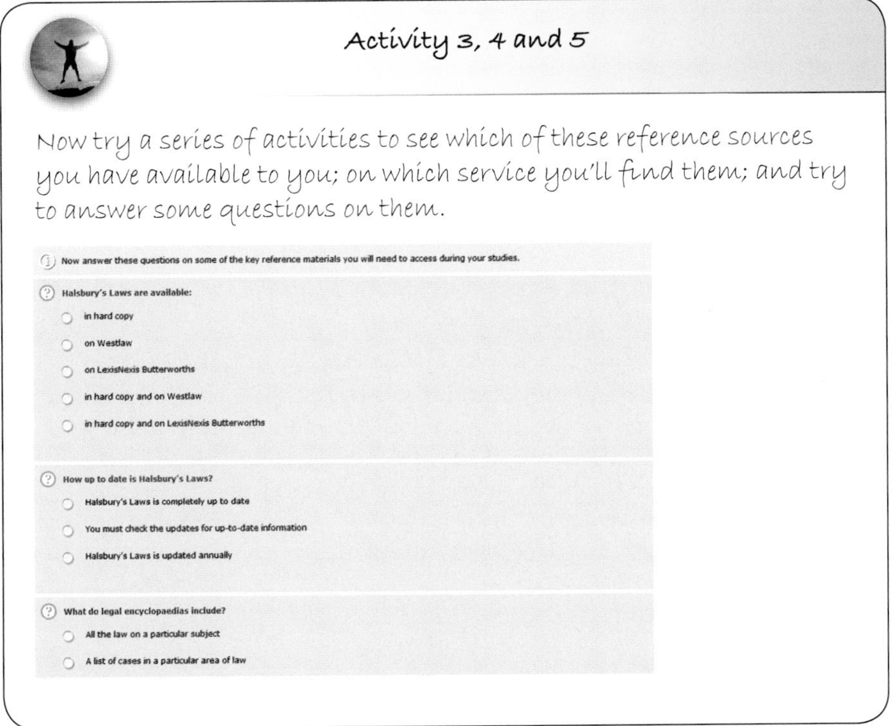

Activity 3, 4 and 5

Now try a series of activities to see which of these reference sources you have available to you; on which service you'll find them; and try to answer some questions on them.

Now answer these questions on some of the key reference materials you will need to access during your studies.

Halsbury's Laws are available:

- in hard copy
- on Westlaw
- on LexisNexis Butterworths
- in hard copy and on Westlaw
- in hard copy and on LexisNexis Butterworths

How up to date is Halsbury's Laws?

- Halsbury's Laws is completely up to date
- You must check the updates for up-to-date information
- Halsbury's Laws is updated annually

What do legal encyclopaedias include?

- All the law on a particular subject
- A list of cases in a particular area of law

Other reference materials

In addition to these legal works, there is a huge range of non-legal encyclopaedias and other reference works which you may well want to consult during your time as a student. Works such as the **Encyclopaedia of Philosophy** and the **International Encyclopaedia of the Social Sciences** will be helpful in finding articles on more theoretical concepts related to jurisprudence. Look in the reference sections of your library to see what works of this kind you have available, and check your online resources to see what is available online.

Online reference materials

Most people, when faced with finding out about a topic, will type the search into Google, and will probably end up with an article on Wikipedia. While it is very useful for quick reference, you should always cross-check with a legal authority, such as the ones described above. As Wikipedia can be edited by anyone, there is no guarantee that the material is entirely accurate. Certainly, it will not be accepted as a source for any essay or assessment you write, unless the information is backed up with an authoritative legal source.

Cross reference Chapter 7, Avoiding plagiarism, will give you further guidance on this.

Having said that, an internet search will dig up a lot of useful information, and provided you are scrupulous about checking the source and acknowledging it, you can use it as an additional source of reference.

Key Point

Wikipedia should not be used as a reference source. There is a danger that if you use material from Wikipedia it may be inaccurate and you may inadvertently be plagiarising.

Conclusion

In this chapter we have concentrated on the major legal reference works. Explore them and use them, and your work will gain in accuracy and authority.

Links

Oxford dictionaries http://www.askoxford.com/shoponline/dicts/

Oxford English Dictionary http://www.oed.com/

Oxford Reference Online http://www.oxfordreference.com/

www.oxfordinteract.com

» Part 3 Legal method skills «

Part 3

Legal method

www.oxfordinteract.com

Chapter 19

Reading statutes and the legislative process

Rationale

Statutes or Acts of Parliament are probably your most important tool of trade as a lawyer. Moreover, as society becomes increasingly complex and regulated, their significance is increasing. Many answers to the questions we get asked as lawyers, whether as students, practitioners or academics, are contained within statutes. There is nothing mysterious about reading statutes but it is useful if you understand the problem that the statute is designed to address, are familiar with statutory structure and language, and practise reading statutes.

This chapter is devised to:

- Outline the ways in which a statute comes into force and help you locate the policy discussions which have informed the statute
- Help you locate up-to-date statutes
- Describe the structure of a statute and give examples of statutory language
- Give examples of statutory material with exercises so that you can check your understanding.

The life cycle of a statute

An outline

Statutes start life as bills. There are two main types of bill – public and private, and also a hybrid type.

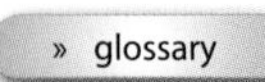

- Public bills relate to matters of public policy, and are introduced directly by members of Parliament. Ones which are introduced by members of the government are known as government bills. Others are introduced by individual MPs, and are referred to as Private Members' bills (NB: don't confuse these with private bills). Government bills usually have explanatory notes attached, which are useful for finding out the background to the proposed legislation. Amendments are also published on the web.

» glossary

» glossary

- Private bills relate to individuals, groups of individuals, public corporations or specific places, and their application is limited to those people or places. There are around 20 a year.

» glossary

- Hybrid bills are public bills which may affect the private rights of people or bodies. An example of a hybrid bill is the Channel Tunnel Rail Link Bill 1994.

Example

You can see the bills before Parliament at http://www.publications.parliament.uk/pa/pabills.htm

The House of Commons produces a useful series of Factsheets which you can find at http://www.parliament.uk/parliamentary_publications_and_archives/factsheets.cfm

Remember that the final version of a bill may be quite different from its beginning, as it can be substantively amended on the way.

Most bills are government bills, which means they are sponsored by a government minister. The formal process starts when the bill is presented to Parliament by the minister responsible for it. This is known as the first reading. The bill is then published, and at the same time the government also publishes explanatory notes to the bill. These provide an invaluable source of information for people trying to understand the clauses of the bill. You can find bills and explanatory notes on http://www.publications.parliament.uk (the parliamentary website).

There are a series of readings, committee scrutiny and debates on the bill. The bill is amended and republished at various stages throughout the process. Eventually the bill, if it does not fail, receives the **Royal Assent** which marks its transformation into an Act of Parliament. Acts of Parliament are published very quickly after Royal Assent on the HMSO website.

» glossary

Even after the Act receives the Royal Assent there is often a long delay before sections are brought into effect. We have provided you with advice on how to find out the implementation date of particular sections of statutes further on in this chapter.

Cross reference
See 'Finding implementation dates' on p. 262.

From bill to Act – the passage of a bill through Parliament

A bill may be introduced in the House of Commons or the **House of Lords**. The procedure is more or less the same in each House. This is the procedure for a government bill, which is introduced into the House of Commons.

» glossary

The bill is introduced to the House of Commons

The **First Reading** of a bill is a formality. Once formally presented to the House, the bill is printed, and proceeds to the second reading

In the **Second Reading** the minister proposes the bill, and there is a debate on the main principles of the legislation.

» glossary

The bill then proceeds to the committee stage. The bill is referred to a **Public Bill Committee** (formerly known as a **Standing Committee**), where the bill is considered in detail, clause by clause, and amendments may be made. Occasionally the whole House sits as a Committee. This is known as a **Committee of the Whole House**, and is used for bills of national constitutional importance, bills requiring very rapid passage, and Finance Bills.

The bill then returns to the full House for the **Report Stage**, where the amendments are debated. Further amendments may be made at this stage.

This is followed by the **Third Reading**, which is an overview of the bill. No substantive amendments may be made at this stage.

When a bill has completed all its stages in the House in which it was introduced, it is referred to the other House.

It then goes through the same stages as in the first House, and further amendments may be made.

Amendments must be agreed by both Houses, and a bill may go to and fro to each House several times until agreement is reached. When agreement has been reached, the bill receives the Royal Assent, and becomes an Act of Parliament.

If no agreement can be reached, the Commons may invoke the Parliament Acts, and the bill is passed in the following session of Parliament without the consent of the Lords. This happens only rarely (an example was the European Parliamentary Elections Bill in 1998).

When agreement has been reached, the bill receives the Royal Assent, and becomes an Act of Parliament.

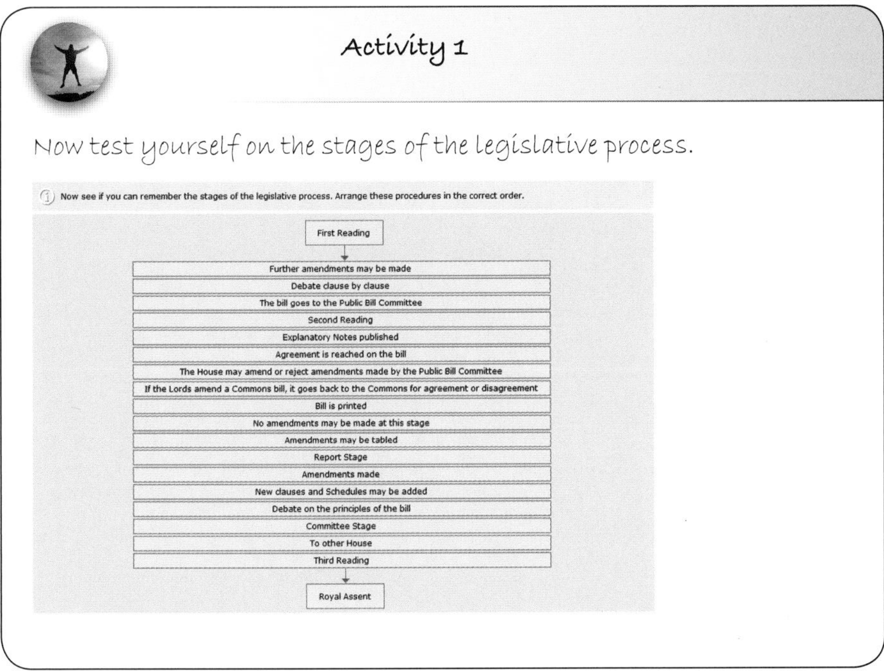

Consultation

The origins of legislation are far-reaching, and are a response to party policy, expert lobbying and public opinion. Moreover, parliamentary time is a scarce and expensive resource. This means that there must be significant political commitment to an idea even before it becomes a bill. There are a number of mechanisms designed to ensure that there is sufficient discussion of the subject matter of a bill before it gets to Parliament. Sometimes the government will publish a **Green Paper** which sets out proposals to change the law and ask for comments. Green Papers are so called because in the past they were published with green covers. Following this consultation process the government may set out its revised policy objectives in a **White Paper**. You will not be surprised to learn that the name derives from the fact that originally White Papers were published with white covers. More recently government has started to publish some bills in draft form before they are introduced into Parliament as formal bills. This enables consultation and pre-legislative scrutiny before the parliamentary process begins which should mean that amendments to the draft can be considered more carefully. The Mental Capacity Act 2005 is an example of a piece of legislation which was originally published as a draft bill and was extensively debated prior to its introduction to Parliament.

» glossary

» glossary

One of the most important originators of legislation is the **Law Commission** http://www.lawcom.gov.uk/ which is the official law reform organisation. This looks at legislation in detail and makes recommendations for changes in the law.

» glossary

The Land Registration Act 2002, for example, originated from a joint project between HM Land Registry and the Law Commission which commenced in 1996. The initial proposals for reform were published in *Land Registration for the Twenty-First Century: A Consultative Document* in September 1998 and then amended following consultation. A final report and draft bill were published in *Land Registration for the Twenty-First Century: A Conveyancing Revolution* on 10 July. The joint report contains a detailed discussion of the policy behind the recommendations, a draft bill and full explanatory notes. To a great extent the final Act implemented the Law Commission and HM Land Registry proposals.

Cross reference
See more about Green Papers, White Papers and other official publications in chapter 13, Sources of law.

You can get full details of current draft bills at http://www.parliament.uk/business/bills_and_legislation/draft_bills.cfm

Activity 2

Now answer some questions on draft bill procedure.

Now answer some questions on the draft bill procedure.

In what circumstances is a government likely to use the draft bill procedure?

- Legislation required to enact a government's manifesto proposals
- Politically controversial legislation
- Legislation which requires broad policy consultation
- Legislation designed to consolidate and update existing law

What types of proposed legislation are best suited to detailed consideration by the Law Commission?

- Legislation required to enact a government's manifesto proposals
- Politically controversial legislation
- Legislation which requires broad policy consultation
- Legislation designed to consolidate and update existing law

Not all bills are subject to detailed consideration and consultation. Sometimes a bill contains proposals which are so politically significant that the government's imperative is to get the bill enacted quickly and with minimum amendments. Many bills sponsored by the Home Office fall into this category. Sometimes there is a public outcry about an issue, and the government is forced to act by public opinion. One example of a hurried response to a particular problem is the Dangerous Dogs Act 1991.

Cross reference
For further details on Private Members' bills see the factsheet L2 Private Members' Bills Procedures published on the Parliament website http://www.parliament.uk/documents/upload/l02.pdf.

A significant number of Acts start life as Private Members' bills, for instance the Homeless Persons Act 1977.

Drafting bills

Bills are drafted by **Parliamentary draftsmen** who are lawyers with professional qualifications who have received specialist training. Parliamentary draftsmen are generally instructed by government lawyers who attempt to achieve the policy objectives which other civil servants and politicians have formulated. Drafting a bill is a difficult process, and even before the bill reaches Parliament it is likely to have been through a number of versions as the lawyers discuss the best ways to achieve what the government wants. Drafting is made more difficult in the later stages of the parliamentary process where amendments may be agreed overly hastily in order to ensure that a bill survives.

Bills are drafted in **clauses** which are numbered. If you wish to discuss a bill in your work, you should refer to clause numbers. Clause numbers change with each publication of the bill – so don't forget to state which version of the bill you are working from.

Parliamentary debate

When MPs debate a bill they frequently explain, or challenge the meaning of its clauses and/or criticise the political objectives. This means that their debates are a very useful source of information and critical opinion on a legislative measure. Debates are recorded in Hansard which can be found at http://www.publications.parliament.uk/pa/cm/cmhansrd.htm

» glossary

Hansard is the edited verbatim report of proceedings in both Houses. It is also known as the Official Report. Commons Hansard covers proceedings in the Commons Chamber, Westminster Hall and Standing Committees. Lords Hansard covers proceedings in the Lords Chamber and its Grand Committees. Both contain Written Ministerial Statements and Written Answers. Daily Debates are published on this website the next working day at 8 am.

Key Point

Hansard is the daily record of the debates in both houses of Parliament. It is published on the Parliament site. You can read the verbatim account of speeches in the House of Commons and House of Lords the following day, and there is an archive going back to 1988. The web version follows the terminology and format of the printed version (which you may have in your library), which refers to 'columns' rather than pages, and 'bound volumes' for the annual cumulations.

There is also Hansard for Standing Committee debates, including Standing Committee debates on bills.

If you are looking for a clear explanation of a bill, it is much better to search Hansard for the debates held during the second reading rather than the first reading, which is a very abbreviated parliamentary process. Moreover, debates at the committee stage in the House of Lords are far more useful to outsiders than the much more party political discussions which take place in the House of Commons.

Activity 3

Think about what you have just read and jot down the various sources of information about bills going through Parliament. Work out how useful these sources are likely to be.

Go online to read our thoughts on this and to see which other sources you should consider.

Finding implementation dates

The date an Act comes into force is contained within the commencement provisions, which are contained in the last or penultimate section of the Act. In the absence of specific commencement provisions, the Act comes into force as soon as it has received the Royal Assent. Otherwise, there are several different ways in which an Act may be brought into force:

- A date for implementation may be contained within the Act's commencement provisions.
- A period (e.g. three months) may be given until the Act is implemented, the actual date depending on the date of the Royal Assent.
- The Act may indicate that it will come into force on a date to be appointed by the Secretary of State, or another official.
- The Act may specify different implementation dates for different parts of the Act, or for different jurisdictions (Wales, Scotland, etc.).

The implementation dates are specified in Statutory Instruments known as Commencement Orders.

» glossary

The dates at which an Act is brought into force can be extremely complicated, and when you are applying an Act it is obviously crucial to know whether a particular section is in force or not. Moreover, the dates may be set and subsequently changed by later Commencement Orders. Some legislation depends on a complex regulatory infrastructure which is mostly specified by means of delegated legislation. Variable implementation of a statute is a way of ensuring that the regulatory framework is in place before the Act comes fully into force.

A good example of this is the Mental Capacity Act 2005. This is s. 68, the commencement provisions:

> **68 Commencement and extent**
>
> (1) This Act, other than sections 30 to 41, comes into force in accordance with provision made by order by the Lord Chancellor.
>
> (2) Sections 30 to 41 come into force in accordance with provision made by order by—
>
> (a) the Secretary of State, in relation to England, and
>
> (b) the National Assembly for Wales, in relation to Wales.
>
> (3) An order under this section may appoint different days for different provisions and different purposes.
>
> (4) Subject to subsections (5) and (6), this Act extends to England and Wales only.
>
> (5) The following provisions extend to the United Kingdom—
>
> (a) paragraph 16(1) of Schedule 1 (evidence of instruments and of registration of lasting powers of attorney),
>
> (b) paragraph 15(3) of Schedule 4 (evidence of instruments and of registration of enduring powers of attorney).
>
> (6) Subject to any provision made in Schedule 6, the amendments and repeals made by Schedules 6 and 7 have the same extent as the enactments to which they relate

This only tells you what provisions will be made for implementation. You then have to find out the detail, which is contained in the Commencement Orders.

You can find these quite easily on Westlaw or LexisNexis Butterworths, which have links to the commencement SIs, and on the Statute Law Database, which contains the commencement SIs in the Table of Legislative Effects. LNB, in addition, has a separate database called *Is It In Force?* You will not, however, find this information on the Acts of Parliament website (OPSI), which only has the text of the Act as passed.

» glossary

» abbreviation

Westlaw links to the commencement SIs from its *Legislation Analysis* under s. 68.

LexisNexis Butterworths links to the commencement SIs from s. 68. You can also link to *Is It In Force?* From the 'next steps' drop down menu: this gives the commencement provisions in tabular form.

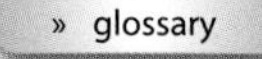

Justis links to the commencement SIs through its sister service called **JustCite.** There is an automatic link to JustCite from the legislation on Justis.

The **Statute Law Database** links to the commencement SIs on its *Table of Legislative Effects*. You have to specify the year of the affecting legislation, so you need to do separate searches for the 2006 and 2007 SIs.

Activity 4

The next activity asks you to do some research on implementation dates using the Mental Capacity Act 2005.

Now do some research on implementation dates using the Mental Capacity Act 2005. For this activity you can use any of the databases we have discussed in the text. Read the statements below and match the sections to the date they were enforced.

- Sections 5–29 of the Act came into force on...
- Sections 30–34 of the Act (for the purposes of enabling applications in relation to research to be made...) came into force on...
- Sections 35–41 of the Act (for the purposes of enabling the Secretary of State to make arrangements under s 35 of the Act in accordance with the Mental Capacity Act 2005 (independent Mental Capacity Advocates) (General) Regulations 2006) came into force on...
- Section 44 of the Act came into force on...

1 November 2006
1 April 2007
1 October 2007
1 July 2007

Amendments and repeals

Once enacted, statutes can be and frequently are altered, a process known as **amendment**. Primary legislation can only be altered by another statute; otherwise it would be easy for the government to subvert the will of Parliament. There are a number of reasons why Parliament might want to amend a statute. First of all, when the courts interpret a statute, the meaning that they decide it has may be different from the meaning that Parliament had intended. We explain judicial interpretation of statutes in the next chapter. Parliament may well then pass legislation to amend the initial statute. Secondly, Parliament may decide to implement legislation which introduces new terms or procedures. Previous statutes may require amendment to make them consistent with the new provisions. Of course, a new set of provisions may render old statutes obsolete. In these circumstances the new legislation **repeals** the old legislation.

» glossary

Sometimes legislation becomes obsolete through the passage of time. For example, there is no longer a need to have legislation levying taxes on cargo ships using the port of Sunderland, those taxes being used to support the poor of that town. We now have a national system of welfare support. See http://www.lawcom.gov.uk/docs/background_notes.pdf (link to an interview with the head of the statute law reform team) for an explanation of the work of the statutory law reform team at the Law Commission which focuses on modernising the law through the repeal of obsolete legislation.

Cross reference
See chapter 20, Understanding judicial interpretation of statutes.

Looking at a statute

The list below explains the different parts of a statute. Go online for a visual representation of where these would appear in a statute:

Title *The official name of the Act, sometimes called the Short Title. Acts also have long titles, and the use of a short title was only established at the end of the 19th century*

Chapter number *The chapter number is the number of an Act in any year. It is abbreviated to c. or sometimes ch.*

» glossary

Headings *These are headings which subdivide the sections by topic. Some Acts are divided into Part I, Part II, Part III etc.*

Sections *Sections are numbered consecutively through the Act. They are abbreviated to s. (or ss. in the plural). Sections are subdivided into subsections.*

Section 3 subsection 4 of this Act would be cited Animal Welfare Act 2006 s. 3(4).

There are 69 sections in this Act. The last section usually contains provisions for the Commencement of the Act (the date it comes into force) and the Extent (whether it applies to the UK, or to its constituent jurisdictions, in whole or in part).

Long Title *The Long Title sets out in detail the purpose of the Act.*

Royal Assent *Date of Royal Assent.*

NB: this does not indicate the date of coming into force (known as the Commencement date) which may vary considerably from this, and which is contained in the penultimate section of the Act.

Schedules *Appended to the Act are the Schedules. These contain matters of detail such as amendments to existing legislation consequent on the Act, forms, procedural rules, tables of fees, etc.*

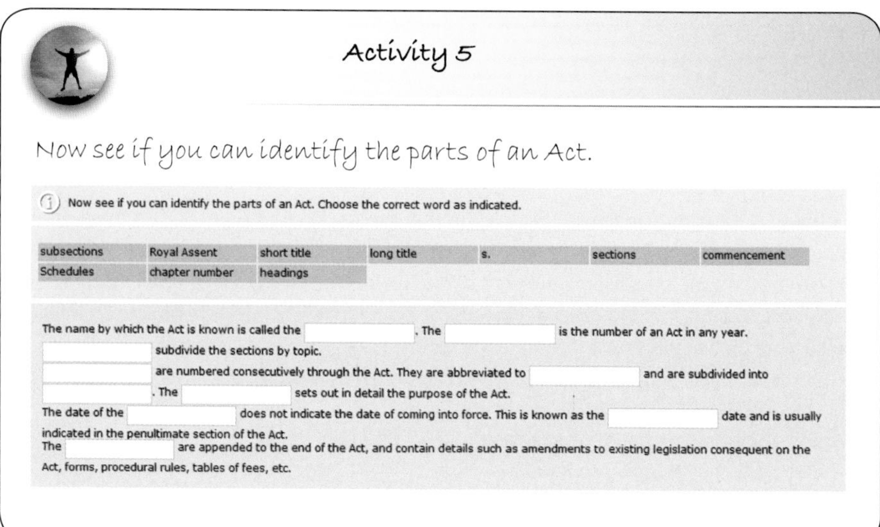

Activity 5

Now see if you can identify the parts of an Act.

Now see if you can identify the parts of an Act. Choose the correct word as indicated.

subsections	Royal Assent	short title	long title	s.	sections	commencement
Schedules	chapter number	headings				

The name by which the Act is known is called the ______. The ______ is the number of an Act in any year.
______ subdivide the sections by topic.
______ are numbered consecutively through the Act. They are abbreviated to ______ and are subdivided into ______. The ______ sets out in detail the purpose of the Act.
The date of the ______ does not indicate the date of coming into force. This is known as the ______ date and is usually indicated in the penultimate section of the Act.
The ______ are appended to the end of the Act, and contain details such as amendments to existing legislation consequent on the Act, forms, procedural rules, tables of fees, etc.

Delegated legislation

No matter how long Parliament sits, it still will not be able to pass sufficient legislation in the detail that the running of a sophisticated democracy requires. Moreover, as we have already discussed, the procedure of amendment is as longwinded as the procedures for enacting the initial legislation. Therefore it is sensible to put provisions which will require frequent updating in a form which can be changed more easily. You will find, in most Acts of Parliament, a power for delegated legislation which provides a solution to both of these problems. We look at a power to provide delegated legislation when we consider the legislation banning smoking in public places below.

Delegated legislation, as its name implies, gives the power to some person or body to pass legislation that has the same effect as if it had been passed by Parliament through its normal process of legislation. For the delegated legislation to come into force, it is normally 'laid before Parliament'. This requires a copy of the proposed delegated legislation to be placed (or laid) in the House of Commons and the House of Lords for a specified number of days. After that, the legislation comes into force. It may require a vote without a debate, or alternatively may come into effect by 'negative resolution'. This means it will come into force unless sufficient members of Parliament put their names down so as to require a vote to be taken. There is a constitutional issue here. The power in a statute must not be so wide as to enable government to defeat the intention of Parliament. A great deal of attention is paid in Parliament to clauses in bills which delegate powers to ministers to avoid this consequence.

Statutory Instruments

Most delegated legislation is in the form of Statutory Instruments (SIs), which are regulations and orders made under the authority of a statute, known as the enabling Act.

- Many Statutory Instruments lay out the rules and regulations for the detailed application of an Act.
- Many are purely local in application, or may be in force for only a brief period.
- Some provide for the commencement of a statute – i.e. they give details on when and how the statute will be brought into force.

Other subordinate legislation

There are many other regulations such as Codes of Practice, Rules, Orders and Circulars which are issued by departments or professional bodies with the authority to do so. You can usually find them on the government department or organisation's website.

Guidance

In certain areas of law, especially social services and social welfare law, government gives extensive guidance on the implementation of legislation. The status of guidance can be confusing. Guidance does not have the full force of a statute, but it must be followed unless there are justifiable reasons for not doing so. On the other hand following guidance does not guarantee that the person or organisation is acting within the law. Guidance issued by a government department will always only amount to a view of what the department thinks the law is. It is perhaps the clearest expression of the government's wish as to what the law should mean. However, it remains the function of the court to actually decide what legislation means. We discuss the court's role in interpreting statutes and the 'rules' it uses in doing this in the next chapter.

↳ **Cross reference**
See chapter 20, Understanding judicial interpretation of statutes.

Orders in Council

Where the enabling power is delegated to the Crown, the subordinate legislation is made by the Privy Council. Most, but not all, are in the form of SIs, and are known as Orders in Council. You can find out more about these from the Privy Council website http://www.privy-council.org.uk/

» glossary

Devolution

» glossary

Devolution in the UK involves the transfer of some legislative power from Parliament to Scotland, Northern Ireland and Wales. The legislative basis for devolution is set out in the Scotland Act 1998, the Government of Wales Act 1998 and the Northern Ireland Act 1998. There is also a non-legislative framework of agreements between government departments and the devolved institutions. Certain areas of responsibility are devolved, i.e. have been passed to the new political bodies, while other matters are reserved for the UK Parliament. The devolution of power differs between Scotland, Northern Ireland and Wales, and you should also note that pressure for further devolution of power continues. The consequences of devolution are that in some areas (university fees being an example) there are different policies in the different parts of the UK.

You will look at devolution in the course of your public law/constitutional and administrative law course. For full details at this stage you should look at the relevant websites.

The Northern Ireland Assembly

The Assembly is the prime source of authority for all devolved responsibilities and has full legislative and executive authority. Its website is http://www.niassembly.gov.uk/

National Assembly for Wales

The Assembly is a devolved body that decides on its priorities and allocates the funds made available to it by the UK Government. Powers devolved to the Assembly include health, education, economic development, planning and culture. Within its powers, the Assembly develops policy and passes legislation affecting the people of Wales. Its website is http://www.wales.gov.uk/

The Scottish Parliament

The Scottish Parliament powers include education, health and prisons. Its website is http://www.scottish.parliament.uk/, and you can find a description of its powers on http://www.scottish.parliament.uk/corporate/powers/index.htm.

There is a very useful parliamentary research paper explaining the background and the institutional framework of devolution at http://www.parliament.uk/commons/lib/research/rp2003/rp03-084.pdf.

Statutes as lawyers' tools

Reading statutes

↳ **Cross reference**
See chapter 13, Sources of law, to see details of the sources.

There are a number of sources for statutes, and you will find them in print in your law library as well as online. It is important that you read the fully amended up-to-date version of the statute. To do this you should use the official Statute Law Database, or one of the commercial legal databases. Using these, you can see which sections of a particular statute are in force. Acts published on the OPSI website are not updated as they are amended.

You must be sure that you are using the latest version of a statute, including all the amendments.

Once you have located the statute you are looking for, and checked that it is in force, you must read the statute. We use the Human Rights Act 1998 to give you some guidance on reading a statute. In this case, we suggest that you look at the Act on the OPSI website http://www.opsi.gov.uk/acts/acts1998/19980042.htm, which is the version as passed by Parliament, without amendments.

The Human Rights Act 1998

The Human Rights Act 1998 is a hugely important statute that you will refer to constantly throughout your career as a lawyer. However, at this stage we are going to consider it simply as a typical example of a modern statute and provide you with a simple explanation of what you can see when you look at this statute on the OPSI website.

The year, 1998, is the year the Human Rights Act received Royal Assent. This was not the year the statute was implemented. The Human Rights Act, like many other statutes, contains complex provisions which need to be prepared for. In many cases delegated legislation has to be prepared and published. In the case of the Human Rights Act an extensive programme of training of the judiciary and public authorities had to be completed before the Act came into force.

The front cover of the statute has the royal coat of arms in the left-hand corner (which we are not allowed to reproduce), the name of the statute and the words 'Chapter 42'. What this refers to is that it is the 42nd statute of that particular parliamentary session. You can ignore the chapter number in reality. The front cover also contains a statement of crown copyright. You are allowed to reproduce free of charge the text of the Act, but not the Queen's printer imprints or the Royal Arms. You do not need to worry about copyright at this stage. If you are looking at a print version of the Act you will see a note to say that explanatory notes have been produced to assist in the understanding of this Act and are available separately. These can easily be found on the HMSO website.

If you scroll down the page you will see the contents of the Act. Many Acts are divided into parts and each part consists of a number of chapters. However, the Human Rights Act is a relatively short statute so there are neither parts nor chapters. The contents page provides you with a very useful navigation tool for the whole of the statute. If, for instance, you were looking to find out what judicial remedies are available to respond to breaches of the Human Rights Act you would see very quickly that you should be considering s. 8.

If you now scroll down to one of the sections of the Act, say s. 6, you can now see the typical layout for a section of an Act. The section has a heading, in this case 'public authorities'. It is then divided into subsections which are numbered in brackets. If you want to refer to a particular subsection then you should say 'section six subsection one'. If you are referring to this subsection in writing you would write s. 6(1). Now have a look at s. 22. Section 22(2) tells us that ss. 18, 20 and 21(5) and s. 22 come into force on the passing of the Act. Section 22(3) states that the other provisions of the Act come into force on such day as the Secretary of State may by order appoint; and different days may be appointed for different purposes. You will have to look at later commencement orders – i.e. secondary legislation to find out the relevant dates.

Schedules

Not everything is contained in the body of the statute. Most Acts have schedules attached which contain further material usually of a more detailed kind. The Human Rights Act has four schedules. They are listed beneath the contents of the Act. Schedules are set out slightly differently from the main body of the Act. If you turn to Schedule 2 you will see its title, 'Remedial Orders'. The Schedule is then set out in paragraphs and subparagraphs. If you wish to refer to a subparagraph within a schedule then you refer to it as 'paragraph 1(2) of Schedule 2 to the Act'. We say 'to' the Act rather than 'of' the Act because the Schedule is attached to the Act.

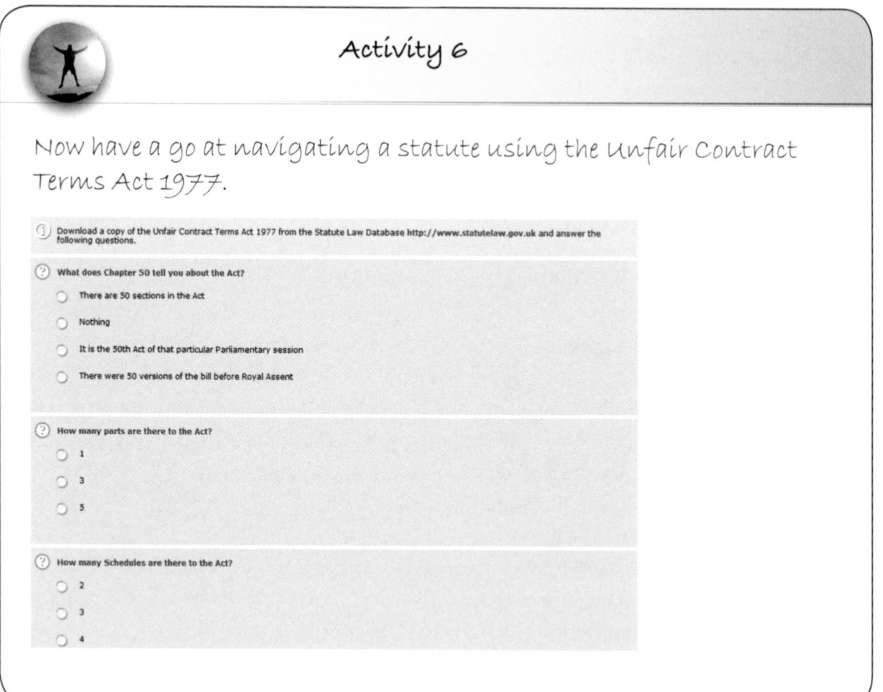

Activity 6
Now have a go at navigating a statute using the Unfair Contract Terms Act 1977.
Download a copy of the Unfair Contract Terms Act 1977 from the Statute Law Database http://www.statutelaw.gov.uk and answer the following questions.
What does Chapter 50 tell you about the Act?
There are 50 sections in the Act
Nothing
It is the 50th Act of that particular Parliamentary session
There were 50 versions of the bill before Royal Assent
How many parts are there to the Act?
1
3
5
How many Schedules are there to the Act?
2
3
4

Reading statutory provisions

So far, in this chapter, we have concentrated on the structure of a statute. It is very useful to understand how a statute is laid out, how to understand repeals and amendments and what you can expect to find in schedules. The next step is to practise reading some statutory provisions.

We will continue to use the Unfair Contract Terms Act 1977. What you will learn is that simply to understand one section of the Act, you need to refer to other parts of the legislation, and that you need to read and understand every word of a section.

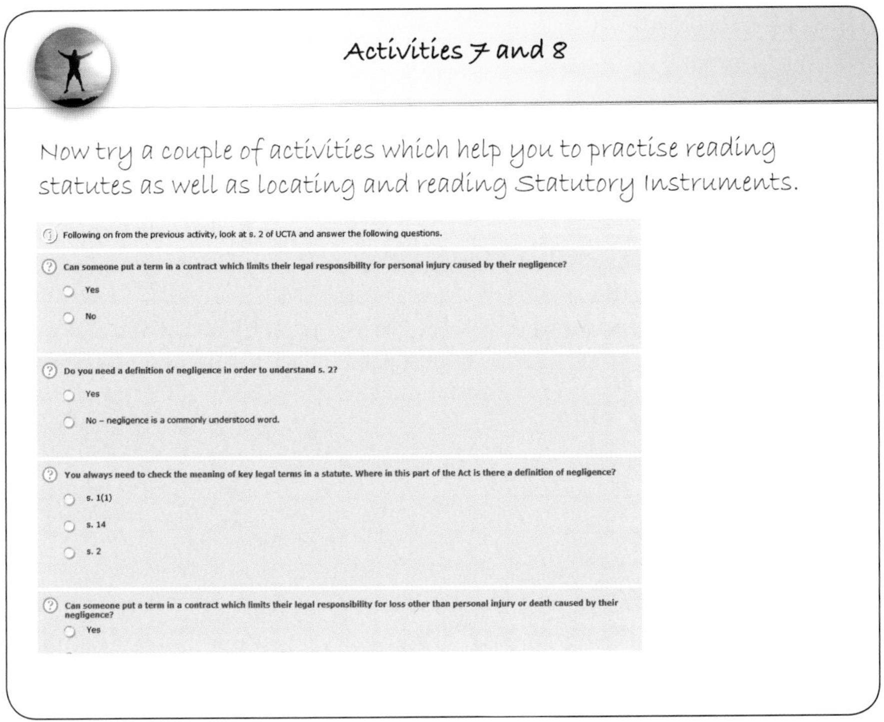

Activities 7 and 8

Now try a couple of activities which help you to practise reading statutes as well as locating and reading Statutory Instruments.

Following on from the previous activity, look at s. 2 of UCTA and answer the following questions.

Can someone put a term in a contract which limits their legal responsibility for personal injury caused by their negligence?

- Yes
- No

Do you need a definition of negligence in order to understand s. 2?

- Yes
- No – negligence is a commonly understood word.

You always need to check the meaning of key legal terms in a statute. Where in this part of the Act is there a definition of negligence?

- s. 1(1)
- s. 14
- s. 2

Can someone put a term in a contract which limits their legal responsibility for loss other than personal injury or death caused by their negligence?

- Yes

Statutory interpretation

Having been through all the procedures and amplification outline above, you would have thought that the law would be perfectly clear. However, it is not as straightforward as that. There will always be disputes as to what is the particular meaning of a statute, or indeed what is the meaning of a particular word within a statute. This is partly because English is not a particularly precise language. It is the function of courts to interpret statutes. This process is called statutory interpretation. Statutory interpretation has evolved over centuries. When courts have had to decide what a statute says, there has developed a series of so-called 'rules' that guide the courts. Their effect is to set out the approach that should be adopted by the courts. There are three main 'rules': first the literal rule, which says that the words in a statute are taken to have their literal meaning unless such an interpretation produces a nonsensical result. In that case the golden rule applies, which says that if the literal meaning produces an absurd result then you look at it in the overall context of the statute. If these two 'rules' do not help then the mischief rule is applied. This rule states that you interpret the meaning of the word in the light of what the problem or mischief was that the statute was passed to deal with. The Human Rights Act has an impact on statutory interpretation, in that it provides that courts must strive to interpret legislation in a way which is compatible with Convention rights and the intention

» glossary
» glossary
» glossary
» glossary

of Parliament. When it is not possible to interpret the legislation in this way, the senior courts may strike down **delegated** legislation but not **primary** legislation (although they may make a **declaration of incompatibility**, which should prompt government action).

We look in more detail at judicial interpretation of statutes in the next chapter.

Conclusion

This chapter has provided you with an introduction to statutory material. We hope that the task of reading sections, schedules and amendments will be made easier with the explanations we have provided of the way statutes are drafted and enacted, and with the activities which should help familiarise you with the standard layout and language of a statute. You will read a great deal of statutory information during your law degree, and you will find that, with practice it becomes easier. Nonetheless, there will always be statutory provisions which cause lawyers and the courts particular difficulties, and our next chapter turns to the techniques that the courts use for solving these problems.

Links

For more detail on the parliamentary procedure, see *Making New Law*

http://www.parliament.uk/works/newlaw.cfm
Parliament produces many useful publications which you can find on its website.

House of Commons Factsheets include:
The Parliamentary Stages of a Government Bill
Private Members' Bill Procedure
You can see the full list of Factsheets here
http://www.parliament.uk/parliamentary_publications_and_archives/factsheets.cfm

There is a wealth of information on the Parliament website: www.parliament.uk
The ePolitix site www.epolitix.com provides links to Parliament and enables you to track the passage of a particular bill through the parliamentary process. This can be extremely useful if you are interested in the progress of a bill and its amendments.

» glossary

www.oxfordinteract.com

Chapter 20

Understanding judicial interpretation of statutes

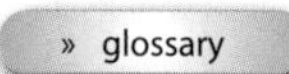

Rationale

In the last chapter we concentrated on the skills you need to develop to feel confident reading statutes. Here we consider the ways that judges read or interpret statutes in order to decide what particular provisions mean in the context of particular legal disputes. You will need to understand judicial interpretation of statutes for a number of reasons:

- **To help solve legal problems.** If you know how judges will approach statutory provisions you will be able to advise, both in the context of academic legal problem solving and in practice, on the likely interpretation of statutory provisions.
- **To understand the meaning of cases involving statutory interpretation.** When you are reading cases which involve judicial interpretation of statutes you will be able to develop a critical understanding of particular judges' approaches to the legal dispute they are deciding.
- **To develop legal arguments.** When you want to urge a particular interpretation of a provision in a statute or in a legal document you can use the 'rules' to inform your argument. For example, if you want to say that a provision in a lease must relate to the landlord's responsibility to maintain the windows you can suggest that the literal meaning of the words suggests this, and that the mischief which the lease is trying to remedy, was the necessity of dealing with the maintenance of the building as a whole.

There are a number of books which provide extensive detail on judicial interpretation of statutes. One we particularly recommend is *Learning Legal Rules* by Holland and Webb published by Oxford University Press. There is no need for us to replicate the useful explanations these books provide, although we would advise you to spend some time working through the relevant chapters of Holland and Webb's book. What we are going to do in this chapter is to summarise the approaches to judicial interpretation, to provide a checklist of useful aids to statutory interpretation and finally to consider three particular cases with the aim of understanding how the judge approached the task of statutory interpretation.

This chapter has been devised to ensure that you:

- Are familiar with the 'rules' of statutory interpretation
- Have some knowledge of some conventions relating to judicial interpretation of statutes
- Understand the implications of the Human Rights Act 1998 for statutory interpretation
- Have considered statutory interpretation in three different cases
- Have considered critically one student's work on statutory interpretation.

'Approaches to' rather than 'rules of' statutory interpretation

You will frequently read about the 'rules' of statutory interpretation but these are not rules in any commonly understood form. They are more like summary descriptions of particular judicial approaches to the task of statutory interpretation. Unfortunately judges do not approach the task with a clear statement of the approach they intend to apply. You have to read their decisions very carefully and decide for yourself on the basis of the evidence in their judgments about their approach. However, the rules give you an indication of the type of approaches they may utilise. Note also it is likely that judges adopt an approach which can be described as an amalgam of those identified by the 'rules'. What this indicates is that trying to interpret statutes cannot be reduced to a set of rules. A statutory provision is a complex statement of law written by someone other than the person trying to interpret it. Legal words, just like many other words in the English language, can be ambiguous, and interpretation can be a challenge. Moreover legal interpretations, just like other interpretations of the written word, are an art and not a science. However, it is an art that is being practised by judges who have had years of legal experience, so they share common approaches and understandings. Some knowledge of the 'rules' can guide you in understanding their approach.

The approaches in summary

- The literal rule. The words must be interpreted in their ordinary literal meaning because that is the only meaning that we can be sure that the draftsman intended. » glossary
- The golden rule. The word or section to be interpreted must be placed in the context of the statute as a whole and then the word must be given its ordinary meaning, unless to do so would lead to absurdity, in which case the judge must do his or her best to give the words another meaning which is consistent with the context. » glossary
- The purposive rule. The word(s) must be given a meaning which is consistent with the general purpose of the section bearing in mind the social, economic or political context of the legislative/documentary provision. » glossary
- The mischief rule. The starting point is the problem that the provision is attempting to remedy. So in the legislative context you should consider the problem of the prior common law position and the history of the statutory response and decide the meaning in the context of the mischief that the draftsman was trying to solve. » glossary » glossary

The application of the 'rules' in themselves is not sufficient to provide all the tools required by the judiciary. There are a number of other judicially sanctioned aids which can facilitate statutory interpretation. We consider these in the next section of this chapter.

Aids in the interpretation of statutes

There are a number of organisational or informational devices which appear in a statute or are part of the deliberations leading to its enactment which may help the courts in deciding what a particular phrase may or may not mean. We list these in the box below. What is important to note is that these pieces of information will not determine what the provision in question means, but may, at the discretion of the court, assist the court in reaching a decision on meaning.

Commonly used devices to aid statutory interpretation

Device	Example	**Comment**
The title of the Act	See *Stevenson v Rogers below and Coltman v Bibby Tankers* [1988] interpreting the Employers Liability (Defective Equipment) Act 1969.	Not very often used because the words of the statute are more significant than its title.
The Interpretation Act 1978	This Act states that certain words should be treated as having certain meanings such as the use of 'he' including 'she' and the use of the singular including the plural.	Not as useful as one might have hoped as it is very limited in the words it explains.
Punctuation and marginal notes	These can be used since the decision in *R v Montilla* [2004] UKHL 50; [2004] 1 WLR 3141	Like all of these matters, it is up to the court to decide the value of marginal notes in any particular case.
Explanatory notes	Whilst explanatory notes contain a warning that they have not been endorsed by **Parliament** and therefore are not part of the Act they have been used to aid in interpretation and even to correct drafting errors; see for example, *Regina (Confederation of Passenger Transport Uk) v Humber Bridge Board and Another* [2003] EWCA Civ 842.	
Dictionaries	These can be used by judges for help in deciding the meaning of non-legal words.	Note that dictionaries can give subtly different explanations of even quite straightforward words.
Travaux Preparatoires/work done in preparation for a **bill**	This could include for instance **Law Commission** reports, **White Papers**, etc.	More commonly used in European courts, but increasingly used here.
Hansard	The rule in *Pepper v Hart* [1992] is the crucial authority here. The **House of Lords** decided that Hansard could be used in certain circumstances to aid statutory interpretation. The circumstances were: • where **legislation** is ambiguous or obscure, or leads to an absurdity; • the material relied upon consists of one or more statements by a minister together if necessary with such other parliamentary material; • the statements relied upon are clear.	The **Law Lords** considered that use of Hansard should be very rare; initially, however, references were frequent, but the rule is now much more understood as an exceptional rather than a standard tool of interpretation.

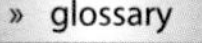

The problems of lists

There are a great many statutes which rely on lists of words for instance to indicate types of methods of service of documents or to set out what specific types of activity are covered by a particular generic term. One recent example of the latter comes from the Animal Welfare Act 2006. The Act in s. 11(1) creates an offence of selling an animal to a young person aged under 16. Section 11(2) explains that 'For the purposes of subsection (1), selling an animal includes transferring, or agreeing to transfer, ownership of the animal in consideration of entry by the transferee into another transaction'.

Lists create particular problems for statutory interpretation. The first question is whether the list is comprehensive and complete. Draftsmen try to insure against the future by using the word 'include' – therefore if new examples crop up, they may be covered by the provision. But the word 'include' also leads to problems. Does the use of 'includes' mean that:

- everything which follows is a complete list of what is meant, so that 'includes' in effect means 'means and includes'?
- is it by way of example only?
- or, as in the case of the Animal Welfare Act, is it a further elaboration of what selling might include, in order to prevent avoidance of the provision?

Common sense would suggest that the answer depends upon what was meant by the drafters of the statute. This is what the House of Lords decided in *Cotman v Bibby Tankers* [1988] AC 276. Clearly then the judge in deciding the meaning of lists and the use of the word 'includes' will have to turn to his or her standard repertoire of interpretative techniques. However, there are some legal Latin maxims which can be used by judges to help them with the interpretative task. We have set these out with their meanings below.

Expressio unius ext exculsio alterius	The expression or inclusion of one thing is the exclusion of another.	However, where the word 'includes' is used then the maxim does not apply.
Eiusdem generis	When an Act uses a generic but non-exhaustive list then the meaning of any general word in the list must be limited by the specific examples given in the list. So, for example, in the Housing Act 1996 s. 189(1)(d) provides that people who have become homeless as a result of an emergency 'such as fire, flood or other disaster' the nature of the emergency is limited to those emergencies which are similar in cause to flood and fire.	This is a rule of grammar which can be rebutted by judicial interpretation of the statute.
Noscitur a Sociis	A word is known by its associates. This does not apply where the word 'other' is used – in such circumstances eiusdem generis would be the appropriate rule.	

Judicial interpretation – some examples

1. The example of the Sale of Goods Act 1979

In this first example we are going to 'talk' you through the decision of Potter LJ in *Stevenson v Rogers* [1999] QB. We will begin by considering the legal problem in the case.

The problem

» glossary

The common law of contract is based upon the principle of caveat emptor – let the buyer beware. For a number of reasons, in particular the imbalance of power between the consumer and the supplier, usually a business and often a large corporate entity, the idea underpinning caveat emptor, that parties to a contract have equality of bargaining power, is outdated. There have been a number of interventions over the years to provide greater protections for the consumer. The particular intervention that we are concerned with is the Sale of Goods Act 1979 which implies certain terms into contracts for the sale of goods. However, these implied terms, which relate to satisfactory quality and fitness for purpose, are not implied into private sales but only sales of goods sold 'in the course of a business'. Now in most situations the distinction is clear. If you buy goods from a shop or a wholesaler then you are buying goods sold in the course of a business. If you are buying a second-hand sofa from your auntie, then that is a private sale and you, as the buyer must take care. However, there are a number of transactions where the distinction is less clear. The case we are going to consider revolves around the meaning of 'in the course of a business' where it was unclear whether the transaction attracted the protections of the legislation. What we are looking for are the methods that the judges used to interpret the meaning of the statutory phrase, 'in the course of a business'. You will need a copy of the case to refer to.

The case – Stevenson v Rogers [1999] QB 1028

The facts can be briefly stated.

» glossary

» glossary

The Stevensons (the plaintiffs) bought a fishing boat, *Jelle*, at a price of £600,000 for commercial use from Rogers (the defendant) who intended to obtain another boat for continuation of his business. The *Jelle* was found to need repair, the cost of which the Stevensons claimed from Rogers. The legal dispute hinged upon whether Rogers, a fisherman, in selling his boat to the Stevensons, was dealing as a trader in the course of business, or as a private individual selling his property and hence exempt from the provision of the Sale of Goods Act 1979. The Stevensons' claim was rejected by the High Court, which decided that the sale was not in the course of business and therefore not covered by s. 14(2) of the Act since boat selling was not integral to Rogers' work as a fisherman. The plaintiffs appealed to the Court of Appeal where they were successful. It decided that as both parties were acting as businesses with regard to one another, hence the sale was in the course of a business and therefore the implied terms as to quality did apply.

The statutory provision

Section 14(2) Sale of Goods Act 1979 states:

> Where the seller sells goods in the course of a business, there is an implied condition that the goods supplied under the contract are of merchantable quality...

The judgment

The leading judgment was given by Potter LJ and was agreed by the other two judges hearing the case, Sir Patrick Russell and Butler-Sloss LJ. We will concentrate on Potter LJ's judgment to see what methods he suggests may be employed to decide the meaning of the words 'in the course of a business' and to see which method he decides to employ. Read the judgment and then carry out the activities below.

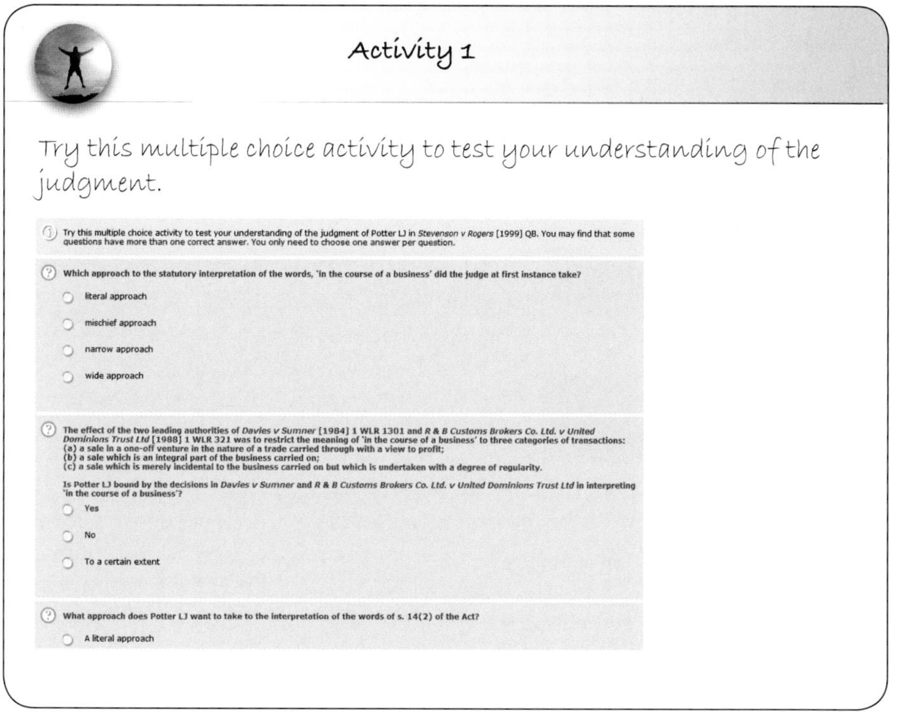

Activity 1

Try this multiple choice activity to test your understanding of the judgment.

Try this multiple choice activity to test your understanding of the judgment of Potter LJ in *Stevenson v Rogers* [1999] QB. You may find that some questions have more than one correct answer. You only need to choose one answer per question.

Which approach to the statutory interpretation of the words, 'in the course of a business' did the judge at first instance take?

- literal approach
- mischief approach
- narrow approach
- wide approach

The effect of the two leading authorities of *Davies v Sumner* [1984] 1 WLR 1301 and *R & B Customs Brokers Co. Ltd. v United Dominions Trust Ltd* [1988] 1 WLR 321 was to restrict the meaning of 'in the course of a business' to three categories of transactions:
(a) a sale in a one-off venture in the nature of a trade carried through with a view to profit;
(b) a sale which is an integral part of the business carried on;
(c) a sale which is merely incidental to the business carried on but which is undertaken with a degree of regularity.

Is Potter LJ bound by the decisions in *Davies v Sumner* and *R & B Customs Brokers Co. Ltd. v United Dominions Trust Ltd* in interpreting 'in the course of a business'?

- Yes
- No
- To a certain extent

What approach does Potter LJ want to take to the interpretation of the words of s. 14(2) of the Act?

- A literal approach

Potter LJ justifies his approach as follows:

> Reference to Hansard and the First Report makes clear that the mischief which parliament intended to rectify in relation to section 14(2) was that section 14(2) of the 1893 Act had a restrictive effect and was inadequate to impose on every business seller (whether or not habitually dealing in goods of the type sold) the implied condition as to merchantable quality. It was in that context that the draft clause annexed to the First Report was enacted without modification in section 3 of the Supply of Goods (Implied Terms) Act 1973. Thus resort to the mischief rule confirms my view formed at first impression that the changed wording of section 14(2) should not be read as to bear [a restrictive ambit].

He dismisses limiting the construction of the phrase to meaning given in the other cases, in a forceful manner:

> To apply the reasoning in the R & B Customs case in the interests only of consistency, thereby undermining the wide protection for buyers which section 14(2) [of the Sale of Goods Act] was intended to introduce, would in my view be an unacceptable example of the tail wagging the dog.

Cross reference
If you do not know how to do this refer to chapters 11–18 in Part II of this resource.

Now we have talked you through the decision, your next step in developing your understanding of this case is to locate and read some case notes and articles which consider it.

Activity 2

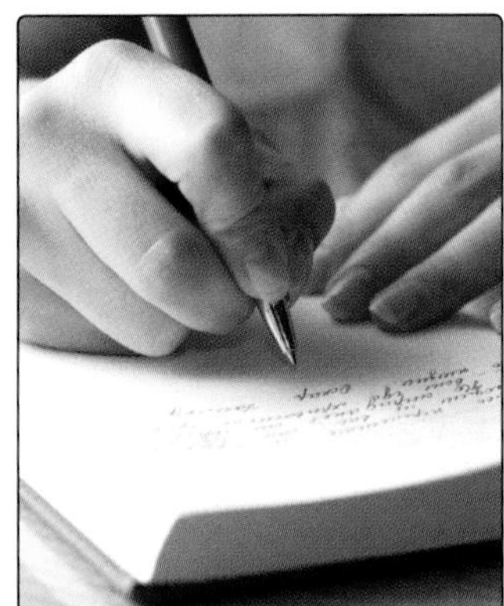

Students' understanding of statutory interpretation is frequently assessed by asking them to write a case report on the use of statutory interpretation in a particular case.

Go online to see an example of such a report written about *Stevenson v Rogers*. This report was marked at a low 2.2 level. We provide comments on the strengths and weaknesses of the analysis.

2. The example of the Crime and Disorder Act 1998

We are now going to look at the case of *R v Rogers* [2007] UKHL 8 [2007] S All ER 433. We want you to work out the approach of the House of Lords to the interpretation of s. 28(4) of the Crime and Disorder Act 1998. You will need to refer to Baroness Hale's judgment. This is a much shorter judgment than the one we have just looked at.

The problem

If the offence of using abusive words and behaviour with intent to cause fear or provoke violence contrary to s. 4 of the Public Order Act 1986 includes racial or religious features then ss. 29–32 of the Crime and Disorder Act 1998 (the Act) transform it into the racially aggravated form of the offence which means that the perpetrator faces more serious penalties. The offence is racially or religiously aggravated if at the time of committing the offence, or immediately before or after doing so, the offender demonstrates towards the victim hostility based on the victim's membership (or presumed membership) of a racial or religious group – s. 28(1) of the Act. These aggravated offences are part of the government drive to eliminate hate crime, and to recognise its seriousness. The problem in this particular case is whether calling people 'bloody foreigners' is a demonstration of hostility based upon the victims' membership of a racial group.

The case

Rogers, the defendant, encountered three young Spanish women when he was riding his motorised mobility scooter along the pavement. Rogers got into a dispute with the young women, during which he called them 'bloody foreigners' and told them to 'go back to your own country'. He then pursued them to a kebab shop in an aggressive manner. He was charged with an offence of using racially aggravated abusive or insulting words or behaviour with intent to cause fear or provoke violence, contrary to s. 31(1) of the Crime and Disorder Act 1998 (the Act). At the end of the prosecution case the defence submitted that there was no case to answer on the ground that the words used by the defendant were not in law capable of demonstrating hostility based on membership of a racial group because foreigners did not constitute a racial group as defined in s. 28(4) of the Act. The judge rejected that submission and the jury convicted the defendant. The Court of Appeal dismissed the defendant's appeal and held that 'foreigners' did constitute a racial group within the meaning of s. 28(4).

The statutory provision

Section 28(4) of the Crime and Disorder Act:

> In this section, 'racial group' means a group of persons defined by reference to race, colour, nationality (including citizenship), or ethnic or national origins.

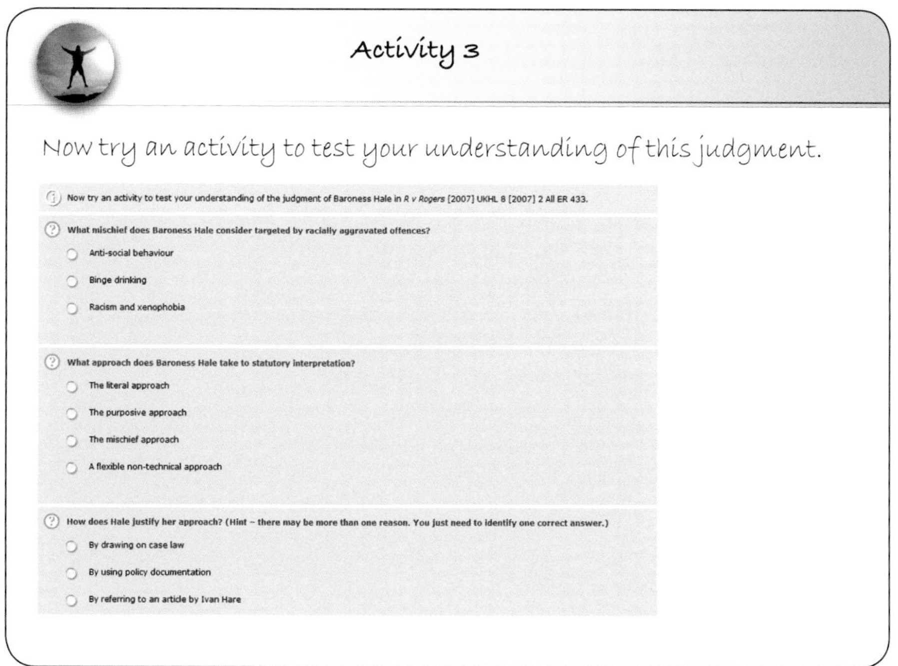

Activity 3

Now try an activity to test your understanding of this judgment.

Now try an activity to test your understanding of the judgment of Baroness Hale in *R v Rogers* [2007] UKHL 8 [2007] 2 All ER 433.

What mischief does Baroness Hale consider targeted by racially aggravated offences?

- Anti-social behaviour
- Binge drinking
- Racism and xenophobia

What approach does Baroness Hale take to statutory interpretation?

- The literal approach
- The purposive approach
- The mischief approach
- A flexible non-technical approach

How does Hale justify her approach? (Hint – there may be more than one reason. You just need to identify one correct answer.)

- By drawing on case law
- By using policy documentation
- By referring to an article by Ivan Hare

» glossary

The decision of the House of Lords in *R v Rogers* may suggest that statutory interpretation is a much more flexible art than textbooks often suggest. You may want to use this decision to think critically about the relationship between judges and Parliament.

Activity 4

Do you think that it is right for judges to take such a flexible approach to the interpretation of statutes? Whose interests are served by the decision in *R v Rogers*? Who loses out?

Go online to read our thoughts on these questions.

3. The example of the Housing Act 1985

The next example we consider is from the succession provisions of the Housing Act 1985. Again the purpose of the activities is for you to practise understanding judicial approaches to statutory interpretation. The case we consider is *Birmingham City Council v Walker* [2007] UKHL 22 [2007] 2 WLR.

The problem

The Housing Act 1985 (the Act) regulates the provision of council housing to tenants and gives tenants certain rights. One particular right is the right to succeed to a tenancy – s. 88 of the Act. If a tenant dies the tenant's partner, or a member of their family who is living in the property, is entitled to succeed to the tenancy. That means that they take it over, and have the same security of tenure as the original tenant. The Act only allows one succession to take place. The reason to restrict succession to one succession is that low cost housing is a scarce resource and is generally allocated according to need. However, the restriction to one succession can cause problems in circumstances where the original tenant died a long time ago, his or her successor remains in the property with an adult child who cares for them as they age. When the successor dies, the local authority landlord is entitled to evict the adult child, potentially causing hardship and upheaval.

The case

In 1965 Birmingham Council granted a joint periodic tenancy of a three-bedroom property to the defendant's parents, with whom he lived. On the father's death in 1969 the mother became the sole contractual tenant by right of survivorship. Following the introduction of secure tenancies by the Housing Act 1980, the mother became a secure tenant. The relevant provision relating to secure tenancies were re-enacted in consolidating legislation in Part IV of the Housing Act 1985. In 2004 the mother died leaving the defendant in occupation. The council issued proceedings against him claiming possession of the property. The deputy district judge decided that the mother was a successor within the meaning of s. 88(1) of the Housing Act 1985 so no further succession could take place. This decision was confirmed on appeal. However, the Court of Appeal allowed the defendant's appeal. The council appealed.

The statutory provision

Housing Act 1985 s. 88(1):

> The tenant is himself a successor if – (a) the tenancy vested in him by virtue of section 89 (succession to a periodic tenancy), or (b) he was a joint tenant and has become the sole tenant, or (c) the tenancy arose by virtue of section 86 (periodic tenancy arising on ending of term certain) and the first tenancy there mentioned was granted to another person or jointly to him and another person, or (d) he became the tenant on the tenancy being assigned to him (but subject to subsection s(2) and (3)) or (e) he became the tenant on the tenancy being vested in him on the death of the previous tenant or (f) the tenancy was previously an introductory tenancy and he was a successor to the introductory tenancy.

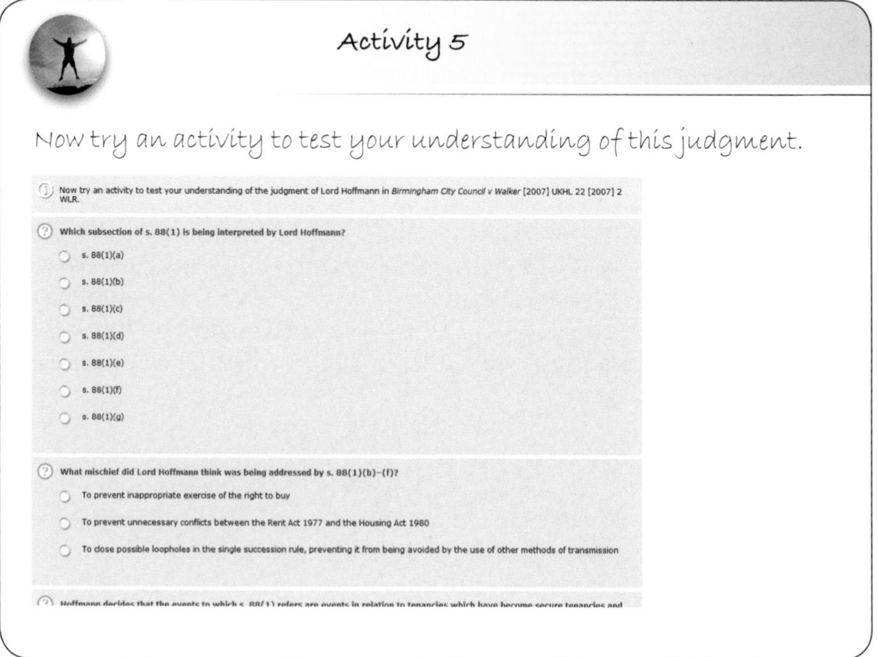

Activity 5
Now try an activity to test your understanding of this judgment.
Now try an activity to test your understanding of the judgment of Lord Hoffmann in Birmingham City Council v Walker [2007] UKHL 22 [2007] 2 WLR.
Which subsection of s. 88(1) is being interpreted by Lord Hoffmann?
s. 88(1)(a)
s. 88(1)(b)
s. 88(1)(c)
s. 88(1)(d)
s. 88(1)(e)
s. 88(1)(f)
s. 88(1)(g)
What mischief did Lord Hoffmann think was being addressed by s. 88(1)(b)–(f)?
To prevent inappropriate exercise of the right to buy
To prevent unnecessary conflicts between the Rent Act 1977 and the Housing Act 1980
To close possible loopholes in the single succession rule, preventing it from being avoided by the use of other methods of transmission

This decision demonstrates that it is difficult to characterise judicial approaches. We would encourage you to use the formal approaches, but to be confident in arguing that their relevance is limited.

Presumptions

» glossary

In *Birmingham City Council v Walker* the House of Lords refers to a legal presumption against retrospective operation of statute. This is an important limit on judicial interpretation of statutes. There are other presumptions that you should be aware of. We have set these out below. Presumptions can be rebutted if there are clear statutory words that do so although judges are reluctant to exclude the right to judicial review. Notice how close these presumptions are to the protections offered by the Human Rights Act 1998.

Presumption...

- Against deprivation of liberty
- Against alteration of the common law
- Against binding the Crown 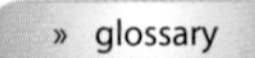 » glossary
- Against deprivation of property and against interference with private rights
- Against ousting the jurisdiction of the courts
- Against criminal liability without *mens rea* » glossary

Statutory interpretation and the Human Rights Act 1998

What we have been suggesting up to this point is that the 'rules' of statutory interpretation represent the methods that judges employ to enable them to make sense of legislation whilst respecting the sovereignty of Parliament. The passing of the Human Rights Act 1998, which enacts the fundamental rights contained in the European Convention on Human Rights, makes this judicial balancing act more complex. The nature of the impact of the Human Rights Act on parliamentary sovereignty is a controversial subject which will no doubt be dealt with extensively in your public law course. However, you need to be aware of the impact of the Human Rights Act on statutory interpretation even before you consider the constitutional issues. There are two distinct issues. First: how should the Human Rights Act be interpreted? Second: what effect does the Human Rights Act have on the interpretation of statutes? The answers to these questions will be succinct; the complexities are much better dealt with by your public law lecturers!

How is the Human Rights Act to be interpreted?

The Human Rights Act has a different status from the majority of legislation enacted by Parliament. It is a constitutional instrument that gives effect to fundamental rights. Therefore, when interpreting it, judges should respect its distinct character. Nonetheless, the wording of the statute is important – it was carefully drafted by a senior parliamentary draftsman who was well aware of its significance.

In the recent case of *YL v Birmingham City Council and Others (Secretary of State for Constitutional Affairs Intervening)* [2007] UKHL 27, [2007] 3 WLR 112, the House of Lords had to consider the meaning of a particular section of the Human Rights Act. Their Lordships took a more narrow approach to the interpretation of the Act than the Government was advocating.

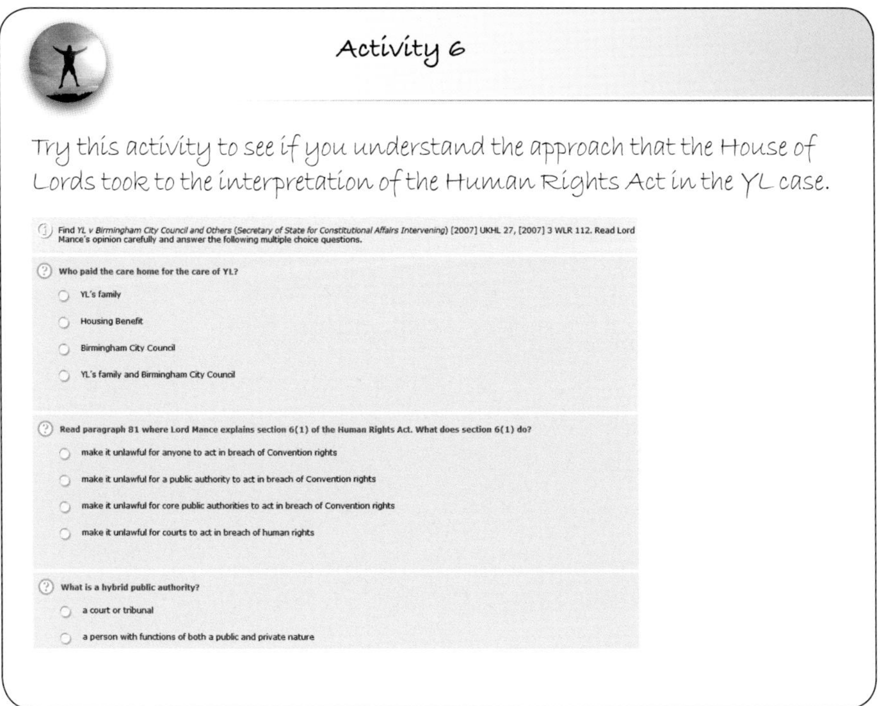

Activity 6

Try this activity to see if you understand the approach that the House of Lords took to the interpretation of the Human Rights Act in the YL case.

Find *YL v Birmingham City Council and Others (Secretary of State for Constitutional Affairs Intervening)* [2007] UKHL 27, [2007] 3 WLR 112. Read Lord Mance's opinion carefully and answer the following multiple choice questions.

Who paid the care home for the care of YL?

- YL's family
- Housing Benefit
- Birmingham City Council
- YL's family and Birmingham City Council

Read paragraph 81 where Lord Mance explains section 6(1) of the Human Rights Act. What does section 6(1) do?

- make it unlawful for anyone to act in breach of Convention rights
- make it unlawful for a public authority to act in breach of Convention rights
- make it unlawful for core public authorities to act in breach of Convention rights
- make it unlawful for courts to act in breach of human rights

What is a hybrid public authority?

- a court or tribunal
- a person with functions of both a public and private nature

The consequence of the House of Lords' decision was that the Government decided to amend the Human Rights Act to ensure that people who are in private care homes but are funded by the state are given the protection of the European Convention on Human Rights. However, residents of private care homes who are privately funded are not protected by the Convention. You should note that the judges in the House of Lords were split 3 to 2. Clearly, there is disagreement about how the Act is to be interpreted.

What impact does the Human Rights Act have on the interpretation of statutes?

Section 3 of the Human Rights Act provides that:

> So far as it is possible to do so, primary legislation … must be read and given effect in a way which is compatible with the Convention rights.

You have already studied law long enough to know that this is not a straightforward provision. The judges have to decide which primary legislation it is possible to read in a way that is compatible with Convention rights.

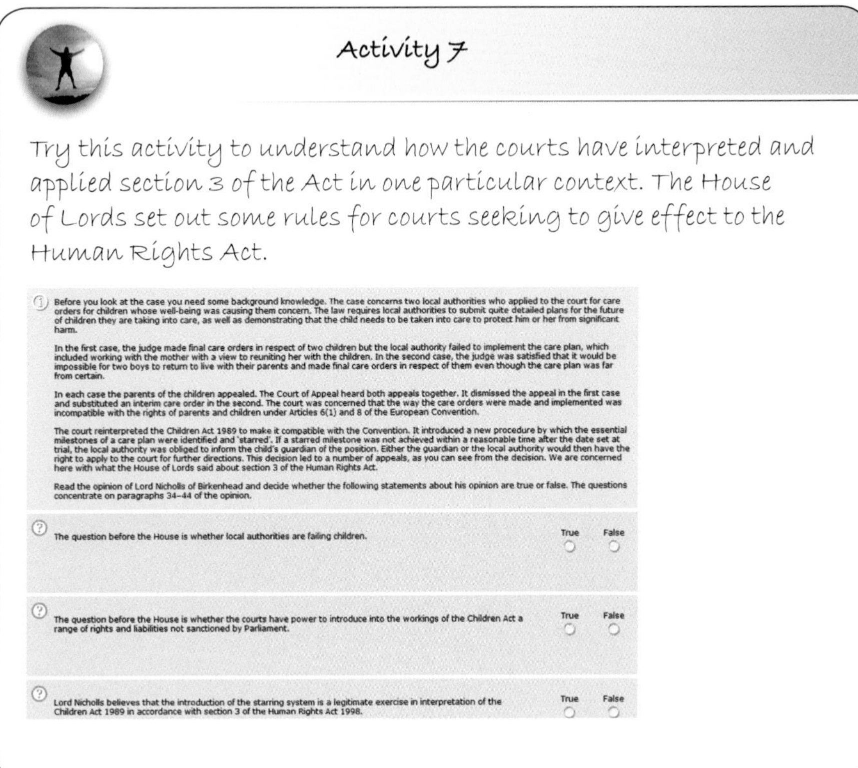

Activity 7

Try this activity to understand how the courts have interpreted and applied section 3 of the Act in one particular context. The House of Lords set out some rules for courts seeking to give effect to the Human Rights Act.

Before you look at the case you need some background knowledge. The case concerns two local authorities who applied to the court for care orders for children whose well-being was causing them concern. The law requires local authorities to submit quite detailed plans for the future of children they are taking into care, as well as demonstrating that the child needs to be taken into care to protect him or her from significant harm.

In the first case, the judge made final care orders in respect of two children but the local authority failed to implement the care plan, which included working with the mother with a view to reuniting her with the children. In the second case, the judge was satisfied that it would be impossible for two boys to return to live with their parents and made final care orders in respect of them even though the care plan was far from certain.

In each case the parents of the children appealed. The Court of Appeal heard both appeals together. It dismissed the appeal in the first case and substituted an interim care order in the second. The court was concerned that the way the care orders were made and implemented was incompatible with the rights of parents and children under Articles 6(1) and 8 of the European Convention.

The court reinterpreted the Children Act 1989 to make it compatible with the Convention. It introduced a new procedure by which the essential milestones of a care plan were identified and 'starred'. If a starred milestone was not achieved within a reasonable time after the date set at trial, the local authority was obliged to inform the child's guardian of the position. Either the guardian or the local authority would then have the right to apply to the court for further directions. This decision led to a number of appeals, as you can see from the decision. We are concerned here with what the House of Lords said about section 3 of the Human Rights Act.

Read the opinion of Lord Nicholls of Birkenhead and decide whether the following statements about his opinion are true or false. The questions concentrate on paragraphs 34–44 of the opinion.

	True	False
The question before the House is whether local authorities are failing children.	○	○
The question before the House is whether the courts have power to introduce into the workings of the Children Act a range of rights and liabilities not sanctioned by Parliament.	○	○
Lord Nicholls believes that the introduction of the starring system is a legitimate exercise in interpretation of the Children Act 1989 in accordance with section 3 of the Human Rights Act 1998.	○	○

Re S (Minors) (Care Order: Implementation of Care Plan) [2002] UKHL 10 demonstrates that there are constraints on judges – they must still respect the authority of Parliament. However, the issue is not as clear cut as the advice the House of Lords gave to the Court of Appeal would suggest. In the activity below we ask you to read *Ghaidan v Godin-Mendoza* [2004] UKHL 30, [2004] 2 AC 557.

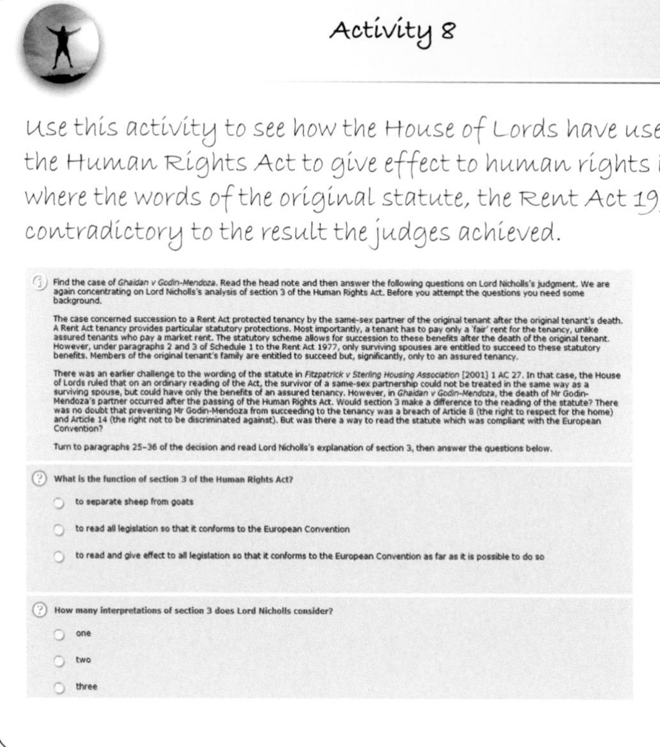

Activity 8

Use this activity to see how the House of Lords have used section 3 of the Human Rights Act to give effect to human rights in a context where the words of the original statute, the Rent Act 1977, seem contradictory to the result the judges achieved.

Find the case of *Ghaidan v Godin-Mendoza*. Read the head note and then answer the following questions on Lord Nicholls's judgment. We are again concentrating on Lord Nicholls's analysis of section 3 of the Human Rights Act. Before you attempt the questions you need some background.

The case concerned succession to a Rent Act protected tenancy by the same-sex partner of the original tenant after the original tenant's death. A Rent Act tenancy provides particular statutory protections. Most importantly, a tenant has to pay only a 'fair' rent for the tenancy, unlike assured tenants who pay a market rent. The statutory scheme allows for succession to these benefits after the death of the original tenant. However, under paragraphs 2 and 3 of Schedule 1 to the Rent Act 1977, only surviving spouses are entitled to succeed to these statutory benefits. Members of the original tenant's family are entitled to succeed but, significantly, only to an assured tenancy.

There was an earlier challenge to the wording of the statute in *Fitzpatrick v Sterling Housing Association* [2001] 1 AC 27. In that case, the House of Lords ruled that on an ordinary reading of the Act, the survivor of a same-sex partnership could not be treated in the same way as a surviving spouse, but could have only the benefits of an assured tenancy. However, in *Ghaidan v Godin-Mendoza*, the death of Mr Godin-Mendoza's partner occurred after the passing of the Human Rights Act. Would section 3 make a difference to the reading of the statute? There was no doubt that preventing Mr Godin-Mendoza from succeeding to the tenancy was a breach of Article 8 (the right to respect for the home) and Article 14 (the right not to be discriminated against). But was there a way to read the statute which was compliant with the European Convention?

Turn to paragraphs 25–36 of the decision and read Lord Nicholls's explanation of section 3, then answer the questions below.

What is the function of section 3 of the Human Rights Act?

- to separate sheep from goats
- to read all legislation so that it conforms to the European Convention
- to read and give effect to all legislation so that it conforms to the European Convention as far as it is possible to do so

How many interpretations of section 3 does Lord Nicholls consider?

- one
- two
- three

Lord Nicholls makes it clear in *Ghaidan v Godin-Mendoza* that there is no clear answer to the problem of statutory interpretation under section 3 of the Human Rights Act:

> A comprehensive answer to this question is proving elusive. The courts, including your Lordships' House, are still cautiously feeling their way forward as experience in the application of section 3 gradually accumulates.

Watching the development of the application of section 3 will undoubtedly form a major part of your legal studies.

Conclusion

This chapter has provided you with an outline of the operation of judicial statutory interpretation and enabled you to practise identifying judicial approaches by guiding you through some decisions on the interpretation of statutes. You should now feel more confident in carrying out the task yourself.

Don't panic

It is not easy to decide how judges are approaching statutory interpretation. Nor are judges consistent. However, if you remain alert to identifying their approaches, you will gain a great deal of insight into the way judges operate both institutionally and individually. This will help you develop a critical approach to the law. You will get increasingly adept at identifying judicial strategies as you become more experienced in reading cases.

www.oxfordinteract.com

Chapter 21

Reading cases 1: the basics

» glossary

Rationale

Case reports or law reports are the bread and butter of your work as a law student. You encounter them from your first day in law school and you will be using them in your final piece of assessment. The requirement to read cases is probably the single most distinct feature of studying law at university. In the first few weeks of your studies it can seem a daunting requirement. However, with practice and some guidance you will soon feel confident in reading cases. This chapter is the first of a series of chapters on the important legal skill of case reading. The chapters are designed to guide you from your first encounter with a law report to the stage where you are ready to tackle more complex cases on your own.

This chapter is devised to cover the basics of reading a case. It will enable you to:

- Understand what a law report is
- Understand why you are being required to read cases
- Recognise the standard layout and key features of English law reports
- Use the headnote and other aids to understanding judgments.

What are law reports?

Law reports are reports of cases decided by the courts which set out the facts of the case and the reasons given for the decision of the court. They are an extremely important tool in the common law system as they provide a record of judicial decisions and reasoning. Law reports are not written by the judges in the case but by law reporters who are qualified lawyers. The Incorporated Council of Law Reporting for England and Wales – a private company established in 1865 – publishes the official Law Reports. Their reports are written by barristers and solicitors who are present at court during the hearing and present when the judgment is handed down and their reports are approved by the judges in the case. There are many other series of law reports published on a commercial basis which are not approved by the judges.

Cross reference
You will learn more about law reports and how they are cited (referred to) in chapter 14, Citing legal authorities.

Law reports are – for the new law student - an entirely different form of presentation of information. They are designed for and written by experienced lawyers. It is entirely reasonable that you find reading law reports a challenge.

The challenges facing you

When you first start there are likely to be several problems you face:

- You are not necessarily given simple cases to read at the beginning of your studies. That is because you have to read the cases that are relevant to the topics you are studying rather than the easiest cases. It is possible that right from your first seminar you are faced with cases which are challenging to read – inevitably you feel thrown in at the deep end.
- Case reports appear bewildering and take a long time to read. Your normal strategies of reading – starting at the beginning and working through to the end – seem to be counter-productive. You may become perplexed by the language and the technical details, the report appears to be going nowhere and you give up before the end.
- Cases are not linear – they are more like Russian dolls, because they are in layers. The judge is not just concerned with the decision in front of him or her but, because of the rule of precedent, with previous decisions on the same legal point and with responding to the arguments of counsel in the case. This can be very confusing for the reader if he or she has not worked out where these arguments come from or how they fit together in the particular case.
- Even when, by some extraordinary feat of stamina you reach the end of the case, you realise that you did not know what you were looking for; however, you think you have worked hard on the case and you know the facts and the result, but then you go to the seminar and discover you cannot answer the questions you are being asked.

» glossary

» glossary

Why read cases?

There is one overwhelming reason why lawyers read cases – to find out the law. English law is described and developed in part through the medium of cases. This sounds obvious, but if you hold on to this understanding when you read a case it should make it easier for you to know what you are looking for. We look at this in more depth when we consider the rule of precedent in the next chapter. In brief, however, judges are deciding what the law is on the particular point that is being argued in front of them. They can decide either to confirm the previous views of the court, to distinguish the point of law from other legal decisions in related areas or to develop a legal answer to a new legal problem that is in front of them. When you finish reading a case, ask yourself, what is the law on the particular point that was in front of the judge? If you don't know the answer, go back to the case and work it out!

» glossary

» glossary

The second, and almost equally important reason for reading cases, is to learn about judicial reasoning. You will be studying the ratio decidendi of the decision – the reasoning the judge uses in the particular case to reach his decision. The skill of finding and appreciating the ratio decidendi is considered in the next chapter. Appreciating the legal reasoning of judges is an

» glossary

important legal skill for you to acquire. The judges in our higher courts have extremely well-trained legal minds. You will learn how lawyers think by reading their arguments, noting how they structure their thoughts, what approaches they find compelling, what resources they use to justify their decisions. Understanding legal reasoning teaches you to think like a lawyer and enables you to be able to predict how courts will approach particular legal problems. This is invaluable both in your academic work, when you will be asked to analyse hypothetical legal problems and to criticise particular legal decisions, and if and when you practise as a lawyer when you will be required to find solutions to legal problems.

» glossary

This leads straight to the third reason for reading cases – which is to develop a critical understanding of the law. This is at the heart of what you do as a student of law. It means that when you read a case you must pay particular attention to the judge's reasoning. Ask yourself how the judge develops his or her line of reasoning, how does he or she use the evidence and the authorities before the court? Do you agree with his or her approach, and can you work out how that approach differs from other judges' legal reasoning in the case? It is particularly fruitful to consider the reasoning of judges who disagree with each other. So when the Court of Appeal is overruled by the House of Lords, don't just assume that the House of Lords is right – work out whose legal reasoning you prefer and why.

Key Point

As you read a case always bear in mind why you are reading it – usually you are reading the case to:

- *find out the law*
- *follow the legal reasoning and*
- *develop a critical understanding of the law.*

Your seminars and your assessments will be testing that you have read with understanding the cases you have been set.

First steps

Now you know what you are reading and why you are reading it. However, before you immerse yourself in the judgment in any case, you should take some time to:

- work out what the case is about
- identify those parts of the case which require the most attention.

This will ensure the most efficient and effective use of your time. Fortunately cases are set out in a standard way and utilise a standard vocabulary. As you become familiar with the layout and the standard features and as you gain experience in law you will become increasingly confident in reading and using cases. Most importantly you can learn a lot about the case from the first few pages of the law report.

Navigating the case

The first few pages of a law report, before the judgment(s) begin, provide an invaluable aid to the reading and understanding of cases. They can be seen as a map which provides an indication of the key features of the case you are about to read, or as a theatre programme which, with its cast list of lawyers, its brief synopsis of the plot and its indication of the production history, gives you a rich insight into the legal production you are about to experience.

Key Point

If you are reading a case on-screen print off the page(s) of the decision prior to the commencement of the judgment. Read those pages – following our guide below - and note the information they contain. Keep referring back to them as you read the body of the case – it will stop you getting lost. So, for example, when the judge refers to an argument put forward by Mr Brown, you can work out exactly who he is – for instance, counsel for the defendant.

» glossary

There are standard features to these first few pages of law reports which we set out in the table below.

» glossary

Standard features of law reports

Feature	Comment
The name of the case	In English law civil cases are named by the names of the parties bringing the case. The name of the person bringing the case, whether claimant or appellant comes first, followed by the name of the defendant or respondent. The 'v' means versus, i.e. against, and is usually spoken as 'and'. In family cases names are not disclosed to preserve anonymity, so cases are named with letters. In order to avoid confusion there is often some indication of the subject matter of case. Judicial review cases are named slightly differently. Prior to 2001 judicial review cases are cited as the Crown against a particular body *ex parte* (on behalf of) an applicant. Judicial review cases after 2001 are cited with the applicant's name in brackets after the R. When we say the name of these cases out loud we say 'the Crown on the application of X against the (name of the public body). Criminal cases are cases taken against individual citizens by the Crown. Criminal case names are written *R v Martin*, where the *R* stands for Regina. The case name is said, Crown against Martin, and not R versus Martin.

Continued

The court in which it was heard	The more senior the court the more influential the decision is.
The name of the judge or judges	Notice who the judges are; as you get more experienced in reading case law you will begin to notice that you agree with some judges' decisions more than you do with others. You will also notice that senior judges make the decisions on the more difficult and controversial areas. You can find out more about the current judges in the Court of Appeal and the House of Lords at http://www.judiciary.gov.uk/
The hearing date(s)	
The headnote	This provides a summary of the case. It sets out the material facts, it indicates the key legal questions to be considered by the court and it summarises the court's decision. We discuss how you should use the headnote more below. We also provide a guide to the terminology of the headnote.
A list of cases referred to	The list is divided into two parts – those cases which the judges refer to in their decision and those cases which counsel refer to in argument. It is the cases which the judges refer to that are the most important. These cases provide one of the layers of complexity that we talked about above. In order to be fully conversant with the decision in front of you, you should be familiar with the arguments in those cases.
Details of the appeal	This gives the legal history of the case setting out the previous hearings and the previous findings of the courts. The legal history is the second key layer of the case – if you can get a grip on what happened to the case previously then you are prepared for those parts of the judge's reasoning which deals with the previous judicial decision making in the case.
The name of counsel appearing in the case	Note who counsel are and which party they are representing. Their arguments are a third key layer which the judgment will have to respond to. Moreover noting their names will ensure that you are not totally thrown when a judge suddenly refers to someone by name.
The judgment(s)	This is the most important part of the case. Each judge sitting is entitled to give his or her own opinion, although often the judges simply concur – agree – with each other. The most senior judge gives his or her opinion first and then the others give either supporting speeches or dissenting speeches. These opinions will deal with greater or lesser sophistication with the layers of arguments in the case. There is no set format to the judgment although it tends to be traditional and courteous in style and often begins by setting out the facts in more or less detail. Nowadays each paragraph is numbered – this enables you to refer to the relevant paragraph when you are quoting from cases in your essays and other written work. We will look much more closely at judgments in the next section of the chapter. Notice the words 'cur adv vult' which precede the judgment. This is an abbreviation of the Latin phrase *curia advisaria vult* which means the court wishes to be advised. Note, in cases reported in the AC series, the judgments do not being until after the arguments of counsel have been reported. These arguments can take up several pages of text. When you first read a case you do not need to read counsels' arguments.

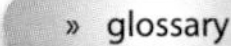

Cross reference

Chapter 14, Citing legal authorities, provides more comprehensive information on the names of cases.

See chapter 20, Understanding judicial interpretation of statutes.

Example

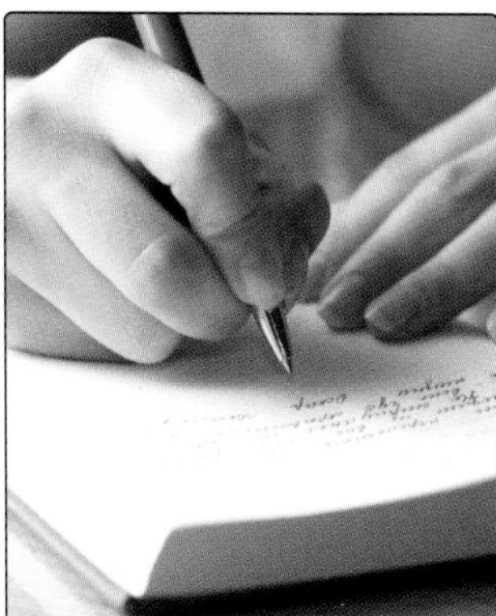

Now go online to have a look at an example of a case which helps you become familiar with the key features of a law report.

Activities 1, 2 and 3

Now test yourself on how to read preliminary information and the headnote of a property case, a public law case and a criminal case.

Now test yourself on how to read preliminary information and the headnote of a property case.

To do this activity you will need to have two browser windows open. There are three ways of doing this:

either click on your browser button to open a second window;
or click Window > New window on the top browser menu;
or type Ctrl N: this will open a new window.

You will find it useful to resize the windows so that they sit side by side, and don't overlap.

To complete this activity you will need to access the case *Bruton v London & Quadrant Housing Trust* [2000] 1 AC 406.

To do this you will need to:
- Login to your institution's library or learning resources centre.
- Login to Westlaw or LexisNexis.
- Search for *Bruton v London & Quadrant Housing Trust* [2000] 1 AC 406.

See chapter 17 if you need more information on using legal databases.

Now read the preliminary information and headnote for *Bruton v London & Quadrant Housing Trust* [2000] 1 AC 406 and answer the following multiple choice questions.

How would you say the name of the case?

- Bruton versus London Quadrant Housing Trust
- Bruton and London Quadrant Housing Trust

In which court is the case being heard?

- The High Court
- The Court of Appeal
- The House of Lords

Using the headnote and other aids to reading cases

The headnote provides a summary of the case which can help you with understanding the full judgment. One particularly useful feature of a headnote is that it tells you the effect of the decision on existing case law. This information is crucial because of the operation of the rule of precedent which we discuss in the next chapter. We are concerned with two different things. First, we need to know the effect of this decision on the previous decisions made by lower courts on this particular case. In this instance the decision of the lower court can be either:

- **Affirmed** – that is, the judgment of the court is in agreement with the decision of the lower court or
- **Reversed** – that is, the court overrules the decision of the lower court.

Secondly we need to know how the judgment both uses and responds to other cases which cover similar legal points. Here the court may have:

- **Applied** a particular case – which means that the court considered that case provided a precedent for this case and therefore it followed the legal reasoning of the judgment in that case.
- **Approved** a particular case – which means that the court agreed with the decision of a lower court in that case.
- **Considered** a particular case – which means that the court discussed that case. Generally courts consider decisions in cases which have been made at the same level of hierarchy of court.
- **Distinguished** a particular case – this means that the court has discussed a particular case which may have been argued to be binding upon it; however, it has decided that there is sufficient difference between that case and the case it is deciding to prevent it from being bound.
- **Overruled** a particular case – which means that the court has decided to overturn the decision in that case. Usually the court only overturns cases in courts at a lower level; however, it is possible to overturn decisions at the same level in the hierarchy.

There are other words you will find in headnotes. For instance, the Latin word 'semble' is used to indicate that the court has given its opinion on a matter that is not directly at issue in the case. The Latin phrase 'per curiam' is particularly important for students. A per curiam statement is an explicit statement of the law which is given by one judge on behalf of the whole court, rather than the standard practice which is that judgments are the opinion of that judge alone. The per curiam statement will probably not be part of the ratio decidendi of the case, but is intended to be an authoritative statement of the law. The phrase literally means 'through the senate' which you can understand as 'through the court'.

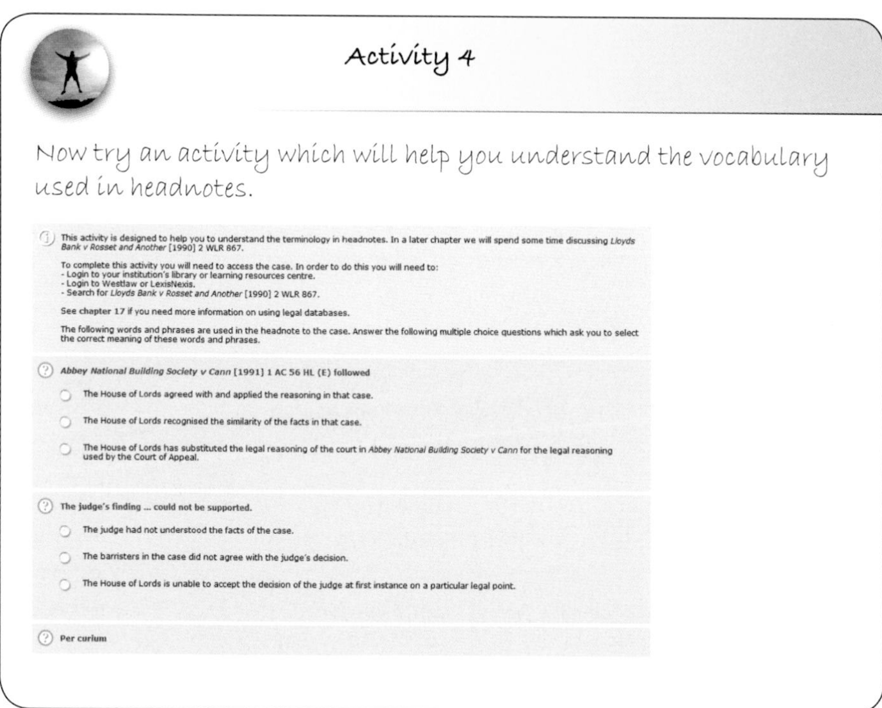

Activity 4

Now try an activity which will help you understand the vocabulary used in headnotes.

This activity is designed to help you to understand the terminology in headnotes. In a later chapter we will spend some time discussing *Lloyds Bank v Rosset and Another* [1990] 2 WLR 867.

To complete this activity you will need to access the case. In order to do this you will need to:
- Login to your institution's library or learning resources centre.
- Login to Westlaw or LexisNexis.
- Search for *Lloyds Bank v Rosset and Another* [1990] 2 WLR 867.

See chapter 17 if you need more information on using legal databases.

The following words and phrases are used in the headnote to the case. Answer the following multiple choice questions which ask you to select the correct meaning of these words and phrases.

Abbey National Building Society v Cann [1991] 1 AC 56 HL (E) followed

- The House of Lords agreed with and applied the reasoning in that case.
- The House of Lords recognised the similarity of the facts in that case.
- The House of Lords has substituted the legal reasoning of the court in *Abbey National Building Society v Cann* for the legal reasoning used by the Court of Appeal.

The judge's finding ... could not be supported.

- The judge had not understood the facts of the case.
- The barristers in the case did not agree with the judge's decision.
- The House of Lords is unable to accept the decision of the judge at first instance on a particular legal point.

Per curium

It's perfectly reasonable for a law student to ask why they need to read the full case when the headnote to the case provides a succinct summary of the decision. One answer is that the headnote is not authoritative and can be wrong. It is written by the court reporter, who is likely to be an experienced barrister, but who is not the judge in the case. Moreover, its very brevity means that it inevitably reduces the complexity of the decision making to a simplified form. That is not to say that headnotes are not helpful – read them before embarking on reading the judgment so that you understand the contours of the decision. The second reason is that there is not sufficient information in the headnote to enable you to develop a critical understanding of the case. Remember you are reading cases for more than straightforward legal information.

This is a convenient point to consider the value of textbooks and cases and materials books. The authors of these books are generally experienced teachers of law and have well-developed legal skills. What they say about the meaning of cases is very useful and should not be ignored. They can provide really useful contextual information – about why the particular dispute poses a problem, and about how the case got to court. They can give you the benefit of their perspective on the development of the law. However, their opinions on the meaning of judgments are only that – opinions. Moreover, they may be using the case to illustrate a particular point in their own argument, and so they may emphasise something that actually distorts the meaning of the decision. Reading casebooks and textbooks helps you with understanding the case; it does not substitute for reading the case.

» glossary

» glossary

Key Point

Do not read the headnote as an alternative to reading the decision. Use the headnote and comments and context from textbooks to help you with reading cases and not as a substitute for doing so.

Judgments

In chapter 23 we are going to help you develop a strategy for reading judgments – at this stage we want to explain why judgments are a complex as well as a rich source of law.

The layers of the case

Even only having read to the end of the headnote of a case we can get some idea of the complexity of the legal reasoning that will be contained in the judgment. The judgment(s) will have to respond to:

- the arguments of counsel
- the arguments used in cases on related areas
- the arguments of the lower courts

as well as developing their own line of legal argument. What this means when you are reading judgments is that you must be aware of how these different arguments are embedded in the judgment. As you read the judge's reasoning, ask yourself which argument he or she is responding to, and how persuasive he considers that argument to be. Being aware of these different arguments is extremely helpful in understanding the decision.

Thinking about how experts approach the reading of cases

One of the best ways to master any skill is to consider how experienced practitioners demonstrate the skill.

Activities 5, 6 and 7

Now go online to watch two law lecturers explaining what two different cases are about. We want you to watch these files and (a) consider how lecturers explain cases and (b) answer some questions about the cases.

The decision

Just before you embark on reading the judgment there is one other thing we would advise you to do. Find that part of the judgment where the judge makes his or her decision and tells the parties what their remedies are to be. Note the decision, or cut and paste it into a document which will be used for your notes of the case. Not only is it important in itself, it also means that before you start your reading you know where the judgment is going to end up – your destination on the map or the denouement of the play. However you understand it, knowing where you are going makes it far easier to understand the stages of the journey or the complexity of the plot.

Using cases in your work

In this final part of the chapter we remind you that you are required to use cases in your assessed work.

Remember that what is being assessed is your:

- knowledge of the law as set out in the case;
- your appreciation of the legal reasoning in the case;
- your critical understanding of the case.

If you have read the case properly and taken good notes you will have no difficulty in persuading those assessing you that you have understood the case. What lecturers do not want to see is cases being used simply to demonstrate that you recognise the case as relevant to the topic under consideration. You have to think about why the case is relevant and demonstrate that it is relevant.

Key Point

Citing cases in your work

You will be expected to cite cases properly in your essays and coursework. Be precise about citations – it demonstrates that you have paid the necessary attention to detail. You are not expected to cite cases fully in examinations. You should, however, remember the proper name of the case, and in significant cases a good candidate would know the name of the judge who gave the leading judgment.

» glossary

Conclusion

» glossary

In this chapter we have introduced you to the basic information you need to enable you to navigate a law report. You can gather essential information from the preliminary pages and the headnote to a case and you can use textbooks and lectures to help orientate you. If you identify the decision within the judgment then you will know where you are going. This means you can concentrate on reading the judgment and following the legal reasoning. You can then use cases effectively in your assessed work. In the next chapter we concentrate more on legal reasoning because we introduce you to the rule of precedent and the ratio decidendi.

www.oxfordinteract.com

Chapter 22

Reading cases 2: the rule of precedent and the operation of ratio decidendi

Rationale

We introduced you to the basics of case reading and law reports in our last chapter. In this chapter we explain more about the operation of the rule of precedent and the ratio decidendi. You need to understand these in order to fully appreciate the cases you are reading. This chapter is quite demanding. Don't worry if you find that you don't understand all of it at this stage – you can keep returning to it.

The chapter is devised to help you:

- Understand what the rule of precedent is and the reason for it
- Understand the operation of the rule of precedent in English courts and the scope for judicial flexibility
- Understand when precedent is persuasive rather than authoritative
- Know what a ratio decidendi is and how to identify it.

Introduction

» glossary

Most of us, when we begin to study law, think that what is important is who wins a case. However, whilst that may be the crucial issue for the parties, for lawyers, including law students, the most important aspects of a case are the legal reasoning and the extent to which the decision of the court provides a precedent for future cases. The creation and development of precedents, which lies at the heart of the common law system, is critical to the study of law. Understanding the operation of the rule of precedent is an essential skill which you need to master, not only for your legal studies, but also for legal practice.

A precedent is a statement of law made by a court in the course of its judgment which binds other courts which are of equal or lesser importance than the court making the precedent. Not all of the judgment binds other courts, only that part of the reasoning which is relevant to the legal decision that is being made. We spend much of this chapter elaborating upon this. At this point you should note the points below.

Key Point

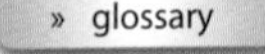

» glossary

- Precedent is relevant not only to the development of the common law, but also to the interpretation of statutes which is largely done through cases.
- The operation of the rule of precedent dovetails with the hierarchical system of the courts. This book is not the place to explain in detail that hierarchy. However, just to remind you we have set out below a simplified diagram of the hierarchy of the courts which it will be useful for you to bear in mind as you study this chapter.

Key Point (Continued)

- For the purposes of this chapter we are using the phrase 'common law' to describe those rules of law developed by the courts as opposed to those created by statute.

The doctrine of precedent has generated a specialised vocabulary – some of it Latin – which we will use throughout this chapter. We set out the main terms in the table below.

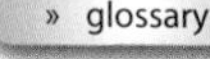

Phrase	Meaning
Stare decisis	The usual and acceptable form of the longer more accurate Latin phrase *stare rationibus decidendis* – let the reasoning of the decision stand, or in its shortened form, let the decision stand. The phrase means the rule of precedent
Ratio decidendi	The reason for the decision
Rationes decidendi	The plural of ratio decidendi – however, it is perfectly acceptable to write 'ratios'
Obiter dictum(s) Obiter dicta(pl) Dicta	Something or some things said in the decision which are not part of the ratio. Dicta can never be more than persuasive.
Per incuriam	Through carelessness – without due regard for the correct law
Authoritative precedent	Binding precedents – statements of law which fall within the rule of precedent
Persuasive precedent	Decisions by courts which are not binding, because they do not fall within the rule of precedent, but may be taken into account by other courts making other decisions
Leading case	A case which contains an authoritative precedent

Don't panic

The Latin vocabulary will initially seem difficult and unwieldy but you will soon become familiar with it from listening to lectures and from reading cases and you will quickly feel able to use it appropriately.

The purpose of the rule of precedent

The purpose of the rule is to provide a degree of legal certainty in a system of law generated by cases. People need to know what the law is and how it is likely to impact upon their disputes. In theory it also means that legal rules are developed by the most experienced and accomplished legal minds. However, the operation of the rule of precedent has other implications. Judges may not be able to deliver what they consider to be the right outcome in individual cases they hear; in other words the rule that ensures that the system as a whole delivers justice may not provide justice to the individuals before the court. Moreover, the rule means that in England and Wales it can be difficult to get rid of an awkward decision. The general responses to these criticisms are that:

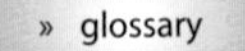

- it is for Parliament and not for the judges to amend the law and
- there is more flexibility built into the operation of precedent than might first appear.

We will look at the means whereby judges evade the strict operation of the rule below. However, we will begin the discussion by a more explicit discussion of the operation of the rule.

A simple statement of the rule of precedent

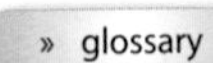

In straightforward terms the doctrine of precedent in the English common law system means that a court in England or Wales is bound to follow the decision reached by a superior court in a previous case on the same legal issue and that the appellate courts other than the House of Lords are bound by their previous decisions. What that means in concrete terms is that:

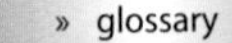

- a decision by the Court of Appeal is binding on all lower courts and is generally binding upon itself – we discuss the exceptions to this below
- the Court of Appeal is bound by decisions of the House of Lords.

Remember that, in general, the rule of precedent holds even if there are arguably good reasons for changing the law. This has been made clear by many judges, including Buckley LJ in *Produce Brokers Co. v Olympia Oil & Cake Co.* (1915) 21 Com Cas 320, a case quoted in *Young v Bristol Aeroplane* [1944] KB 718 (see below).

> I am unable to adduce any reason to show that the decision which I am about to pronounce is right. On the contrary, if I were free to follow my own opinion, my own powers of reasoning such as they are, I should say that it is wrong. But I am bound by authority – which, of course, it is my duty to follow – and, following authority, I feel bound to pronounce the judgment which I am about to deliver.

The operation of the rule of precedent in the courts of England and Wales

In other words - which courts are bound – and by whom?

The House of Lords

Between the middle of the nineteenth century and 1966 the House of Lords considered itself to be bound by its own decisions. This understanding reinforced the hierarchical structure of the court – the House of Lords provided the final level of appeal and its decisions should therefore be final, providing certainty within the law. However, the rule was increasingly criticised as excessively inflexible. Lord Gardiner, the **Lord Chancellor**, published a practice statement which changed the position of the House of Lords.

» glossary

> Their Lordships regard the use of precedent as an indispensable foundation upon which to decide what is the law and its application to individual cases. It provides at least some degree of certainty upon which individuals can rely in the conduct of their affairs, as well as a basis for orderly development of legal rules.
>
> Their Lordships nevertheless recognise that too rigid adherence to precedent may lead to injustice in a particular case and also unduly restrict the proper development of the law. They propose, therefore, to modify their present practice and, while treating former decisions of this House as normally binding, to depart from a previous decision when it appears right to do so.
>
> In this connection they will bear in mind the danger of disturbing retrospectively the basis on which contracts, settlements of property and fiscal arrangements have been entered into and also the especial need for certainty as to the criminal law.
>
> This announcement is not intended to affect the use of precedent elsewhere than in this. The practice statement is reported as Practice Statement (Judicial Precedent) [1966] 1 WLR 1234

Notice that the practice statement explains that decisions of the House of Lords are normally binding and that Lord Gardiner emphasised the especial need for certainty in the criminal law. It was not until twenty years later in the case of *R v Shivpuri* [1986] 2 All ER 334 that the practice statement was applied in a criminal case. In that case the House of Lords overruled its own decision about the meaning of s. 1(2) of the Criminal Attempts Act 1981 made one year earlier in *Anderton v Ryan* [1985] AC 560.

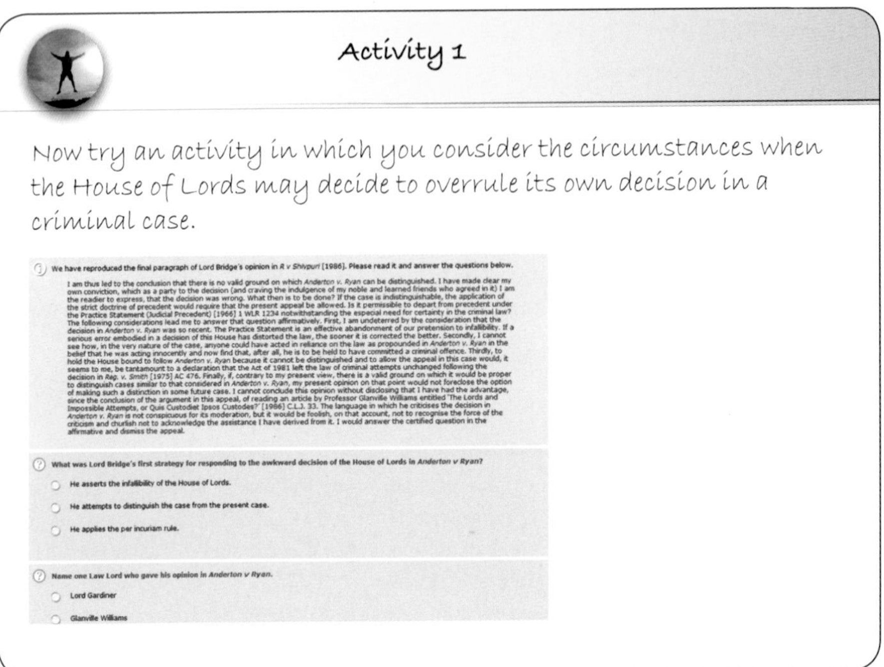

Activity 1

Now try an activity in which you consider the circumstances when the House of Lords may decide to overrule its own decision in a criminal case.

We have reproduced the final paragraph of Lord Bridge's opinion in *R v Shivpuri* [1986]. Please read it and answer the questions below.

I am thus led to the conclusion that there is no valid ground on which *Anderton v. Ryan* can be distinguished. I have made clear my own conviction, which as a party to the decision (and craving the indulgence of my noble and learned friends who agreed in it) I am the readier to express, that the decision was wrong. What then is to be done? If the case is indistinguishable, the application of the strict doctrine of precedent would require that the present appeal be allowed. Is it permissible to depart from precedent under the Practice Statement (Judicial Precedent) [1966] 1 WLR 1234 notwithstanding the especial need for certainty in the criminal law? The following considerations lead me to answer that question affirmatively. First, I am undeterred by the consideration that the decision in *Anderton v. Ryan* was so recent. The Practice Statement is an effective abandonment of our pretension to infallibility. If a serious error embodied in a decision of this House has distorted the law, the sooner it is corrected the better. Secondly, I cannot see how, in the very nature of the case, anyone could have acted in reliance on the law as propounded in *Anderton v. Ryan* in the belief that he was acting innocently and now find that, after all, he is to be held to have committed a criminal offence. Thirdly, to hold the House bound to follow *Anderton v. Ryan* because it cannot be distinguished and to allow the appeal in this case would, it seems to me, be tantamount to a declaration that the Act of 1981 left the law of criminal attempts unchanged following the decision in *Reg. v. Smith* [1975] AC 476. Finally, if, contrary to my present view, there is a valid ground on which it would be proper to distinguish cases similar to that considered in *Anderton v. Ryan*, my present opinion on that point would not foreclose the option of making such a distinction in some future case. I cannot conclude this opinion without disclosing that I have had the advantage, since the conclusion of the argument in this appeal, of reading an article by Professor Glanville Williams entitled 'The Lords and Impossible Attempts, or Quis Custodiet Ipsos Custodes?' [1986] C.L.J. 33. The language in which he criticises the decision in *Anderton v. Ryan* is not conspicuous for its moderation, but it would be foolish, on that account, not to recognise the force of the criticism and churlish not to acknowledge the assistance I have derived from it. I would answer the certified question in the affirmative and dismiss the appeal.

What was Lord Bridge's first strategy for responding to the awkward decision of the House of Lords in *Anderton v Ryan*?

- He asserts the infallibility of the House of Lords.
- He attempts to distinguish the case from the present case.
- He applies the per incuriam rule.

Name one Law Lord who gave his opinion in *Anderton v Ryan*.

- Lord Gardiner
- Glanville Williams

» glossary

Even though the House of Lords now has the power to overrule its own decisions mistakes of law made by the Law Lords may still cause legal difficulties over a long period. This is because it may take a very long time for an appropriate case to reach the Lords. In 2006 the House of Lords took an unusual step to put right a mistake that otherwise could have taken a very long time to correct. The issue is discussed by Clare Dyer, Legal Editor of the *Guardian*, in an article headlined 'Privy council overrules Lords to put judgment back on track', dated 30 January 2006.

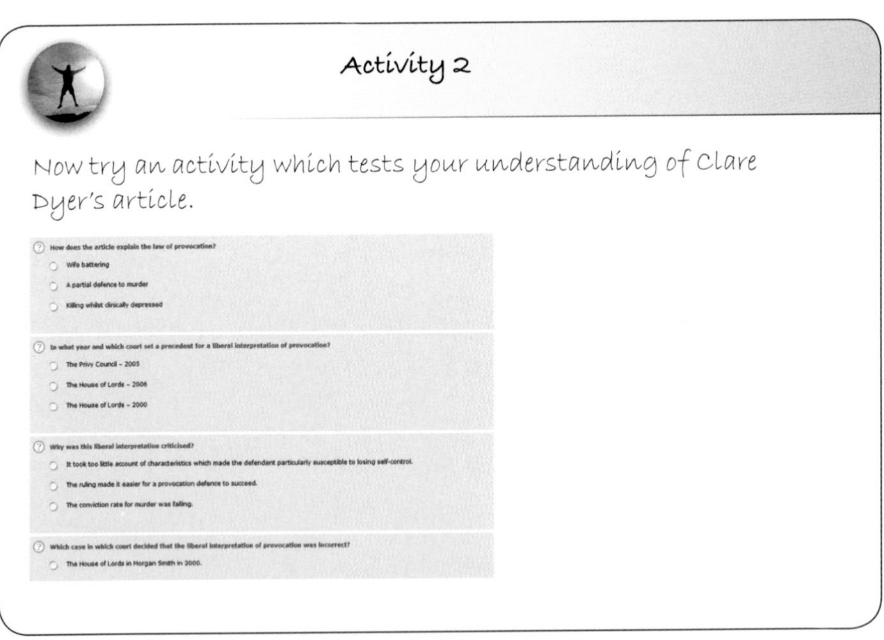

Activity 2

Now try an activity which tests your understanding of Clare Dyer's article.

How does the article explain the law of provocation?

- Wife battering
- A partial defence to murder
- Killing whilst clinically depressed

In what year and which court set a precedent for a liberal interpretation of provocation?

- The Privy Council – 2005
- The House of Lords – 2006
- The House of Lords – 2000

Why was this liberal interpretation criticised?

- It took too little account of characteristics which made the defendant particularly susceptible to losing self-control.
- The ruling made it easier for a provocation defence to succeed.
- The conviction rate for murder was falling.

Which case in which court decided that the liberal interpretation of provocation was incorrect?

- The House of Lords in Morgan Smith in 2000.

The Court of Appeal

In *Young v Bristol Aeroplane Co Ltd* 1944 KB 718 the full Court of Appeal (a court made up of five or in this case six judges rather than the more usual three) decided that in the interests of certainty and uniformity it would be absolutely bound by its prior decisions. However, Lord Greene, Master of the Rolls, outlined three exceptions to this general rule:

- The court is entitled and bound to decide which of two conflicting decisions of its own it will follow.
- The court is bound to refuse to follow a decision of its own, which, though not expressly overruled, cannot in its opinion, stand with a decision of the House of Lords.
- The Court of Appeal is not bound to follow a decision of its own if it is satisfied that the decision was given per incuriam. You will recall that per incuriam means that the decision was inaccurate because of carelessness.

There is greater flexibility in decisions made by the Criminal Division of the Court of Appeal – see *R v Gould* [1968] 2 QB 65 because a more flexible adherence to the rule of precedent is appropriate when the liberty of an individual may be at risk. In other words, stare decisis does not apply as rigidly in the criminal division as in the civil decision of the Court of Appeal.

Decisions made per incuriam

The per incuriam rule means that a court reached its decision having failed to take into account all the relevant and necessary legal material and that this failure impacted upon the decision. It does not mean that the court made a mistake, but that, through carelessness it reached its decision without having full knowledge of the law, and that the lack of knowledge had an impact on the decision. This is an important distinction.

Key Point

The per incuriam rule cannot be used to put right decisions which the Court of Appeal disagrees with, otherwise it would totally distort the operation of stare decisis.

The Divisional Court and the High Court

The Divisional Courts operate at a higher level than the High Court in the hierarchy of the courts because their jurisdictions are mainly appellate. What this means is that their decisions are binding on the High Court and that they bind themselves – although subject to the same exceptions as the Court of Appeal set out in *Young v Bristol Aeroplanes*. Decisions of the High Court are binding on the lower courts but not on other High Court judges.

The Crown Court, county and magistrates' courts and tribunals

The Crown Court is not bound by its previous decisions. However, because it is particularly important to ensure certainty in the criminal law, its previous decisions are considered to be strongly persuasive.

» glossary

Neither county courts nor magistrates' courts nor **tribunals** are bound by their own decisions.

Persuasive authority

We have made several references to decisions which are persuasive rather than authoritative. One attempt at an amusing definition of persuasive authority is *authority which you cite when you are desperate!* More usefully we describe authorities as persuasive when they are not binding. So, decisions of lower courts are persuasive only – they cannot bind superior courts. Decisions of the High Court when it is not exercising its appellate function are persuasive upon the High Court when it is, but are not binding. Decisions of the Privy Council are persuasive only (but see below). Decisions of courts in other common law jurisdictions, and decisions of the Scottish and Northern Irish courts are also persuasive.

Techniques ensuring judicial flexibility

» glossary

There is scope within the doctrine of precedent for a judge to **distinguish** cases which he or she considers to have been inappropriately decided from the decision he or she has to make. That is because not everything said by a judge when giving judgment constitutes a precedent. The rule of precedent only applies to statements of the law. Most disputes are only concerned with the facts. But we are not even concerned with everything the judge says about the law. It is only those parts of the judgment which the judge considers necessary for the decision on the law which form part of the ratio decidendi and thus amount to more than an obiter dictum.

Key Point

Noting the tactics and strategies that judges use to distinguish cases and avoid being bound is when law gets interesting.

The process of deciding whether or not the judge is bound by a previous decision is:

- to decide what the ratio decidendi of the previous case is
- then consider whether the material facts in that case are sufficiently similar to the facts in the case under consideration for that ratio to be considered to be in point.

The judge can then distinguish the case by arguing that either:

- the fact situation in the earlier case is not sufficiently similar for the ratio to be regarded as in point or
- the proposition of law relied upon by one of the parties in the case was not part of the ratio decidendi for the previous case but was made obiter and therefore is not binding on the court.

Other methods of distinguishing cases are to argue that:

- the rule laid down was wider than necessary for the decision
- that the decision is obscure
- that the decision is in conflict with other authorities or legal principles
- that the reasoning of the judge was deficient in some respect
- that the judge primarily had one fact situation in mind when he or she gave the decision and his or her reasoning cannot by analogy be applied to the fact situation in the present case.

Activity 3 and 4

Now try two activities which help you to identify some strategies that judges use when avoiding 'awkward' precedents.

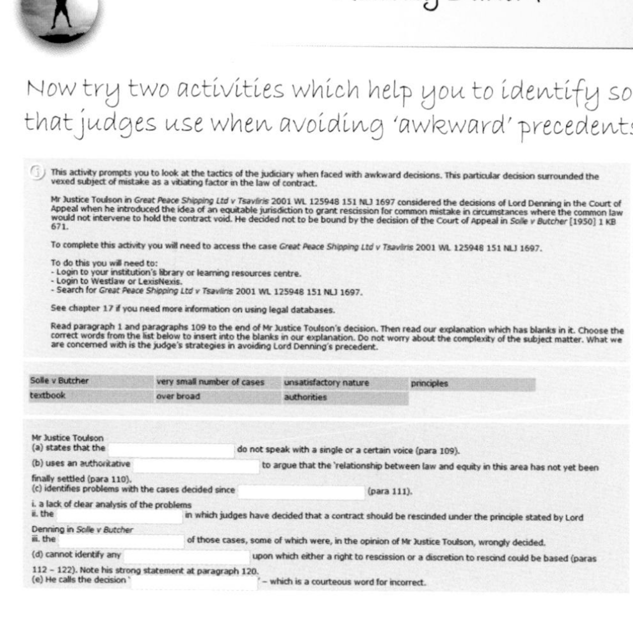

This activity prompts you to look at the tactics of the judiciary when faced with awkward decisions. This particular decision surrounded the vexed subject of mistake as a vitiating factor in the law of contract.

Mr Justice Toulson in *Great Peace Shipping Ltd v Tsavliris* 2001 WL 125948 151 NLJ 1697 considered the decisions of Lord Denning in the Court of Appeal when he introduced the idea of an equitable jurisdiction to grant rescission for common mistake in circumstances where the common law would not intervene to hold the contract void. He decided not to be bound by the decision of the Court of Appeal in *Solle v Butcher* [1950] 1 KB 671.

To complete this activity you will need to access the case *Great Peace Shipping Ltd v Tsavliris* 2001 WL 125948 151 NLJ 1697.

To do this you will need to:
- Login to your institution's library or learning resources centre.
- Login to Westlaw or LexisNexis.
- Search for *Great Peace Shipping Ltd v Tsavliris* 2001 WL 125948 151 NLJ 1697.

See chapter 17 if you need more information on using legal databases.

Read paragraph 1 and paragraphs 109 to the end of Mr Justice Toulson's decision. Then read our explanation which has blanks in it. Choose the correct words from the list below to insert into the blanks in our explanation. Do not worry about the complexity of the subject matter. What we are concerned with is the judge's strategies in avoiding Lord Denning's precedent.

Solle v Butcher	very small number of cases	unsatisfactory nature	principles
textbook	over broad	authorities	

Mr Justice Toulson
(a) states that the ______ do not speak with a single or a certain voice (para 109).
(b) uses an authoritative ______ to argue that the 'relationship between law and equity in this area has not yet been finally settled (para 110).
(c) identifies problems with the cases decided since ______ (para 111).
i. a lack of clear analysis of the problems
ii. the ______ in which judges have decided that a contract should be rescinded under the principle stated by Lord Denning in *Solle v Butcher*
iii. the ______ of those cases, some of which were, in the opinion of Mr Justice Toulson, wrongly decided.
(d) cannot identify any ______ upon which either a right to rescission or a discretion to rescind could be based (paras 112 – 122). Note his strong statement at paragraph 120.
(e) He calls the decision '______' – which is a courteous word for incorrect.

Finding the ratio decidendi for yourself

As we have already made clear it is not all of the decision which provides a binding precedent, but only that part of the legal decision that represents the legal reasoning of the judges in the case. It is that part which is described as the ratio decidendi or the ratio for short. The skill you need to develop is the ability to recognise the ratio of a case – that part of the decision which will bind inferior courts in the future. This can be difficult.

- You are not told by the judge what the ratio of the case is.
- It may be difficult to find buried in a broader discussion.
- Judges often give more than one reason for the decision they make, and in many cases there will be more than one judgment, and the different judges will base their decision upon different reasons.

Don't panic

Finding the ratio of cases is one of the most difficult legal skills. That is because the ratio can prove elusive and can often only be deduced by reading what judges in subsequent cases decide the ratio to be. You will get better at finding the ratio with practice – and much of what you study in law provides you with practice in identifying ratios. Every time you read a case you are practising finding the ratio.

Some key points

Sir Rupert Cross in his definitive work, *Precedent in English Law*, gave some useful pointers to finding ratios.

They arise from the reasoning of the judge

> The ratio decidendi of a case is any rule of law expressly or impliedly treated by the judge as a necessary step in reaching his conclusion, having regard to the line of reasoning adopted by him...

It is a matter of interpretation and argument

> No doubt the ratio decidendi of a previous case has to be gathered from the language of the judge who decided that case, but it is trite learning that the interpreter has nearly as much to say as the speaker so far as the meaning of words is concerned.

The context is crucial

> Judgements must be read in the light of the facts of the cases in which they are delivered

and

> Every judgment must be read in the light of judgments in other cases.

We look more at understanding judicial reasoning and identifying bases for decisions in the following chapters on how to read a case.

Our final set of activities in this chapter concern the mechanisms for development of the common law. We will first locate an important ratio, and then see how the common law developed in response to changing social expectations – but slowly and carefully!

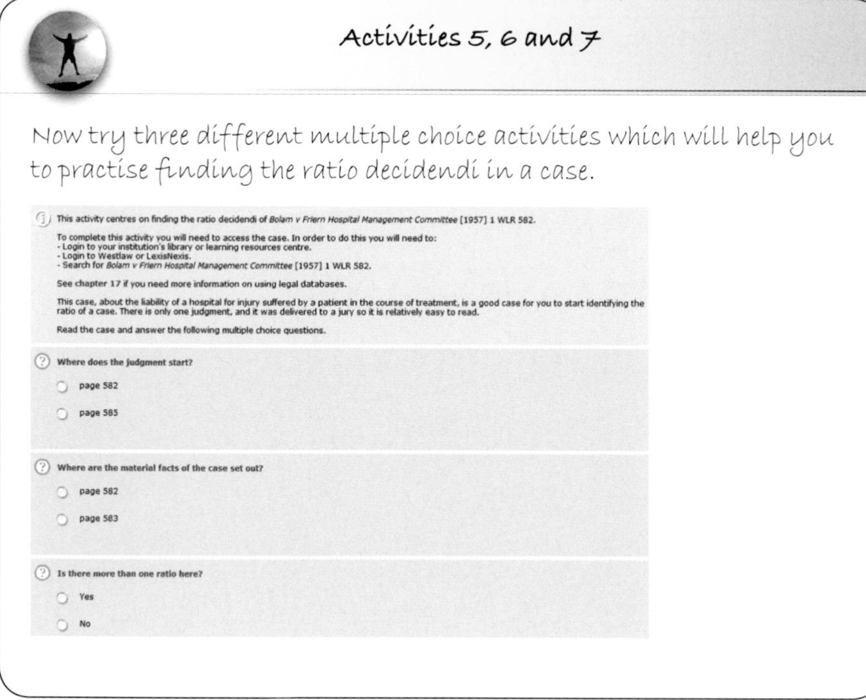

Activities 5, 6 and 7

Now try three different multiple choice activities which will help you to practise finding the ratio decidendi in a case.

This activity centres on finding the ratio decidendi of *Bolam v Friern Hospital Management Committee* [1957] 1 WLR 582.

To complete this activity you will need to access the case. In order to do this you will need to:
- Login to your institution's library or learning resources centre.
- Login to Westlaw or LexisNexis.
- Search for *Bolam v Friern Hospital Management Committee* [1957] 1 WLR 582.

See chapter 17 if you need more information on using legal databases.

This case, about the liability of a hospital for injury suffered by a patient in the course of treatment, is a good case for you to start identifying the ratio of a case. There is only one judgment, and it was delivered to a jury so it is relatively easy to read.

Read the case and answer the following multiple choice questions.

Where does the judgment start?
- page 582
- page 585

Where are the material facts of the case set out?
- page 582
- page 583

Is there more than one ratio here?
- Yes
- No

Conclusion

This chapter has been concerned with introducing you to common law method and the impact of the doctrine of stare decisis on English law. We have looked at the mechanics of the operation of the rule of precedent in the courts; considered the scope for flexibility and considered the difficulties inherent in identifying rationes. The following chapters aim to develop your skills in reading cases and understanding the rule of precedent.

Key Point

When you read cases you are concerned with the rule of precedent. You want to learn how the judge uses precedent, attempt to distinguish the current case from earlier cases, and how he or she creates new precedents.

Chapter 23

Reading cases 3: developing a strategy for reading judgments

Rationale

In this chapter we are going to help you develop a strategy for reading judgments. We describe one possible strategy for you to use. We suggest that you read this strategy through and then apply it to the case we discuss below, or to a case you are preparing for a seminar. Think about what works, and what does not work for you, and develop the strategy to fit your particular needs. Remember that the strategy is there to help you not only to acquire necessary information from the case, but also to help you locate the ratio decidendi, develop your appreciation of legal reasoning and to develop your critical understanding of the law.

This chapter is devised to:

- Explain the standard structure of a judgment
- Propose a strategy for reading judgments
- Illustrate that strategy by applying it to a particular case.

The standard structure of a judgment

A judgment is a judge's opinion on the correct resolution of the legal dispute in front of the court. It explains what the dispute is about, it explains how the judge has approached resolving the dispute and it explains what the resolution of the dispute is. All judgments are written to achieve these goals. This means that there is a standard structure to the case.

» glossary

The judge usually starts by explaining the facts of the case – the events which led to the legal dispute. The judge will usually emphasise those facts which he or she considered to be important in helping him or her reach a decision. Sometimes the account of the facts is full and clear; other times it can be unclear. Either way, it is important that you understand the facts of the case, and understand which aspects of the facts were particularly important to the judge deciding the case.

Quite often (but not always) the case will contain a section on the legal/procedural history of the case. This is an account of what has happened since legal proceedings were issued. It will explain which courts have heard the case, what their decisions were, who has appealed and why.

The judgment then usually turns to the law. The law is discussed in two sections. First, there is frequently a general discussion of the legal principles applicable to the case. These principles might be derived from statute, from the European Convention on Human Rights, from European Union law

» glossary

» glossary

or from the common law. Then the judge will discuss how he or she has applied those principles to the particular case in front of him or her.

» glossary

» glossary

Each part of the judgment is important to you. In particular, do not underestimate the importance of the facts of the case. Once you have read the chapter on the rule of precedent you will know that when you read the law part of the case you are looking out for the ratio decidendi and any dicta made by the judge. You will also know that the ratio is more important than dicta. Now that you have a general idea of the structure of judgments you can start to develop a strategic approach to reading cases. Note that not every case has to be read as fully as we suggest below. Your lecturers will indicate which cases require the closest attention.

Key Point

When you read a case make sure that you have identified:

- The facts
- The legal history
- The relevant legal principles
- The application of the legal principles to the facts of the case.

Reading cases – a strategic approach

Here is our suggested strategy for reading cases.

1. Gather together some material to help you understand the context of the case – use textbooks, lectures and your notes from seminars. If you are using a casebook which suggests questions at the end of cases, then use those questions as a prompt for your reading. Ensure you have any seminar questions about the case to hand.
2. Read the introductory pages of the case, picking up the information we suggested in chapter 21, Reading cases I – the basics. Print out those pages as an aid to your work.
3. Find and record the decision.
4. Read the case through quickly, noting only the location of the key constituents of the decision, the facts, the matter(s) in dispute, the legal history, the legal reasoning, and any general rule – precedent – which emerges. Remember the layers of decision

making we discussed earlier. Note when the judgment refers to an argument in the lower courts, or an argument from counsel. Make a mental or a marginal note of these structural points. As you read, pay particular attention to anything in the text that indicates it is important. Quite often judges state – *It is particularly important to note that*…or *One fundamental question that must be asked*…. These are vital clues to understanding the text. You may even resort to doing a 'search and find' scan of the text on screen to look for the word 'important'.

» glossary

5. Highlight words that you do not understand and look them up in a legal dictionary.
6. The next step is to spend more time on the facts and the matter in dispute. Make sure you have got these clear in your head before you move on to the judicial reasoning.
7. Now read the case through slowly, employing strategies which ensure that you engage with the text as you read. For instance, you should:
   - Make marginal notes.
   - Ask questions of the text – Why is the judge saying this? What is he or she saying?
   - Try to work out why the judge is referring to a particular authority or line of argument.
   - If you really get lost whilst trying to decipher a complex part of the decision, then read the passage out loud. That often helps you focus and follow the text.
   - If you are doing your reading on screen, you could try cutting and pasting various parts of the decision under the headings we set out in 2 above. In our experience simply highlighting parts of the case does not work. Students frequently turn up to seminars with the highlighted text and then have little idea why they highlighted those particular points, and are certainly not able to navigate around the case to answer the questions seminar leaders ask.
8. As you read, think about the sort of questions you might be asked by your seminar leader and think of some questions to ask your seminar leader.
9. Finally read the case through again. You are not going to understand it or remember it until you have read it two or three times. Check your understanding by explaining the case to someone. However, if there are parts of the case you do not understand even after re-reading, make a note and ask your seminar leader.

Activity 1

Now try an activity which is designed to help you apply this strategy to a particular case – *Lloyds Bank v Rosset* [1991] 1 AC 107.

The activity guides you through the six key steps below.

Applying the strategy to the judgment of Lord Bridge in *Lloyds Bank v Rosset* [1991] 1 AC 107

Step 1: The preliminaries – before starting to read the judgment

» glossary

(a) Open the case and open a Word document. Head the document with the name of the case and the citation. Then put headings for the following – the facts – the matter(s) in dispute – the legal history – the legal reasoning – any general rule which emerges. You should also have a heading for any additional comments you want to make about the case.

(b) Look in your property law text book and at your lecture notes for references to the case – make a note of what you think is important in your Word document.

(c) Read and then print out the preliminary pages of the decision to keep beside you as you read the screen.

» glossary

(d) You know from reading the headnote that part of the decision is per curiam. Find those paragraphs of the judgment and paste these into your document under the proper heading.

(e) Find Lord Bridge's decision (hint, it is at the end of his judgment) and cut and paste that decision into your Word document.

Note this is a working document – you can refine it as you progress with your reading of the case and you should return to it after you have attended a seminar on the case to ensure you are happy with it as a record of your understanding of the case.

Step 2

Read the case quickly and mark out roughly its key components. We have done this on screen for you. Notice any vocabulary in the decision that suggests that a point is of particular importance.

Step 3

The next step is to spend quite a lot of time making sure you have understood and properly recorded the facts and the legal history of the case. Set out the facts in your word document under the decision. We have provided a summary of the facts for you to compare and contrast with your own version. Work out the legal history and put that into your Word document at the appropriate point.

Step 4

Now read the judgment through slowly and carefully, engaging with the text. Look words up in a dictionary if you do not understand them. If you have to answer seminar questions bear these in mind as you read. Follow the suggestions we made earlier to ensure that you engage with the text. When you have done this compare your notes and questions with ours. Make notes in the Word document under the appropriate headings as you read.

Step 5

Read the judgment through again and then refine your notes of the decision, ensuring that you have something under each heading in your Word document. If there are questions arising from the decision that you need to ask your seminar teacher, make a note of them on your Word document. You should print out both the case and your Word document to take to the seminar.

Step 6

Following the seminar add what you have learned about the case to your notes. The Word document should provide you with sufficient information for revision purposes, as you will not have time to return to the original case.

We will return to this case when we consider how you use cases in essays, in problem questions and in exams. You can assess the value of your notes by considering the extent to which they help you answer the questions that are set. In the next chapter we are going to consider how you need to develop your skills in order to deal with a more complex case.

» glossary

Key Point

One problem in learning law is that it is not possible to introduce students to cases in order of increasing difficulty. Basic legal principles may be contained in very complex cases, so you may be required to read difficult cases early in your legal career. You need to develop strategies in order to deal with this.

Conclusion

You will not use your time and energy effectively by reading a case, like a novel, from beginning to end. Such an approach would be counter-productive and confusing. We suggest you take a strategic approach to reading cases. This requires that you understand the normal structure of judgments, and that you absorb the necessary information from headnotes and textbooks and lectures. We are not trying to prescribe how you should develop your strategy. Instead we have suggested one approach which you can adapt. Use it, evaluate it and develop it for your own needs.

www.oxfordinteract.com

Chapter 24

Reading cases 4: a complex case

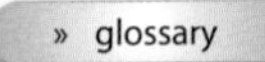

Rationale

In earlier chapters we have introduced you to cases and the rule of precedent, and helped you develop a strategy for reading cases. In this chapter we suggest ways in which you can develop your case reading skills by applying them to a more complex and longer case.

The chapter is devised to provide you with:

- Guidance for reading a complex case
- Activities to check your understanding
- Suggestions to develop your case reading skills.

Reading a more complex case: *A v Secretary of State for the Home Department* [2005] 2 AC 68

This is an important and complex case concerning the appropriate relationship between Parliament and the judiciary in the contentious field of human rights and terrorism. It is one which is essential for you to read and understand. However, we accept that the task can seem daunting. The decision is very long – over 100 pages. It refers to a number of other decisions, treaties, legal opinions and academic articles. The purpose of this chapter is to provide you with some hands-on guidance as to how you can develop the strategy we have already outlined to master this case. Note that you are going to need at least two to three hours to read this case – you cannot wait till just before your seminar! If you are using these notes online, you should ensure that the text of the case is open alongside the notes. If you are doing this from the printed page, you will need to have the case in front of you alongside this resource. Note we are going to make the task easier by looking only at Lord Bingham's judgment.

Why are you reading this case?

This takes us back to the first of our case reading chapters. We suggested that if you know in general what you hope to gain from reading a case, then you may better be able to manage the task. The question also relates to the rule of precedent and the need to identify the ratio of the case.

Activity 1

Consider why you are reading this case. Go online to read our thoughts on this matter.

The starting point

With such a long case, it is particularly important to start by getting an overview of the case. Open a Word document and head it with the name of the case and the citation. Put the headings as we suggested in our last chapter, for facts, matters in dispute, legal history, legal reasoning, precedent and additional comments. Check what your lecturer has said about the case. Then check how your textbook deals with the case. Both these sources are likely to be very helpful. Note anything useful in the additional comments part of your Word document. Read the preliminary information and the headnote as well, note what is significant, and print it out to have it beside you as you work. Next, cut and paste the decision in this case into your Word document. You now know what answer Lord Bingham gave to the legal problem facing the House of Lords. The much more difficult task is to work out how he got to his decision.

» glossary

» glossary

» glossary

» glossary

Cross reference
See chapter 23, Reading cases III.

Step 2

Move now to step 2 of our general strategy. Read Lord Bingham's judgment quickly and mark out its key components. One way to manage Lord Bingham's 73 paragraphs is to note down how he breaks them up into sections with headings.

Activity 2

Now try an activity to check that you have understood how Lord Bingham organises his judgment.

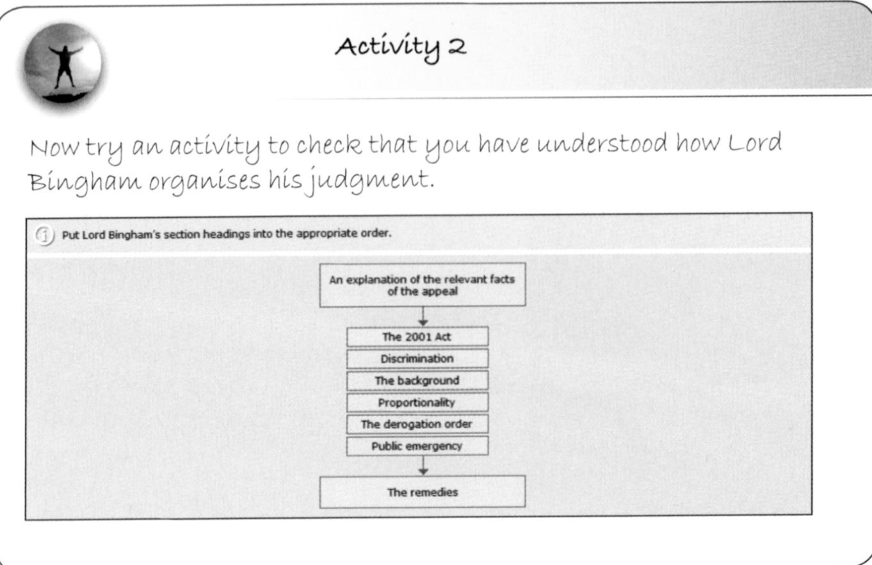
Put Lord Bingham's section headings into the appropriate order.
An explanation of the relevant facts of the appeal
The 2001 Act
Discrimination
The background
Proportionality
The derogation order
Public emergency
The remedies

Another useful strategy in managing such a lot of text is to colour code the case, shading the appellants' argument one colour, the Attorney General's arguments another colour, and the points where the judge makes a decision in another colour. It is important to get this right. Students often make mistakes because they have confused those parts of the judgment where the judge is talking about the submissions of the parties with those parts of the judgment where he or she is explaining his or her decision making.

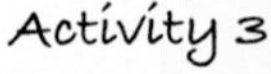

Activity 3

Colour code the case and then go online to compare your colour coding with ours.

Step 3

You have now got a basic outline of the case. However, you need to spend some time on working out its history and its legislative context, so set yourself some simple tasks:

- Set out all of the forums where the appellants' case has been heard.
- Make a note of the relevant facts.
- List the relevant legislative provisions.

In noting the relevant law ensure that you refer to the relevant statutory provisions of the Anti-Terrorism, Crime and Security Act 2001 (which is primary legislation) and the Human Rights (Designated Derogation) Order 2001 (secondary legislation) and the relevant articles of the European Convention on Human Rights (ECHR). Just make a note of the necessary information in bullet point form at this moment. You can provide further elaboration of the facts and the law as you gain a greater understanding of the case.

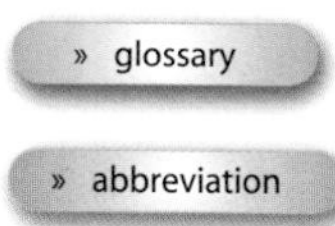

Next we suggest that you:

- Summarise the basis of the appeal – 'the matter in dispute' – in your Word document.
- Note how the decision differs from the decision in the Court of Appeal.

Do not only think about the point of law upon which the appellants succeeded. Also consider the point(s) on which it failed.

Cross reference
For further information on primary and secondary legislation see chapter 19, Reading statutes and the legislative process.

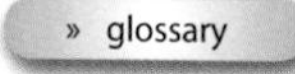

Step 4: Developing your understanding of the decision

The next step is for you to get to grips with the decision and start forming your own opinion about it.

Note where Lord Bingham concentrates his efforts. He has a lot to say about the public emergency, proportionality, and discrimination. That might suggest to you which areas are the most contentious.

The first thing to do here is to read the background paragraphs carefully (from 1–15). Once you are happy that you have understood what has been going on both legally and politically, then you are ready to tackle the more substantive parts of Bingham's decision.

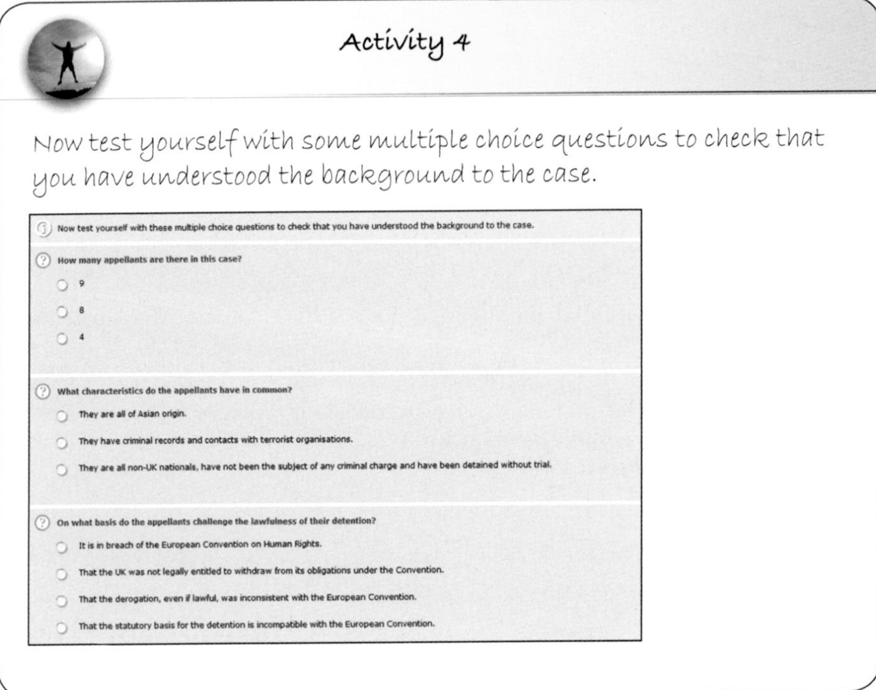

Activity 4

Now test yourself with some multiple choice questions to check that you have understood the background to the case.

Now test yourself with these multiple choice questions to check that you have understood the background to the case.

How many appellants are there in this case?

- 9
- 8
- 4

What characteristics do the appellants have in common?

- They are all of Asian origin.
- They have criminal records and contacts with terrorist organisations.
- They are all non-UK nationals, have not been the subject of any criminal charge and have been detained without trial.

On what basis do the appellants challenge the lawfulness of their detention?

- It is in breach of the European Convention on Human Rights.
- That the UK was not legally entitled to withdraw from its obligations under the Convention.
- That the derogation, even if lawful, was inconsistent with the European Convention.
- That the statutory basis for the detention is incompatible with the European Convention.

On your preliminary read through you may have noticed references to a number of other sources of opinion about the reconciliation of anti-terrorism legislation and the ECHR. You will need to understand the sources of these opinions.

Check that you know what the following are:

SIAC

The Newton Committee

The Joint Committee on Human Rights

The ICCPR

The Commissioner for Human Rights

UN Human Rights Committee

The Siracusa Principles

↳ Cross reference
For suggestions on how to do this see chapter 13, Sources of law.

If you do not know what they are, then find out!

The following discussion is going to concentrate on the most important elements of Lord Bingham's decision. In effect, we are going to talk you through Lord Bingham's reasoning, raising some questions for you to answer for yourself.

Public emergency

There must be a public emergency threatening the life of the nation before there can be a derogation from article 5 of the ECHR – see Article 15.

Lord Bingham begins with the appellants' assertion, that there neither was, nor is, a 'public emergency threatening the life of the nation' within the meaning of article 15(1). How does Lord Bingham respond to this assertion? He uses decisions of both the European Court and the ICCPR.

- **Decisions of the European Court.** Lord Bingham looks at European Court cases which consider the meaning of article 15(1). At this point you should list the names of the cases and note Lord Bingham's conclusions. What he highlights is that in each of the cases the European Court finds that there was a public emergency within the meaning of article 15(1), and that the Court is careful to note the important role of national authorities in deciding whether or not there is a public emergency. He also notes that there remains a role for the courts in supervising the decision about the public emergency.
- **The International Covenant on Civil and Political Rights.** At para. 19 of the decision Lord Bingham refers to the ICCPR.

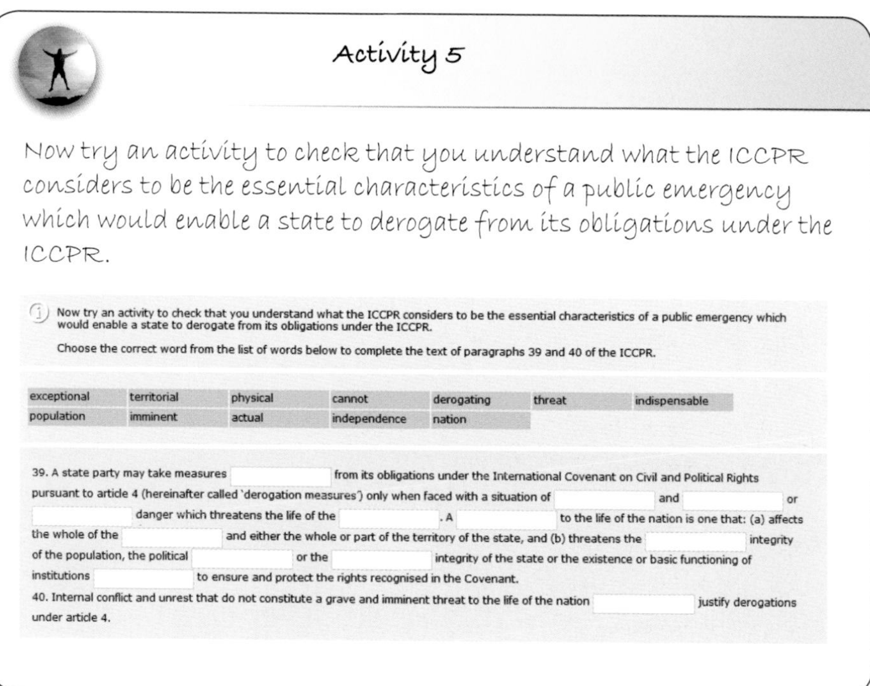

Activity 5

Now try an activity to check that you understand what the ICCPR considers to be the essential characteristics of a public emergency which would enable a state to derogate from its obligations under the ICCPR.

Now try an activity to check that you understand what the ICCPR considers to be the essential characteristics of a public emergency which would enable a state to derogate from its obligations under the ICCPR.

Choose the correct word from the list of words below to complete the text of paragraphs 39 and 40 of the ICCPR.

exceptional	territorial	physical	cannot	derogating	threat	indispensable
population	imminent	actual	independence	nation		

39. A state party may take measures ______ from its obligations under the International Covenant on Civil and Political Rights pursuant to article 4 (hereinafter called 'derogation measures') only when faced with a situation of ______ and ______ or ______ danger which threatens the life of the ______. A ______ to the life of the nation is one that: (a) affects the whole of the ______ and either the whole or part of the territory of the state, and (b) threatens the ______ integrity of the population, the political ______ or the ______ integrity of the state or the existence or basic functioning of institutions ______ to ensure and protect the rights recognised in the Covenant.

40. Internal conflict and unrest that do not constitute a grave and imminent threat to the life of the nation ______ justify derogations under article 4.

So far Lord Bingham's reasoning is not looking good for the appellants. At this point he returns to the appellants' argument and the way in which they have developed it to respond to the cases. What they say is threefold. For there to be a public emergency within the meaning of article 15(1):

- it must be imminent
- it must be of a temporary nature
- and in some sense there should be a shared understanding within Europe that it is a public emergency.

In the opinion of the appellants, these features are essential and none of these features are in place. Lord Bingham also considers the Attorney General's rebuttal of these points.

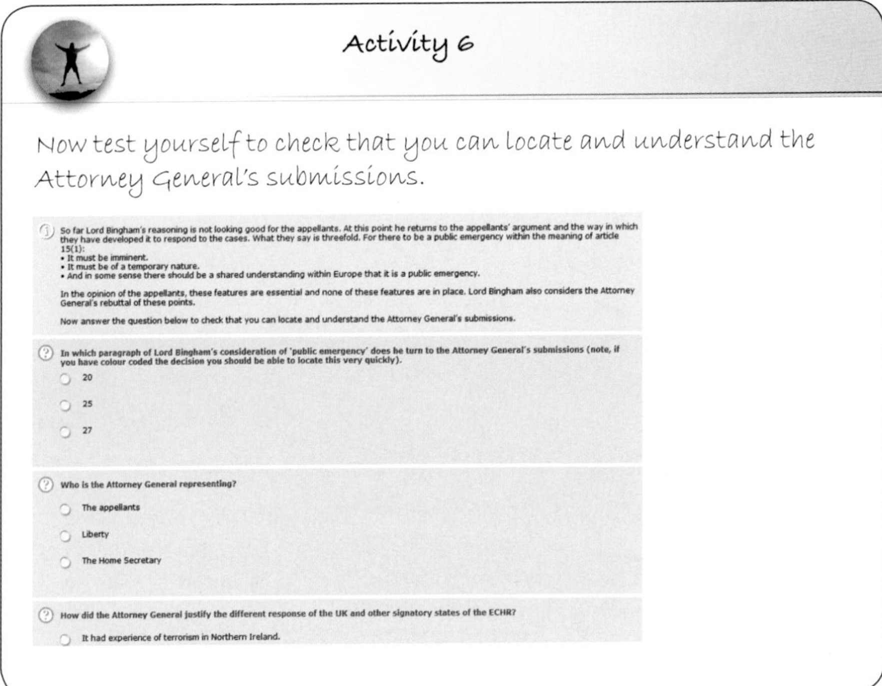

Activity 6

Now test yourself to check that you can locate and understand the Attorney General's submissions.

So far Lord Bingham's reasoning is not looking good for the appellants. At this point he returns to the appellants' argument and the way in which they have developed it to respond to the cases. What they say is threefold. For there to be a public emergency within the meaning of article 15(1):

- It must be imminent.
- It must be of a temporary nature.
- And in some sense there should be a shared understanding within Europe that it is a public emergency.

In the opinion of the appellants, these features are essential and none of these features are in place. Lord Bingham also considers the Attorney General's rebuttal of these points.

Now answer the question below to check that you can locate and understand the Attorney General's submissions.

In which paragraph of Lord Bingham's consideration of 'public emergency' does he turn to the Attorney General's submissions (note, if you have colour coded the decision you should be able to locate this very quickly).

- 20
- 25
- 27

Who is the Attorney General representing?

- The appellants
- Liberty
- The Home Secretary

How did the Attorney General justify the different response of the UK and other signatory states of the ECHR?

- It had experience of terrorism in Northern Ireland.

Lord Bingham's decision on public emergency

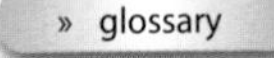

Lord Bingham takes the appellants' arguments about the necessary characteristics of a public emergency very seriously. Look at what he says in para. 26. If you are preparing this case for an essay question, it would be worth looking at the thoughts of the Joint Committee on Human Rights, the observations of the Commissioner for Human Rights and the warnings of the UN Human Rights Committee. You should also look at the opinion of Lord Hoffmann. You will have to make up your own mind as to whether Lord Bingham's decision to disagree with Lord Hoffmann is the right decision.

Lord Bingham decides to reject the appellants' arguments on the meaning of public emergency.

Activity 7

Jot down the three reasons why Lord Bingham rejected the appellants' arguments on the meaning of public emergency.

Go online to read our thoughts on this matter.

Proportionality

The question of proportionality in *A v Home Secretary* is framed in the following terms: Were the measures 'strictly required by the exigencies of the situation?'

The easiest place to start to unravel Lord Bingham's decision is with the arguments of the appellants. The main thrust of their argument is set out in para. 30. 'They submitted that even if it were accepted that the legislative objective of protecting the British people against the risk of catastrophic Al-Qaeda terrorism was sufficiently important to justify limiting the fundamental right to personal freedom of those facing no criminal accusation, the 2001 Act was not designed to meet that objective and was not rationally connected to it. Furthermore, the legislative objective could have been achieved by means which did not, or did not so severely, restrict the fundamental right to personal freedom'. Note that the appellants' argument survives the failure of their argument on the nature of the public emergency.

One way to approach Lord Bingham's decision on proportionality is to split it into three. He considers:

1. Whether the measures are a logical response to the situation.
2. The judicial deference required when the issue at stake is the liberty of the individual.

3. As appeals from SIAC are limited to points of law, whether SIAC's decision to reject the appellants' challenge can be appealed?

We will consider these three points separately.

Were the measures a logical response to the terrorist threat?

Let's summarise the relevant points of the appellants' argument here.

- The threat to the UK did not derive solely from foreign nationals who could not be deported because they would face torture etc. in their home countries. In particular, ss. 21 and 23 of the Act did not rationally address the threat to the security of the UK because:
  - They did not address the threat presented by UK nationals.
  - They permitted foreign nationals suspected of being Al-Qaeda terrorists or their supporters to pursue their activities abroad if there was any country to which they were able to go.
  - They permitted the certification and detention of persons as Al-Qaeda terrorists or supporters those who were not suspected of presenting any threat to the security of the UK
  - If threats posed by UK nationals can be addressed without infringing their right to personal liberty, then similar measures could address the threat posed by foreign nationals.

Lord Bingham looks at evidence from SIAC, from the European Commissioner for Human Rights, and from the Newton Committee to evaluate the appellants' arguments and finds it compelling.

The question of judicial deference when the issue at stake is the liberty of the individual

The sixth step of the appellants' argument was concerned with the fundamental importance of the right to personal freedom. Here Lord Bingham mentions:

- The Magna Carta
- Statements in recent English cases
- Statements of the European Court
- The Siracusa Principles.

It is at this point that Lord Bingham addresses the submission of the Attorney General which is concerned with the significance of judicial deference. It is fully set out in para. 37. The crucial point the Attorney General makes is 'that it was for Parliament and the executive to assess the threat facing the nation, so it was for those bodies and not the courts to judge the response necessary to protect the security of the public'.

Lord Bingham takes the argument very seriously and weighs up the European and domestic legal authorities to decide what degree of judicial respect should be accorded to political decisions. He observes that judicial deference will depend upon the nature of the political decision, and considers the particular importance of the right to individual liberty. Here he draws on Canadian and United States decisions, as well as European cases and the opinions of the European Commissioner for Human Rights and the Newton Committee. He refers to the House of Lords decision in *R (Daly) v Secretary of State for the Home Department* [2001] 2 AC 532, paras. 23, 27: 'domestic courts must themselves form a judgement whether a Convention right has been breached' and that 'the intensity of review is somewhat greater under the proportionality approach'. The logic of these authorities leads to his decision, which is set out in paras. 42 and 43. In summary:

- The appellants are entitled to invite the courts to review, on proportionality grounds, the Derogation Order and the compatibility with the Convention of s. 23 Anti-terrorism, Crime and Security Act 2001.
- The courts are not precluded from doing so by any doctrine of deference.
- The Human Rights Act 1998 gives the courts a very specific, wholly democratic mandate.
- The appellants' proportionality challenge is sound.

His conclusion is that the Order and s. 23 in Convention terms are disproportionate.

The decision of SIAC

Lord Bingham's argument is set out in para. 44. He notes SIAC's four reasons for rejecting the appellants' challenge on proportionality. However, he considers that the reasons given by SIAC do not warrant its conclusion. 'The first reason does not explain why the measures are directed only to foreign nationals. The second reason no doubt has some validity, but is subject to the same weakness. The third reason does not explain why a terrorist, if a serious threat to the UK, ceases to be so on the French side of the English Channel or elsewhere. The fourth reason is intelligible if the foreign national is not really thought to be a serious threat to the UK, but hard to understand if he is'. However, this is not sufficient for Lord Bingham. He also has to deal with the Court of Appeal's decision that SIAC's findings are findings of fact, and therefore are unappealable. What he decides is that SIAC's findings go to the heart of proportionality and therefore cannot be described as simple findings of fact:

> The greater intensity of review now required in determining questions of proportionality, and the duty of the courts to protect Convention rights, would in my view be emasculated if a judgement at first instance on such a question were conclusively to preclude any further review... In my opinion SIAC erred in law and the Court of Appeal erred in failing to correct its error.

Activity 8

Now try an activity to check that you have understood Lord Bingham's reasoning on proportionality.

Answer the questions below to check that you have understood Lord Bingham's reasoning on proportionality.

Into how many separate steps does Lord Bingham organise the appellants' submission?

- 5
- 6
- 7

What does this sentence, 'But the evidence before us demonstrates beyond argument that the threat is not so confined', from para. 95 of SIAC's judgment mean?

- That SIAC agreed with the Home Secretary that serious threats to the nation emanated predominantly from foreign nations.
- That SIAC considered that far more foreign nationals required detention than the 9 appellants in this case.
- That SIAC disagreed with the Home Secretary that serious threats to the nation emanated predominantly from foreign nations.

Which of the following is NOT a comment made by the European Commissioner for Human Rights in his Opinion 1/2002?

- That the derogating measures of the Anti-terrorism, Crime and Security Act allow for the detention of those presenting no direct threat to the UK.
- That the derogating measures of the Anti-terrorism, Crime and Security Act allow for the release of those of whom it is alleged to present a threat to the UK.
- That an individual who has links with a terrorist organisation must be released and deported to a safe receiving country should one become available.
- That the exigencies of the situation justify the harsh although paradoxical measures implemented by the UK government.

Discrimination

Article 14 of the ECHR is a very important article, with wide-reaching implications which have not yet been fully explored in the cases.

Lord Bingham approaches the article as relating to equality before the law. Note that article 14 'piggy-backs' on other articles. What that means is that the obligation on the state not to discriminate applies only to rights which it is bound to protect under the Convention.

Lord Bingham made two important points before considering the dispute between the parties which you must understand.

- The UK did not derogate from article 14 of the ECHR in the legislation under review.
- The foreign nationality of the appellants does not preclude them from claiming the protection of their Convention rights.

The question in dispute was: 'Did the Secretary of State discriminate against the appellants on the ground of their nationality or immigration status?'

Lord Bingham answers this question by drawing on the questions posed in para. 42 of *R (S) v Chief Constable of the South Yorkshire Police* [2004] 1 WLR 2196.

Activity 9

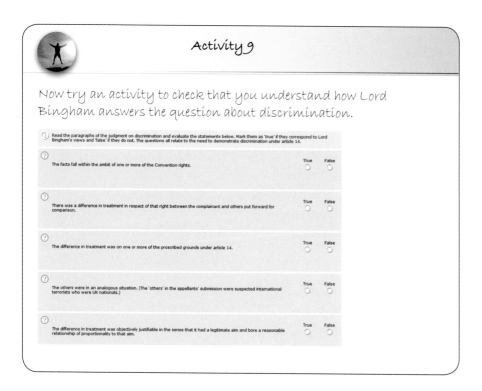

Now try an activity to check that you understand how Lord Bingham answers the question about discrimination.

Read the paragraphs of the judgment on discrimination and evaluate the statements below. Mark them as 'true' if they correspond to Lord Bingham's views and 'false' if they do not. The questions all relate to the need to demonstrate discrimination under article 14.

Statement	True	False
The facts fall within the ambit of one or more of the Convention rights.	○	○
There was a difference in treatment in respect of that right between the complainant and others put forward for comparison.	○	○
The difference in treatment was on one or more of the proscribed grounds under article 14.	○	○
The others were in an analogous situation. (The 'others' in the appellants' submission were suspected international terrorists who were UK nationals.)	○	○
The difference in treatment was objectively justifiable in the sense that it had a legitimate aim and bore a reasonable relationship of proportionality to that aim.	○	○

The final question of activity 9 – was the difference in treatment objectively justifiable in the sense that it had a legitimate aim and bore a reasonable relationship of proportionality to that aim? – attracted detailed submissions from the Attorney General which we need to pay more attention to.

The Attorney General made three important points in his attempt to suggest that the difference in treatment was objectively justifiable. First, he suggested that the relevant comparators were non-UK nationals who represented a threat to the security of the UK but who could be removed to their own or to safe third countries. The relevant difference between them and the appellants was that the appellants could not be removed. A difference of treatment of the two groups was accordingly justified and it was reasonable and necessary to detain the appellants – see para. 52.

Secondly, in para. 55, Lord Bingham records the Attorney General's submission that the Convention permits the differential treatment of aliens as compared with nationals, and that international law sanctions the differential treatment, including detention, of aliens in times of war or public emergency. Lord Bingham draws on a wide range of materials in paras. 55–62 to rebut these submissions. He accepts that the materials he cites are not legally binding on the United Kingdom, but concludes that 'these materials are inimical to the submission that a state may lawfully discriminate against foreign nationals by detaining them but not nationals presenting the same threat in a time of public emergency' – para. 63. He then turns to para. 194 of the Newton Committee report, and the relevant reports of the Joint Committee on Human Rights which together provide strong condemnation of the government's approach. Moreover, SIAC also concluded that s. 23 was discriminatory and in breach of article 14 of the Convention. Lord Bingham has to respond to the Court of Appeal decision that there was no breach of article 14. He rejects its analysis.

> Any discriminatory measure inevitably affects a smaller rather than a larger group, but cannot be justified on the ground that more people would be adversely affected if the measure were applied generally. What has to be justified is not the measure in issue but the difference in treatment between one person or group and another. What cannot be justified here is the decision to detain one group of suspected international terrorists, defined by nationality or immigration status, and not another. (para. 68)

The final point that Lord Bingham attends to here is the claim that there is some historic or public international law argument which allows states to treat aliens in a discriminatory way. Brooke LJ in the Court of Appeal accepted the public international law argument. However, whilst Lord Bingham considers the international law instruments to which the Attorney General drew his attention, together with some cases from the United States, he decides at para. 70, that he is not convinced. 'Neither singly nor cumulatively do these materials, in my opinion, support a conclusion other than that which I have expressed' – specifically that article 14 had been breached.

Remedies

The final point you should note in relation to Lord Bingham's decision is the remedies he provides for the appellants. In para. 73 he states:

> there will be a quashing order in respect of the Human Rights Act 1998 (Designated Derogation) Order 2001. There will also be a declaration under section 4 of the Human Rights Act 1998 that section 23 of the Anti-Terrorism, Crime and Security Act 2001 is incompatible with articles 5 and 14 of the European Convention in so far as it is disproportionate and permits detention of suspected international terrorists in a way that discriminates on the ground of nationality or immigration status.

Remember the provisions of the Human Rights Act 1998; the courts can quash secondary legislation but only make declarations of incompatibility where they consider that primary legislation is in breach of the Convention.

What next? Completing step 5

You have now worked your way through one of the speeches in the case. Don't worry, the other judgments are shorter. Moreover by reading one speech very carefully you are much better prepared to tackle the others. Remember that each judgment will have a different ratio. However, at this point we want to check that you have gathered the necessary information from reading the case.

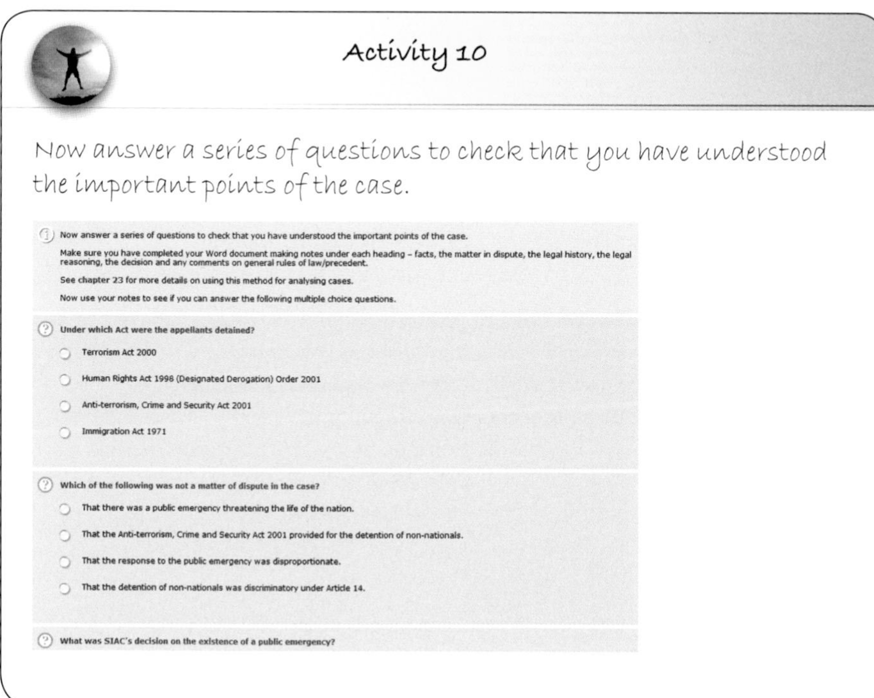

Activity 10

Now answer a series of questions to check that you have understood the important points of the case.

Now answer a series of questions to check that you have understood the important points of the case.

Make sure you have completed your Word document making notes under each heading – facts, the matter in dispute, the legal history, the legal reasoning, the decision and any comments on general rules of law/precedent.

See chapter 23 for more details on using this method for analysing cases.

Now use your notes to see if you can answer the following multiple choice questions.

Under which Act were the appellants detained?

- Terrorism Act 2000
- Human Rights Act 1998 (Designated Derogation) Order 2001
- Anti-terrorism, Crime and Security Act 2001
- Immigration Act 1971

Which of the following was not a matter of dispute in the case?

- That there was a public emergency threatening the life of the nation.
- That the Anti-terrorism, Crime and Security Act 2001 provided for the detention of non-nationals.
- That the response to the public emergency was disproportionate.
- That the detention of non-nationals was discriminatory under Article 14.

What was SIAC's decision on the existence of a public emergency?

Learning through reflection

We have just guided you through reading a difficult case. Neither we, nor your lecturers can provide this level of help on every case you read. What you have to do is to treat this as one model for reading a complex case. We suggest that you reflect on the strategy we have suggested, work out what has been helpful to you and what you did not find useful.

Think about the value of using colour codings to separate out appellants' and the Attorney General's arguments from the actual decisions of the judge, and using boxes to keep track of answers to the questions that the judge raises in his analysis of the arguments. Are these ideas you could adopt? When you have read the other judgments carry out step 5 of our strategy again – read Lord Bingham's judgment through again and refine your notes of the decision, ensuring that you have something under each heading in your Word document. It's at this point that you should start to form a critical view of the judgment. To help you do this think about the following questions:

- How do Lord Bingham and the other judges view the relationship between the courts, the executive and Parliament? Does this accord with your view of the relationship, or the standard textbook explanation?
- Put the decision into the context of your understanding of the rule of law. Why did the government legislate on this issue, and to what extent was the legislative process itself shaped by human rights?

- What light does the case shed on the impact of human rights on the judicial review process?

These are hard questions, but by engaging with them and using the text of the case you can begin to develop a critical understanding of the case.

Conclusion

Not every case will require the same level of intellectual energy. However, there will be several cases which you will come across in your first term and in your first year which will be equally demanding. You cannot avoid hard intellectual work when you are unravelling these cases. However, we are sure that with our suggestions and practice you will learn how to use your time effectively.

www.oxfordinteract.com

Part 4

Academic and assessment skills

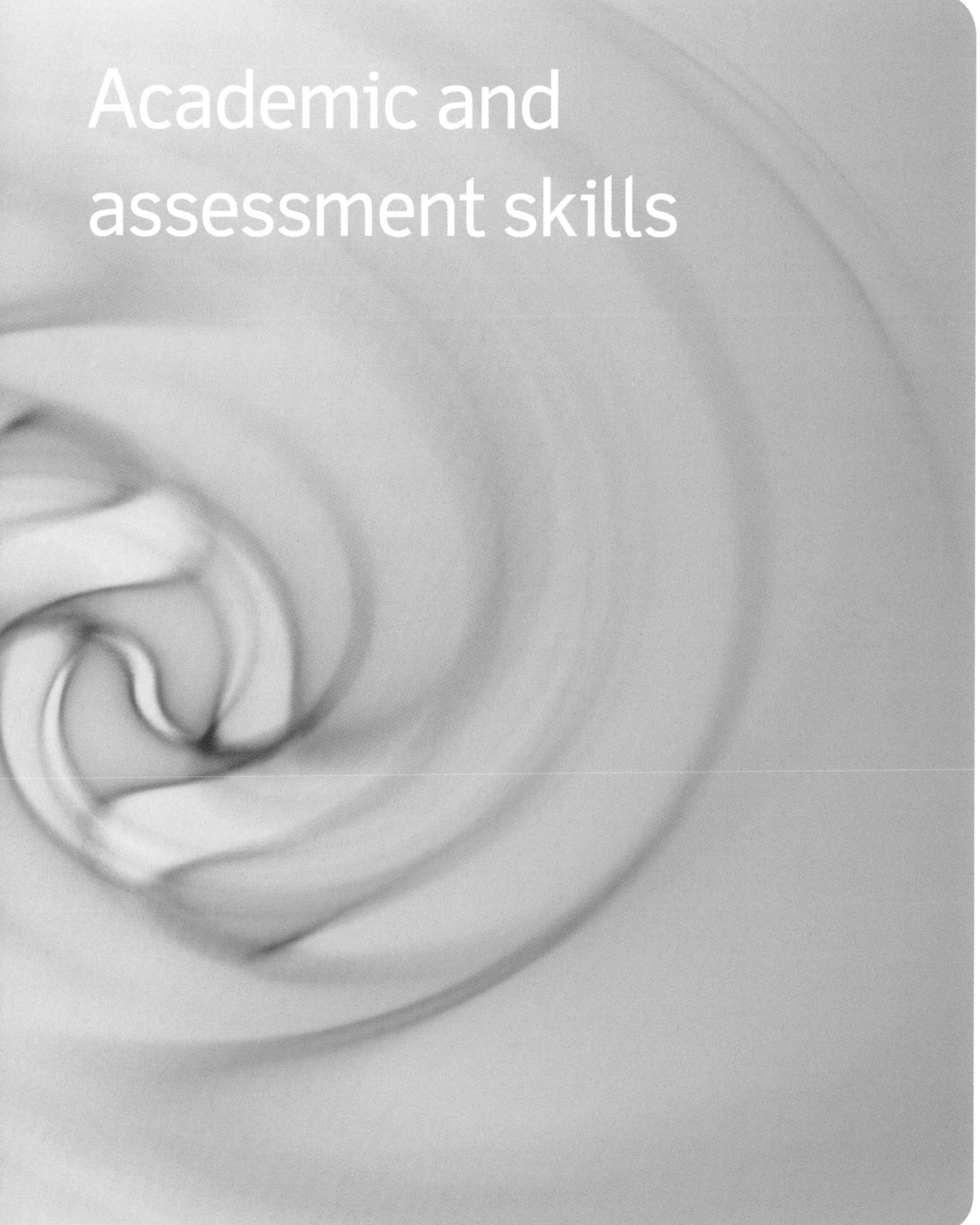

www.oxfordinteract.com

Chapter 25

Writing essays

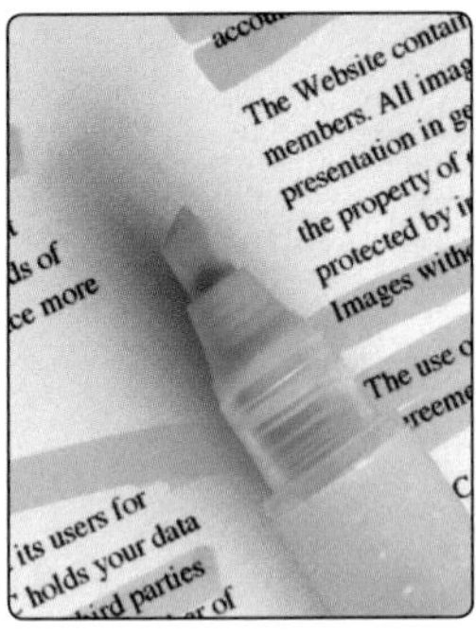

Rationale

Essay writing is one of the most widely used and important forms of assessment in undergraduate law degrees. It is also a form of assessment that many students find very difficult to master. There are probably good reasons for this. You may have had little experience of writing essays before, or the essays you have been asked to write have been much shorter. The content of the essay may have been descriptive rather than analytical. At school you are often given a great deal of guidance by your teachers on what is expected, but at university there is much more emphasis on independent learning, and on critical thought. In general you will be expected to work out an answer to an essay question on your own and the focus of your work will be critical rather than descriptive.

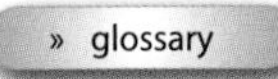

Lecturers are looking for a variety of things from your essays. These are likely to include:

- **Knowledge** – this requires legal research skills. Your knowledge must be accurate, up to date, and appropriate for the question that has been set and must be referenced. You will have to demonstrate this, through proper referencing and a bibliography.
- **Relevance** – you must exercise judgement about what material you will use in your essay. Not everything you know about the subject will be relevant. A key skill is the ability to discard the irrelevant and ensure that the relevance of what you retain is made clear to your reader.
- **Analysis** – it is not enough to describe the knowledge you have acquired: you must also be prepared to evaluate that knowledge, to point out the problems with it, to weigh up its significance and long-term implications.
- **Focus** – your essay must demonstrate that you have understood the question that is being asked and must answer that question.
- **Written skills** – your writing must be fluent and structured. You must use appropriate language and referencing.
- **Originality** – your work must not be plagiarised. More than that, it should in some sense be creative. You should take an original approach to the question you are set, work out an argument which demonstrates that approach and your essay should deliver your argument.

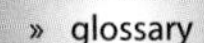

Some of these requirements – such as legal research, creative thinking and plagiarism – are addressed elsewhere in this resource. You will also need to refer to our sections on bibliographies and referencing. Do not forget they are all essential if you want to achieve a good mark.

Our list setting out the requirements for a good essay looks intimidating. It is an intellectual challenge to write a good essay. However, at stage 1 of your degree the level of skill that is expected of you is quite different from level 3 or from postgraduate writing. So, for instance, the originality that is required at stage 1 is relatively limited. All that is required is that you develop your own well-informed opinion about the subject matter you have been studying and present it in a coherent manner. Putting this another way, what we are asking you to do is to ask yourself what you know and what you think about a particular area of law, and then to demonstrate your knowledge and your opinions to a well-informed reader.

This chapter will focus on how to develop an argument in answer to a question and how to present that argument well and in an essay format. It is targeted at the typical undergraduate essay of between 2,000 and 3,500 words. We provide additional information about longer pieces of writing and dissertations in a separate chapter. We also consider essay writing in examinations elsewhere. However, a great deal of what we say in this chapter is relevant to all writing tasks.

This chapter is devised to help you:

- Write a good essay
- Choose a question and develop an original argument
- Plan your essay
- Determine the contents of introductions and conclusions
- Write your essay.

How to write a good essay

Here are three key points to bear in mind before you start work on any essay:

1. Before you start writing an essay, check the assessment criteria for the piece of work that you have been set. Assessment criteria are usually in your module handbook. If you cannot find them, or do not understand them, ask your seminar teacher. Make sure your work addresses the criteria.
2. There is a huge difference between A-level standard essays and undergraduate work. If your first piece of work does not achieve a high mark, do not give up! Writing is a skill that takes practice. Read the comments made, take them constructively and not personally, ask for clarification if appropriate, and work at your weaknesses. Get additional help if you need to. Your marks will improve as the course goes on, as long as you keep working.
3. Read the feedback on the last essay you wrote and use that feedback to improve your work. If your lecturer has suggested that your work is insufficiently analytical, then ensure that you address that weakness. If your lecturer suggests that you have not been sufficiently accurate or precise, then concentrate on that. Whilst students complain that lecturers give insufficient feedback or give their feedback too slowly, lecturers complain that students don't take any notice of what is written. Don't fall into that trap! We discuss the best way to respond to feedback below.

» glossary

The components of a good essay

There is no simple formula for success because a good essay is a combination of:

- Critical thinking about the question which you have to address.
- Wide but focused and critical reading which is then appropriately applied to the problem in hand. You should read carefully and pay close attention to the ideas which inform the material you are considering. As you read, develop your own ideas in response. Ask yourself, do you agree or disagree with the author?
- Effective writing, which means you must pay attention to the following:
  - Planning the structure of your essay so it allows you to develop a coherent argument about the question you have been set.
  - Constructing an introduction which sets out the argument you wish to present.
  - Summarising your argument in the conclusion.
  - The fluency of your writing. Your sentences and your paragraphs must be well structured and purposeful.
  - You will almost inevitably need to redraft all, or parts of your essay as part of the writing process.

Activity 1

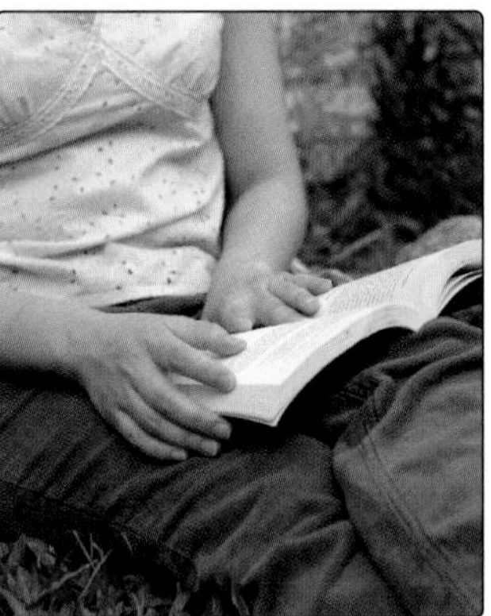

Now try an activity to help you think about the relationship between thinking, reading and writing when you are working on an essay.

Here is a diagram which represents one approach to the processes involved in working on an essay.

Thinking about the question
↓
searching for information
↓
collecting books and articles
↓
reading books and articles
↓
writing essay

Is this the approach you adopt? Yes/no
Go online to read our thoughts on this question.

Time management

It should immediately be obvious that writing a good essay takes time.

The first step (once you have chosen the question you want to answer – see below) is to work out how much time you have before it has to be handed in. In that time you will have to carry out a series of steps.

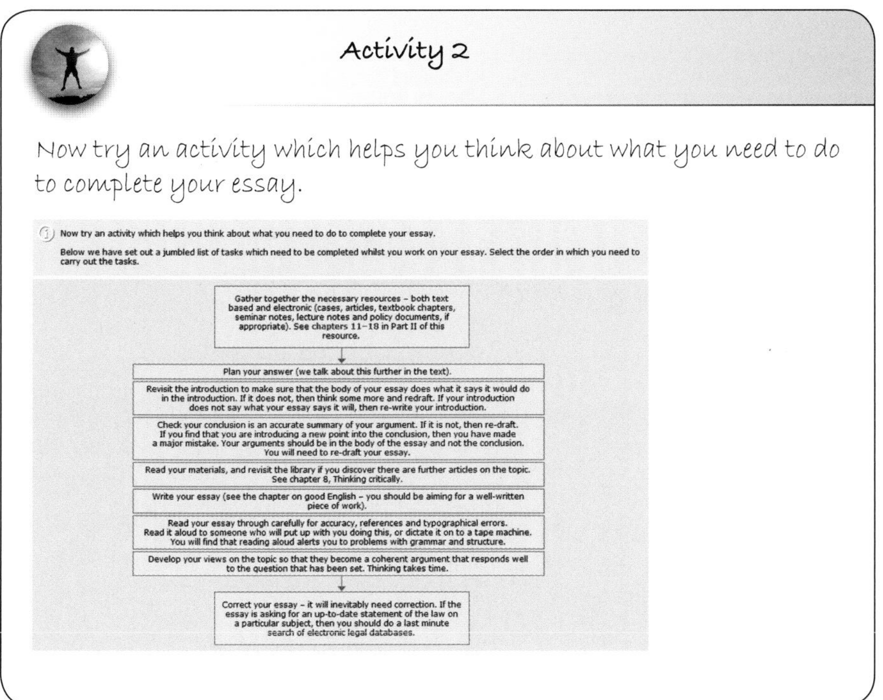

Activity 2
Now try an activity which helps you think about what you need to do to complete your essay.
Now try an activity which helps you think about what you need to do to complete your essay.
Below we have set out a jumbled list of tasks which need to be completed whilst you work on your essay. Select the order in which you need to carry out the tasks.
Gather together the necessary resources – both text based and electronic (cases, articles, textbook chapters, seminar notes, lecture notes and policy documents, if appropriate). See chapters 11–18 in Part II of this resource.
Plan your answer (we talk about this further in the text).
Revisit the introduction to make sure that the body of your essay does what it says it would do in the introduction. If it does not, then think some more and redraft. If your introduction does not say what your essay says it will, then re-write your introduction.
Check your conclusion is an accurate summary of your argument. If it is not, then re-draft. If you find that you are introducing a new point into the conclusion, then you have made a major mistake. Your arguments should be in the body of the essay and not the conclusion. You will need to re-draft your essay.
Read your materials, and revisit the library if you discover there are further articles on the topic. See chapter 8, Thinking critically.
Write your essay (see the chapter on good English – you should be aiming for a well-written piece of work).
Read your essay through carefully for accuracy, references and typographical errors. Read it aloud to someone who will put up with you doing this, or dictate it on to a tape machine. You will find that reading aloud alerts you to problems with grammar and structure.
Develop your views on the topic so that they become a coherent argument that responds well to the question that has been set. Thinking takes time.
Correct your essay – it will inevitably need correction. If the essay is asking for an up-to-date statement of the law on a particular subject, then you should do a last minute search of electronic legal databases.

Work out a realistic timetable for yourself, counting back from the hand-in date. Work out what other assessments are due in, and don't forget to factor in seminar preparation and lecture and seminar attendance. Your first draft of your essay should be completed some time before the hand-in date, to allow time for re-reading, re-writing and last minute corrections. Check our resources for effective time management.

» glossary

↳ Cross reference
You can use the timetable we provided in chapter 2, Managing your time, to work out the dates by which you should have completed key tasks.

Choosing a question

Typically you will be given a number of essay questions and you will be required to choose the one you wish to answer. Students often waste a lot of time deciding which question to answer, and then can quite easily choose a question which does not play to their strengths. Often their

choice is determined by which answer seems the easiest to understand and has the greatest amount of material available. You can be more constructive in your choice than this. What you have to do is to work out:

- Your intellectual strengths. Ask yourself questions:
  - Are you better at case analysis than structuring arguments?
  - Are you interested in the social/economic/political context of law?
  - Is your strength in describing technical provisions of the law?

  Your answers will help you choose a question that suits your skills.
- What has interested you in the course:
  - Which lectures/seminars caught your interest?
  - Were there issues you felt strongly about?
- How much extra research is required to answer the question:
  - Sometimes you will have covered the subject at some length in the course.
  - Other questions will require a great deal of additional research. Have you got the time, the inclination, and the skills to do this?

Activity 3

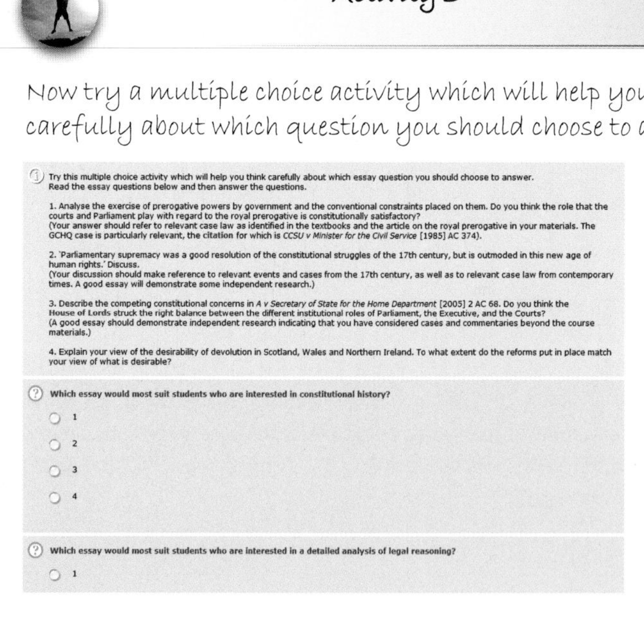

Now try a multiple choice activity which will help you think carefully about which question you should choose to answer.

Try this multiple choice activity which will help you think carefully about which essay question you should choose to answer.
Read the essay questions below and then answer the questions.

1. Analyse the exercise of prerogative powers by government and the conventional constraints placed on them. Do you think the role that the courts and Parliament play with regard to the royal prerogative is constitutionally satisfactory?
(Your answer should refer to relevant case law as identified in the textbooks and the article on the royal prerogative in your materials. The GCHQ case is particularly relevant, the citation for which is *CCSU v Minister for the Civil Service* [1985] AC 374).

2. 'Parliamentary supremacy was a good resolution of the constitutional struggles of the 17th century, but is outmoded in this new age of human rights.' Discuss.
(Your discussion should make reference to relevant events and cases from the 17th century, as well as to relevant case law from contemporary times. A good essay will demonstrate some independent research.)

3. Describe the competing constitutional concerns in *A v Secretary of State for the Home Department* [2005] 2 AC 68. Do you think the House of Lords struck the right balance between the different institutional roles of Parliament, the Executive, and the Courts?
(A good essay should demonstrate independent research indicating that you have considered cases and commentaries beyond the course materials.)

4. Explain your view of the desirability of devolution in Scotland, Wales and Northern Ireland. To what extent do the reforms put in place match your view of what is desirable?

Which essay would most suit students who are interested in constitutional history?

○ 1
○ 2
○ 3
○ 4

Which essay would most suit students who are interested in a detailed analysis of legal reasoning?

○ 1

Active words in questions

Once you have chosen your question you must think about what that question requires you to do. All essay questions require that you do something with the information you have to hand. What you have to do is set out in the question and described by an active word. Whatever the active word is in the essay, whether it is 'consider' or 'assess' for instance, make sure that the whole of your essay does just that! Whenever you read an essay question locate the active word or words in it, make sure that you understand what they require of you, and then deliver that action in your essay. As you write, keep referring back to the active word to remind yourself what you are required to do.

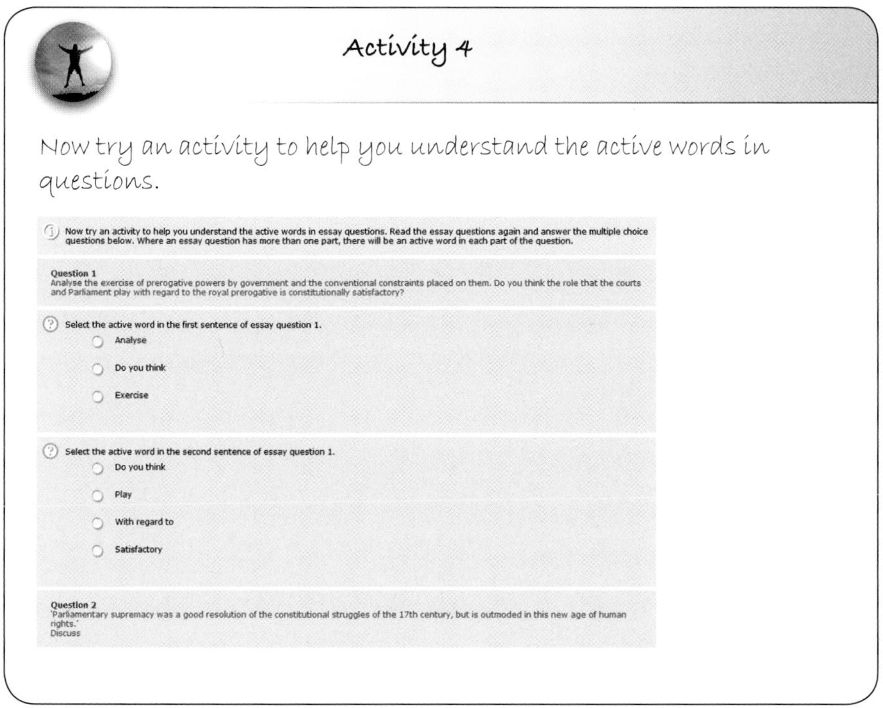

Activity 4

Now try an activity to help you understand the active words in questions.

Now try an activity to help you understand the active words in essay questions. Read the essay questions again and answer the multiple choice questions below. Where an essay question has more than one part, there will be an active word in each part of the question.

Question 1
Analyse the exercise of prerogative powers by government and the conventional constraints placed on them. Do you think the role that the courts and Parliament play with regard to the royal prerogative is constitutionally satisfactory?

Select the active word in the first sentence of essay question 1.

- Analyse
- Do you think
- Exercise

Select the active word in the second sentence of essay question 1.

- Do you think
- Play
- With regard to
- Satisfactory

Question 2
'Parliamentary supremacy was a good resolution of the constitutional struggles of the 17th century, but is outmoded in this new age of human rights.'
Discuss

Developing an original argument

One crucial component of a successful essay is a clear argument, which you present in a structured form. Students often find it difficult to develop an argument. The first step is to think carefully about the question you have chosen to answer. We are going to use the example of a question set on devolution to illustrate how you might go about developing an argument.

» glossary

Example

Explain your view of the desirability of devolution in Scotland, Wales and Northern Ireland. To what extent do the reforms put in place match your view of what is desirable?

This question is quite explicit about what it wants you to do. You must set out your views about the desirability of devolution in Scotland, Wales and Northern Ireland. It is not asking you for the pros and cons of devolution. It wants your views – in other words it wants you to tell your story about devolution. However, remember that your views must be authoritative. Even though the question is asking you what you think, it is probably best to avoid the phrase 'I think' in the answer. It is better to use 'I prefer the argument of…' or 'I consider that …' or 'I give greater weight to the opinion of X' and then explain why you think in that way.

The obvious trap the unwary student will fall into is writing a description of the devolution frameworks in Scotland, Wales and Northern Ireland. That would be hard work, almost inevitably tedious to write and certainly tedious to read, and would probably result in a low mark. You can avoid this trap by concentrating on what the question asks you to do. Once you have worked out what is, in your opinion, based on the informed opinions of commentators, desirable about devolution in Scotland, Wales and Northern Ireland, then you can go on to measure the reforms against your own criteria. This is bound to provide you with an original argument, because it is your ideas and your evaluation.

How do you go about developing an opinion about devolution in the UK? It may be that you have strong views already. That's fine – you just have to express those views appropriately in the essay, without ranting and supported by authority. However, many students find it difficult to formulate an opinion.

» glossary

One place to start is your lectures and seminars – did your lecturer give you any indication of the range of views of the desirability of devolution? That should give you a starting point. If you cannot glean anything from your lecture notes, then what do your textbooks suggest? Is there a perspective that is appealing to you?

» glossary

Another thing to think about is the themes that run through the teaching of the course. Some course leaders may make it clear that they are interested in concepts such as democracy, majoritarianism, the nation state, globalism, power, and government. These are big ideas, but indicate the sort of issues that may be relevant and they may help you decide what you think is desirable about devolution in Scotland, Wales and Northern Ireland. For example, if you think that a strong nation state is very desirable, then that suggests that you might think that devolution in Scotland, for instance, has gone too far.

Something else you might like to consider: Without doing very much reading, you will be aware that each of the devolution settlements is quite distinct. Therefore if you decide that one is desirable, that inevitably raises questions about the value of what the others provide for their citizens.

One place where strong opinions are always expressed is in the comment columns of the broadsheets. If you look through old editions of *The Times* – perhaps at the time of the passing of the relevant statutes – you should find some strong views. Do you agree with them, or disagree? (This may be a tall order for very old statutes, but for more recent legislation should be relatively straightforward.)

» glossary

» glossary

And that leads us to another source of strongly expressed opinion – Parliament. If you look in Hansard (the official record of debates in Parliament) you will find the debates on the devolution bills. These may be helpful to you to understand the range of views expressed.

» glossary

However, nothing is as valuable in developing your own ideas as careful and critical reading of informed opinions. Make sure you have read every article which is on your reading list. Remind yourself of the importance of active reading. If you read articles closely you will develop your own critical thinking skills.

Cross reference
For more information see chapter 8, Thinking critically.

Let's imagine that after doing some basic research you have come up with a range of ideas about what is desirable about devolution in the UK. Perhaps you would argue that devolution of power improves democracy because it improves participation, that localism allows political decisions to reflect the concerns of the electorate, that national cultures should not be repressed by the English majority. Whatever it is you work out, now you have to think it through. Are the Welsh being served by the devolution settlement they have received? Why is the Northern Ireland solution so radically different? If you value participation most, then why isn't proportional representation available throughout the UK? And why should Scottish MPs decide on laws for the English? Once you start thinking devolution through, you surely begin to think about the English position. If localism is so important for Scotland, Wales and Northern Ireland, then surely it is equally important for England? Perhaps this gives you one way to work on an argument that you can develop in your essay. Don't forget to stress the constitutional aspects of devolution – this is after all a law essay.

Another approach might be to suggest that the UK Parliament has simply given as little power away as possible – that it is the strength of the political demands which has determined the shape of the solution. That may not seem very desirable. It suggests that the UK Parliament is not driven by principle but by pragmatism. Perhaps there is an argument that you can develop here. You could think about whether the limited solutions adopted are going to satisfy demand in the long run. We have already seen an amendment to the Welsh devolution settlement, and the suggestion is that there is now an increasing demand for Scottish independence. Perhaps it is not possible for a pragmatic solution to work?

» glossary

Another possibility would be to think about whether the nation state can survive devolution. Is it important for the nation state to survive? Can it survive anyway in the light of supranational developments such as the European Union? Is devolution of power to a more local level the natural reaction to the pressures that the nation state is under?

We are not trying to tell you the answer. All we are trying to do here is to suggest some triggers for you to start developing an argument. Once you have the glimmer of an idea, then you can read more about it, make sure that your opinion is informed, and that it is supported by authority. Gradually you will develop an argument that you can sustain throughout your essay. It will take a lot of thought, some discussion perhaps with your fellow students, perhaps some more reading, but you should be beginning to get there.

It's at this stage you should start planning your essay.

Planning your essay

When we ask students if they plan their essays there is a tendency to avoid answering the question. We suspect that many undergraduates do not know how to plan an essay, or even what a useful essay plan looks like. An essay plan takes as its starting point the argument you intend to present in your answer to your essay. In the introduction it sets out the main points of the argument, and then the plan indicates how paragraph by paragraph the argument will be delivered in the essay. Finally the plan sets out the main points of the conclusion which will be a summing up of the argument.

We can take the essay question on devolution to demonstrate this.

> *Explain your view of the desirability of devolution in Scotland, Wales and Northern Ireland. To what extent do the reforms put in place match your view of what is desirable?*

Let's say your argument is that devolution in Scotland, Wales and Northern Ireland is desirable and perhaps essential because it operates to revitalise democracy and the nation state by increasing political engagement at a local level. Because local political conditions are distinct, then different devolution settlements are appropriate. However, the result both of the transfer of power and the variations is to set up further demands for devolution which paradoxically undermine the nation state and may result eventually in its dissolution. Thus whilst devolution is desirable, it is ultimately uncontrollable.

This is quite a complex argument to deliver in only 2,000 words. What you have to do is to split it up into the main thoughts underpinning the argument and devote paragraphs to those thoughts.

So:

Introduction

Set out the argument, and then describe how you are going to present it.

You might want to split the essay into two. In the first half you could demonstrate the desirability of devolution as a means of increasing democratic engagement and through this the political validity of the nation state. In the second half you could demonstrate how it is likely to set up uncontrollable demands which will defeat the purpose of revitalising the nation state. You should explain this structure in your introduction. Your introduction is likely to take 250–300 words.

Paragraph 1

The first paragraph will be about the desirability of devolution. Here you might talk about the democratic deficit and general political disengagement. You might introduce ideas of globalism. You could draw on the undermining of political sovereignty by the European Union (probably about 250 words).

Paragraphs 2, 3 and 4

Here you are going to have to briefly explain your thought that devolution settlements are a response to local and historical circumstances. You will illustrate this by setting out the significant features of the Scotland, Wales and Northern Ireland schemes of devolution. For instance, you will talk about the strength and long-standing nature of the demand for a transfer of political power in Scotland, the complexities of the Northern Ireland situation, and the different nature of the demand for devolution in Wales.

You will have to avoid the trap of simply describing each settlement. Perhaps you could do this by taking two or three themes of the settlements, for instance participation and the results of devolution referenda, the political history, and the political culture. One theme could be explained in each paragraph (up to 750 words).

Paragraphs 5 and 6

At this stage you enter the second part of your argument, which is to suggest that once having started the process of devolution of power from the centre, the process may be unstoppable. You will draw here on developments since the initiation of devolution in Wales and Scotland, and in particular on the debates about the future of Scotland (up to 500 words).

Paragraph 7

An important element of the argument will be the political position of England. You could devote a paragraph to explaining how the political position of England is undermined by the devolution settlements, which then allows you to explore the paradox of the nation state being undermined by the transfer of power but faced with overwhelming arguments to do just that for the survival of democracy. Don't forget to consider the 'West Lothian' question – if you don't know what this is, look it up on the web.

Conclusion

Here you will have to sum up your argument. You may want to say that what you have demonstrated in this essay is the desirability of devolution because of its role in the democratic project which seems to be at risk in a global world, but that the complexity and contingency of the devolution of power serves to undermine the nation state and probably cannot be controlled. Whatever your argument has been, try to sum up what you have said. The most important thing is not to introduce new material here.

Next steps in planning

If you set out your plan in the right way you will ensure that you have made argument and analysis the centre of the essay. The process is not a simple one; it requires a lot of thought, but is really a crucial step in a successful essay. The next step is to think over the plan and consider which references and authorities you are going to use to back up your argument. If you have not got authority for a point, then you are going to have to do further research, or abandon that point. An important focus of your plan is the introduction. If this is not strong and well-thought through, then your essay is not going to work. The next section considers introductions more fully, and looks at some examples from students' work.

Introductions

The introduction to an essay is where you set out your argument. To put it in sales terms, it is where you pitch your ideas. If your argument is not clear or convincing then this becomes apparent in the introduction. If it is too simple, or if it sets out how you are going to describe the law, but gives no indication of any analysis, then your essay is not going to work. Writing the introduction is therefore an important step in helping you formulate your argument, and ultimately in delivering an effective essay.

Of course your thinking process will not be complete as you plan your essay. It will continue right up to the time you finish writing. So there is nothing wrong, and indeed everything in favour of continually re-visiting your introduction, making it more sophisticated and more reflective of the argument that you are developing in the body of the essay. Many academics set out a relatively simple introduction in the first draft of an article. They then develop their thoughts as they write. They return to the introduction at the end of the process to make it more complex so that it accurately introduces what they have argued.

Remember – you have very few words to explain and develop your answer to an essay question. Do not waste them by repeating the essay title as part of the introduction. This does not mean that you should not put the essay title at the top of your essay. You must, and you must constantly refer back to it and to the active word(s) in the question to remind you of what you are required to do.

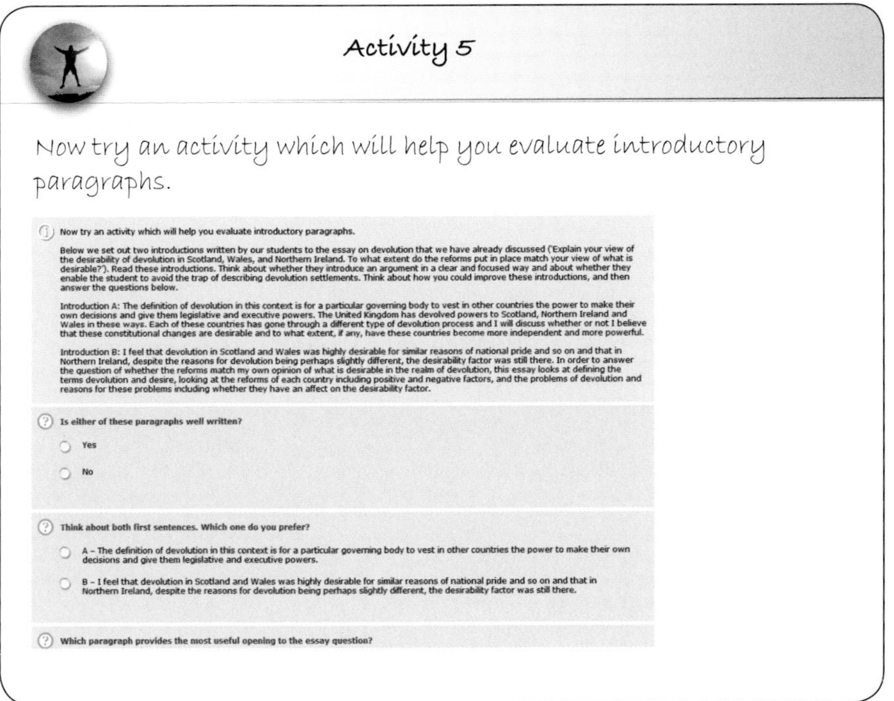

Activity 5

Now try an activity which will help you evaluate introductory paragraphs.

Now try an activity which will help you evaluate introductory paragraphs.

Below we set out two introductions written by our students to the essay on devolution that we have already discussed ('Explain your view of the desirability of devolution in Scotland, Wales, and Northern Ireland. To what extent do the reforms put in place match your view of what is desirable?'). Read these introductions. Think about whether they introduce an argument in a clear and focused way and about whether they enable the student to avoid the trap of describing devolution settlements. Think about how you could improve these introductions, and then answer the questions below.

Introduction A: The definition of devolution in this context is for a particular governing body to vest in other countries the power to make their own decisions and give them legislative and executive powers. The United Kingdom has devolved powers to Scotland, Northern Ireland and Wales in these ways. Each of these countries has gone through a different type of devolution process and I will discuss whether or not I believe that these constitutional changes are desirable and to what extent, if any, have these countries become more independent and more powerful.

Introduction B: I feel that devolution in Scotland and Wales was highly desirable for similar reasons of national pride and so on and that in Northern Ireland, despite the reasons for devolution being perhaps slightly different, the desirability factor was still there. In order to answer the question of whether the reforms match my own opinion of what is desirable in the realm of devolution, this essay looks at defining the terms devolution and desire, looking at the reforms of each country including positive and negative factors, and the problems of devolution and reasons for these problems including whether they have an affect on the desirability factor.

Is either of these paragraphs well written?

- Yes
- No

Think about both first sentences. Which one do you prefer?

- A – The definition of devolution in this context is for a particular governing body to vest in other countries the power to make their own decisions and give them legislative and executive powers.
- B – I feel that devolution in Scotland and Wales was highly desirable for similar reasons of national pride and so on and that in Northern Ireland, despite the reasons for devolution being perhaps slightly different, the desirability factor was still there.

Which paragraph provides the most useful opening to the essay question?

Strong beginnings are essential in your essay. They give the impression of thoughtfulness and confidence. If they reflect the body of your essay and provide an indication that you will tackle some complex issues, they will ensure that your essay is structured, is sufficiently sophisticated and they should help you avoid describing rather than analysing the law. Don't worry if your first draft of your introduction does not achieve everything that you want it to, you can keep redrafting and refining the introduction throughout the process of writing your essay.

Activity 6

Now try an activity to help you recognise the need for a strong introduction.

This activity is designed to help you recognise the need for a strong introduction. First of all, read the introduction, reproduced below, to Helen Reece's article, 'The End of Domestic Violence' (2006) 69 MLR 770–91.

> There was no significant opposition to the two additions that the Domestic Violence, Crime and Victims Act 2004 recently made to the list of associated persons in section 62(3) of the Family Law Act 1996. Neither was there much objection when Part IV of the Family Law Act 1996 created the list. Despite, or perhaps because of this marked consensus, rigorous examination of the merits of both the existence and the parameters of the category of associated persons is long overdue. In this article, I tackle this task by identifying three rationales that have been given for the category, which I describe as the empirical, the principled and the ideological. I argue that the empirical and principled rationales are unfounded and that the ideological rationale is reactionary. Hence, I conclude that the category of associated persons is misguided.

Now read our analysis of the introduction and select the missing words from the list below to complete the gaps.

conclusions	associated persons	purpose	reactionary	context	misguided
consensus	rationales				

This is a very strong and clear introduction. It sets the ______ of the article – the passage of the Domestic Violence, Crime and Victims Act 2004 and the extension of the list of associated persons who are protected by the Act. It explains the ______ of the article – to challenge the ______ about the existence and parameters of the category of ______. It introduces the reader to the argument that the author is going to use, and to the way in which she structures the article. What she is going to do is to take three potential ______ for the changes to the law and decide whether they are. She also introduces us to her ______. She is not looking to surprise the reader but to help the reader follow her argument. What the author argues is that because the empirical and principled rationales are unfounded and the ideological rationale is ______, the category of associated persons is ______. The introduction seems simple, because it is so well structured. However, the argument is complex and controversial. The reader is almost inevitably going to enjoy watching the author's thought processes unfold.

Using cases in your essay

» glossary

There are two types of essay questions in which you will have to use cases. One signals the fact very clearly because it asks your opinion about a case. For example: 'Has *Lloyds Band v Rosset* [1991] AC 107 provided an adequate template with which to handle constructive trusts of land?'

» glossary

You should not write an essay about a case without carrying out some further research into case notes and articles written about the case.

↳ Cross reference
Check chapter 13, Sources of law, and chapter 14, Citing legal authorities, if you are in any doubt how to do this.

The second type of essay is more general. For instance, in public law you could be asked a question along these lines:

1. "The emergence of proportionality in judicial review has led to greater protection of human rights. However it has also distorted the institutional balance between the judiciary, administration and Parliament."
2. "Human rights in the UK tend to have a vertical operation – that is, they regulate the relationship between the individual and the state. They also tend to be subject to limitation if it is deemed 'necessary in a democratic society'. This is no way protect human rights."

↳ Cross reference
See chapters 21–24, Reading cases 1–4.

A v Home Secretary – a case we pay some attention to in our chapters on how to read cases – could play a part in answering either of these questions. Indeed, if you have got to grips with the case you could use it to demonstrate the contemporary significance of proportionality, or by thinking about how Lord Bingham curtailed the court's interference with decisions about public emergency, you could argue that it demonstrates the serious limitations of human rights jurisprudence. There is nothing wrong with placing a great deal of emphasis in an essay on one particular case as long as it is of sufficient significance, and you demonstrate wider knowledge by drawing on other cases to back up your points. Again you should ensure that you have located appropriate case notes and articles.

Key Point

When you use cases in your essays you must:

- *cite the case properly*
- *quote from the judgments and not from what a textbook tells you about the case*
- *use the case to enhance your arguments and not simply to demonstrate that you have read the case*
- *you can use opinions from authoritative textbooks and articles as evidence – but you should evaluate these opinions and explain why you prefer one interpretation to another.*

Writing your essay

We have considered writing skills elsewhere. However, there are some particular points it is worth making in the context of essay writing, for it is in marking your essays that your lecturers pay most attention to your writing skills.

Cross reference
See chapter 3, Writing good English.

It is good practice in an essay to:

- Start paragraphs with a strong sentence to indicate the importance of the point you are making. A strong beginning to the introduction to your essay is particularly useful to suggest that you are confident in the argument you are putting forward.
- Link one paragraph with the one which follows it. Sometimes that means you have to be explicit, writing, 'I will now go on to discuss....' If your lecturer does not like the use of the first person, you can write, 'The discussion will now move to...' These are acceptable devices as they help your reader navigate your essay.

- End paragraphs with a short summary of the contents of the paragraph. This will emphasise the coherence of your work, and remind you that each paragraph must focus on and develop one main idea.
- Use quotations, but you must use them well. Remember, quotations do not speak for themselves, and people's opinions need evaluating. Do not use up too much of your word count in quotations. You can use quotations from cases, articles and authoritative textbooks. Remember, however, that if you are going to use extracts from primary sources, such as cases or legislation, then you should quote directly from these, and not from a textbook digest of them.
- Vary the length of your sentences. Short sentences are easy to read, but can sound too staccato. Long sentences are often disastrous, because students fail to communicate with their reader. Split long sentences into shorter ones. You will find that it forces you to think through, and to develop your point effectively.
- Voice your opinions, but ensure that your opinions are authoritative. Use cases, quotations from authoritative textbooks or from articles to give weight to your opinions. Explain why you prefer one opinion to another.
- Remind yourself throughout the writing process of the essay title and of the active word in the essay title. Ensure that you are delivering what you are required to deliver.

You should avoid thoughtlessness. There are a number of signs in your writing that you have been thoughtless. Here are some of them.

Rhetorical questions

They indicate to the marker that whilst you have thought of a question that your argument raises, you do not know how to answer it. This is a bad sign in writing an essay. Here are some examples from constitutional and administrative law essays. Do you agree that the rhetorical question does not add anything to the essay, and if it achieves anything, does it suggest that the student is flummoxed?

Example

'However as concerns the relatively new structure of devolution, I feel that government are actually doing the task to the best of their ability whilst still taking into account what they have to deal with. Is that not all we can ask for from a government under constant constraint?'

'How then is it possible to safeguard Parliament's sovereign power from being exercised in an undesirable way? It would seem there isn't a way.'

'Even more to the point is that as Parliament does not know what Ministers can do until it's done how could it possibly be safeguarded or controlled?'

Carelessness

There are a number of ways of writing essays which suggest that you have been careless and are not taking the task seriously. Some sentences, for instance, suggest you are not concentrating as you write. What impression is given by the following sentence?

> 'I now realise in the competing constitutional society, government must adapt to there appears to be somewhat of a growing development balance shown through New Labours regular improvements.'

Probably the student had a good clear thought that they wanted to express. However, it has got lost between the thinking and the writing. Read over your work carefully to avoid this. It is particularly helpful if you read it out loud. If no one is prepared to listen to you, then read it into a digital recorder and play it back to yourself. You will be surprised how many mistakes you will spot.

Unreasonable assertions

Sometimes students seem to reach untenable conclusions. Does the student who wrote this really think this?

> 'The worldwide acceptance of fundamental protection of human rights seems to have isolated the UK.'

Make sure that anything that you say makes sense and is backed up with authority, either from cases or articles or textbooks. Check your essay for sentences which give opinions which are supported by references. If those sentences do not flow from your previous argument you need to think again.

Gaps

Students often leave gaps in their essays when they cannot quite think how to make their point. They usually intend to finish the sentence when they complete the essay, but they then forget. Why not put a hash (#) in your essay, and then when you think you have finished your work, do a quick search for # just to pick up any gaps you have left. You should also search for any obvious typographical blunders. When one of the authors worked on the Public Law team at the Law Commission the team always ensured that documents were searched before publication for the word 'pubic', an obvious and embarrassing typographical error for public (and one which a spell-check will not pick up!)

» glossary

Repetition

Read through your essay to check that you have not repeated yourself. One of the useful comments on a sixth form essay that one of the authors was given was – once you have made a good point once, there is no reason to keep on repeating it. Develop your points in your essay, and avoid simply repeating it. However, repetition is not necessarily limited to ideas; writers frequently repeat particular sentences. For example, several paragraphs might begin 'In this paragraph I will demonstrate…' Read your joining sentences and make sure you have not repeated yourself.

Clichés

A final thought on thoughtlessness: avoid clichés. They suggest you are not thinking critically. Here is an example:

> 'We need to go back in time to understand how the prerogative powers came into effect and how they have adapted to present day life.'

This is not only an unnecessary sentence but it suggests to the marker that the student is not taking a critical perspective on the essay title.

Assessment criteria

When you are writing your essay you should pay attention to the assessment criteria. These will vary in detail and specificity from institution to institution. However, most law schools will have clear criteria on how you should present your work. They will probably specify that you should:

- cite references properly
- use correct spelling and accurate grammar and syntax
- comply with a word limit
- word-process your essay.

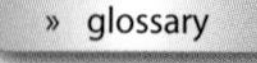

They may also prescribe how you are to use footnotes and whether or not you use a **bibliography**.

↳ Cross reference
We discuss how to cite references in chapter 14, Citing legal authorities; how to proofread your work and write good English in chapter 3, Writing good English; and how to use footnotes and how to prune your work to comply with a word limit in chapter 26, Writing dissertations.

Key Point

Read the assessment criteria carefully and ensure you comply with the requirements. A properly presented essay demonstrates that you have taken the task seriously and paid sufficient attention to the academic requirements. If you are in any doubt seek advice from your lecturer.

Conclusions

The conclusion to your essay is not only your opportunity to sum up the argument that you have presented, but also a chance to ensure that your essay is going to work. If you cannot sum up the points that you have made in the body of the essay, or if those points do not match the argument that you said you were going to develop in the introduction, then something has gone wrong. Think through the essay again, adjust your paragraphs so that you make the points that you intend to make, and then rewrite your conclusion so that it reflects those arguments.

The important indicator that something has gone wrong in your thought processes in writing the essay is when you find that you are introducing new material in the conclusion. This should never happen. It means that your argument has developed whilst you are writing. That's fine; indeed it is probably inevitable. However, it means you have to adjust your essay to ensure that the body of the essay delivers your argument, and not the conclusion. So in our devolution example, if you find yourself referring to the 'West Lothian' question in the conclusion, you need to rethink your essay, and start a new draft. Don't worry; it often takes three or more drafts to produce an effective piece of work. With word processors, new drafts should not be too time-consuming.

Key Point

Do not introduce new material, either facts or ideas, into the conclusion of your essay. If this happens you need to re-draft the essay so that you explore the new material properly within the body of your essay.

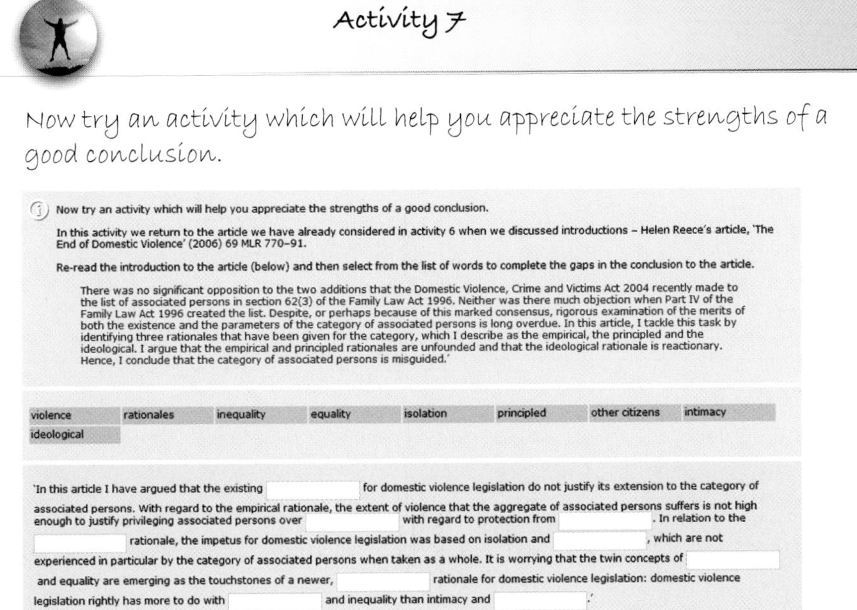

Activity 7

Now try an activity which will help you appreciate the strengths of a good conclusion.

Now try an activity which will help you appreciate the strengths of a good conclusion.

In this activity we return to the article we have already considered in activity 6 when we discussed introductions – Helen Reece's article, 'The End of Domestic Violence' (2006) 69 MLR 770–91.

Re-read the introduction to the article (below) and then select from the list of words to complete the gaps in the conclusion to the article.

> There was no significant opposition to the two additions that the Domestic Violence, Crime and Victims Act 2004 recently made to the list of associated persons in section 62(3) of the Family Law Act 1996. Neither was there much objection when Part IV of the Family Law Act 1996 created the list. Despite, or perhaps because of this marked consensus, rigorous examination of the merits of both the existence and the parameters of the category of associated persons is long overdue. In this article, I tackle this task by identifying three rationales that have been given for the category, which I describe as the empirical, the principled and the ideological. I argue that the empirical and principled rationales are unfounded and that the ideological rationale is reactionary. Hence, I conclude that the category of associated persons is misguided.'

violence	rationales	inequality	equality	isolation	principled	other citizens	intimacy
ideological							

'In this article I have argued that the existing _____ for domestic violence legislation do not justify its extension to the category of associated persons. With regard to the empirical rationale, the extent of violence that the aggregate of associated persons suffers is not high enough to justify privileging associated persons over _____ with regard to protection from _____. In relation to the _____ rationale, the impetus for domestic violence legislation was based on isolation and _____, which are not experienced in particular by the category of associated persons when taken as a whole. It is worrying that the twin concepts of _____ and equality are emerging as the touchstones of a newer, _____ rationale for domestic violence legislation: domestic violence legislation rightly has more to do with _____ and inequality than intimacy and _____.'

The pitfalls

One way to write a good essay is to avoid the characteristics of a bad essay. Now that you have almost completed this chapter you should be able to work out what these are and how to avoid them.

We have designed an online activity to check that you are aware of the pitfalls you should avoid when writing an essay.

Activity 8

List the eight most important things to avoid when writing an essay.

Go online to see if your list matches ours!

Key Point

Remember that plagiarism must be avoided at all costs. It will be fatal to your assessment and may mean the end of your academic career!

If you have any doubt about what plagiarism means and how to avoid it:

- read chapter 7, Avoiding plagiarism
- talk to your lecturers.

Feedback

One important and useful way to improve your essay writing skills is to use effectively the feedback you have been given on earlier essays.

Key Point

Students in their first year at university are often surprised that lecturers do not routinely give feedback on drafts of essays – a practice that is commonplace in schools. There are probably two reasons for this. First, lecturers expect that your essay will be your own work and therefore do not comment on drafts as this will mean they have too much input into the final product. Secondly, lecturers are teaching too many students for them to be able to devote adequate time to one-to-one feedback.

In taking note of feedback you receive you should first distinguish between feedback that relates to the subject matter of the essay – that will be useful in any further assessments you have in that subject – and then consider the feedback that relates to more general essay writing skills. You should not take the comments personally but see them as indications of where you need to improve your work.

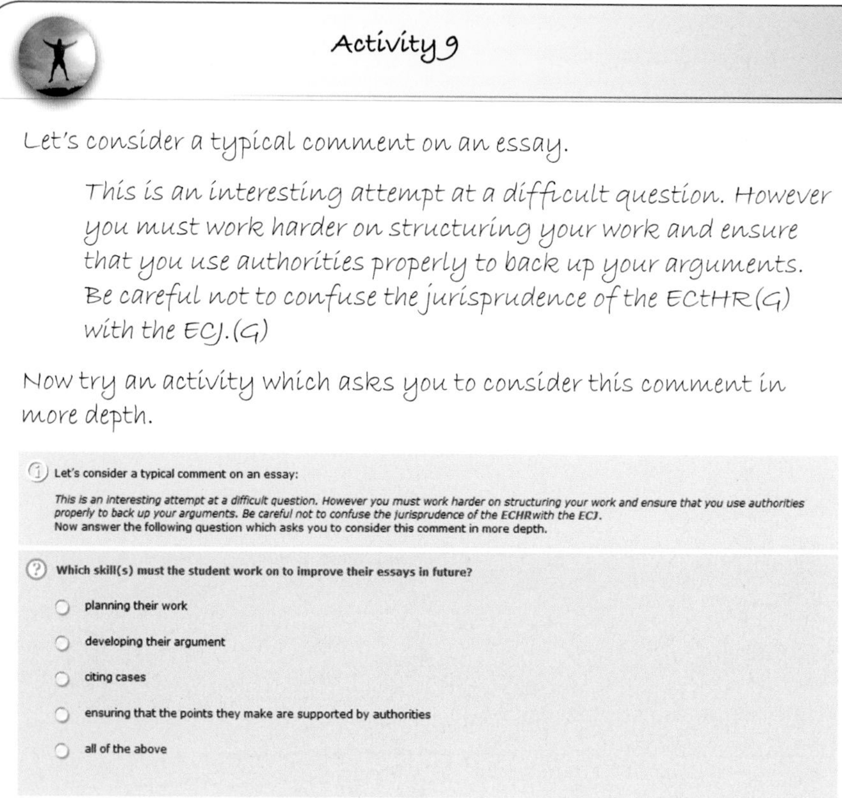

Activity 9

Let's consider a typical comment on an essay.

> This is an interesting attempt at a difficult question. However you must work harder on structuring your work and ensure that you use authorities properly to back up your arguments. Be careful not to confuse the jurisprudence of the ECtHR(G) with the ECJ.(G)

Now try an activity which asks you to consider this comment in more depth.

Let's consider a typical comment on an essay:

This is an interesting attempt at a difficult question. However you must work harder on structuring your work and ensure that you use authorities properly to back up your arguments. Be careful not to confuse the jurisprudence of the ECHRwith the ECJ.

Now answer the following question which asks you to consider this comment in more depth.

Which skill(s) must the student work on to improve their essays in future?

- planning their work
- developing their argument
- citing cases
- ensuring that the points they make are supported by authorities
- all of the above

Receiving feedback from your lecturer

Sometimes you genuinely do not understand where you have gone wrong, and you get little help from the written feedback. You may want to approach your lecturer to make sure that in future you avoid the mistakes that have reduced your mark this time. If you decide to speak to the lecturer about the feedback you have been given, make an appointment and ensure that you turn up on time. Take your essay with you, and paper and pen to make notes. However much you feel you deserved a higher mark than you were given, it is better not to approach the meeting feeling aggrieved. (If you genuinely think that your work has been improperly marked you should consult your personal tutor and find out how to use your university appeals procedures.)

Most lecturers mark work very carefully, and have a great deal more experience than you of what makes a good law essay. Moreover, if you behave aggressively, they will spend the time defending the mark and the feedback, rather than helping you learn how to improve your work.

Activity 10

Now watch a video clip of a student, Tom, receiving feedback on his essay from his lecturer.

Go online to watch the video and note down any learning points. You can then read our thoughts on this feedback session.

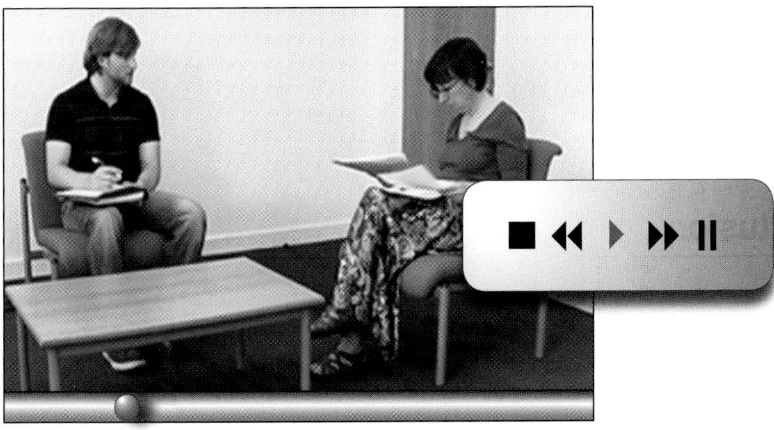

Now it's your turn!

One of the best ways you can learn how to improve your work is to reflect critically but constructively upon someone else's work. It is often far easier to spot their strengths and weaknesses and then apply what you have learned to your own work.

Activity 11

We have provided you with a copy of Tom's essay online, together with a suggested set of questions which enable you to evaluate that piece of work. Once you have worked through the essay, you will have experience of assessing an undergraduate law essay which you can then apply to your own work.

Conclusion

This chapter focuses on one of the most important skills you acquire as an undergraduate: the ability to present an argument in the form of an essay. Whatever essay writing skills you have developed up to this point will need more thought and more work if you are going to achieve high marks. However, if you work carefully through our suggested activities we are confident you will succeed.

Don't panic

Writing is a skill. We all need to practise it and we all get better with practice!

Key Point

The most effective ways to improve your essay writing skills are to

- Understand that when you are assessed by means of an essay you are demonstrating not only your understanding of the law, but also your essay writing skills. Practise writing essays and reflect carefully upon the criticism your writing receives. Become, if possible, your own critic.
- Learn how to read your own work and in particular the importance of re-drafting. Your first effort will not be good enough!
- Read your legal textbooks and articles with an awareness of the writing skills that the author is using. So, do not limit your attention to the legal arguments. Think about the techniques the writer uses to communicate his or her argument. What articles do you particularly enjoy reading? Can you work out why? Does the author use methods you could adapt for your own work?
- Enjoy your writing! This will make your work better, and help you devote the time and thought that good writing requires.

Chapter 26

Writing extended essays and dissertations

Rationale

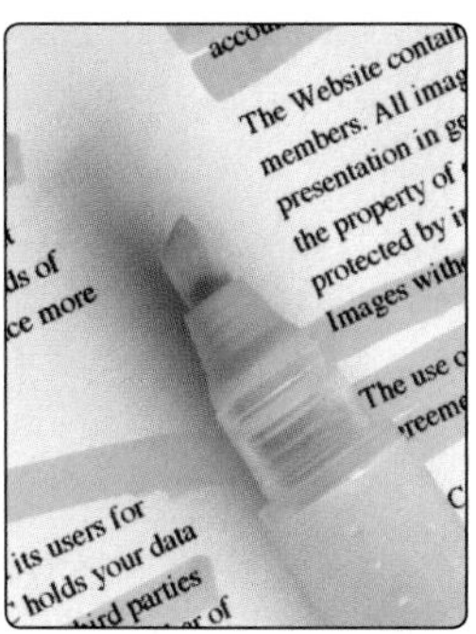

It is very likely that during the course of your law degree you will be offered the opportunity of writing an extended essay of more than 3,000 words, which may be described as an extended essay or as a dissertation. In many courses the extended essay or dissertation is a compulsory form of assessment.

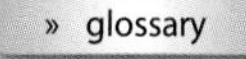

If you enjoy independent academic study, you will probably enjoy writing an extended essay. It gives you the opportunity to develop a personal interest in a particular area of law, which can be very rewarding. There are other more practical advantages in completing dissertations. Employers are often very interested in your ability to carry out an extended piece of research. It demonstrates independence, strategic and organisational skills and intellectual energy and stamina – all of which are valuable commodities in the workplace.

This chapter has been devised to help you write a successful dissertation. We have divided the task of writing a dissertation into three stages, the preliminary stage, the development stage and the completion stage. However, you should note that the stages overlap, and in particular you should be thinking about the final product throughout.

The chapter is devised to help you:

- Understand the importance of conforming to the module requirements for a dissertation
- Consider how to choose a topic for your dissertation
- Think about what makes a good title
- Develop a research strategy and a timetable for your dissertation
- Plan your dissertation
- Understand particular stylistic requirements
- Consider what makes a successful dissertation.

Preliminary stage

Module requirements

Your starting point for a successful dissertation or extended essay is your own university requirements. Most are set out in a module format. The module outline will provide you with information about word length, deadlines, supervision, resources, style etc.

» glossary

Before you commit yourself to writing a dissertation (and for the rest of this chapter we are going to use the term dissertation rather than extended essay but the suggestions

are applicable whatever name is given to the long essay you are required to write) you must:

- Ensure you know the timetable both for choosing the dissertation module and for submission.
- Establish a relationship with your supervisor, and understand what he or she will expect from you.
- Understand the importance of research and writing skills, and consider what additional help your law school may provide for dissertation students.
- Choose a topic and a working title for your dissertation (you can usually refine your title as your research progresses).
- Know what the word limit is, and whether it includes footnotes and bibliography.

» glossary

Preliminary activities

Committing yourself to writing a dissertation requires you to complete a number of preliminary activities which are all necessary to ensure that you are ultimately successful.

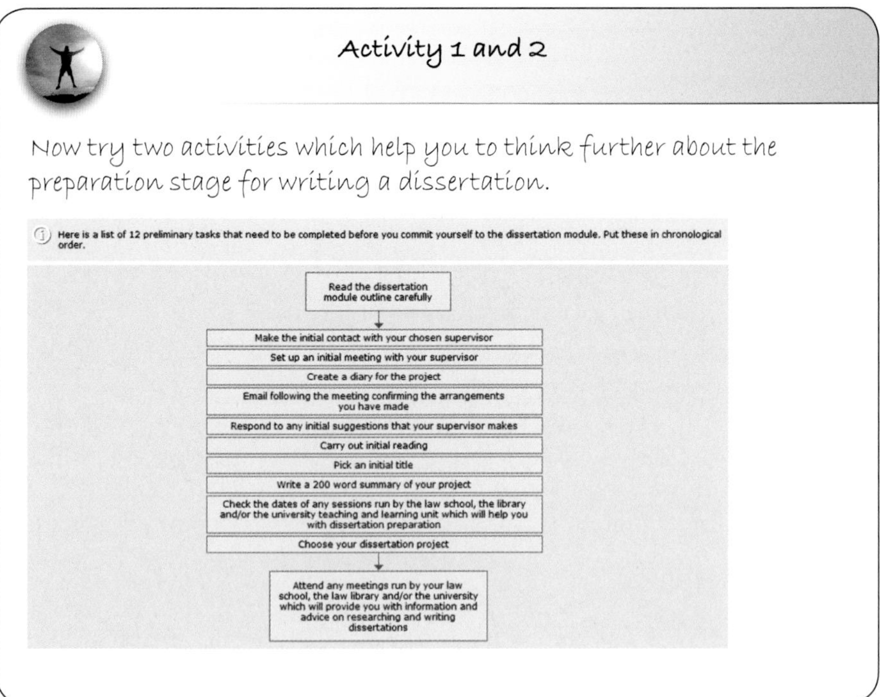

Activity 1 and 2
Now try two activities which help you to think further about the preparation stage for writing a dissertation.
Here is a list of 12 preliminary tasks that need to be completed before you commit yourself to the dissertation module. Put these in chronological order.
Read the dissertation module outline carefully
Make the initial contact with your chosen supervisor
Set up an initial meeting with your supervisor
Create a diary for the project
Email following the meeting confirming the arrangements you have made
Respond to any initial suggestions that your supervisor makes
Carry out initial reading
Pick an initial title
Write a 200 word summary of your project
Check the dates of any sessions run by the law school, the library and/or the university teaching and learning unit which will help you with dissertation preparation
Choose your dissertation project
Attend any meetings run by your law school, the law library and/or the university which will provide you with information and advice on researching and writing dissertations

There are a number of important choices you have to make in the initial stages of your dissertation. You have to think very carefully about these choices because the decisions you make will have long-lasting implications.

Important initial decisions

Choosing a topic

One important step towards completing a successful dissertation is to choose something that interests you. Think of your choice of topic as choosing a puzzle you would like to solve. A successful dissertation is a response to a puzzle which has sustained your interest during the period of research. Equally importantly, you need to choose a topic that you can present in a way which captures and sustains the interests of your marker. To do this, you have to write with enthusiasm about the topic. So start by deciding what areas of law have attracted your interest or aroused your curiosity and about which you would like to learn more. Think about other essays you have written, were there issues in these which you would have liked to think about further but were unable to follow through because of time or word limits?

If you want more ideas you could try the following:

- The **Law Commission** website tells you those areas of law that are currently being considered by them. » glossary
- The **ePolitix** website tells you which **bills** are currently going through **Parliament** (www.epolitix.com). **Legislation** is often drafted in response to a problem with the current law. » glossary
- Judicial websites provide information about recently decided **cases**. Again, recently decided cases are likely to be concerned with interesting legal dilemmas. » glossary
- The law pages of quality newspapers and the websites of radio programmes such as *Unreliable Evidence* on BBC Radio 4, which focus on areas of topical legal interest. These may reveal puzzles about the law which capture your interest.

There is another important choice you will have to make in choosing your topic. Are you going to choose a totally new area of law, or are you going to develop your knowledge of something you have already studied? It is always exciting to look at a different area of law. However, there are drawbacks. It will take you time to develop a basic understanding of the legal framework of a new area, time that will not be necessary if you choose something you have some familiarity with. Moreover, you may be tempted to think that simply describing a new area of law will be sufficient. It will not be enough for a good mark. Even if your chosen area of work is technically complex, a good dissertation will require that you take a critical approach to that knowledge. We will discuss different approaches to solving legal puzzles below. However, first of all you must find out whether the legal puzzle that you are interested in has attracted academic interest.

Initial research

Your next step is to ensure that the topic you choose has attracted the attention of academics. This will mean that there are plenty of **academic articles** available for you to read and reference in your work. » glossary You should carry out some preliminary research by looking at a range of authoritative recent **textbooks** and academic journals to see what has been written about your preferred topic. » glossary Do not leave out professional journals. Practitioners often write about complexities and dilemmas which face them in practice. However, you should be aware that academic articles are given considerably more weight, so if there is no academic work on your topic of interest it is probably not a good idea to pursue it. If you have difficulties with carrying out this type of research you should read our chapter on legal research. Don't forget this is just the preliminary stage of your research. You will have to develop your research strategy much further in the next stage of the dissertation.

↳ **Cross reference**
See chapter 11, Embarking on research.

Activity 3

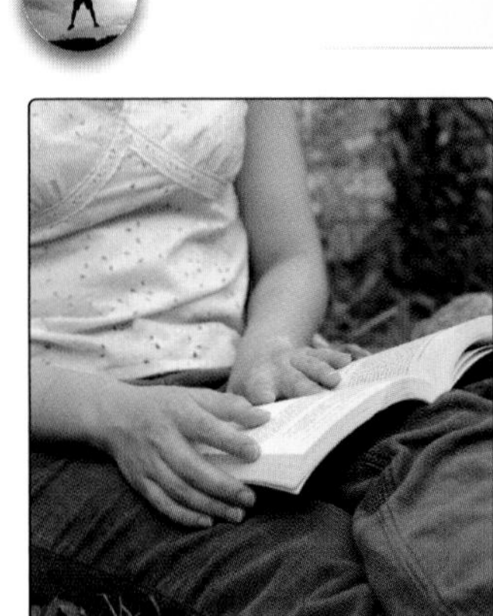

Now try an activity which is designed to help you think about relevant journals to consult to locate relevant articles.

Choosing your approach

Students often work very hard on their dissertations and are disappointed when after a lot of hard work they do not achieve a high 2.1 or a first. Unfortunately you do not achieve high marks simply because you are diligent. A critical perspective on the topic is absolutely necessary if you are to achieve a high mark. It is not enough to describe the law, however technical and complex the area that you have chosen. So the next step, once you have an idea about your topic, and made sure that there is sufficient information available to you on that topic, is to develop a critical perspective on that topic. This requires creative thinking. You must gather together your thoughts and knowledge about your chosen topic and construct from that something new and original. We gave you some suggestions about this in our chapters on writing essays, on critical thinking and on creative thinking.

However, there are other choices to be made about how you might approach your research. Below we suggest ways you might consider in deciding how to solve the problem you have set for yourself.

Black letter/doctrinal approaches

This approach is probably the one that you are most familiar with as you have probably been set several essays which require this form of analysis. It involves a careful analysis of the legal constituents of a legal problem. It is likely to focus on complex legal puzzles such as conflicting **precedents** or the emergence of legal principles in a particularly complex area of law. It requires you to take a careful and forensic approach to the law, paying attention to the ratios of leading cases for instance, or scrutinising legislative provisions. Don't forget that you must also be critical. It is not sufficient to describe the complexities of the law – you must also think about the consequences of these complexities and whose interests they serve.

» glossary

Theoretical approaches

By a theoretical perspective we mean that you approach the topic using a general explanatory framework which you then apply to that particular topic. We illustrate what we mean by this through two examples.

Feminist perspectives on law

A feminist perspective on law can be summarised as seeking to challenge the gendered assumptions of law and to replace the authoritative male voice with a voice that acknowledges gender and difference. There are some very useful resources on feminism and law. Routledge publishes a series of books entitled Feminist Perspectives on Law, the latest of which, *Feminist Perspectives on Land Law* was published in 2007 and Springer publishes the journal Feminist Legal Studies three times a year.

Regulation and law

Regulation and law scholars are interested in the role of law as a regulator of economic and social behaviour. They see law as one example of the tools available to both state and supranational bodies to regulate behaviour. They are interested in what makes for effective regulation, how regulation is legitimised, tracing the evolution of regulatory instruments amongst other things. There are a number of useful texts, in particular Morgan and Yeung, *Cases and Materials on Regulation*, published by Cambridge University Press in 2007.

Empirical work

Another way of developing an original piece of work is to carry out some empirical work on an area of law. What we mean by empirical work is research designed to discover how people experience law. So, for instance, you could find out whether law students are better at reading contracts than other students by researching the extent to which they have read and understood the lettings agreements they have signed with the university or with private landlords and comparing the results with other students. An empirical approach would work well as part of a law-in-action dissertation. This is often very enjoyable work. However, be careful. Your law school might not allow empirical work, or they might require that you study a social science module which teaches you about empirical methodologies before allowing you to engage in an empirical project. Get advice at this point. Even if you do not have to study a methodology module you must become familiar with the literature on designing questionnaires for instance, and selecting samples for interview.

Key Point

Whilst empirical work can provide a very useful basis for a dissertation you must ensure that you have an understanding of the methodologies and approaches of empirical work before you start on the project.

There are a number of useful resources you can consult. Hamersley and Atkinson first published their classic text, *Ethnography: Principles in Practice* in 1983 and it remains very useful. Nigel Gilbert, *Researching Social Life*, published by Sage, is also a very useful introductory text. The Journal of Law and Society intends to publish a special edition on law and empirical work in 2008.

Comparative approaches

One particular approach which can be very enlightening is to consider a comparative approach. So, for instance, you could consider the statutory response to the events of 11 September in the USA, the UK and France. You have to accept the challenge of researching in different jurisdictions and you also need to ensure that your literature search covers international journals. However, the end result is likely to be very rewarding. Note that it is easier than you might think to locate **statutes** in other English-speaking jurisdictions by using websites. Nor should you worry about your ability to understand them. Australian legislation in particular tends to be written in very plain English, and most **common law** jurisdictions statutes are accessible with a little work.

» glossary

» glossary

Comparative work can be theoretical or black letter. You should, however, be sensitive to the different meanings that different societies place on what might seem to you to be commonplace legal assumptions. For instance, the British approach to the exercise of discretion may be quite distinct from how other European cultures view granting discretionary powers to the state. These differences are cultural, historical and political and you should take account of them. In other words, simply because you are taking a comparative approach does not mean that you do not need to be critical in your thinking.

Interdisciplinary approaches

You are not necessarily limited to legal analysis in your research. If your supervisor agrees, you may find historical or textual based approaches to researching the law very interesting. You may also be interested in the links between the law and political thought drawing on the work of Foucault or Marx for instance. This could be particularly relevant when looking at topics such as sentencing, surveillance or mental health.

Key Point

We have suggested a number of approaches you might take. The approach you choose to take to the puzzle you are trying to solve should be one which enables you to find out some answers which you find interesting.

Choosing a title

One common feature of a dissertation is that you are required to devise your own essay title. This is a really important stage of the assessment because a good title enables you to produce a good piece of work and a poor title will mean that you are inevitably going to get a poor mark.

A good title is one which:

- is clear and focused
- gives a good indication of the legal puzzle you are attempting to solve
- allows you to develop the critical perspective on a particular area of law which we have suggested is vital to success
- is manageable in terms of the coverage it demands of the subject area
- allows you to discuss the topic in sufficient detail within the word limit
- enables you to refer to research which will support your work.

Perhaps most important, a good title is one which interests you, and will sustain your interest over the period of research. This means the marker is likely to share your interest once you have completed your task. What you ideally want is for your supervisor to say, 'now that's an interesting angle on that topic, I look forward to reading your work'. In short, a good title makes someone want to read your work.

A poor title is one which:

- allows you to answer the question simply by describing an area of law
- is too long, or contains too many questions to be answered in the essay
- is too broad in scope
- is too obscure, so that you are unable to find academic work to support your own research.

You have to steer a careful path between too simple and too complex a title. This means that you cannot choose your title until you have done some reading around the topic that you are interested in. Make sure that you read the articles which your lecturers have recommended. These

» glossary

should give you some ideas. Quite often footnotes in articles raise questions of interest. Look at other academic journals such as the Journal of Law and Society or the Modern Law Review to see the sort of topics which they publish, and the titles that academics have chosen for their articles. You should also read government publications in the area to see what problems government and policy makers are concerned with. Consultation papers are a particularly rich source of inspiration since they ask readers to respond to questions which are of interest to government. You should also look at magazines and policy documents produced by legal pressure groups such as Shelter, Citizens Advice and Legal Action Group. They will give you some good ideas about topical issues.

It is a good idea to choose a title which reflects the angle you take on the research. So if you decide to utilise a feminist perspective on anti-social behaviour, then you could use the title, 'A feminist perspective on anti-social behaviour'. Another example might be 'Tenancy deposits in the UK and New South Wales – an analysis of effective regulation'. You, your supervisor and any reader knows exactly what you are trying to do.

Don't panic

We are putting a lot of emphasis on choosing a title at this stage. However, don't panic. You will have lots of opportunity to refine and adapt your title as your dissertation progresses.

Activity 4

Now try an activity which asks you to evaluate effective titles for a dissertation.

You are going to have to answer a number of questions at the preliminary stages of your dissertation. We have summarised these in the box below.

Key Point

- What are my interests?
- Do I want to study something new?
- Can I find a puzzle I want to solve?
- Is it a puzzle which has attracted academic interest?
- What are my objectives in searching for the solution?
- How do I want to approach the problem?
- Does my approach serve my objectives?
- Does my title reflect what I am trying to do?

When you have begun to answer these questions then you are ready to move on to the next stage of your dissertation.

The development stage

Time planning

Once you have made your initial decisions about your dissertation you must work out how you are going to complete the dissertation in the time available.

Key Point

You cannot produce a dissertation at the last minute – you must plan your time effectively.

Time planning is crucial to the successful completion of your dissertation and you need to take this seriously. What you need to do is to consider are:

- those deadlines within the task that must be complied with

- the key milestones that you must achieve in order to meet those deadlines – these are more variable and you should ensure that they are realistic
- the most effective use of your time and the effective deployment of the resources available to you
- deadlines that you must meet in other areas of your study
- your commitments outside of your study such as work and family.

↳ Cross reference
We talk more about effective time management in chapter 2, Managing your time.

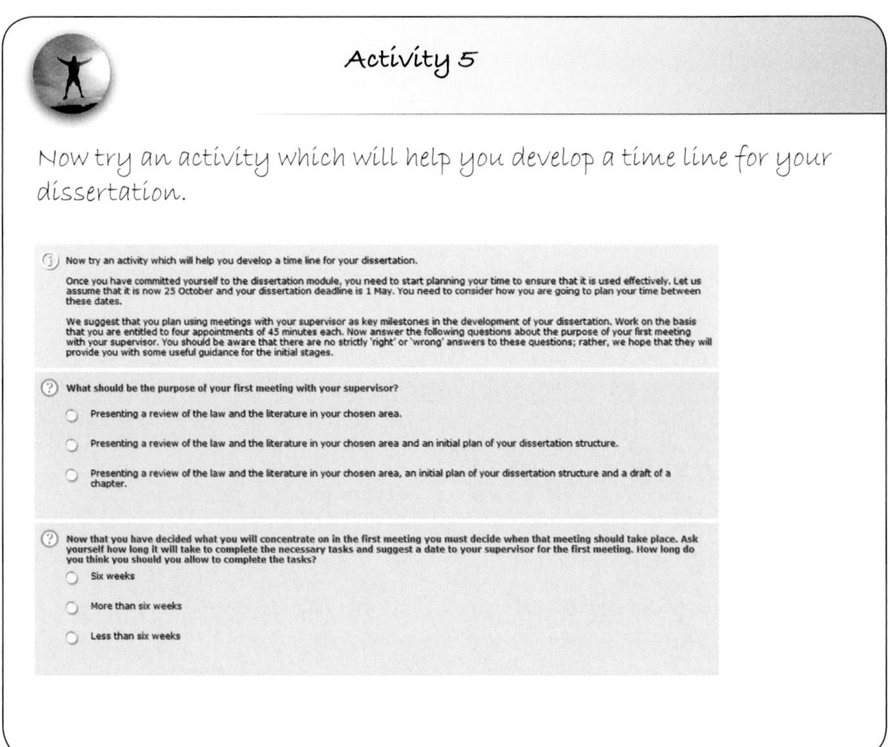

Activity 5

Now try an activity which will help you develop a time line for your dissertation.

Now try an activity which will help you develop a time line for your dissertation.

Once you have committed yourself to the dissertation module, you need to start planning your time to ensure that it is used effectively. Let us assume that it is now 25 October and your dissertation deadline is 1 May. You need to consider how you are going to plan your time between these dates.

We suggest that you plan using meetings with your supervisor as key milestones in the development of your dissertation. Work on the basis that you are entitled to four appointments of 45 minutes each. Now answer the following questions about the purpose of your first meeting with your supervisor. You should be aware that there are no strictly 'right' or 'wrong' answers to these questions; rather, we hope that they will provide you with some useful guidance for the initial stages.

What should be the purpose of your first meeting with your supervisor?

- Presenting a review of the law and the literature in your chosen area.
- Presenting a review of the law and the literature in your chosen area and an initial plan of your dissertation structure.
- Presenting a review of the law and the literature in your chosen area, an initial plan of your dissertation structure and a draft of a chapter.

Now that you have decided what you will concentrate on in the first meeting you must decide when that meeting should take place. Ask yourself how long it will take to complete the necessary tasks and suggest a date to your supervisor for the first meeting. How long do you think you should you allow to complete the tasks?

- Six weeks
- More than six weeks
- Less than six weeks

Planning for your first meeting

In Box 1 we set out our suggestions for the tasks you need to complete for the first meeting.

Box 1 – preparing for your first supervision meeting

Stage	Steps to be taken	Comments
Preparing for Meeting 1 with your supervisor	You should start to carry out the tasks you have agreed should be completed prior to that meeting. These are likely to include...	
	Researching your dissertation area, including the law and the literature and preparing a summary of these	Send this by email to your supervisor prior to the meeting
	Initial planning of your dissertation into chapters (see below)	Send this by email to your supervisor prior to your meeting
	Re-considering your project outline and your project title	Send this by email to your supervisor prior to your meeting
Meeting 1	Checking the initial tasks, developing the focus of the dissertation and agreeing the agenda for the next meeting	Ask your supervisor for any additional suggestions for research and ask their opinion as to the initial structure of your dissertation. Is the supervisor happy with your title and does your project outline continue to reflect the aims of your dissertation?

Following the meeting we suggest that you email your supervisor to confirm the decisions made in Meeting 1 and to confirm the date and agenda for Meeting 2. Note that we have included thinking about the second meeting as part of your agenda for the first meeting – it is important that you are always thinking about the next stage of your dissertation as well as carrying out the necessary tasks for the current stage.

Developing a research strategy

One of the most important tasks at this early stage of your dissertation is developing an effective research strategy.

Let's take three potential topic areas:

- the implications of terrorism for civil liberties
- the issue of consent in rape law
- the reform of public health law.

The first two topics are related to your studies in the compulsory curriculum for most LLB degrees. The reform of public health law is likely to be an entirely new area for most students. Your general approach to research will be the same for each topic. However, your specific focus will depend upon what approach you decide to take to your research.

You will need to:

- identify both basic and specialist texts in the area
- check the relevant statutory framework

- research the relevant cases
- identify relevant articles
- locate the specialist journals in the topic area and search for relevant articles in these
- check relevant websites, including pressure groups, government websites, and professional websites
- ensure that you have the theoretical work to support your approach. For instance, if you are going to look at surveillance from a Foucauldian perspective you will need to read *Discipline and Punish*.

As your research question becomes more focused you will be able to assess your research findings for relevance. So your search starts general and gradually becomes more refined, providing you with in-depth knowledge of a very particular area. The final general point is that you must remember to constantly update your research for new articles, cases and statutory developments.

Implementing your research strategy

To help you develop your research skills we are going to look in some depth at research strategies in the three areas mentioned above.

To start with, look at the chapters in Part II, Research and technical skills, which will give you some general guidance on how to embark on research. Now let's see how you could tackle these three topics.

1. The implications of terrorism for civil liberties

Starting point

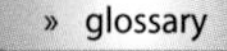

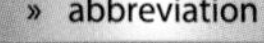

The first thing you will need to do is to check the law on terrorism. **Halsbury's** Laws (in hard copy or on **LexisNexis Butterworths** (**LNB**)) is always an excellent place to start if you want an overview of the law. A good search might be terrorism and human rights (you will find that the term civil liberty is not the used term). You will get a number of entries: note the appropriate volumes and sections to find the relevant ones.

Books

When you come to look up books on terrorism in your library catalogue you will find a great many books on international terrorism, 9/11, international law etc., but very few which deal with it in the domestic context, although you might come across:

> Steve Hewitt, *The British War on Terror: Terrorism and Counterterrorism on the Home Front Since 9–11* (Continuum 2007, in press)

The absence of books indicates that this is a new area of interest, and therefore you should concentrate on looking for academic writing in journals, while keeping your eyes open for new books which may be a useful way into the subject.

Statutes

You will probably have identified the legislation from Halsbury's, but you can also see a list of the Acts on terrorism by checking on one or another of the databases, e.g. Westlaw or LNB or the Statute Law Database (SLD).

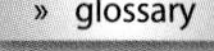

» abbreviation

Example

SLD: If you enter *terrorism* and look for UK Public General Acts only, you get a list of All Acts with Terrorism in their title, up to date. You would note especially the Terrorism Act 2006 and the Prevention of Terrorism Act 2005.

LNB: If you look these up on LNB, you can link to Halsbury's annotations. These include a note of the parliamentary debates leading up to the Act, which you could then look up in Hansard.

Westlaw: When you look up an Act, you can link directly to cases and journal articles citing it. The Explanatory Note is included.

Acts of Parliament on the OPSI site: Here you can get the Explanatory Notes provided by the government for each Act.

» glossary

» abbreviation

Cases

You can search for cases in Westlaw, LNB or Justis, using search terms such as *terrorism* and *human rights* (remember to put the phrase "human rights" in quotes for Westlaw). If you search in full text you will get far too many cases to deal with, so make sure you enter them in the subject/keyword field.

» glossary

Or you can search for cases which cite the Terrorism Act 2006 and/or the Prevention of Terrorism Act 2005.

Articles

Using the Legal Journals Index (LJI)on Westlaw, or the Index to Legal Periodicals, you can search using the terms *terrorism and "human rights"*. Remember that if you search in full text you will get far too many hits, so confine your search to the subject/keywords. These are the kind of results you would get:

» abbreviation

LJI – subject/keywords – *terrorism and "human rights"* 500+ articles

LJI – article title – *terrorism and "human rights*" 30+ articles

LJI – subject keyword *terrorism* and free text *"civil liberties"* 40+ articles

You can also search very effectively for articles which cite a particular case, or an Act. Remember, too, that even if you get an overwhelming number of hits, you may only want to look at the most recent ones.

Websites, pressure groups etc.

Government department websites contain the current policy and a great amount of research. The Home Office **Research Development and Statistics** website has a great deal of material which isn't immediately apparent from the home page.

Pressure groups can provide invaluable information, but you need to exercise some care and discrimination when looking for these. Be sure you know that the site is genuine and has some authority. **Liberty** and the **Legal Action Group** would be obvious pressure groups to look at. **Statewatch** monitors the state and civil liberties in Europe and has a large amount of material on its website.

Official publications

You can search for materials on the Official Documents site. If you search using the term *terrorism* you come across some key documents, from any of which you will get referred to others.

↳ Cross reference
For more details on the Official Documents site, see chapter 13, Sources of law.

Example

Official Documents site search for terrorism

The definition of terrorism: a report by Lord Carlile of Berriew Q.C. Independent Reviewer of Terrorism Legislation Cm 7052, Session 2007

Countering international terrorism: the United Kingdom's strategy Cm 6888, Session 2006

Terrorism detention powers: the Government reply to the fourth report from the Home Affairs Committee session 2005–06 HC 910

The Government reply to the report by Lord Carlile of Berriew Q.C. Independent Reviewer of Terrorism Legislation: the definition of terrorism Cm7058, Session 2007

2. The issue of consent in rape law

Use the same methodology as outlined above.

Starting point

Halsbury's Laws is the best way of starting your research for this topic. If you search for *rape and consent* you see that there is a section on each of these terms: Criminal Law Vol 11(1) para 163: Consent and Vol 11(1) para 165: Rape. Make sure you check the updates for recent judgments and changes in the law.

Books

There are a great many books about rape and sexual offences. It's easy to get diverted away from the essential legal problem of consent if you're not careful, and you must also be aware that most of the publication on the subject is American, and therefore has limited relevance. Two books you're sure to come across are:

> Sue Lees, *Carnal Knowledge: Rape on Trial* (2nd edn, Women's Press, Ltd, London 2002)
>
> Jennifer Temkin, *Rape and the Legal Process* (2nd edn, Oxford University Press, Oxford 2002)

Statutes

Having looked at Halsbury's Laws you will be aware that the relevant legislation is the Sexual Offences Act 2003, which redefined the law in this area.

Look at the Explanatory Notes to the Act, which will also refer you to the background documents, and the Halsbury Annotations on LNB.

Case law

If you look on Westlaw or Lexis using *rape and consent* as search terms, this brings up a great many cases, which you can narrow down by looking at **House of Lords** cases only. Remember that if you find a recent House of Lords judgment, it will refer to other leading cases.

» glossary

Articles

The Legal Journals Index on Westlaw brings up over 150 articles using the subject/keyword search *rape and consent*. You get fewer if you search in the article titles.

Google Scholar is a Google search facility which searches for scholarly articles only. These can be useful for finding unpublished or semi-published articles such as working papers from university departments, and can be a valuable source if used with discretion. Remember that you must cite these properly, and on no account copy and paste without attribution.

Websites and official publications

Look on the Home Office and Law Commission websites as described above.

Official publications

This is a problematic area to search, as the search terms bring up a great many irrelevant publications, which may include the terms, but are too broad to be of use. It's better, in this case, to look for references in articles which lead you to official publications.

News

Look for articles on BBC, Guardian online, etc. You can search daily newspapers on LNB.

3. The reform of public health law

This topic requires a rather different approach, because it is not an identifiable area of law in the same way as the previous two topics. As well as the strategies we have used for the other two topics, you could try the following:

Starting point

Rather than search Halsbury's, it is useful in this case to browse the list of Titles (volumes). You then find *Protection of the Environment and Public Health* (vol. 38). This lists the principal legislation, both British and European, and then goes into the separates topics of public health. This will repay some close reading, and you can pick up references to all the principal documents.

» glossary

Another starting point might be to look at government policy on the Department of Health website. You will also probably need to search in **European Union** legislation and policy, by looking on the **Europa** website.

Books and articles

The term 'public health law' tends to be used in America rather than in Britain. You may therefore be disappointed to find that relevant-looking books are, in fact, completely US-focused. However, there may well be interesting parallels between US approaches to the reform of public health law and anything that might be proposed in the United Kingdom.

Entering *public health* as a subject/keyword search brings up numerous articles in the Legal Journals Index, which may be useful. Many of them relate to specific areas, such as anti-smoking legislation, but are worth trawling through.

Expanding your research

» glossary

This topic is one which you will certainly need to expand outside the boundaries of legal materials. There are lots of journals in subjects such as social policy which contain relevant articles. A very good database for doing is this is known as the **Web of Science**, which is part of a larger service called the Web of Knowledge. Look on your library website for it, and ask advice from the library if you need to. Entering a search for *"public health law"* (using the inverted commas to ensure that you search for the phrase) will retrieve a large number of relevant articles from these journals. You will, of course, need to make sure that they are not exclusively American in their focus.

You may be surprised to learn that a search for theoretical articles looking at the regulation of public health is likely to be fruitful. Foucauldian perspectives are particularly in evidence. So, for instance, a quick review of the literature produced this abstract of an article by Sarah Sanford and S. Harris Ali:

> Social Theory & Health (2005) 3, 105–125
>
> The 2003 Severe Acute Respiratory Syndrome (SARS) outbreak presented a challenging period for public health in Toronto. Many old and new public health measures were implemented at local, national and global levels, in an attempt to control the outbreak of the disease. Among these, surveillance mechanisms dominated, which involved new epidemiological techniques and statistical profiling strategies. In this paper, Gramsci's concept of hegemony is used to further understandings of public health governance during the outbreak of emerging infectious diseases. Specifically, the function of the discourse of 'risk' in public health governance is examined, along with public health as a 'moral agent' in the naturalization of specific public health measures. In addition, the pervasive discourse of 'security' is discussed in relation to current public health practices. These characteristics of public health are examined with consideration of their potential for propagating social exclusion and stigmatization of individuals and communities.

The specific case of SARS in Toronto is used to examine the implications of public health as a mechanism for social control and reproduction rather than the promotion of equality in health throughout the population.

Moreover historical research may reveal interesting insights on contemporary problems. For instance the sanitation reforms of the 1830s carried out in response to the threat of cholera may be interesting at a time when the government in the UK is questioning whether we have the necessary legal infrastructure to respond to global threats like SARS.

The research cycle

All we have been able to do in suggesting how to develop a research strategy is to start you on the research process. It will be up to you to decide how to develop your line of enquiry and what to focus on in your research.

At this stage of your academic career you probably think of the research stage as a linear process which starts when you gather books and articles together, which you then read and then you write your dissertation. This is not the most effective way to carry out research. It is better to see research as a cycle. You have begun the cycle when you carried out some initial research to see what academic interest there was in your chosen topic. You will have thought about what you have read and what questions it raised in your mind. Those questions should stimulate further research as your ideas get more focused. Once you gather further materials you read these and question them. Then you repeat the process, and keep repeating it even after you have started writing. You repeat it until you have finished your thinking, and you probably don't finish thinking until you have finished writing.

Planning your dissertation

We have also suggested that at this stage you should start to plan your dissertation. You should plan your dissertation following the advice of your supervisor. However, we can give you some rules of thumb. You should spend some time thinking about a logical subdivision of the topic you are researching. You should identify what the key issues are and how these break down into sub-issues. This task should be informed by your research, by the puzzle you are trying to solve and by the approach you are taking to solving that puzzle. Once you have decided on the key issue and the sub issues we would advise that you organise the dissertation into chapters which reflect these subdivisions. At an undergraduate level dissertation chapters should be between 2,000 and 2,500 words. Introductions and conclusions are likely to be shorter. Therefore in a 12,000 word dissertation we would expect that you would write an introduction of around 1,000 words and a conclusion of a similar length. The remaining 10,000 words should consist of 4–5 chapters of around 2,000–2,500 words in length. Your first chapter may be concerned with the history of the legal problem for instance, or consist of an explanation of the political context. Your next two or three chapters will provide a more in-depth analysis of the legal issues. Each of your chapters should have an introduction which explains how it relates to the key issue you are investigating and a conclusion.

Your introductory chapter should explain your theoretical perspective or your research hypothesis if you have carried out empirical work. You should also explain the structure of the dissertation, and why you have divided it into the chapters you have. Don't abandon your perspective once you have explained it; ensure that it is built into every chapter of the dissertation. Your concluding chapter should summarise your research project, and suggest new questions for research if relevant.

You should begin preparing your plan as soon as possible, ideally after you have carried out your initial search for cases, statutes and articles. This means that you can discuss it with your supervisor at an early stage and that you develop a clear understanding of the task you have set yourself.

You can learn a lot about how to subdivide your work from reading academic articles.

Activity 6

Now try an activity which helps you think about how to subdivide your work into chapters by considering the structure of a typical academic article.

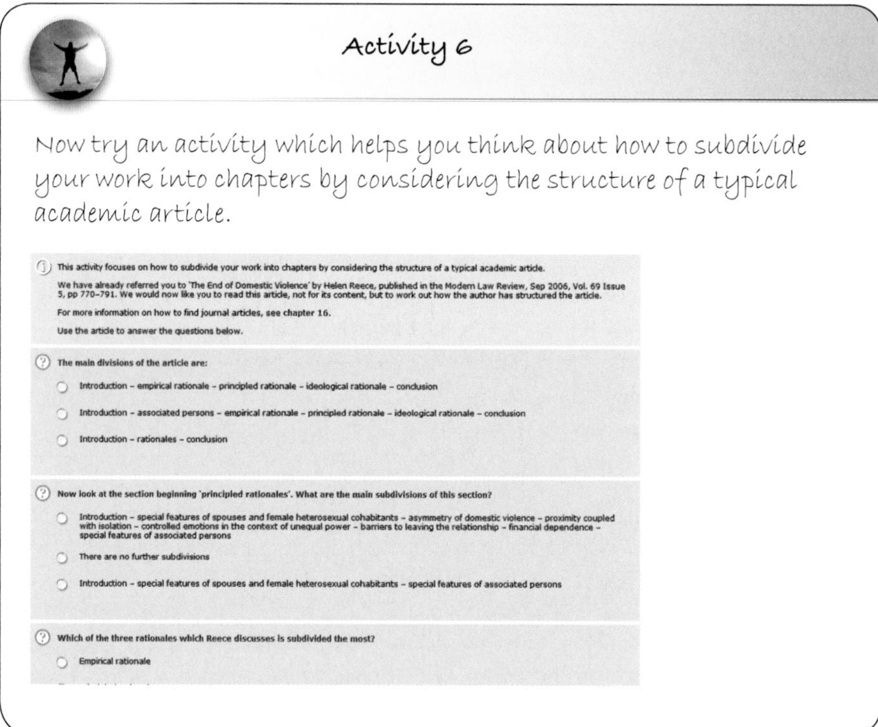

This activity focuses on how to subdivide your work into chapters by considering the structure of a typical academic article.

We have already referred you to 'The End of Domestic Violence' by Helen Reece, published in the Modern Law Review, Sep 2006, Vol. 69 Issue 5, pp 770–791. We would now like you to read this article, not for its content, but to work out how the author has structured the article.

For more information on how to find journal articles, see chapter 16.

Use the article to answer the questions below.

The main divisions of the article are:

- Introduction – empirical rationale – principled rationale – ideological rationale – conclusion
- Introduction – associated persons – empirical rationale – principled rationale – ideological rationale – conclusion
- Introduction – rationales – conclusion

Now look at the section beginning 'principled rationales'. What are the main subdivisions of this section?

- Introduction – special features of spouses and female heterosexual cohabitants – asymmetry of domestic violence – proximity coupled with isolation – controlled emotions in the context of unequal power – barriers to leaving the relationship – financial dependence – special features of associated persons
- There are no further subdivisions
- Introduction – special features of spouses and female heterosexual cohabitants – special features of associated persons

Which of the three rationales which Reece discusses is subdivided the most?

- Empirical rationale

Once you have become immersed into the research cycle and started planning the structure of your dissertation you should begin the completion stage of the dissertation.

The completion stage

This is a very important stage of your work. You will continue to research and you will be rethinking your title and your structure. In this section of the chapter we return to the need for good time management, and we provide some guidance on the writing process.

Time planning

The deadline for submission of the dissertation is drawing closer and you still have lots to do. Time management is even more important than ever.

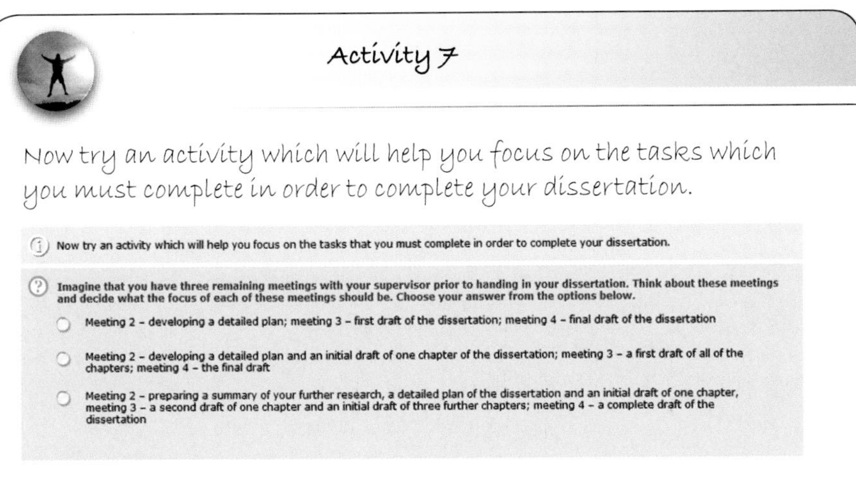

Activity 7

Now try an activity which will help you focus on the tasks which you must complete in order to complete your dissertation.

Now try an activity which will help you focus on the tasks that you must complete in order to complete your dissertation.

Imagine that you have three remaining meetings with your supervisor prior to handing in your dissertation. Think about these meetings and decide what the focus of each of these meetings should be. Choose your answer from the options below.

- Meeting 2 – developing a detailed plan; meeting 3 – first draft of the dissertation; meeting 4 – final draft of the dissertation
- Meeting 2 – developing a detailed plan and an initial draft of one chapter of the dissertation; meeting 3 – a first draft of all of the chapters; meeting 4 – the final draft
- Meeting 2 – preparing a summary of your further research, a detailed plan of the dissertation and an initial draft of one chapter, meeting 3 – a second draft of one chapter and an initial draft of three further chapters; meeting 4 – a complete draft of the dissertation

We have set out a suggested plan for the remainder of the dissertation period in Box 2 below. We have left columns blank for you to complete with the relevant dates. Don't forget to build in time for contingencies – what this means is that you allow a week or so's grace at each deadline, for last minute crises. If you do not need the extra time, you carry on with your tasks, just in case an emergency crops up later. Note also the importance of other major academic deadlines, so when planning your time you should plot in when other essays have to be handed and when examinations take place. Dissertation deadlines frequently coincide with the commencement of the examination period. If that is the case for you, you must include time for exam preparation as well as completion of your dissertation. Finally, don't forget to allow sufficient time after the fourth meeting to complete your dissertation including responding appropriately to any criticisms made by your supervisor. Once you have decided when it would be appropriate to have these meetings, email your supervisor for their agreement. Note that effective supervision does not necessarily have to be face to face. Feedback can often be usefully provided by email if you and your supervisor agree. This means that your time away from the university can also be used for supervisions.

Box 2 – from the end of meeting 1 to submission…

Stage	Steps to be taken	Comments	By (insert date)	Completion date
Preparing for Meeting 2 with the supervisor	Email your supervisor to confirm the decisions made in Meeting 1 and to confirm the date of the second meeting			
	Prepare for the next meeting. The most important tasks at this stage are…			
	To continue with your research, in particular following up any suggestions made by your supervisor			
	To develop a more detailed plan of the dissertation, in particular planning each chapter of the dissertation	Make sure you send this to your supervisor in sufficient time..		
	Write an initial draft of one or two chapters	Make sure you send these to your supervisor in sufficient time.		
Meeting 2	The purpose of this meeting is to ensure that your plan is effective to deliver an answer to the title you have chosen and that your initial draft of your chapters is well written, critical, and focused on the title.	Discuss the plan, take a careful note of its strengths and weaknesses and agree. Agree what you need to do to develop the plan. Discuss your draft chapters – what does your supervisor like, what does he or she think needs developing. Agree the tasks for the next meeting.		
	Following the meeting send an email confirming the decisions you have made, agreeing the agenda for the next meeting, and confirming the meeting date and time.			
Preparing for Meeting 3 with the supervisor	Prepare for the next meeting. The most important tasks at this stage are…			
	To write second drafts of those chapters you have already submitted to your supervisor and to write the initial drafts of the remaining chapters (depending upon what you have agreed with your supervisor). It may be that the drafts of the introduction and conclusion will be deferred to Meeting 4.	Ensure that you get drafts to the supervisor well in advance of the meeting. The feedback you get at this stage is especially important because you still have time to do a lot more work on the dissertation if that is shown to be necessary.		
Meeting 3	The purpose of this meeting is to get detailed feedback on your work to date.	You should take notes of the feedback. What you want is to know how to complete the dissertation in time and to a high level.		

Preparing for Meeting 4	The task at this stage is to prepare a complete draft of your dissertation including the introduction and conclusion.	Ensure that you send the draft to your supervisor in sufficient time for the feedback to be thoughtful and useful.
Meeting 4	The purpose of this meeting is to learn how to improve the dissertation prior to submission	Take notes, and decide what action you are gong to take in the time you have remaining
	Following the meeting send an email to your supervisor confirming the steps you are going to take.	
Preparing for submission	You are going to be redrafting those chapters you have written and responding to the criticisms made by your supervisor. Don't forget to carry out all those editing tasks we discussed in the chapter on writing essays, such as updating your research, spell checking etc.	This will take some time!
Completing your bibliography	Ensure that your bibliography is complete, accurate and uses the proper **citation** method.	This will also take longer than you might anticipate.
Hand in your dissertation	Congratulate yourself on a job well done!	

» glossary

The writing task

We have provided extensive advice on academic writing throughout the book. You should pay particular attention to our chapter on writing good English and on writing essays. The advice given there is of critical importance when you are involved in a sustained piece of writing. If you plan your time properly you will have the opportunity for good advice from your supervisor.

Cross reference
See chapter 3, Writing good English and chapter 25, Writing essays.

Key Point

Make sure that all of your writing focuses on achieving the task that you have set yourself. Keep referring back to the title and ask yourself if you are continuing to answer the question.

There are three specific issues involved in the writing task that cause students difficulties, which we have not discussed elsewhere. These are footnotes, bibliographies and editing work.

Footnotes

Most dissertations utilise footnotes. Students are often perplexed about what should go into a footnote. Footnotes are used in three different ways:

- To indicate the source of the information used in the main body of the text.
- To indicate further research on the point being made.
- To elaborate on a point made in the body of the text which does not necessarily fit with the flow of the text in the main article.

ibid

You may want to cite some sources more than once in your dissertation. Each time you cite a source for the first time, you must use the full footnote form, including the author's full name, the complete title of the work, and full publication information You will often see the word *ibid* which is short for *ibidem* which is a Latin word meaning 'the same' in footnotes. This may be used when a source is cited for the second and subsequent times. It indicates that the citation information is exactly the same. Using *ibid* means you do not have to write the full footnote form each time. When you cite the same source but use a different page number from that source, you may still use *ibid* followed by a comma and then the page number. We would urge you to be cautious in the use of *ibid*. As your work develops you will move chunks of text around, and delete some. Your original use of the source may end up in a place which you have not anticipated, and your *ibid* may precede it. Alternatively you may delete the original footnote. To avoid these problems you should simply repeat the full citation each time you use it. With word processing, it is not such an arduous task.

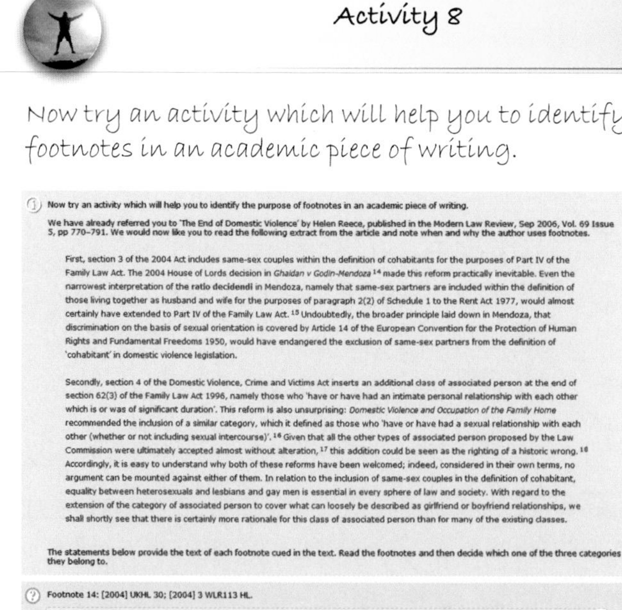

Activity 8

Now try an activity which will help you to identify the purpose of footnotes in an academic piece of writing.

Now try an activity which will help you to identify the purpose of footnotes in an academic piece of writing.

We have already referred you to 'The End of Domestic Violence' by Helen Reece, published in the Modern Law Review, Sep 2006, Vol. 69 Issue 5, pp 770–791. We would now like you to read the following extract from the article and note when and why the author uses footnotes.

First, section 3 of the 2004 Act includes same-sex couples within the definition of cohabitants for the purposes of Part IV of the Family Law Act. The 2004 House of Lords decision in *Ghaidan v Godin-Mendoza* [14] made this reform practically inevitable. Even the narrowest interpretation of the **ratio decidendi** in Mendoza, namely that same-sex partners are included within the definition of those living together as husband and wife for the purposes of paragraph 2(2) of Schedule 1 to the Rent Act 1977, would almost certainly have extended to Part IV of the Family Law Act. [15] Undoubtedly, the broader principle laid down in Mendoza, that discrimination on the basis of sexual orientation is covered by Article 14 of the European Convention for the Protection of Human Rights and Fundamental Freedoms 1950, would have endangered the exclusion of same-sex partners from the definition of 'cohabitant' in domestic violence legislation.

Secondly, section 4 of the Domestic Violence, Crime and Victims Act inserts an additional class of associated person at the end of section 62(3) of the Family Law Act 1996, namely those who 'have or have had an intimate personal relationship with each other which is or was of significant duration'. This reform is also unsurprising: *Domestic Violence and Occupation of the Family Home* recommended the inclusion of a similar category, which it defined as those who 'have or have had a sexual relationship with each other (whether or not including sexual intercourse)'. [16] Given that all the other types of associated person proposed by the Law Commission were ultimately accepted almost without alteration, [17] this addition could be seen as the righting of a historic wrong. [18] Accordingly, it is easy to understand why both of these reforms have been welcomed; indeed, considered in their own terms, no argument can be mounted against either of them. In relation to the inclusion of same-sex couples in the definition of cohabitant, equality between heterosexuals and lesbians and gay men is essential in every sphere of law and society. With regard to the extension of the category of associated person to cover what can loosely be described as girlfriend or boyfriend relationships, we shall shortly see that there is certainly more rationale for this class of associated person than for many of the existing classes.

The statements below provide the text of each footnote cued in the text. Read the footnotes and then decide which one of the three categories they belong to.

Footnote 14: [2004] UKHL 30; [2004] 3 WLR113 HL.

Bibliographies

Your module requirements will probably indicate that you must include a bibliography. A bibliography is an alphabetical list of all materials consulted in the preparation of your dissertation. This is more than the works you have specifically referred to in your writing. It includes all your reading matter. You need to ensure that you conform to the style guidelines for bibliographies which are determined by your institution. A good bibliography means that you must keep records of everything you have read from the commencement of your research.

Editing your text

One unexpected problem can cause students difficulty as they complete the writing process. Despite what seemed at the start of the process an overly generous word limit, they find that they have exceeded the word limit for the dissertation. This means that they must edit their work.

Don't panic

Although the first reaction to the need to cut words is that it is not possible without destroying your work, this is rarely the case. The editing process can add value to your work by removing unnecessary words and phrases.

Read your work carefully:

- Are there paragraphs which are longer than others which could be rewritten in a more concise form?
- Can you delete repeated or redundant words?
- Have you have made the same point more than once?
- Are there places where your writing can be simplified?
- Can your quotations be shortened?

Activity 9

Now try an activity where you have to practise editing text.

Conclusion

A good dissertation demonstrates a high level of intellectual qualities and skills. It differs from an essay because these qualities and skills must be sustained over the full length of the work. This means that the task should be well planned and well finished. A good dissertation is therefore well

- researched
- referenced
- planned
- written.

It is also well argued, which means that it is:

- creative
- critical
- logical
- coherent
- interesting
- sustained.

It is therefore a significant intellectual challenge, but one for which your university education to date has been preparing you. As we said at the beginning of the chapter, it should be an enjoyable exercise. Writing is a real pleasure and for many people their ideal life would be writing. If you want to take a more utilitarian approach a good mark for a dissertation demonstrates to employers that you are organised and motivated, and it should also demonstrate to you whether or not you are suited for master's level work. If you can read critically and widely, write effectively and plan your time in the ways we have suggested, we are confident that you will succeed.

Chapter 27

Answering problem questions

Rationale

Alongside writing essays, answering legal problem questions is likely to be one of the primary ways you are assessed while doing a law degree. A problem question usually takes the form of a factual scenario describing some event or events that have occurred. You are asked to 'sort out' this scenario in a legal sense – often by being asked to 'advise' one of the parties. This, in a way, is 'practice' for the real world of law, where you may be engaged in this sort of thing on a daily basis, so is probably one of the best forms of early legal training.

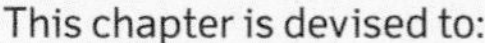

This chapter is devised to:

- Help you to understand what you are required to do when faced with a problem question
- Enable you to work out how to identify the issues you need to discuss in your answer, and apply the law to them
- Help you to give your answer a good structure – a key part of problem question answering.

What are problem questions for?

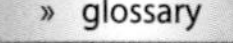

Answering problem questions requires a wholly different approach to essay writing and employs a different set of skills. It helps if you understand what a problem question is **for**, i.e. what is it trying to achieve (or what is the person who set the question trying to get you to achieve?)? Problem questions are where you apply your knowledge of the law to supposedly real-life factual situations, such as a dispute between X and Y, or a crime that might have been perpetrated on A by B. What this means is that you need not only to **know** the law you have been studying, but also how to **use** it.

Note

If you try to write an answer to a problem question in the same way as you would write an essay, it will not be very good! An answer to a problem question should not be an exploration of a number of ideas, but should be punchy, concise and to the point.

Imagine yourself as a professional lawyer, being confronted by a client who comes to you with a problem. They explain their situation to you: what happened when, who said what, who did what, etc. It would then be your job to advise this client about how the law would treat their problem. If it's a criminal case, would they be acquitted of the crime they have been accused of? And if so, why is this? Is it because there is a flaw in the case against them, or because they have an adequate defence? Or, if it is a civil dispute, are they likely to win? If so, might they receive any compensation? And, is the case actually as clear cut as this? That is, is there actually 'an answer' or might there be more than one possible outcome? Problem questions are often designed like this – to get you to see the various alternative outcomes and debate with yourself which is the most likely and why.

» glossary

These are also the real-life everyday tasks of lawyers, and possibly what you intend to be doing in the future. A big part of being a lawyer is constructing convincing or winning arguments by using and manipulating the law – and also being aware of the arguments that will come at you from the other side. You can see that this is why problem questions are used during a law degree – an essential part of your early training. Even if you don't intend to practise law, however, this type of exercise helps you to develop some essential skills in constructing and supporting convincing arguments of any type.

As indicated previously, unlike in real life, problem questions are unlikely to be a clear-cut sequence of events that indicate an obvious answer (not that this is always the case in real life!). If they did this, they would not be 'problem' questions! There will be twists and turns and complications built into the question, put there by the person writing it to assess the following:

- Can you identify all the issues arising from the question? There may be more than one issue to deal with and many more 'sub-issues'. Being able to spot all of these is a skill in itself.
- Can you select the appropriate legal sources to help you deal with the issues that you have identified? You can't just say what you think the law would do. Instead you have to work out what would happen by using cases and statutes etc. to support your contentions.
- Can you evaluate the way the law applies to the scenario and come up with good 'advice' at the end? As well as identifying and using the law you ought to know how good your own arguments are – i.e. what the likelihood of success might be – as well as the counter-arguments.

» glossary

How do I answer a problem question?

To tackle a problem question effectively, you need to think it through carefully, breaking it down into its component parts. The approach can be illustrated through a fairly straightforward example (taken from the law of contract, but the general method can be applied in other subjects).

Example

X agrees to fit new windows in Y's block of flats for £50,000. After X has done half the job she tells Y that she has run out of money and will not be able to complete it. Y promises X an extra £5,000 if the job is finished. X then finishes the job, but Y refuses to pay more than £50,000. Advise X.

The kind of response expected

'Advise X' is the classic way a problem question is posed. It has a conventional and restricted meaning in the context of legal education, and it is important that you realise what is meant by it. In essence, you are expected to offer a reasoned application of relevant law to the facts – effectively, this a prediction of how a court might decide the matter. You are **not** expected to do any of the following: debate the morality of the protagonists' behaviour; debate matters of proof (you must take the facts as given) or give X tactical advice (e.g. about how to avoid legal action)! Nor should you, despite the use of 'advise', present an account of what a lawyer would actually say to a client. You are simply expected to state the arguments likely to be made and to carry weight before a court if the case were litigated, bearing in mind the interests of the parties in the situation. And, where there is more than one possible argument, or 'route', that could be adopted to reach the 'client's' goal, you are expected where possible to suggest the best route, based on an assessment of their relative chances of success, as well as to take into consideration, when advising X, 'what will Y argue?'. Imagine your task is to provide X with a full account of all the legal arguments on both sides of the equation – giving them the full picture so that they are aware of the potential pitfalls and risks of their own argument, as well as its strengths, and vice versa in respect of Y's arguments.

The steps in the analysis

Problem questions are designed to probe particular points of law, and the key to them is identifying what the issues are and assessing how they would be resolved in a court. It is useful to break this down into five steps when planning your answer:

1. What remedy/outcome is the litigant likely to want? Here, this is clear – the payment of the extra £5,000. In other situations you will need to think about what the parties might want and to have knowledge of the range of available remedies.
2. What are the factual and legal issues on which the availability of the remedy hinges? The issue here that needs to be identified as relevant is whether the promise by Y of the extra £5,000 (fact) is supported by 'consideration' (legal issue), i.e., roughly, whether the law treats X as having given anything in return for the promise. Without consideration, Y will not here be held to her promise.
3. What are the legal principles or rules at stake? This involves stating the relevant 'ingredients' of consideration, from case law.

4. How can the relevant ingredients be assessed to determine whether there is anything here which is likely to count as consideration? This is where one considers whether, on the facts given, X did provide any consideration for Y's promise.
5. Finally, which way is the 'hinge' issue likely to go, and why? What will the likely outcome of the litigant's claim be?

Note

This is a simple problem with only one 'hinge' issue. Usually, the problems set for assessment in exams and coursework have more than one such issue, and these may interrelate in quite a complex way.

» glossary

This five-step structure is offered as a guide to teasing out the issues from a problem. Although other ways of teasing these issues out can be used, it is essential that you think in a structured and systematic way about how the law applies to the facts.

Things to avoid

- Don't jump straight to applying a concept (stage 3) without first establishing why the concept is relevant. This is one of the most common causes of irrelevance in legal analysis. At best, this results in a discussion of the correct issues which is not adequately grounded because the relevance of the issue has not been explained. At worst, it results in striding off vigorously on completely the wrong track where some concept looks at first blush to be relevant but with a bit of thought is not.
- Do not assume that, because the facts of a problem resemble a well-known case, the problem must be resolved the same way as the case. Very often, the author of the problem deliberately tweaks the facts so that it is different from the leading case. What is then needed is an analysis of the law discussed in the case (and other related cases) to assess how it would be applied to the different facts of the problem.
- Do not assume, either, that a leading case that factually resembles the problem is necessarily relevant to the problem at all. Different legal issues can arise on the same facts, and you need to work out from steps 1 and 2 what the relevant issue is.

Don't panic

Don't be scared of problem questions. It is probably easier to get a good mark in a problem question than it is with an essay, as long as you remember at all times what you are doing and why, and as long as you are supporting your analysis of the problem with law. That said, many students do worry about problem questions. However, it is often ironic that students worry about problem questions so much when, in actual fact, writing the answer to a legal problem requires exactly the same skills as solving many of the simpler day-to-day 'problems' we 'analyse' all the time, just with the addition of some law. For example, we all think about things like:

- Can I get a refund on an item I've bought?
- What can I do if the service I had somewhere wasn't up to scratch?
- Is there a way I can get an extension of my essay deadline?

» glossary

Working out the answers to questions such as these requires analysis – you must know 'the rules' and be able to put the facts you have together with the rules to be able to predict what will happen. This is exactly what you do in legal problem questions. Another point to note on this is that you might **not always be able to predict the answer**. For example, on the question of a refund, you might be left with the 'answer' 'Yes, I can, if the item has a fault, but I may not be able to if the item is not faulty'. You will find similar things with problem questions – you'll be left with possible alternative outcomes, but no more. Remember that it is not wrong to reach this as a conclusion – in fact it's far more likely to be exactly what the person setting the question was looking for!

Structuring your answer

Because it is a legal problem with a legal answer, there is usually a pretty clear structure that can be followed when answering problem questions. As with all writing, you should start by carefully **planning** what you are going to say using the analytical steps outlined above and by following the structural steps outlined below, before you even begin to write your full answer. Like an essay, problem questions need an introduction and conclusion – but these are usually a bit easier to manage in a problem question than in an essay. In a sense, they (certainly the introduction) are the easiest bit of your answer to write. Why is this?

↳ **Cross reference**
See chapter 25, Writing essays.

The introduction – as this is a 'real life' situation, and you are being asked to 'advise' your 'client', the first question to address is 'what does my client want to get out of this?' Therefore, summarising this succinctly at the beginning of your answer, alongside a short statement about what the contentious area of law is, operates as a good, clear introduction.

Example

The builder, Mr Jones, needs to know if he is liable to pay for the damage to Mr Smith's property, or whether the exclusion clauses in his contract cover the damage that occurred during the time he was working there. Ordinarily, Mr Jones would be liable for any damage negligently caused by him while working, but his clauses (a) and (b) seek to prevent that liability arising. Whether these clauses are effective depends on the common law on incorporation and construction, as well as the application of the Unfair Contract Terms Act 1977 and the Unfair Terms in Consumer Contract Regulations 1999.

» glossary

Everything else that goes in your problem question will come after this stage and before your conclusion – or your 'advice'. This – the main bulk of your answer – is where you demonstrate your knowledge of the law you have learnt and also your ability to apply it to a set of given facts. Following the guidelines below will help you to construct a good answer.

Identifying the issues (legal and factual)

When you first see them, problem questions can look quite daunting. It seems like you are being given a lot of information (you are) and you may not know where to start. While an essay question may only be one or two lines long (or even shorter!), problem question scenarios **can** take up to a side of A4, although they are not usually this long. Whatever the length, the first step in any problem question is to **identify the issues** at hand.

An example of a problem question is as follows. We will use this question as a basis for discussion of some of the various aspects of answering problem questions throughout the remainder of this chapter, as well as in some of the interactive activities. The example used (as with other examples in this chapter) comes from the law of contract, but problem questions can arise in other areas of law, such as criminal law, tort, and public law. The techniques suggested in this chapter should work for all problem questions, but in terms of explaining the method it is easier to stick to one question as an example for you to use. It doesn't matter if you don't yet know the law – we are just trying at this point to explore the common principles behind answering problem questions:

> In May, Mary won a lot of money on the National Lottery and decided to have a large swimming pool constructed in her garden before the summer. She contracted with Poolside Ltd for the work to be done to an agreed design for a sum of £40,000, payable on completion.
>
> Poolside began work and the construction appeared to go well. When it was three-quarters complete, Mary realised that the pool was not quite as deep as was specified in the design agreed in the contract – the difference was less than one foot (0.3 metres). She considered what to do. In any event, she had second thoughts about having a pool because she had been advised that, as her house was not in a high price bracket, a pool may actually reduce its value. She was considering moving house instead.
>
> Mary decides to use the breach of contract by Poolside as a reason to terminate the contract and tells them to clear off the site as the pool is too shallow. She plans to avoid paying Poolside anything, and then have the shell of the pool levelled and filled in.
>
> Advise Mary.

In all problem questions there will be both factual and legal issues to spot. When you first read a problem question scenario, your task is to 'spot the issues'. First, read through slowly, pausing after each sentence or paragraph to think about what it has said and any potential **factual** issues that might be raised. Use a highlighter on particular passages, or underline key words and phrases so you know what to come back to and analyse later. Of course, there will be a lot of **facts** – but what you are looking for are **factual issues**. These are facts that you are obviously being told for a reason, rather than just those that you have to be told in order to make the scenario make sense, or seem like a real story, or 'set the scene'.

You should note that it is rare in a problem question for all the salient facts to be given – you may have to construct some 'what ifs' for yourself. You should ask the question: 'Are there any other relevant facts that I need to inform my legal analysis?' For example, if someone is injured in a road accident, the age of the victim may be critical in establishing issues of duty and breach in negligence. If the age is not given, you would need to consider alternative outcomes, clearly articulating the legal reasoning and citing relevant case law.

Some points on identifying factual issues:

- Look at **what** the facts are telling you and ask **why** you would need to be told this – for example, if you are told that a contract was made over the phone, ask why you might need to know this. It is likely that it will be relevant to a later legal issue and become something you need to analyse.
- Many of the facts in a problem question may seem unrealistic but remember that the writer of the question has to design it to raise legal issues that you can analyse, so some of the situations may be a bit beyond belief!

- Look out for 'red herrings' – facts that are inserted to lead you off the right track. These are a valid technique designed to see if you know what you're talking about and what is and is not relevant.
- Don't 'make up' any facts that aren't there. You can't make any assumptions and can only discuss the facts as they are given to you.

You may use the factual issues you have identified to more fully 'flesh out' your introduction. Building on the previous example of an introduction, above, you can see that the following example of an introduction contains many more concrete facts of the case.

Example

The builder, Mr Jones, has caused £3,000 worth of damage to Mr Smith's walls and carpets while constructing a conservatory for him. Ordinarily, Mr Jones would be liable for any damage negligently caused by him while working, but his clauses (a) and (b) seek to prevent that liability arising. He needs to know if he is liable to pay for any of the damage to Mr Smith's property, or whether clause (a) in his contract covers the damage to the walls, which were poorly constructed by Mr Jones, and clause (b) in the contract covers the accidental damage to the carpets caused by leaving the taps on. The latter will be the case if the terms are properly incorporated and constructed and not rendered invalid by the application of the Unfair Contract Terms Act 1977 and the Unfair Terms in Consumer Contract Regulations 1999.

What would you write if you were writing a short introduction to the problem question you were given above?

Activity 1

Picking out the key facts in a problem question scenario is a skill in itself, as you will be given quite a complex set of facts to work through. Knowing what is important and what is not in terms of the question will make it easier to write your answer. This activity is designed to help you identify the relevant facts.

Picking out the key facts in a problem question scenario is a skill in itself, as you will be given quite a complex set of facts to work through. Knowing what is important and what is not in terms of the question will make it easier to write your answer. This activity is designed to help you identify the relevant facts.

Read the problem question on Mary and her swimming pool, below. Read the statement below and select anything that you think is a key factual issue. You should select **four** statements in total.

> In May, Mary won a lot of money on the National Lottery and decided to have a large swimming pool constructed in her garden before the summer. She contracted with Poolside Ltd for the work to be done to an agreed design for a sum of £40,000, payable on completion.
>
> Poolside began work and the construction appeared to go well. When it was three-quarters complete, Mary realised that the pool was not quite as deep as was specified in the design agreed in the contract – the difference was less than one foot (0.3 metres). She considered what to do. In any event, she had second thoughts about having a pool because she had been advised that, as her house was not in a high price bracket, a pool may actually reduce its value. She was considering moving house instead.
>
> Mary decides to use the breach of contract by Poolside as a reason to terminate the contract and tells them to clear off the site as the pool is too shallow. She plans to avoid paying Poolside anything, and then have the shell of the pool levelled and filled in.
>
> Advise Mary.

- This happened in **May**
- **Mary won a lot of money on the National Lottery**
- The £40,000 was **payable on completion**
- The work was **three-quarters complete**
- The pool was **not as deep as was specified in the design**
- **Her house was not in a high price bracket**
- **She was considering moving house instead**

Now, having worked through that example, you may be able to more clearly see how the process of identifying the factual issues can work. But this is not the end of the story – from the factual issues you need to go on to identify the **legal** issues. To do this you need to **really** look at what the facts are telling you – as you have seen, some facts are just facts (e.g. from the conservatory building example above, how much it will cost to fix the damage) but many of the facts you are given will be 'signposts', pointing you towards particular legal issues.

A legal issue is one that arises from the facts but gives rise to a question of interpretation and/or analysis. There are 'big' and 'small' legal issues to consider. From the conservatory example above, the overarching (big) legal issue to be considered is whether the law says that the builder should pay for the damage or not. Within this are the smaller legal issues of the two clauses in the contract (each is a separate issue) and whether they are valid. There are general rules about this in terms of the validity of 'exclusion clauses' in contracts in general, which would obviously need to be discussed in an answer. And, breaking this down even further: clause (a), which refers to the damage to the walls, seems to refer to bad workmanship by the builder (which should point you towards a particular part of the legislation referred to); and clause (b) refers to accidental damage, otherwise known as negligently caused damage, which again would point you to a particular part of the relevant legislation. All of these 'big' and 'small' legal issues would need consideration within your answer.

» glossary

Identifying the relevant law

Once you have identified the issues that you are going to consider, you then need to work out what law actually needs to be applied. Remember that many of the factual issues will be 'signposts' to legal issues – and therefore possibly also signposts to point you in the direction of the actual law (cases and/or sections of a statute) that you need to **use** in order to be able to answer the question. The key part of this is to find the **relevant** law – many students fall into the trap of identifying and stating **all** the law on a particular topic, without stopping to think about which bits of that are actually relevant to the actual issue at hand and which are not (similar problems crop up in essay writing – just think, it is highly unlikely that you would ever get an essay title asking you to 'Write all you know about misrepresentation' or 'Discuss everything about defences to murder'. Similarly, a problem question would not require this).

In your plan, use **arrows** or **colour coding** to 'attach' the relevant bits of law to the relevant factual and legal issues, then you won't lose track of them when you come to actually write your answer. When you write, you will be stating what law it is you have selected and saying **why** it is relevant to the issues you have identified. Then you will go on to **apply** the law to the question. When you come to write your answer, deal with one issue at a time. If you try to deal with all the issues together your analysis is likely to become jumbled, as will your structure. Say all you have to say on one point, then move on to the next one. If there are, for example, three main issues within a problem question, you may find using subheadings helpful. These will help to keep your points and analysis distinct.

Applying the law to the facts given

This is the part of answering a problem question that a lot of students have the biggest problem with – and is often where they fail to pick up marks. Many students don't immediately grasp what it means to **apply** the law – many will simply stop at stating what law is relevant to the facts and issues at hand, without going on to do something with it. Being able to describe the law and how it has been used in previous cases does demonstrate a degree of knowledge, but it doesn't really show understanding. To show that you understand the law you must be able to apply it. Applying the law means exactly that: to **do** something with it. What is it that the case you are using actually does to your 'case'? How is the section of the statute you are using going to affect it?

If you can apply the law to the problem, you demonstrate a higher level of understanding than simply being able to identify the issues and the relevant law – and this is where you start to gain higher marks. If you can demonstrate that you can build a convincing legal argument – one that is supported by the law – you will be doing exactly what is required of you. Anything less than this falls short of what is required.

Some dos and don'ts

- Don't bother restating the facts given to you in the question.
- Do make sure you clearly state what the relevant law is and why it is relevant.

- Don't stop at merely stating what the relevant law is.
- Do use cases and/or statutes as authority to back up your statements on the law.
- Do apply these directly to the facts and issues at hand.
- Don't write out all the facts of any case you use.
- Do mention any facts that are directly pertinent, for example if they are comparable to your 'case'.
- Do draw conclusions (or potential conclusions) from your application of the law.
- Don't forget there may be counter-arguments to your contentions and that you should bear these in mind as well.

Activity 2

This multiple choice activity is designed to test if you know when you are simply stating the law, when you are discussing it and when you are actually applying it.

In May, Mary won a lot of money on the National Lottery and decided to have a large swimming pool constructed in her garden before the summer. She contracted with Poolside Ltd for the work to be done to an agreed design for a sum of £40,000, payable on completion.

Poolside began work and the construction appeared to go well. When it was three-quarters complete, Mary realised that the pool was not quite as deep as was specified in the design agreed in the contract – the difference was less than one foot (0.3 metres). She considered what to do. In any event, she had second thoughts about having a pool because she had been advised that, as her house was not in a high price bracket, a pool may actually reduce its value. She was considering moving house instead.

Mary decides to use the breach of contract by Poolside as a reason to terminate the contract and tells them to clear off the site as the pool is too shallow. She plans to avoid paying Poolside anything, and then have the shell of the pool levelled and filled in.

Advise Mary.

Mary wants to avoid paying anything. Advise Mary.

- Mary can only avoid payment if she was correct to terminate the contract. This will be up to the court to decide.
- It first needs to be established whether Mary was entitled to terminate her contract with Poolside. This will depend on the type of breach Poolside committed. The case of *Hong Kong Fir* [1962] tells us when someone is entitled to terminate after the breach of an innominate term.
- Mary will be entitled to terminate if Poolside breached a condition of the contract, or breached an innominate term giving rise to sufficiently serious consequences. In *Hong Kong Fir* [1962] the consequences of the breach of an innominate term were not deemed to be sufficiently serious and so the charterers were not entitled to terminate the contract for the ship.

The work was three-quarters complete, therefore:

- Mary only has to pay Poolside for the work they have completed if it amounts to 'substantial performance' of the contract. Three-quarters of the work is not substantial performance, as was said in *Hoenig v Isaacs* [1952], so Mary will not have to pay.
- Mary only has to pay Poolside for the work they have completed if it amounts to 'substantial performance' of the contract. According to the case of *Hoenig v Isaacs* [1952], where a decorating company did some work leaving defects to be corrected, and the case of *Bolton v Mahadeva* [1972], where central heating was badly installed in a house, Mary will not have to pay.
- Mary only has to pay Poolside for the work they have completed if it amounts to 'substantial performance' of the contract. Three-quarters of the work sits somewhere between the amount of work done in the cases of *Bolton v Mahadeva* [1972] and *Hoenig v Isaacs* [1952]. One-quarter of the work to be finished seems to amount to more than a minor defect so, comparing those cases to ours, there does not seem to be substantial performance here, and Mary will not have to pay.

The best way to apply the law successfully is always to ensure that you are **using** it to demonstrate something, or to prove a point you have made. Then explain to the reader what effect the authority would have on your case, i.e. what would the outcome of relying on that authority be? Always read back over what you have written to see if you are merely saying what the law is, describing it or discussing it. While these things show knowledge, they do not show application – and that is essentially what you are being tested on with problem questions.

Also remember that you need to apply the law objectively to your question. This means that you should take care to remain aware of any counter-arguments to your position (and, if possible, to try and counter those counter-arguments). Remember that there are two sides to every case, and it is rare that one side overwhelmingly has the law on their side (especially in problem questions). It may also be that in advising your 'client', you have to give them some bad news – that is, following your analysis of the authorities you might decide that the law might not work out for them in the way they would like best.

A very useful exercise you can do is to imagine you had been asked the question the other way. For example, what would you write if, following the problem scenario outlined above, you had been asked to 'advise Poolside Ltd?' Your entire starting point would be different, and you would be thinking of the arguments you could make – and what law you could apply to support those arguments – to make Poolside win the case.

Advise X

In a sense, this is your conclusion. Your 'advice' is a summary of the law you have applied and the result of applying it. Be aware that there is not necessarily one 'right answer'. As long as you have constructed your answer by using the law to support your contentions and analysis, you will be right, even if someone else may have come to a slightly different conclusion than you (or even the exact opposite!).

Don't panic

If you think about it, of course there is not always a 'right answer' to a legal problem. There are two sides to every dispute, and each of them will have their own lawyer. It is the lawyers' job to try and win for their client – this means that each side could come up with completely different arguments, analysis or interpretation of the law. As long as you always keep in mind who 'your client' is, you shouldn't go far wrong.

Returning to the earlier example of an introduction to an answer to a problem question, we can see that a conclusion might look as follows:

Example

Mr Jones is likely to be protected from liability by the operation of the exclusion clauses in his contract. The two clauses in question are both incorporated into the contract, properly constructed, and do not fall foul of either the Unfair Contract Terms Act 1977 or the Unfair Terms in Consumer Contracts Regulations 1999. Mr Smith will therefore have to pay for the necessary repairs himself.

This has summed up the overall answer to the question and – without having gone through all the analysis again (such as what sections of the legislation are being used or what cases apply to the incorporation of terms into contracts) – tells the reader what the outcome of the case is likely to be.

Conclusion

Writing answers to legal problem questions is daunting when you first start, as it is likely to be unlike anything you have ever done before. However, this chapter has given you some simple guidelines and tips to follow in order to begin producing good answers. The most important thing to remember is to get the structure right. Once you are used to doing this then the rest (actually knowing what law to include) is down to you. Make sure you **use** the law rather than merely write about it – the better your analysis and interpretation, the better your marks will be.

Key Point

In order to successfully have answered a problem question, all the stages outlined above must be gone through – possibly more than once in a complex question. Before you submit your answer to be marked, ask yourself these questions:

- *Have I shown that I know and understand the relevant law?*
- *Have I demonstrated that I can apply the law to the facts and issues?*
- *Have I fully analysed how the law may be applied?*
- *Have I drawn a conclusion from the application of the law?*

Links

General guidance on answering legal problems
OUP Online Resource Centre for Holland and Webb
http://www.oup.com/uk/orc/bin/9780199282500/01student/legal_probs.pdf
This site contains some good tips on what not to do when answering problem questions, as well as the author's guidance as to what might constitute a first class, 2:1, 2:2 etc. answer.

Solving legal problems
http://www.ncl.ac.uk/nuls/lectures/legprob/legprob.pdf
This is a **transcript** of a lecture given by Bruce Grant, a lecturer at Newcastle Law School, advising law students how to tackle legal problem questions.

» glossary

www.oxfordinteract.com

Chapter 28

Revising for and succeeding in exams

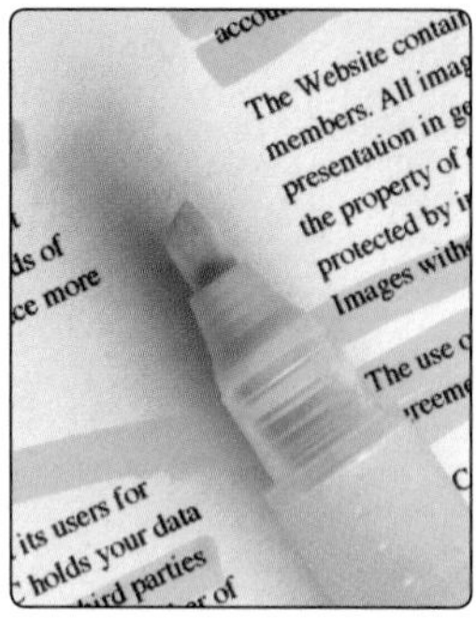

Rationale

Unfortunately, doing a law degree requires that you sit a number of exams. A qualifying law degree requires you to have passed the seven qualifying subjects and it is likely that your other law subjects may have exams at the end of your period of study as well – although you may sometimes be assessed in other ways, such as by dissertation.

That being said, in many law schools there is no formal preparation for exams, although some lecturers may, within their specific modules, offer revision lectures or seminars and/or explain the structure and requirement of the exams to you. Similarly, many legal study skills guides focus little, if at all, on exam skills. So, these are skills that you largely have to develop for yourself, building on exam practices you have cultivated at school or elsewhere. Here, we recognise the importance of preparing students for exams – or in helping students prepare themselves for exams – and focus in particular on preparation and revision aids.

This chapter is devised to:

- Introduce a selection of techniques that may help your revision
- Identify some common pitfalls and how to avoid them
- Provide some suggestions for how to utilise your revision time effectively
- Suggest ways of managing exam stress and gaining some control over the exam experience.

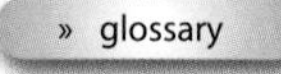

The exam process

No one likes exams, but they remain one of the key ways in which your work and progress at university will be assessed. According to the rules of your institution, you will have to pass exams in a certain number of modules (usually calculated by 'credits' or 'points') at or above a certain level in order to obtain your degree. Furthermore, if you are intent on going into legal practice as a solicitor or a barrister, you will need to have at least a pass in all seven of the qualifying law subjects, as required by the Law Society or Bar Council.

Some of the reasons that we have exams are:

- To demonstrate that the work covered during the course has been understood.
- To show to what level this knowledge has been attained and demonstrated.
- As an opportunity to demonstrate the ability to work alone (without books or other resources and therefore the possibility of plagiarism!)

↳ Cross reference
See chapter 7, Avoiding plagiarism.

Exams have a number of other advantages over coursework-style assessments – for both you as a student and for the lecturers marking them. Unlike coursework, there is less in-depth research required and your answers are obviously not expected to be as long or as detailed as they would be in a formal written assessment, or as clearly referenced (although the more detailed and the more inclusion of references, the better). Similarly, a bibliography would not be required. That said, you are still expected to produce a high-quality answer, using the law (cases, statutes etc.) in support of your arguments or analysis. The good news is that lecturers marking your exam papers are more sympathetic to scrawled handwriting, grammatical errors, spelling mistakes etc.!

» glossary

» glossary

Cross reference
See chapter 25, Writing essays.

Advance preparation for exams

It may sound obvious, but one of the keys to success in any exam is advance preparation and forward planning. The sooner you start preparing, the easier you will find the whole process – those who leave their revision to the last minute or who try to quickly 'cram' for their exams often suffer for it. Their exams won't be as good as they could be and the stress involved may be greater.

Things you can do to prepare for exams **before** you start revision:

1. Find out basic information, including:
    - **Exams** to be taken – are all your modules examined, or are some coursework only? If so, have you completed the coursework in sufficient time?
    - **Exam timetable** – many university websites will have a link to the Exams Timetable when it is published and/or will send out emails notifying students when the timetable is available. Alternatively, it might be available in hard copy, e.g. posted on a notice board.
    - **Past papers** and other information – can you download or access hard copies of exam papers from previous years for your modules? It is worth finding out if and how you can do this as early as possible. Does anything else (like a case list or copy of a piece of legislation) usually come with the exam paper? If so, you might be able to locate previous copies of these, too.
    - **Exam rubrics** – these are the 'instructions' for the exam, often printed on the front page of the question paper. In some universities this information may be available to you before the exam period (or you may be able to find it from past papers, but check the rubric hasn't changed) – it is worth checking this so that you know what to expect, how many questions you need to answer, from what sections of the paper, etc. If you familiarise yourself with these it will save you time and stress in the actual exam.
    - **Using books in the exam** – in some universities (or for some modules, but not others) you are allowed to take, for example, statute books or printed out copies of relevant legislation into the exams. If this is the case for you, make sure that you know the rules regarding this – are your books/legislation etc. allowed to be annotated or highlighted at all?

» glossary

» glossary

Note

The exam rubrics might be different for each module you take. For example, in your criminal law exam you might be required to answer three questions and in contract law you might be required to answer four. Take care when checking rubrics that they are:

- correct for **this year's** exams
- specific to the module you are sitting the exam in.

2. Manage your time effectively

↳ **Cross reference**
See chapter 2, Managing your time.

When it comes to exams you really do need to have excellent time management skills. These skills will be similar to those you have practised all year in relation to your studies but will need to be even more tightly honed. The best way to do this is with a specific **Time Management Schedule** relating to the exam period.

How much time do I have to revise?

In a similar manner to a time management schedule created for your ordinary study, you can make one to help you cope with revision. It is likely that by the time you come to start revising, your lectures and seminars will be over or coming to an end (or, if you have mid-term exams, paused). As a full-time student, you should be aiming to 'work' full-time. Think about what hours are involved in a **full-time job**: about 35–40 hours (minimum – probably even more if you go into legal practice!) per week. If you planned for 35 hours of revision per week, this would mean only an average of 7 hours per day, Monday to Friday, leaving the weekend free for rest, socialising, paid work etc. Or, if you can add more revision time and feel happy doing so, then do so.

Note

Many students these days find that they need to have part-time paid work. How this fits in to your revision schedule is up to you – but you may find that to find time to do substantial revision, you have to jiggle your schedule a little or cut down your hours temporarily. For example, if you have paid work during the day, you may find that some of your revision hours have to be found in the evenings, or at the weekend.

Activity 1

Use the following activity to help you work out exactly how much time you will have to revise per week. Ideally, you should aim to complete this well in advance of your exams, so that you can create and put into place a successful time management schedule for revision.

Use the questions below to build up a picture of how much time you have each week to revise. Your answers should be based on what you usually do, i.e. on your average week. You may be surprised at how much spare time you do actually have! Pay attention to the feedback, as this will help you start to organise your time better, potentially (and hopefully) increasing the effectiveness of your revision period.

Are you spending any time in timetabled classes (revision lectures, seminars, etc) each week and, if so, how much?

- No, all my classes have finished
- Less than 10 hours
- 10 hours or more

How much do you sleep (on average) per night?

- 7 hours or less × 7 = less than 49 hours per week
- approx 8 hours × 7 = about 56 hours per week
- more than 8 hours × 7 = more than 56 hours per week

How much time do you spend doing ordinary daytime activities (eating, getting ready, making cups of tea, etc) per day?

- 3 hours or less × 7 = less than 21 hours per week
- between 3 and 5 hours × 7 = 21–35 hours per week
- more than 5 hours × 7 = more than 35 hours per week

Now, having done the activity, you should take a step back and think about how you organise your revision. If you find you do not have 30–35 hours per week to devote to revision, the solution is **not** to think 'I won't do as much' – rather it is to consider which areas need to be looked at and 'cut down' to allow extra revision time:

- Some **cannot** be cut (e.g. travel)
- Some **should not** be (e.g. sleep)
- Some **could be** (e.g. socialising, but you must still have 'rest' time, even though exams are imminent)
- Some perhaps **should** be (e.g. paid work – the 'enemy' of good results – do some, but not too much, especially at exam time).

You should think of your studies in the same way as you would think of a job. That is, **if you are a full-time student, studying – including revision – should occupy as much of your time per week as a full time job would.**

Suggested time management schedule for revision

Now you should try and draw yourself up a **time management schedule for revision**, using the following tips:

- You should not seek to have a **totally** rigid schedule for every day – this may be very difficult to keep to, and may lead to a sense of frustration or failure.
- Nor should you 'lurch' from day to day with no schedule at all.
- You should seek to have an overview on a weekly basis of your progress, and organise your time the following week accordingly – this may mean adapting the following week's schedule.

The following method of organising time may be helpful. Use a table such as the downloadable one below, and then fill it in for each week of your revision period in the following way (examples are given in downloadable documents, below):

1. **Regular commitments**
   •Construct a schedule of your fixed commitments only – revision lectures and seminars, hours you spend at paid work, other regular activities. These could be added to your table and photocopied (or save a copy on your computer and alter the other details each week).
2. **Weekly schedule**
   •Each week you should add to your schedule any major events occurring – this may even include exams, if one or two are earlier than all the others.
   •Also add the **amount of revision** to be undertaken in each of your subjects/modules that week. If you have five modules, you could allocate a day to each.
3. **Review**
   •Having established your schedule, you should conduct a daily review, **taking into account your progress so far**.
   •The daily review should **not** involve you crossing off something you earlier included, except in exceptional circumstances.
   •You can also conduct a weekly review, looking at your progress in each subject. You may find that you are getting on so well with revision in one module that you want to dedicate less time to it the following week and give more time to others. Or, if one exam is more imminent than others, you may want to dedicate more time to that module for a week, knowing you can 'catch up' on the other modules after the exam is over.

This is an example of the type of table you may want to be creating after completing the analysis of how much time you have, above. The following examples will show how you can build up the table to become a completed time management schedule.

Example

WEEK COMMENCING:

DAY	REGULAR ACTIVITIES	OTHER ACTIVITIES	PLANNED REVISION	DAILY REVIEW
Monday	Criminal law revision lecture 3pm		9–1 Criminal Law 4–6 Contract Law	4 + 2 hrs completed
Tuesday	Contract law revision lecture 10am Work 7–10pm		11–1 Tort 2–6 Tort	2 + 4 hrs completed
Wednesday		Football practice 2–5pm	9–1 Law and Society	Only 3 hours done
Thursday			9–1 Law and Society 2–5 Contract Law	4 + 3 hrs completed Added 1 hr Law and Soc to catch up
Friday	Contract law revision seminar 11am		1–6 European Law	Only 4 hours completed – add more at weekend
Saturday	Work 9am–5pm	John's birthday – night out		
Sunday	Work 10am–4pm			2 hours European Law – on top of this, less next week

Don't panic

Make time not just for study – also schedule breaks, relaxation, exercise, eating properly and **sleep**! *Planning ahead is good, but set realistic goals!.*

Other tips:

- Try to start formal revision at least 6–8 weeks before exams begin – but take into account individual working patterns and how much you realistically have to do.
- Keep your revision schedule flexible – build in spare afternoons/days to allow for the unexpected, especially towards the end.
- Over-estimate the time needed for each module/topic/subject.
- Allow time for a rapid mental recap of the previous session to reassure you 'it's still there' and boost confidence.

Some time management issues that may be specific to exam time

Difficulties of other commitments:

You may have difficulties rescheduling other commitments: a part-time job, sports practice, band rehearsals or childcare may eat up some of your time.

Try to counter some of these problems in advance – for example, arrange to do fewer shifts, play in fewer matches or concerts, or to have some extra childcare in the time leading up to the exams.

Difficulties living in a shared house

It may be hard for you to revise if there is a lot going on in your shared accommodation (with either friends or family!). If this is becoming a problem for you, for example, because your friends don't have exams at the same time as you, or have already finished theirs, then you need to be firm:

- Aim to get the people you live with to take you seriously as a student.
- You have the right to study and for that to be respected. This may mean some change and negotiation within the household.
- If you are responsible for a household, try lowering your housework standards, and/or get others to do their bit.

Revising for your exams

Unfortunately, many students, even if they have developed good academic skills elsewhere, let themselves down in exams. While in part this is down to factors like stress, timing etc., some of it is related to poor revision techniques. We have already highlighted the importance of advance planning for your exams **in general** – the same is true of revision: it will be better and more effective if you have planned exactly **what** you are going to revise and **when**.

Activity 2

Knowing what you can do to revise is as important as finding the time to revise. This next activity looks at various revision techniques and assesses their general effectiveness. Try the activity – you may pick up some tips on how to revise that you hadn't considered before.

Look at the list of statements below. Select all of the statements that reflect the way you normally revise. You can select as many statements as are applicable.

- Re-reading my lecture and seminar notes, in the order they came chronologically.
- Re-reading my lecture and seminar notes, but in order of reference for the topics I think I might answer questions on in the exam.
- Re-reading and redrafting my notes.
- Re-reading textbooks, casebooks, cases, academic articles, etc.
- Reading extra material from textbooks, casebooks, cases, academic articles, etc.
- Reducing my notes to e.g. key cards.
- Making mind-maps on a topic, using my notes and textbooks, casebooks, cases, academic articles, etc.
- Testing myself – e.g. by asking myself questions on a case, then checking to see if I was right.
- Practising answering questions from past papers, or setting my own.
- Working with others – discussing topics in a group and/or testing each other.

Hopefully you should now have some ideas about how to go about your revision to get the best out of it. Remember that there are plenty of ways to revise and that different things (or a combination of different things) work for different people. Experiment to find out what works best for you.

Key Point

Revision does not just mean re-reading and redrafting your notes. Many students fall into this trap. You need to find ways to enhance your learning and memory – this doesn't have to be boring!

The revision process is essentially one of selection – it is for you to decide what you need to revise and how much revision you need to do. Having studied the exam rubrics (see above), make sure you tailor your revision to these. If the rubric says you can be assessed on any or all of the law you have studied, make sure you revise everything. Or, if you know there are eight topics in one module, but you only have four questions to answer in the exam, you may feel confident in 'dropping' one topic (perhaps one you don't like or find very difficult). However, it is advisable to thoroughly revise two more topics than the number of questions you have to answer, with another two revised 'just in case'. You may not like the way the question is worded on your favourite topic, for example.

↳ **Cross reference**
Why not try activity 4 in chapter 25, Writing essays, on identifying the active words in questions.

Choosing revision topics

It is important that you enjoy your revision – or at least that you are not completely bored by it. With this in mind, as well as maximising effectiveness, select topics to revise that have:

- particularly interested you throughout the course
- recur as questions on past papers – check the different ways questions can be asked about the topic – make sure you can answer them all
- you have already completed coursework on – revising using the comments on marked work is usually very helpful.

Once you have chosen your topics:

- Work out answers to a range of possible exam questions for each topic, so you feel able to deal with almost any question that might be set on the topics you have chosen.
- Use 'brainstorming' for answering past questions.
- Prepare and memorise some quotes – the use of quotations, references and paraphrasing in exams is impressive.
- Organise the selected material so that it is easy to remember.

However, take care not to limit your choice of topics. There are big dangers involved in restricting the number of topics you revise within a module – the biggest being that if you only revise three topics for an exam that has three questions, a question on one of your chosen topics **might not come up** or might be phrased in such a way that you **don't know how to answer it.** This may sound like obvious advice, but students do it every year, so the last answer on their exam paper is evidently work they have just tried to remember from the depths of their mind, rather than something they have properly revised. Be aware that the people setting your exams know this – and are likely, therefore, to miss out the odd topic now and again!

Reducing information

Once you have gathered information for each topic you are revising, organise it into hierarchies under headings. Write out the information in the fewest words possible – this process encourages interaction with the material. Use 'keywords' to help you remember topics or parts of a topic.

Once you have done this, there are other things you can do to help you remember the information, such as the use of index cards to recall information. Check these daily and pull out the ones you are having trouble remembering until you have mastered it.

None of this prevents you from going back and reading books, chapters or articles in full. In fact, this is very helpful, and is the way that some people prefer to revise, perhaps jotting down notes as they go.

Revising cases

For many law modules, the knowledge of case law is important – you will need to use cases to support your contentions in exams as much as you would do in a formal written piece of coursework.

When using cases, ensure you know the **most recent** version, e.g. House of Lords decision, rather than Court of Appeal. The decision may be entirely different – stay up to date!

Things that you can do to help you remember cases are:

- Start a 'book' of cases (if you haven't already!) – this should be separate to your other notes, and could include:
  - Brief facts
  - The route through the courts and the eventual outcome
  - The reason for the decision (**ratio decidendi**)
  - The **implication** of the decision – this is often the important part and is most frequently overlooked by students.
- Organise cases into 'groups' or under 'headings' – for example, all cases that relate to the Sale of Goods Act or murder, theft etc.
- Get someone to test you regularly – either by case name, case facts or 'name some cases that relate to offer and acceptance' etc.
- Test yourself – cover the name of a case or the facts of a case and see if you can identify it.
- Ask yourself to jot down (or say aloud) as many cases as you can recall relating to e.g. the Offences Against the Person Act and what they were about/outcome/reason for decision. Try to memorise cases relating to one topic in 'clusters' so that if you remember one of them, you'll remember them all.

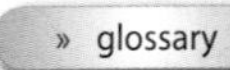

Cross reference
See chapter 22, Reading cases 2 – the rule of precedent and the operation of ratio decidendi.

- If you are given a case list in your exams, try and get hold of one for previous years and use it as a starting point for your case revision. You can tick them off as you go.

Don't panic

If you cannot recall the name of the case in the exam ***at all****, then as a last resort, you can say what it was about (briefly!) – the examiner will know which case you mean!*

Where to revise?

As much as what you revise is important, sometimes where you revise – the atmosphere you are in, how many distractions there are etc. – is equally so. You should aim to revise somewhere that you are comfortable and know you can get on with what you need to.

- For personal revision:
  - Choose somewhere quiet with good light and free from distractions.
  - Have on hand plenty of snacks and drinks to keep you going – and to punctuate your time!
  - Take regular short breaks – for a cup of tea, some fresh air, or just to stretch your legs.
- For group revision:
  - Use group discussion areas in your law library, if you have them (but beware rules on food/drink/mobile phones!).
  - Take turns meeting at others' rooms/house.
  - The great outdoors? The fresh air may inspire you! Try combining group revision with a picnic or a short football game.

Using memory aids

Mnemonics

Any trick that helps you remember is called a mnemonic. One common mnemonic is the use of the first letter of each keyword to make a 'new word'.

Example

G – Good
R – Revision
E – Ensures
A – Actual
S – Success in
E – Exams

The 'new word' does not actually have to be an actual word (or make sense!).

Example

Use 'OACI' to remember the key elements of a contract – if said aloud, this could be made to sound like the word 'OAKY', which might help you to remember it:

O – Offer
A – Acceptance
C – Consideration
I – Intention

It can also be a phrase, rather than a word – again, it need not make sense.

Example

The elements of a successful negligence claim:

D – Duty
B – Breach
C – Causation
D – Defences
(D, B, C, D) – remember as 'Dirty Boys Catch Disease'.

Other types of memory aids

Use of 'lists':

- Learn how many points you have made for a particular topic, then see how many you can recall.
- Repetition of the 'lists' – either by writing them down, saying them aloud or recalling them in your head.
- Use of 'taped information' – recording your own voice and playing it back may help.
- Use of 'colour-coding' for different topics – pens or paper.

Cross reference
See chapter 4, Taking notes, for more information on colour coding.

Some 'silly suggestions' (that just might work!):

- Using body parts

Example

If you want to remember five or ten points of a particular topic, assign a point to each finger on your hand(s).

- Using clothing

Example

Assign each point to a particular jacket/cardigan with e.g. a certain number of buttons that you will wear to the exam as a memory trigger.

- Using visual memory

Example

Assign each point to different part of your car.

- Using song

Example

Recall information to a set tune (one of your favourites? Or something memorable like a nursery rhyme?) or make up your own tune.

Aids to revision

- You can use 'swot books' such as Nutshells/Nutcases as an aid to revision/use as brief checklist, but not your only source of reading! **But** never use 'quotes' from or references to swot books in the exam. They are not authoritative sources
- Visually 'seeing' your notes (in summarised form, or flashcards) can help you remember them. Stick them up where you can see them! Use the edge of your mirror, the back of your bedroom door…
- Group revision:
  - Get together with others – test each other, discuss topics that you have found difficult/interesting and recap on ideas.
  - Work on past problem questions and essay titles together?
  - Select a question: all write a point and pool together.
  - Invent questions?
  - Perhaps provide 'handouts' for each other on different topics as a checklist? This will also confirm you have understood the main issues.

» glossary

Before the exam

So, you've planned ahead and you've done your revision. Now your exams are looming. Is there anything else you can do? You need to be in the right frame of mind to take an exam – hopefully all your hard work on preparation and revision will get you some of the way there. But what else can you do to motivate yourself?

- **Remind** yourself why you are doing the exam and what you hope to ultimately achieve.
- **Plan** your after-exam celebrations.
- Try to get a good night's **sleep.**

- Eat a good breakfast or lunch to stimulate the brain – '**brain food**' includes bananas, nuts, fish.
- Ensure you know what **time** your exam is and how to get to the exam hall.
- Leave plenty of time to **travel** to your exam – allow for traffic/check petrol/bike tyres etc.
- Remember any **ID** you need to take with you to get into the exam, **pens**/pencils and anything else you need.

On arrival at the exam hall/room:

- Check exam hall seating plan – you will be allocated to a particular seat.
- Place bags/books/valuables into the designated holding area – it is unlikely you'll be able to take them in with you.
- Try to avoid others who are overtly panicking – this could make you feel worse!
- Avoid the temptation to listen to others who are revising aloud – they may be using different techniques to you to memorise the information and may put you off. They may even be wrong!

At the beginning of the exam:

- Listen carefully to the instructions provided at the start.
- Don't turn your paper over until told to do so.
- Skim read **all** the questions on the entire paper, then make your selection(s).
- Problem questions – check what is required of you.
- A member of staff responsible will be at the exam hall for the start of the exam. If you don't understand a word or phrase on the paper, ask!
- But, this does not include asking **how** to answer the question!
- Keep an eye on the clock and make a note of your timings.
- Water and extra paper will be provided – just raise your hand.

Exam stress

- Almost everyone suffers from exam stress/nerves.
- A mild degree of stress can be helpful, providing a challenge with stimulation and focus.
- Avoid the temptation to focus on past failures – you've not taken the exam yet, so it's all to play for!

- Don't build the exam out of all proportion – even if you don't pass there are things you can do.
- If you have excessive stress – talk to someone! There may be help available.

Don't panic

What if I go 'blank'?

Don't try too hard to remember – leave a space and go onto the next point. It may come back to you later. Move on to something else and don't waste time panicking.

General points

1. Give equal time to each question:
   - If you spend twice as long on one question, you are unlikely to get twice as many marks.
   - You are more likely to pass/do well if you give reasonable answers to the set number of questions than if you write some brilliant essays but miss one out completely.
2. Be legible – examiners appreciate clear, well-organised structures, good introductions and conclusions. You may lose their goodwill if scripts are messy, illegible and confusing to read.

Answering questions in the exam

A helpful tip is to work out the time required for each question (having checked the exam rubric, see above) before the exam, make a note of these timings at the start and keep sight of them – timing is everything! Be prepared to allow yourself some leeway – for example, you might find that you 'flow' better on one topic than another, writing your answer in **less** time than you have allocated yourself. This is great – it means you have a bit of extra time to complete other (perhaps more difficult for you) questions or to check through your paper at the end of the exam.

Example

Your exam lasts three hours, starting at 2pm, and you have four questions to answer.

Plan the following timings:

2.00–2.10	Read the exam paper carefully, note the questions you will attempt and in what order
2.10–2.50	Question 1
2.50–3.30	Question 2
3.30–4.10	Question 3
4.10–4.50	Question 4
4.50–5.00	Check through your paper to make sure you haven't missed anything.

This plan allows 40 minutes per question (but you will have already prepared for this) as well as 10 minutes at the beginning and end of the exam.

↳ **Cross reference**
See also chapter 25, Writing essays, and chapter 27, Answering problem questions.

» glossary

Essay and problem questions

The skills you needed for writing essays and answers to problem questions throughout the year are exactly the same as the ones needed in your exams – the only caveat is that, because you are writing from memory rather than (usually) using books, academic articles and other sources, the need to reference, use quotes etc. is somewhat lessened. However, if you **can** cite sources in the exam and insert accurate references, this will add weight to your answer.

Selecting your question(s)

- Tick or otherwise indicate all the questions you could answer – tick twice the ones you can answer (and have relevant material for) best.
- If a question sounds like one you have done before, check the wording very carefully. A slight difference in wording might require a very different answer.
- Once selected, highlight key words in the title. You may notice at this stage that the question is not what you originally thought.
- Note how many parts there are to the question. Can you answer all parts?
- At any time, jot down ideas next to that question on the exam paper.

It is important here to note that there are quite a lot of pitfalls when it comes to answering questions – essay questions in particular – in exams. The two biggest of these are not understanding the question, so writing the 'wrong' answer, and what could be termed the 'writing all I know about a topic' answer. The first of these is fairly easy to do, but also very easy to avoid. Just make sure you have carefully read the question and, if you feel it is a little ambiguous, either choose a different topic or state and explain at the outset of your answer that you found the question ambiguous, with reasons why this is so, before going on to say how you have interpreted it.

The second of these pitfalls, however, is far more common. Too often, students come to an exam, see a question on a certain topic, and write down **absolutely everything they remember about it**! This is obviously not what you are being asked to do (if you were, all questions would start with 'write down everything you remember about…'. While this does sometimes apply to problem questions, this can largely be put down to not knowing how to structure an answer, or not understanding that a problem question is different from an essay. With essays, however, doing this alienates examiners (who have heard it all before) as they feel that you are just writing down everything you know in the hope that you'll get some marks as there must be some relevant information in there somewhere! Think hard about what an examination is for – it is not just a memory test, but a test to see what you can **do** with the law. Therefore, pay careful attention to what the question asks you – and answer it!

Key Point

Read the question carefully!

- There are pitfalls in 'seeing' the question you want to answer.
- Even though you should come prepared for your chosen topic: with quotations, paraphrasing, statistical/empirical evidence etc, **don't** use material just because you have prepared to use it! It may not be exactly appropriate.
- Remember to keep tying your material back to the question.

Once you have chosen your question and identified the 'task' you have to do (what is the verb in the essay question asking you to do? What are you being asked to solve in the problem question?), you should make a **plan** (quickly) about how to answer it.

Making a plan

- Brainstorm – remember to cross through your plan in the exam to differentiate between plan and actual answer.
- Prioritise your ideas: start strong, weakest second, then in order until you reach your final point.
- Your answers should have an introduction, main body and conclusion. Make sure you have this in mind before you begin.
- Tell the examiner what you are going to tell them, tell them, then tell them what you told them.

Note

Always ask yourself 'am I answering the actual question asked?'

- One of the most common mistakes made in exams is answering a 'prepared' answer/piece of coursework and not the question being asked.
- Avoid using irrelevant material – this will not impress the examiner and may even detract from your answer, losing you marks.

After the exam

- Avoid the temptation to conduct an 'exam post-mortem'.
- Don't listen to answers other people gave – just because they may be different to yours, does not necessarily mean you are wrong and they are right. In fact you may both be right!
- Worrying about the exam you have just done may distract from your 'celebration/relaxation' time and may hinder your next set of revision for a later exam.

Conclusion

Exams are a stressful time in your university education, but you can make them less frightening by preparing well and thinking about them in advance. Revision, which may sound daunting before you start on it, is not just about reading and re-reading your notes – there is much more that you can do to help you learn and remember the law you need to know. With careful planning, you should be able to make your revision work for you. However, you do need to be motivated in order for the techniques suggested in this chapter to work, and you may need to try more than one of them before you find one that is right for you.

Aim high!

Links

S.I. Strong, 'How to write law essays and exams', 2nd edn (Oxford University Press, Oxford 2006).

Online resource centre accompanying book at http://www.oup.com/uk/orc/bin/9780199287550/

This contains some sample text explaining the author's 'CLEO' writing method, as well as a reported case broken down into its key elements giving you tips on what to consider when reading cases, general tips on citation styles and conventions and frequently asked questions.

» glossary

www.oxfordinteract.com

Part 5

Practical skills

www.oxfordinteract.com

Chapter 29

Making presentations

Rationale

Very few students will have had the opportunity to deliver a presentation prior to their undergraduate degree. However presentations are a common form of teaching and assessment strategies in degrees, so it is very likely that at some point, probably early in your course, you will be required to present your work to your peers for assessment.

But remember:

- Most of your peers will be as inexperienced in making presentations as you
- Very few people are 'natural' advocates
- Presentation skills improve with practice and constructive reflection upon your performance
- There are certain techniques you can use which will ensure that your presentation is competent.

This chapter is devised to help you:

- Understand why your lecturers use presentations as a teaching and assessment tool
- Get started on your presentation
- Know what makes a successful presentation
- Use visual aids to accompany your presentation
- Improve your delivery
- Reflect constructively upon your own performance.

» glossary

The role of presentations

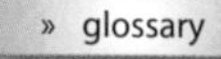

» glossary

Many degrees feature one or more modules in which one of the learning tools is the student presentation. This means that in each seminar one student takes responsibility for researching and presenting a particular issue to the whole class. In law, for instance, students might be required to make presentations on the value of the jury system, or to make a presentation on a significant case. The primary reason for student presentations is to enhance the learning of the student. It is well known that researching something in order to explain it to others is one of the most effective ways of learning. Moreover, the student presentation epitomises the distinction between A-level and undergraduate education. It moves beyond the idea of the passive learner who is dependent upon the teacher for knowledge and makes explicit the student's responsibility for their own learning.

Key Point

Presentations are not designed to humiliate students, but to enhance their learning!

The audience also benefits from the move away from the lecturer. It transforms the way they engage with the material because the student does not have the powerful position of the lecturer and they are therefore more prepared to engage critically with the presentation and challenge the information and ideas presented.

Whilst a seminar presentation feels very demanding to students, it is a relatively safe place to learn presentation skills. Your peers are going to have the same experience as you and they are therefore unlikely to be an overly critical audience. In many modules few, or even no marks, are allocated to seminar presentations. However, most law degrees include one or more compulsory modules which are assessed partly or wholly by presentations. It is very likely therefore that you will be marked on your presentation skills at some point in your degree.

Several law degrees also provide students with opportunities to do other types of presentations. Mooting, for instance, is a more formal and competitive type of presentation. Perhaps your law degree includes a 'street law' module. These involve law students going to schools, community groups and even prisons, explaining legal rights to their audience and responding to questions. Both mooting and street law are great opportunities for students and if your university provides you either of these we would encourage you to consider them. Don't forget that ordinary seminars are an opportunity for you to practise your presentation skills. Think about how you answer questions and put your points across. Are you persuasive? Do you listen and respond to the perspectives of other students? Do you raise your voice, or become incoherent when people challenge your views?

» glossary

Cross reference
For more information see chapter 30, Mooting.

There are a number of other reasons that presentation skills are taken seriously on law degrees:

- Students who decide to become practising lawyers will be expected to be competent at public speaking.
- Even if students do not enter the legal profession, there is still some expectation that a legal education will have included some training in public speaking.
- Many employers require job applicants to make a presentation as part of the interview process.

You may feel reluctant to engage seriously with presentation skills, perhaps thinking that it can be left until the professional stage of your education. However, you have a lot to gain from practising your skills during your undergraduate studies, and constructive reflection upon your practice. If you develop your skills in the supportive atmosphere of your degree you:

- enhance your learning
- gain marks
- are prepared for more demanding presentations in the future.

Key Point

Make the most of the opportunity to learn presentation skills in a safe and supportive environment.

Getting started

Don't forget, you are not starting to acquire presentation skills from scratch. Each time you attend a seminar and participate you are improving your presentation skills. You are learning to think and speak like a lawyer in front of your peers. Make the most of your seminars by participating fully.

Let us assume that you have been asked to give a presentation to your seminar group. The starting point for working on your presentation is the aims you have been set. These will be provided by your lecturer, or, if the presentation is to be assessed, in the assessment criteria.

You must also start thinking about the content – what you are going to say, how you are going to say it and the conclusions you are going to reach. Even at the earliest stage of your preparation, you should be thinking about what you want your audience to think at the end of the presentation. Your presentation must tell your audience something they did not already know – otherwise they will feel that you have wasted their time. This means you must research your topic thoroughly, and plan your presentation so that it highlights some insight that you bring to the topic. You will need to spend some time preparing your information so that it can be delivered effectively. Even from the start of your preparation, you should ensure that you plan your time to ensure you have sufficient opportunity to practise your presentation.

↳ Cross reference
See the chapters in Part II, Research and technical skills

There are four basic elements to organising a presentation. Make sure you have sufficient time to

- *research*
- *plan*

Continued

- prepare
- practise your presentation.

What makes a successful presentation?

A successful presentation is one which delivers its content effectively.

Key Point

This means there are two crucial elements to a successful presentation: **content** and **delivery**. Both of these need to be borne in mind whilst you are preparing your presentation.

The best way to decide what makes a successful presentation is to think about a presentation you have recently watched. It could be a television programme, a lecture or a talk. Was the content coherent? Was it delivered effectively? Did it engage your attention? Did it tell you something that you wanted to know?

Activity 1

Now try an activity which requires you to watch two different presentations and consider the planning and preparation which underpinned the presentations.

Most people find the prospect of standing up and speaking in front of an audience terrifying, and they escalate their fears by imagining everything that might go wrong. In our online activity we suggest a different starting point and ask you to consider what you need to do to deliver a successful presentation.

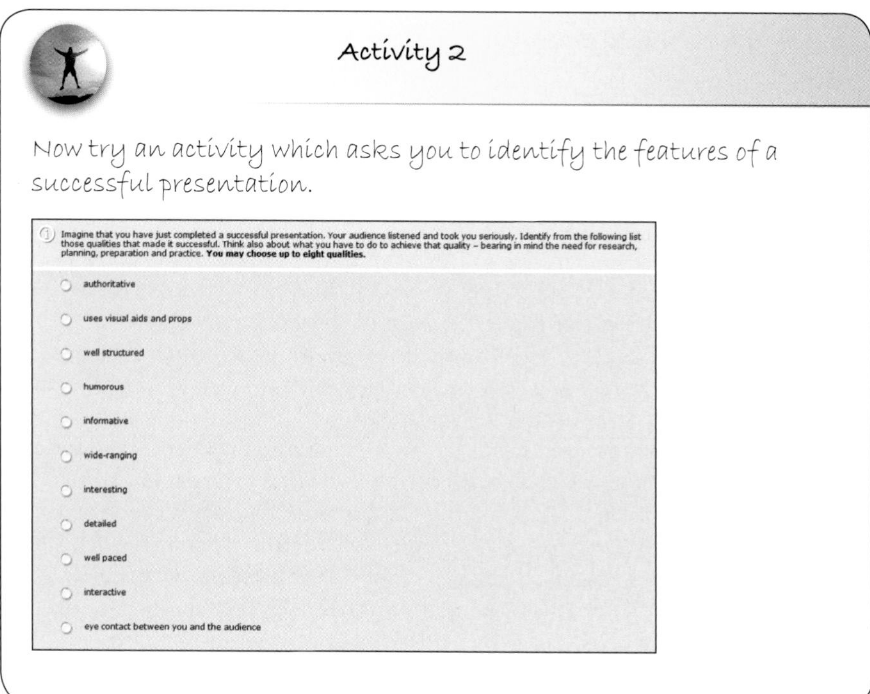

Activity 2

Now try an activity which asks you to identify the features of a successful presentation.

Imagine that you have just completed a successful presentation. Your audience listened and took you seriously. Identify from the following list those qualities that made it successful. Think also about what you have to do to achieve that quality – bearing in mind the need for research, planning, preparation and practice. **You may choose up to eight qualities.**

- authoritative
- uses visual aids and props
- well structured
- humorous
- informative
- wide-ranging
- interesting
- detailed
- well paced
- interactive
- eye contact between you and the audience

Visual aids

Once you have researched the content of your presentation and decided what you want to say, you should start to prepare your visual aids.

There are a number of reasons why you would want to use visual aids to support your presentation. These include:

- Providing a structure for your talk.
- Providing details for instance statistical information, quotations, case references.
- Providing summaries of your points.
- Capturing the attention of your audience.

Key Point

Preparing visual aids makes you focus on preparing your presentation and can make you more confident about delivery. However, you should practise using them and they should complement what you say and be ancillary to your presentation rather than props that you rely on.

Using PowerPoint

The most common visual aid you are likely to have access to is PowerPoint. However, before you prepare PowerPoint slides to accompany your presentation you must check that the room in which you will be presenting has the necessary technology. We are not going to teach you how to use PowerPoint – your university is likely to run courses on the use of PowerPoint, and you can find several tutorials on the web, look for instance at Microsoft's site. Just as important, we think that PowerPoint is fairly intuitive. It is certainly easy to produce a straightforward presentation from the first time you use it. You do not only learn to use tools from courses, you can also learn by modelling your work on other successful practitioners. No doubt many of your lecturers use PowerPoint. Think about what makes a successful PowerPoint presentation and imitate it. Many OUP textbooks also have websites which contain PowerPoint presentations. Look at these and see what works. You will certainly quickly realise that slides should not reproduce exactly what the speaker says – rather they should sum up the key messages of the presentation.

» glossary

» glossary

Some tips and suggestions:

- If you can, use PowerPoint – this is a good time to familiarise yourself with the technology.
- Use a title slide to introduce yourself and your talk.
- Use the next slide to provide an overview of your presentation and introduce your talk by using that slide.
- Ensure that all your slides relate logically to your topic and the points you are making.
- Conclude by using a summary slide. You should be able to summarise your presentation in four or five key points.
- Put a background on your slides – this makes them look more professional and is very easy to do.
- Keep the style of your slides simple – in particular use a consistent font and colours.
- Ensure that your font size is big enough. Think about how it will look to someone in the last row.

- Be wary of animation – it is great fun to do, but much less amusing to watch and can be very irritating.
- Photographs can be very effectively used as part of a PowerPoint presentation – either as a show which runs prior to your talk whilst your audience arrives, or as part of your main presentation. Note, however, that you must leave sufficient time to prepare your presentation, you should review it carefully and be prepared to jettison any photograph which does not work.

Activity 3

Now try an activity on evaluating PowerPoint presentations.

Using an overhead projector

If PowerPoint is not available to you, then you will almost certainly have access to an overhead projector and can prepare transparencies to display during your presentation. We would strongly advise you to print your acetates, if the right quality of acetate is available. You should use a sufficiently large font size, at least 0.5 mm and put no more than six or seven lines of text on each sheet. If you are handwriting the acetates, make sure your writing is legible and sufficiently large to be seen. Be careful about using coloured pens. In general only black, red and blue are sufficiently visible.

Some tips and suggestions:

- Keep the content simple and do not attempt to reproduce exactly what you are going to say.
- Only use one line per point, and use no more than six or seven words in that line.

- Check out the equipment before delivering your talk – the bulbs blow frequently and you may have to ask your IT support desk to replace the bulb. You also want to make sure that the equipment is in the right place for your talk.
- Practise using the slides – in particular you do not want to be removing them from the protective backing during your talk.
- Number your slides – it is very easy for them to get out of order and that will throw you during your presentation.

Handouts

We would always recommend preparing a handout to accompany your presentation. There are a number of advantages to preparing a handout:

- It enables your audience to listen to what you are saying and not be distracted by having to write down every word.
- It enables you to make a lasting impression on your audience because they will physically take away something from your talk.
- It shows respect for your audience and demonstrates that you are taking their learning seriously.
- People like the security of a handout.
- Planning the handout focuses your mind on the presentation in a constructive manner.
- It allows you to provide the level of detail you may feel that your audience needs but cannot be delivered effectively in your presentation.

One important practical point – if you have prepared a handout and the technology fails, you still have something to build your presentation around!

Some tips and suggestions:

- Use the structure of your presentation to structure your handout and then develop your points and provide additional details in a way which is consistent with your talk.
- Think about the layout of the handout and prepare it to a professional standard. If your handout is sloppy your audience will feel cheated. Number your pages so the audience does not get lost.
- Ensure that your handout is prepared in good time. Photocopying at the last minute can be very fraught and lead to a failed presentation. Ensure you have sufficient copies for your audience. If someone is left out, they will feel cheated.
- Rehearse your presentation in front of someone to whom you have given a copy of your handout. Ask them whether they found it helpful and whether they have any suggestions for improvements.

- Think about when you are going to distribute the handout. If you give it out at the beginning the audience may read it rather than concentrate on what you are saying. Moreover, people who arrive late will be looking for a copy of the handout and this will distract you and your audience. On the other hand, there is a benefit to handing it out at the beginning. If the audience has it throughout the presentation they can use it to make notes and follow your talk. You will have to decide when to distribute the handout once you have decided its primary purpose.

Example

Go online to see an example of a handout. It was designed to accompany the first nine slides of presentation 2 in Activity 3.

Delivery

There is no doubt that most people's anxieties focus on the delivery of their presentation. Moreover, it is generally true that it is not what you say but how you say it which has an impact upon your audience.

We have suggested throughout this chapter that you should focus good research, good planning, and good preparation to ensure a successful presentation. However, you do also have to pay attention to your delivery. Below we suggest ways to ensure that your delivery is successful – however, you will have to practise to ensure that your delivery is adequate.

Tips and suggestions:

- Speak clearly and a little slower than normal conversation.
- Avoid a monotone – consciously vary your pitch.
- Speak at a volume that can be heard throughout the room – check that everyone can hear you if you have concerns.
- Face the audience instead of looking at your overheads or the slides.
- Make eye contact with your audience.
- Move your eyes around the room.
- Think of your delivery as an authoritative conversation with the audience, rather than a presentation at the audience.

- Put expression into your voice. Show that you believe in what you are saying – be confident and enthusiastic.
- Accept that mistakes are unavoidable – you will get a little confused, forget an important point or be unable to answer a question. What matters is how you deal with mistakes and not the making of them.
- Pilot your audience through a talk – remind them of your outline, refer them to an earlier point, introduce a new point by stating that this is a different point etc. This makes the audience feel secure that you know what you are saying and where you are going.
- Stand confidently in front of your audience and try not to move around too much. If you are going to move, do it for a purpose, for instance to pass out handouts. Be aware that you may begin to pace back and forwards – try to stop yourself.
- Gestures can help you make your point but if they are overdone, or have no purpose, they can distract your audience.

If you are being assessed on your presentation you should also look at what the criteria are for the assessment. So, for instance, the marker might be looking for a confident delivery of a technical legal point – in which case you should ensure that you deliver just that.

You must practise the delivery of your presentation. However, it is not enough to practise, you must also reflect constructively upon your delivery. The best way to practise is to record yourself. Audio recording is helpful, but it is most useful to see yourself on screen – this gives you plenty of opportunity to reflect on your delivery and improve. It is much easier to record yourself now than it has ever been. Many laptops have built in cameras, as do mobile phones and digital cameras. You may also have access to a webcam. Your institution may have facilities which you can use.

The first time you watch yourself do a presentation you are usually caught up in your horror at seeing and hearing yourself how others see you. That's natural! However, you need to get beyond the stage of embarrassment at your appearance and reflect upon how you can improve your delivery. We suggest that you record yourself and then use our tips and suggestions as a checklist. For instance, did you speak clearly and not too fast? Was your voice a monotone? Do you use gestures that you were not even aware of? Do they enhance what you say, or distract from your presentation? Also ensure that you have your assessment criteria to hand if your presentation is being assessed. Try to think of three good points about your delivery and what needs improving rather than concentrating on all the things you believe you did wrong. Once you have evaluated your performance, try again. See what has improved. By now the novelty of watching yourself on screen should have disappeared and you can become more constructive about your performance. The next step is to work with one or two people you trust. Each of you should record their presentation and then you should watch the rehearsals together and give each other constructive criticism, again utilising our tips and your own assessment criteria. Ensure that you each say as many good things about the delivery as well as suggestions for improvements. You should agree not to say anything destructive by ensuring that your comments are constructive. We have worked this system with students before and found that the improvements in performance following peer review to have been startling.

Activity 4

Go online to watch some videos of law students giving presentations and try an activity which asks you to evaluate their performances.

Note: These videos are of **real** law students filmed for a real assessment!

Nervousness

Nervousness is natural and even experienced speakers get nervous. Good preparation – ensuring that you have done exactly what you were supposed to do – and practice help to overcome it.

Often we get nervous because we imagine terrible scenarios. In the box below we set out some reasons why people panic and suggest how you might respond.

Don't panic

- **The technology might fail** – You can use copies of your slides and your handout to pilot your way through the talk
- **My talk is rubbish** – No it isn't. You have prepared carefully and you are interested in what you are saying. Your audience will be interested too.
- **I lose my place** – Take a deep breath and focus on what you have just said. You have numbered your slides and your notes so it is easy to find where you are.
- **No one can hear me** – Before you start check that your voice can be heard. Nerves often make our voices lower and quieter, so consciously raise your voice. Don't be afraid to say to the audience to let you know if they cannot hear you.
- **I won't know the answer to questions** – Compliment the questioner on an interesting point and open it out to the audience. It might lead to an interesting discussion.

Use these solutions to reassure yourself. Then, just before your presentation, imagine it all going very well and how you will feel when you have successfully completed your presentation. Also arrange for some water to be available. Often when you are nervous your mouth gets dry.

If you are nervous during your presentation you should:

- slow down and take a deep breath
- take a sip of water
- make eye contact with a friendly person in the audience.

Don't worry, all your preparation and practice will pay off!

Conclusion

We have tried to emphasise throughout this chapter that good presentation skills require constant constructive reflection. What this means is that you should note any feedback you receive from your lecturer and decide what you will do to improve in future. If you are given a copy of your presentation, make sure you look at it and work out how you can improve. If you keep all presentations you do during your degree you will notice how you have improved, and begin to think more positively about your skills.

No one is expecting undergraduate students to be full-blown public speakers and this chapter has not aimed to transform you into one. However, what we have done is to give you some common sense advice on how to make the most of the opportunities your undergraduate studies provide for you to improve your presentation skills. We have summarised our main points in the box below.

Key Point

There are very few, if any natural public speakers. Everyone can improve their presentation skills. Take every opportunity to practise your presentation skills. Treat your seminars, for instance, as a presentation of what you have learnt about a topic. You should concentrate on a natural performance that complements your personality.

A good presentation is well researched, well planned, properly prepared and practised.

Good delivery is only one element of a successful presentation. However, it is important and by practising you will improve.

Nervousness is natural and can be overcome.

A competent presenter respects his or her audience.

Constructive reflection upon your presentation will make sure that next time you will do better.

www.oxfordinteract.com

Chapter 30

Mooting

Rationale

Advocacy is one of the main skills of a practising lawyer. Being able to construct and put forward your legal arguments (as well as being aware of what the counter-arguments might be) in the face of questions from the court bench is an invaluable skill and the better it is developed, the more likely it is that your case will be won.

During their law degree and professional qualifying courses, many students have the opportunity to moot – a great way to practise advocacy in a relatively 'safe' environment. Mooting is also a great way to improve your studies in other ways – for example, it hones your research skills and helps with formulating arguments, which is useful when writing essays etc. In addition to internal moots, there are a number of national and international mooting competitions which you can get involved in.

This chapter is devised to:

- Explain what mooting is all about and the processes of a moot
- Give some tips about what you need to do to prepare for a moot
- Give guidance about how to do the type of things expected in planning and preparing for a moot.

What is mooting?

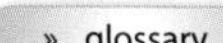

A moot is a mock court case where you are effectively tested on your ability to present a legal argument and, of course, to rebuff the opposition's arguments. It is different from a debate in that you do actually 'pretend' to be in court arguing a case. And, it is different from a mock trial, as moots generally involve appeal cases, to enable you to argue the points of law picked up at trial. Moots are usually set in the Court of Appeal, but sometimes in the House of Lords. The reason for this is that it allows participants to argue and debate points of law, rather than questions of fact (which will have been 'decided' by the fictional lower court that heard the case originally). Students act for either the **appellant** or **respondent** in a problem case given to them in advance, although in some moot competitions (notably national and international competitions) the question is received on the day. Sometimes this is done individually, but sometimes in pairs, within a team of four.

Moots are **always** set in the Court of Appeal or the House of Lords, are **only** about points of law and are **never** a trial on the facts of a case. The facts are given and cannot be disputed.

Mooting is essentially about **research** and **advocacy**. While it is essential to know – and to understand – the area of law in which you are mooting, it helps you to advance your case if you are a good **advocate**. For this reason, lawyers (particularly barristers) are also known as advocates, as this is what they do.

» glossary

Moot (n.) A moot is the raising, arguing and defence of legal issues in a hypothetical case in a fictional court setting.

Moot (v.) To moot is to raise, argue and defend legal arguments in a hypothetical case in a fictional court setting – to participate in a moot. Participants in moots can be called mooters.

» glossary

Advocate (n.) An advocate is someone who argues a case for a client in court or one who speaks on behalf of another, especially (but not always) in a legal context. Used specifically in Scotland to mean a member of the Faculty of Advocates, the professional organisation of the Scots Bar.

» glossary

Advocate (v.) To advocate is to put forward and support a proposition or case.

Advocacy (n.) Advocacy is the skill of being able to put forward and support a proposition or case. It is the active support or defence of an idea or cause etc.; especially the act of pleading or arguing for it.

So, an advocate is the lawyer in a court room (or moot) who presents arguments purely to sway the judge or jury in favour of his client's case – s/he advocates that case, or point of view, or interpretation of the law to the court. It is the opposing side's job to advocate their own position.

Why moot?

In some law schools – as well as in postgraduate and professional legal study – mooting is compulsory as part of the assessment process. In other cases, it is an extra-curricular activity that students can opt to participate in if they want, sometimes for assessment and sometimes only for practice. Despite the hard work and preparation that is involved, mooting can be fun and

» glossary

» glossary

it is good practice for anyone who wants to go to the bar or undertake any advocacy as a solicitor. Even if you don't want to go into practice, mooting is useful because it hones public speaking skills. Mooting is also a unique and effective way of developing your basic research skills and good presentation skills as well as helping students become more organised, as preparation includes creating an outline of the arguments, making legal 'bundles' and ensuring a well-constructed speech.

↳ **Cross reference**
For further information on presentation skills, see chapter 28, Making presentations.

» glossary

Mooting is also not only good preparation for those students who want to go on and become barristers, or solicitors with rights of audience; developing the skills involved in mooting will help any specialist (in law or anything else) to hone the ability to think out arguments clearly and to explain and present them clearly to someone else, often with a view to persuading that person to adopt one or other position. It also helps people to work as a team, deal with counter-arguments or interruptions, develop interpretational skills, answer quick-fire questions while thinking on your feet, and a host of other transferable skills that will be helpful in any chosen profession.

How to prepare for a moot

» glossary

The mooting teams need to start preparing their arguments as soon as they receive their cases. If mooting takes place with teams of two acting for either side, the responsibilities within the team are likely to be divided up as follows (and this is usually the order you will speak in 'court'): **lead** counsel for the appellant, lead counsel for the respondent, **junior counsel** for the appellant, junior counsel for the respondent.

Note

In some university and competition moots the order runs lead appellant, junior appellant, lead respondent, and junior respondent. Check with your mooting co-ordinator which format your moots take before you start.

↳ **Cross reference**
See the chapters in Part II, Research and technical skills, and Part III, Legal method skills.

The team (either all together or split into smaller appellant and respondent 'teams') should then go and research the law that is relevant to the moot problem. Obtaining the skills mentioned in the parts of this resource on 'research and technical skills' and 'legal method skills' will make the preparation of your legal arguments easier.

Remember, you will be arguing points of law rather than points of fact, so you'll need to be aware of where there are possible loopholes or windows where the existing law is unclear or could be interpreted in various ways. You will really need to be aware of the **case law** and **policy** issues covering the aspects of law dealt with in a moot problem question.

Activity 1

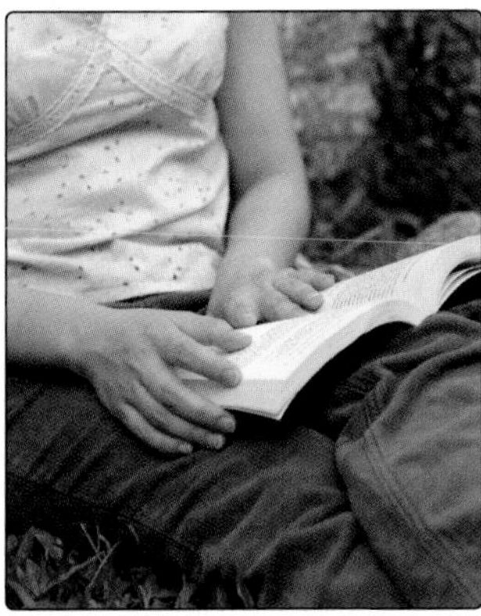

You can work out what needs doing without even seeing the whole question. Look at the example below, which excerpts only the final part of a moot scenario, the finding of the judge in the court below. Then write down what this tells you – information useful before you go on to start the research for your moot.

The trial judge held that:

1. The psychiatric illness was the result of exposure to the asbestos rather than to learning about the possible impact of this exposure, and hence – following *White* – that Joe was a primary victim.
2. Because Joe is a primary victim, it is irrelevant – following *Page v Smith* – whether he is unusually susceptible to this form of psychiatric damage.
3. Following *Fairchild v Glenhaven Funeral Services* and *Barker v Corus* [2006], BuildItRight is liable for the full amount of damages, subject only to a reduction because of Joe's contributory negligence.

Accordingly, the judge assesses damages at £100,000, and awards Joe £50,000.

Go online to read our thoughts on this activity.

Forming an argument

» glossary

Once you have identified the issues that a moot question raises, and which need further research, you – or your team – need to start to form the arguments for each 'side' (appellants and respondents). Each 'side' should begin preparing its skeleton argument, which usually has to be submitted to the 'court officials' (sometimes known as the 'master/mistress of the moots', sometimes less formally as the mooting co-ordinator, or mooting officer) before the date of the moot itself. Timings vary on this, often it will depend on who is judging – if external judges are involved then teams may be asked to submit their skeleton arguments quite early, whereas if the judge(s) will be academic staff only, the date for submission might be later.

To be able to prepare your skeleton argument, you will need to do some research on the law. You will need to know the area of law very well, not just the bits you might need for your own argument. Reading cases related to the area under argument is generally the best way to do this, particularly making note of where judges have said things such as:

> 'there may be exceptions to this rule in future cases if…'

or

> 'in the future, the arguments may well be different…'

» glossary

» glossary

These are 'signposts' to lawyers that let them know that the judge was not prepared to say that their judgment of the case in front of them at that time is the be all and end all of the matter. It leaves an opportunity to argue for an alternative outcome, particularly if arguing upon a different set of facts – and mooters should pick up on this too! You must also know how to distinguish a case, that is, to be able to differentiate the facts of the case before the court from the facts of a case of precedent where there is an apparent similarity. By successfully distinguishing a case, the legal reasoning of the earlier case will either not apply to the current case or will be limited. Whether a case is successfully distinguished often looks to whether the distinguished facts are material to the matter at hand.

An analogy often used to teach about distinguishing cases is that of a case involving black and white spotted cows. A lawyer in a subsequent case involving brown spotted cows might distinguish the facts on the colour of the spots. Whether the colour of the spots on the cow is material to the subsequent case depends on the legal issue. For example, in a case about the value of cows, the colour of the spots may, in fact, be material. However, in a case involving animal cruelty, the colour of the spots is unlikely to be.

Activity 2

Try this activity which asks you to look at a synopsis of two cases from Contract Law and see if you can identify on what grounds the later case may have been distinguished from the other.

This activity asks you to look at a synopsis of two cases from Contract Law and see if you can identify on what grounds the later case may have been distinguished from the other.

Read both of the cases outlined below, then answer true or false to the statements given.

Balfour v Balfour [1919] 2 KB 571
Mr Balfour agreed to give his wife £30 a month as maintenance while he was living and working abroad in Ceylon, as her health was not good enough for her to accompany him. After he had left, the couple separated and Mr Balfour stopped the payments. Mrs Balfour brought an action to enforce the payments, saying that the couple had had a binding contract. At the Court of Appeal, the court held that there was no enforceable agreement as there was not enough evidence to suggest that they were intending to be legally bound by the promise and the 'intention to create legal relations' is one of the *prima facie* requirements of a contract.

Merritt v Merritt [1970] 2 All ER 760
Mr Merritt left his wife and went to live with another woman. Later, he agreed that he would pay his wife £40 per month as maintenance, and she was to make mortgage payments on the house out of this sum, in return for a written agreement from him saying that if she did this, he would transfer the property to her sole ownership. He later refused to transfer ownership of the house to her and she claimed that they had had a binding contract that he would do so. The Court of Appeal agreed, holding that Mrs Merritt was the sole owner of the matrimonial home.

	True	False
The second case could be distinguished because the wife was ill in the first one.	○	○
The second case could be distinguished because the husband went to live abroad in the first one.	○	○
The second case could be distinguished because the couple had separated before the agreement was made.	○	○

Another thing that you need to be able to do is to predict the questions you might be asked – or predict the arguments against your points that the other side may raise. You can only do either of these things if you know the area of law well – that is, you know where judges have hinted that there may be a way round one of the cases **you** are relying on, for example, or a different way in which a section of a statute **might** be able to be interpreted. The best way to anticipate the arguments of the 'other side' is to put yourself in their shoes. As you are reading to prepare your own case, think about what they would be doing – and what cases they would be pulling out etc. – in order to argue for the other party, their client. It might be that they have a far easier task of it than you, in that the law seems to be completely on their side. If this happens to you, don't worry – you get to make the most inventive arguments!

» glossary

Remember *One 'side' may have a much more convincing legal argument than the other (i.e. the law seems to be 'on their side'). This is often the case in real court situations, but it is the job of the advocate to do the best he can for his clients. In a moot, remember it is the* ***advocacy*** *that counts, not whether you 'win' or 'lose' the case.*

Skeletons and bundles

A **skeleton argument** is exactly what it sounds like – it is the bare bones of the argument you (or your 'side') will be presenting to the moot court. It should address the points of law raised by the moot appeal, summarising briefly what points will be raised in argument, in what order, and with which cases supporting them. A skeleton should usually be no more than one side of A4 in length.

Both the appellants and the respondents prepare a skeleton argument, which will be exchanged before the moot takes place, so each side knows what the other will argue. This is similar to what happens in 'real life' but often comes as a surprise to moot participants. However, it is a little less shocking if you remember that an advocate's primary duty is to the court, not to the client!

Note

In most competition moots the skeletons are required to be submitted and exchanged **at least** three working days before the moot – check the rules at your own institution.

Example

Examples of a moot scenario, with good and bad skeleton arguments are provided online.

1) Moot Question / Scenario
2) Appellants' skeleton – good example
3) Respondents' skeleton – bad example

Take a look at these examples and consider why they are good or bad practice. Remember to consider not just what they look like, but also how they work with the points of law/grounds of appeal identified in Activity 2.

Once your skeleton arguments have been submitted and exchanged, they will also be given to the judges of the moot, to allow them time (if wished) to look at the legal issues involved in the case and to refresh their memory on some of the case or statute law being used! After this point, teams should begin working on their 'speeches' – what are you actually going to say in the moot (see 'moot court etiquette', below, for things to bear in mind when preparing your speech).

Teams will usually also be asked to prepare a **bundle of authorities**. Again, this is similar to what happens in real life. When presenting a case to the court, an advocate has to bring with him all the authorities he will be using. So, a bundle should include:

» glossary

- The **full text** of any cases cited or referred to in argument – you must have the full text, rather than just a copy of the passage or passages quoted, in case the judge wants to divert you to another part of the judgment.
- The **full text** of any statutes (or delegated **legislation**) used in argument – or, in some cases, it will be enough just to have the full text of the section you are relying on, check with your court officials.
- Copies of any other sources used.

Cross reference
For further details, see chapter 13, Sources of law; chapter 14, Citing legal authorities; and chapter 17, Using legal databases.

» glossary

Any passages cited (for example, parts of a judgment) should usually be highlighted or otherwise marked in some way, so it is easy to draw the judge's attention to them (and easy for you to see immediately when you need to cite them!). When you write your speech (or note/prompt cards for it, whichever you prefer), you won't need to write these out again, as you can just refer to the appropriate section in the bundle – this will look more professional.

The bundle you prepare should contain all of the cases, statutes and other sources that you will use in argument, even if you don't quote directly from it. There should be identical bundles prepared for the appellants, the respondents and the judge(s). Mooters will refer to passages in the bundle when they cite or quote from cases etc., and should allow the judges time to read around the quote.

What happens in a moot?

If mooting takes place with teams of two acting for either side, as is often the case, the responsibilities within the team are divided up as follows (and this is usually the order you will speak in 'court'):

1. lead counsel for the appellant
2. lead counsel for the respondent
3. junior counsel for the appellant
4. junior counsel for the respondent

» glossary

At the end of the submissions, the lead counsel for the appellant is sometimes given the opportunity for a short **rebuttal**, in which to respond to the arguments presented by the respondent's counsel, but this generally cannot – and should not – be prepared beforehand.

Moots are designed to make students participating feel like they are actually in court, putting forward (advocating) their own case, for their own client(s). Some universities have links with a local court which means that real judges come to preside over the moots, to make the experience even more realistic, although more often academic members of staff are used to judge moots, particularly if they are being undertaken for assessment within a law module.

Because the moot itself is meant to feel like a real case being argued, students have a tendency to get very competitive, even within teams, thinking that they should, for example, keep all their ideas, arguments and sources to themselves, so that the other team does not have the advantage of knowing them. However, this is not actually conducive to a good moot. All members of a mooting team should meet regularly while researching their legal arguments and preparing their submissions. The best moots are those which are approached like a theatre performance, with all parties learning their individual part while being aware of the entire story.

It is possible to 'lose' your case according to the law, but still achieve a high grade for, or win, the moot itself!

As in real life, counsel must exchange their skeleton arguments (see above) with their opponents, usually before their allocated moot date. These arguments are usually then forwarded to the judges and, as such, should contain the structure and content of the arguments counsel will present on the night.

Moot court etiquette

Although a moot court is not a real court, it is usual that certain conventions and rules are followed in the way the moot is run – for example, how the room is set out, how the participants must speak, what they must wear etc. What follows is a short explanation of some of these rules and conventions.

The room

The room in which moots take place may be a designated room for mooting, a seminar room or any other room your university has available. But it will probably be laid out in a way that, as close as is possible, mimics a real courtroom. There should be a 'bench' (where the judges sit to hear the case) and also a dedicated space for the clerk of the court. The advocates sit in front of the bench and clerk, facing inwards. Lead and junior advocates either sit side by side or with the lead counsel in front of the junior. Some universities allow moots to be watched by other students. If this is the case then the 'gallery' should be behind the advocates, facing the judge(s).

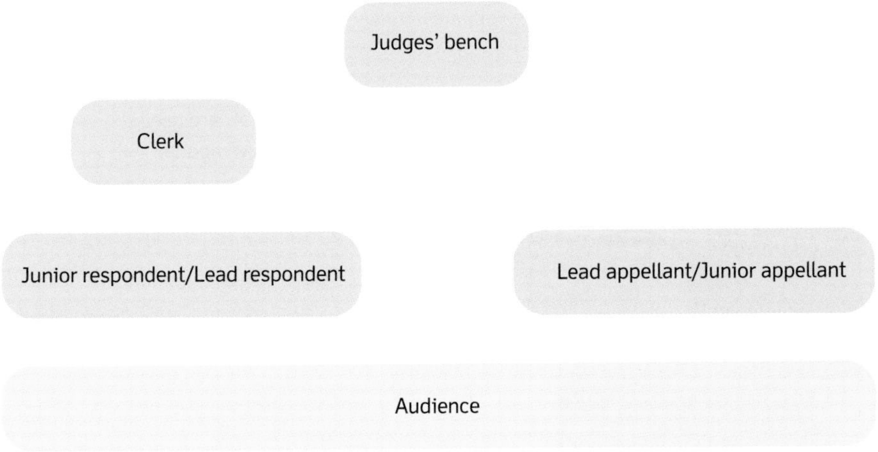

Judges' bench

Clerk

Junior respondent/Lead respondent

Lead appellant/Junior appellant

Audience

Most moots are run in a formal manner and formal dress and court speech is adopted. Men should wear suits and women should wear a smart skirt or trousers and blouse, or a suit.

Starting the moot

The 'case' will normally be introduced by the clerk of the court, who will also announce who the judge(s) presiding over the case are. Then, upon indication that the judge(s) are ready to begin, the moot will start, with the advocates usually speaking in the order outlined above.

Note

This may differ in some cases, particularly if the mooters are dealing with a cross-appeal. If this is the case, check with the mooting co-ordinator or clerk of the court in what order counsel will be required to speak.

Activity 3

Go online to see a video clip of the beginning of a moot.

Speeches

Despite the title, students who are mooting should be aware that the best moots are those that are not so tightly scripted that mooters find it hard to deviate from what's on the page in front of them. While each mooter will have to make their submissions to the court in the form of a 'speech', you should not think of this as a speech in the literal sense.

You do need to prepare what you are going to say in advance – and practise in advance – what you will say to the court, **but** even if you write this all down for the practice runs, when it comes to the moot itself you should try to rely only on notes or bullet points to lead you through what you want to say. If you try to stick to a script, and are then asked a difficult question by the judge (or worse still, told to move on from the point you are making because the judge is satisfied that they have heard enough, or satisfied that your point is not arguable), you will be thrown off track. Remember, you are there to assist the court!

Another reason not to read from a script is that you are likely to be more convincing – both in terms of your arguments and in the way you put them across – if you can maintain good eye-contact with the judge/s you are addressing. This shows confidence and assertiveness – and can be very persuasive! During the presentation of the legal arguments each counsel is likely to be asked questions by the judges, to which they should be able to give a considered answer based on their legal arguments and knowledge.

Bearing these points in mind, here are some dos and don'ts relating to speeches:

DO

- Prepare your submission carefully and in full detail before the moot
- Prepare a bullet-point version of your submission (or on e.g. prompt cards)
- Think about where in your speech you might get asked questions and what these might be
- Think about the weak points of your argument, as you may be asked to move on
- Make eye-contact with the judges
- Speak clearly
- Ask the judges if they need any points expanded (e.g. when you cite a case)
- Allow judges time to read any passages you have referred them to
- Answer any questions the judges ask of you.

DO NOT

- Rely on a script when putting forward your submission
- Read what you have written and avoid making eye-contact
- Mumble
- Race through your points without pause for thought
- Point judges towards a passage of a case or section of a statute without giving them time to read it
- Respond to a judge's question by saying e.g. 'I'm coming to that later' – answer the question there and then!

Note

Work on the **speech** might continue right up to five minutes before the moot itself!

Addressing the court

A common stumbling point amongst mooting students is about how to properly address the court, or specific members of 'the bench'. This depends on what court you are (hypothetically) in – the Court of Appeal or House of Lords – which is probably why there is so much confusion.

Judges in the real Court of Appeal are written as, for example, 'Phillips LJ' – this stands for Lord Justice, but is not how you would address them individually or collectively. The correct way to do this would be to say 'My Lord' or 'My Lady' if referring or replying to one member of the bench

» glossary

at Court of Appeal, or 'My Lords' if referring to them collectively (even if there is a woman on the bench!). Law Lords sit in the House of Lords and would be referred to individually and collectively the same way. However, there are many common mistakes made in moots, some of which are listed below. Try to avoid these!

Your Honour	Should be 'My Lord/s'
Your Worship	Should be 'My Lord/s'
Your Lord/Lordships	Should be 'My Lord/s' unless referring indirectly, such as 'if it pleases your Lordships'
My Lordship/s	Should be 'My Lord/s' unless referring indirectly, such as 'if it pleases your Lordships'

In one moot we have seen, a mooter even referred to a member of the bench as 'Your Majesty'!

Other terminology issues

Of course, speaking to the bench is not the only place where you will be required to use the correct terminology. The way you speak to and introduce other members of your team and opposing counsel, the way you introduce cases, the way you ask judges if they would like you to do (or not to do) something – all of these require use of legal language which is often, at first, difficult to get used to.

Some examples of good practice are set out below. These are not prescriptive, but are included so as to give you some idea of how you should be speaking to the court.

Activity 4

Each example also has a corresponding video clip that you can watch to see how it should be done!

Following the examples of good practice, there is one example of 'bad practice'. We have singled out:

	Example of good practice
Introducing yourself: lead appellant	If it pleases your Lordship/s, my name is X and I am leading/senior counsel for the appellant, C Ltd. To my right is my junior counsel, Y, who will be dealing with the second point of appeal in this case. Opposite me are my learned friends Miss A and Mr B, who are lead/senior and junior counsel for the respondent, D. Would your Lordship/s like a summary of the case and the grounds for appeal?
Introducing the appeal: Lead appellant	My Lord/s, I am dealing with the first point of appeal, namely that.... My submission relies on two grounds: first...; and second,...
Summarising and concluding the appeal: Junior appellant	My Lord/s, you were given the first point of appeal by my learned senior, who showed you that.... I have further addressed you on the second point of appeal, namely that if your Lordship/s **did** find that.... Accordingly, unless you have any further questions you would like me to address, I would invite you to find in favour of the appellant and overturn the decision of the court below.
Introducing the case for the respondent: Lead respondent	If it pleases your Lordship/s, my name is Miss A and I appear on behalf of the respondent, D, alongside my learned junior, Mr B. I shall be addressing the first point of appeal, and my learned junior will address the second. My Lord/s, you have heard from my learned counsel opposite that.... However, the authorities show that in this case.... We contend that...
Summary of the respondents' arguments and conclusion: Junior respondent	My Lord/s, you have now been addressed on both points of appeal. Having heard the respondents' arguments, namely that...; we invite you to uphold the decision of the lower court. Unless I can be of any further assistance, this concludes the submissions for the respondents.
Introducing a case in your submission	To support my contention that (e.g.) because the terms of the advertisement **were** sufficiently certain, so that no supply and demand issues would be raised and no further negotiations would be necessary before acceptance could take place, the advertisement can be viewed as a legal offer, I would like to draw your Lordship'/s' attention to the case of Carlill and Carbolic Smoke Ball Company, which was reported in the first volume of the Queen's Bench reports in 1893 at page 256. Would your Lordship/s like a summary of the facts of that case...?
Referring to a quote from the case in your bundle	I refer your Lordship/s to the case of X, which was reported in the X volume of the X reports in 2007 at page X. Your Lordship/s will find this in the bundle at (e.g) the second tab [pause]. In particular, I would like to direct your Lordship/s to the passage on page X of the judgment, which is highlighted in the bundle, about a third of the way down the page, the sentence beginning '...'.

	Example of bad practice
Introducing a case in your submission	In support of my submission, I would like to draw your attention to a case where (e.g.) a magazine advertisement was held to be an invitation to treat. This was the case of Partridge v Crittenden, 1968, two all ER, 421.

Activity 5

Why was this last example one of 'bad practice'?

Go online to read our thoughts on this question.

Timekeeping

One thing that we have not yet gone into in any detail is the fact that most moots are timed, and that keeping to your allotted time is part of the skill in mooting. This can be difficult, particularly if the judges ask you a lot of questions.

Often, what the judges say to you does not come off your allocated time, although what you say in answer to them does. It is worth checking the rules of your particular university or competition regarding this, so that you can work out what you need to say accordingly. As a general rule of thumb, you should aim **not to** fill the time you are allocated with your speech. If, for example, your speaking time is 10 minutes, aim to write a speech that takes up 7 minutes. This gives you some leeway regarding any questions from the bench or explanations you need to give – one of the worst things is to run out of time – as you will feel like you haven't been able to fully argue your case. You will also look more in control if you pace your arguments well.

Within the time you have for your speech (e.g. 7 minutes, as above), think about how many points you need to make. If you have one ground of the appeal to argue, think about how many points there are to your argument. If there are three, divide your time up roughly equally, depending upon the complexity of the points you need to get across. So, following the 7-minute example, if you have three points to make, your timekeeping may follow a pattern something like this:

Time	Speech
Up to 30 secs	Intro
30 secs – 3 min 30 secs	Point one

3 min 30 secs – 4 min	Questions on point one
4 min – 7 min	Point two
7 min – 7 min 30 secs	Questions on point two

You will notice that the allocated time, including some time built in for introductions and questions finishes after 7 minutes and 30 seconds – leaving 2 minutes and 30 seconds 'free' for you to use, either to develop the detail of one of your arguments or to answer questions from the bench.

Of course, when you are actually standing up and presenting your arguments, you may have no idea what the time is and how long you have been speaking. In terms of timekeeping while you advocate, your co-counsel could look at the plan you have devised (something like the above) and keep time for you – giving you a surreptitious signal when you are coming to the end of your allotted time on one of your grounds of appeal, for example – so that you know that you need to wind up on that point and move on to the next one. But **listen** to the judges as well; for example, you may hear signals that they are far more interested in one of your lines of argument than the other, in which case you may choose to focus more strongly on that.

If you find that you are actually running out of time, tell the judges! You could say something like: 'as it appears that I am coming to the end of my allotted time, my Lord/s, I will just summarise briefly my remaining points'. If they want to hear more, they will ask you!

Remember It is better to answer the judges questions, be diverted off the point if they want you to and then just summarise your remaining points quickly at the end than it is to rush and try and garble everything you wanted to say when you started!

Conclusion

Mooting is a great thing to do while you are a law student. It helps you to develop your skills as an advocate and will look impressive on applications for professional legal training, such as the BVC and LPC. Even if you don't intend to practise law, however, mooting will help you gain confidence in research, making presentations, forming and supporting arguments and thinking on your feet – all invaluable – and transferable – skills.

» abbreviation

Links

MootingNet
http://www.mootingnet.org.uk/
MootingNet is a web resource for mooters in England and Wales set up and run by ex-law students. If you are going to take part in a legal moot, then you can find information and support on this site, including a list of helpful books and other resources on mooting.

What is mooting and how is it done?
http://www.oup.co.uk/oxfordtextbooks/law/mooting/more/
Information from OUP about mooting, including how to set up a mooting competition and some links to other helpful sites.

The KLS mooting programme
http://www.kent.ac.uk/law/currentug/mooting/index.htm
An example of a mooting competition run internally at the University of Kent, with some good advice for students.

www.oxfordinteract.com

Chapter 31

Interviewing

» glossary

Rationale

Interviewing is one of the most important tasks carried out by practising lawyers. Solicitors and, to a lesser but still significant extent, barristers deploy a range of skills during the course of an interview to ensure that they have the necessary information upon which to base their legal advice. If you decide to enter the legal profession you will spend a lot of time during your professional training practising interviewing skills. However, good interviewing skills are also useful in a broad range of occupations, so the skills we highlight here are easily transferable.

At this stage of your legal education we are going to provide only a brief outline of the bundle of skills required for effective interviewing. In particular we will not deal with matters of professional conduct, money laundering requirements and fees. These are more appropriately dealt with during the professional stage of your education. Nonetheless, our chapter will serve as a useful introduction, and should be helpful if you are asked to carry out an interviewing exercise as part of your undergraduate studies. You may also find it useful if you decide to enter the UK heats of the International Client Counselling Competition, in which teams of law students compete with each other to demonstrate their competence at simulated interview scenarios.

There are several reasons why you might be asked to carry out a simulated interview as part of your undergraduate studies. Practising interviewing:

- Improves your listening and questioning skills because you have to rely on those skills to gather information
- Enhances your note-taking skills – you will need to take effective notes from information which is not necessarily delivered in a structured form
- Checks your understanding of legal concepts because it requires you to explain the law to someone using plain English rather than legal language
- Reminds you of the social and economic context of law. For instance, the lease/licence distinction may seem a relatively obscure branch of land law, but it is of vital importance to a social landlord seeking to evict an occupier from short-term housing
- Underlines the significance of remedies – clients want their problems solved rather than to understand the subtleties of the law. Suddenly the equitable, and therefore discretionary, nature of injunctions becomes real when your client wants someone to stop doing something in breach of their legal rights rather than seeking compensation for the breach
- It's an enjoyable and challenging way of learning law.

This chapter has been devised to:

- Introduce you to the range of skills used during an interview
- Demonstrate the value of a well-structured interview
- Highlight both the difficulties and the necessity of note taking
- Help you practise explaining legal concepts in plain English.

The significance of the first interview

This chapter concentrates on the first interview between the lawyer and the client. This interview is crucial. You will have to:

- develop a rapport with the client
- find out the relevant facts
- discover the client's priorities
- advise her
- plan the next steps
- ensure that you have a good record of the interview.

» glossary

You will also be operating under time constraints. In **legal aid** cases, you may have as little as half an hour to achieve everything you need to achieve. You will have to structure the interview and deploy a range of skills in order to be effective. This is best illustrated by thinking about a practical scenario.

Activity 1

Now try an activity which highlights what you have to achieve during the first interview with a client.

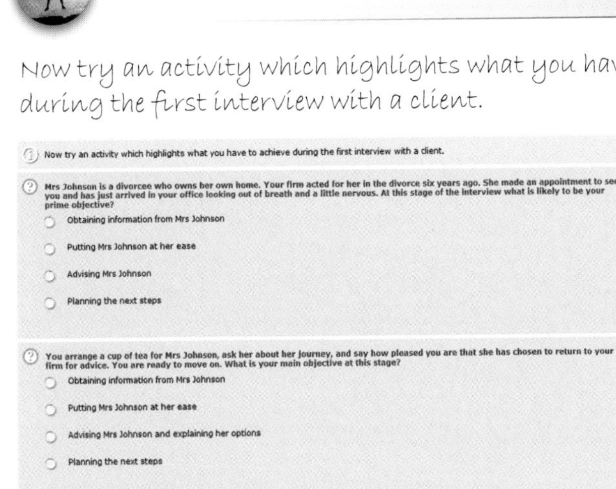

Now try an activity which highlights what you have to achieve during the first interview with a client.

Mrs Johnson is a divorcee who owns her own home. Your firm acted for her in the divorce six years ago. She made an appointment to see you and has just arrived in your office looking out of breath and a little nervous. At this stage of the interview what is likely to be your prime objective?

- Obtaining information from Mrs Johnson
- Putting Mrs Johnson at her ease
- Advising Mrs Johnson
- Planning the next steps

You arrange a cup of tea for Mrs Johnson, ask her about her journey, and say how pleased you are that she has chosen to return to your firm for advice. You are ready to move on. What is your main objective at this stage?

- Obtaining information from Mrs Johnson
- Putting Mrs Johnson at her ease
- Advising Mrs Johnson and explaining her options
- Planning the next steps

You have now heard Mrs Johnson's story in her own words. What is your next objective?

- Obtaining information from Mrs Johnson
- Putting Mrs Johnson at her ease

Even this much simplified account of the first interview demonstrates that:

- there are different priorities at different stages of the interview
- you need to deploy a complex array of skills and
- structure the interview in order to achieve those priorities
- listening to your client takes up a major proportion of the interview.

Key Point

The client and not the lawyer is the expert in the facts of the case. This is why a large proportion of the interview is spent listening to the client and checking your own understanding of the facts.

Preparation

You should prepare as much as possible for the interview. Get as many details as possible from the receptionist about what was said when the appointment was made, find out whether the client has used your firm before, and, if she has, read the previous files. However, there is often little you can do in the way of preparation. You are going to have to listen carefully and think on your feet.

Note taking

We have already said that you must ensure that you have a useful record of the meeting. It can be very difficult to listen, reassure, advise and take notes. The story will emerge in a very different way from the facts in an examination. It is unlikely to be coherent, you will not be able to understand why certain things are relevant until later, and the person telling the story is emotionally involved. Because of this it can be counter-productive to take notes from the beginning of the interview or during the stage when the client is telling you the story in his or her own words. We would suggest taking notes at the stage of checking that you have understood the story. This allows you to have a feel for the full story, and will work well alongside your questions. When you are taking notes remember what you will be using them for. Your next task after the interview will be to write to the client confirming your instructions, the advice you have given, and the next steps that you have both agreed. Your notes, at the very least, should be sufficient to enable you to write that letter.

↳ **Cross reference**
Don't forget you practise note taking in lectures and seminars – look back at chapter 4, Taking notes, for hints on how to focus on the most important points.

Summary of the structure of an interview

The stages of the interview can be explained diagrammatically as set out below.

Tasks	Purpose	Skills	Note taking
Greeting and introductions	Putting the client at ease – establishing a relationship	Social skills	Not yet appropriate
The client's story	Allow the client to tell their story uninterrupted	Listening skills – with prompts if necessary	Not yet appropriate
	Question the client about the story, filling in gaps and elaborating necessary details. Don't forget to ask if the client has brought any documents with her	Questioning skills	Note taking begins here Arrange to have any documents copied to keep with your notes
	Summing up the client's story, and checking that the client has agreed your version	Questioning skills	Check your notes of the story are complete – don't be nervous about checking spelling of names and other details
Advising and explaining options	Analyse the client's problem in legal terms, and evaluate the options	Legal problem analysis	Take full notes of any advice you give.
	Explain the relevant law in plain English, checking that the client has understood. Help the client decide upon the best course of action	Explanatory skills	
	Sum up your advice and check that it is understood		
Planning the next steps	Decide what is to happen next and who will take responsibility for this. For instance, you may say that you will write a letter confirming your advice, and you would like to hear from the client with additional information and instructions.		Take full notes of the next steps
Terminating the interview	Reassurance and goodbyes. See the client to the door and shake their hand.	Social skills	Your note taking will have stopped now – make sure you give the client your full attention
After the interview		Write a letter confirming your instructions, advice and next steps	Your notes will be invaluable here

More on interviewing skills

The skills involved in effective interviewing comprise:

- social skills
- listening
- questioning

- problem analysis
- explaining.

Social skills

Sometimes inexperienced lawyers are so concerned about performing their role as a lawyer that they forget that the interview experience may be nerve-wracking for the client. Even if the client is not nervous, this is their first contact with you and they want to be confident that their legal problems are going to be properly handled. You need to be aware of the client's feelings and needs throughout the interview and, in particular, to reassure them at the beginning of the interview that you are interested in their story and their problems and will give them ample time to explain their position. Pay proper attention to greeting your client. Come out from behind the desk and shake their hand. Offer them a seat and a drink. Let them catch their breath before starting to question them. At the end of the interview, the client wants to feel confident that their problem is in competent hands and that things will start to happen. They should leave your office clear about the next steps, and consider that, however difficult their problem, the interview has been a positive experience. Even if your next client is waiting, take time to say goodbye and re-assure the client that she or he is in safe hands.

There is another element to social skills. When you are listening to your client's story you must not be judgmental about decisions the client has made or actions they have taken. That is not your role. Also, avoid jumping to conclusions, or making stereotypical assumptions about why things happened or what the client wants. Let the story unfold and the client set out their own priorities.

It can be easy to get embarrassed about asking for information. However, you must overcome your embarrassment and ensure that you obtain all the crucial information. Catching people's names can be particularly difficult, and we all feel very uneasy admitting that we have not remembered someone's name. One way to ensure that you have got the client's name right is to repeat it to them straight away. Refer to them throughout the interview by their name. Always ask them to spell their name, and check it back to them. If you have failed to note their name, and only realise this late in the interview, you are going to have to apologise. Say something like, 'I am really sorry, but I have failed to note your name properly. Can you just repeat it again for me, so I can ensure that my records are accurate?'

Listening

We have already suggested that listening is the most important skill that is used during an interview. Yet effective listening does not come naturally. There are a variety of reasons why we might find it difficult to listen carefully to what people are telling us. We are busy and we really do not have time to let the client's story unravel slowly; we are bored and we have heard it all before; we are tired and cannot concentrate and anyway tomorrow's court case is a more pressing concern.

Whatever the situation, you must prioritise the client's story, use effective listening techniques, and consciously demonstrate to the client that you are listening to them.

Effective listening involves:

- Good eye contact – don't stare at your client, but don't avoid his or her gaze.
- Positive body language – psychologists suggest that we unconsciously imitate the body language of people with whom we feel comfortable. If you consciously imitate your client's body language this is likely to increase the rapport between you. Encouraging smiles, head nodding, and expressions of concern are also useful.
- Allowing silences – clients need time to think about the events they are recounting, try to avoid the natural desire to fill silences.
- Encouraging the client with the story by phrases such as 'yes I understand', 'go on', and 'so that happened when she visited . . .'.
- Articulating empathy – not only should you feel concern, you should try to articulate it – 'I can understand why you felt that way', 'it would make most people anxious', etc.

Avoid

- Staring at the client or looking away from them. Even if you think it helps you concentrate both are very off-putting for someone who is trying to communicate with you.
- Talking too much – something you might be tempted to do if you are nervous.
- Distracting mannerisms such as fiddling with your pen, or drumming your fingers on the desk.
- Making pre-emptory judgments about the client and their story.

Note taking can interfere with effective listening. It is better to postpone taking notes until later in the interview.

Listening is often enhanced by observing your client's body language.

One way that you can demonstrate to the client that you have listened, and at the same time check that you have understood what you have been told is by summarising what you have heard. Summarising should include a summary of the facts, but also what you consider to be the client's priorities and main concerns.

Questioning

You need to ask questions in order to gather together the information upon which you will advise your client. Different types of questions are relevant to different forms of information gathering. The two types of questions are open questions and closed questions. We define these in the table below.

Types of question	Characteristics
Open questions are questions which do not assume any particular type of answer and are likely to be answered at length	They ask the client to think and reflect. They will include opinions and feelings. They hand control of the conversation to the respondent.
Closed questions assume the subject matter of the answer and can be answered briefly	They give you facts. They are easy to answer. They are quick to answer. They keep control of the conversation with the questioner

We ask **open questions** in order to encourage the client to tell the story in their own words and to provide the opportunity for the client to raise all matters that are relevant. We ask **closed questions** to obtain more detailed information, to clarify matters and to prompt memory. You have to use both forms of questions to ensure that you obtain adequate information.

Open questions include:

- What's on your mind?
- Tell me all about it.
- What happened next?
- Go on.
- Is there anything else which is worrying you?

Closed questions include:

- Exactly where were you when this happened?
- What words did he actually use?
- So what happened after he threatened you?
- Just demonstrate exactly how he did that.

Interviews tend to start with open questions, and then move to closed questions as details are checked and gaps are filled. This sequence of questioning is often described as a T funnel. Be careful not to move to the closed question stage too quickly as this can mean that important details are omitted from the client's account. Provide opportunities for the client to tell you about other matters by using open questions again once you have finished your detailed questioning. This will hand control of the interview back to the client. So, for instance, remember to ask – is there anything else on your mind? Or – is there any other business you would like me to consider? Remember that clients do not always tell you straightaway about the matter that concerns them most. One further question that you should always ask – have you brought any documents with you? Clients often forget that they have brought a contract, or a lease along with them. You should never assume that they have no relevant documentation, but prompt them to show it to you.

Style of questioning

Questions need to be asked in a supportive manner. You are trying to piece the whole story together, not demolish it. Lawyers can unconsciously adopt cross-examination techniques with their client. The first interview is not the time to test the client's story. At this point you want the client to feel confident that you are taking them seriously by listening to what they have to say.

Remember, as you end one set of questions, to check your understanding of the client's story by summarising what you have heard, and asking questions to confirm that understanding.

Problem analysis

You will spend a great deal of your undergraduate studies learning how to think like a lawyer. By this we mean learning the law and learning to apply it to particular factual situations. In many ways you are well prepared for this stage of the interview. However, you will face new challenges. Unfortunately clients do not bring problems to lawyers in the same way that your lecturers provide problems for you to answer. You do not know if the subject matter is going to be tort, or contract, for instance, and you will soon learn that the traditional subject boundaries are irrelevant in the office. Moreover, clients' priorities are not necessarily those that the lawyer will recognise. Relatively few clients, for instance, want to go to court to enforce their legal rights. One major concern for inexperienced lawyers is that they will not know the answers to the questions they have been asked. Fortunately, an interview is not an exam. You do not lose marks or face by admitting to the need to research the law.

Don't panic

No one is expected to know all the answers. Moreover, you have a duty to act in the best interests of your client when you provide advice. It is not only perfectly legitimate, it is also your professional duty to tell a client that you do not know the answer and that you will have to research the law on that particular point.

In many cases there will be a range of options facing the client. You need to outline these to the client, and work with them in finding a solution to their problem. Check that your client has understood any advice you have given, provide opportunities for asking questions about your advice, and reassure them that you will repeat the advice in a follow-up letter.

Explaining

Even if you have analysed the client's problems with skill, and provided excellent advice, you will not have looked after the best interests of the client if they do not understand your advice.

Activity 2

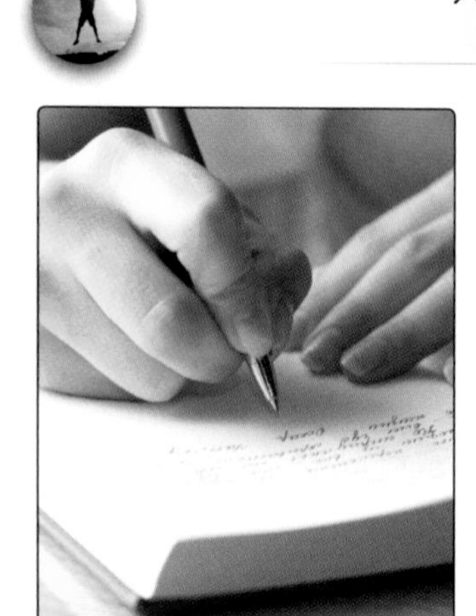

Now try an activity to help you practise explaining important legal concepts in plain English.

Over time you will develop your own personal style of explaining legal concepts in lay terms. At this stage of your legal education it can be very useful to practise putting legal jargon into plain English. It ensures that you have really understood the concept you are trying to explain.

Once you have explained your advice to your client, then check their understanding and offer to go through it again if necessary. If you think it would be useful summarise your advice. Remember to reassure the client that you will write to him or her reiterating your advice.

Conclusion

In this chapter we have considered the bundle of skills which are required for effective interviewing and suggested a model structure for the typical interview. We have provided you with some suggestions for developing your skills of listening, questioning, problem analysis and explaining. This will provide you with the necessary skills for interviewing exercises during the undergraduate stage of the degree and a good foundation for your professional studies. We hope it will also give you the confidence to enter the client counselling competition.

Chapter 32

Negotiating and alternative dispute resolution

Rationale

It is easy for law students to assume that all disputes that concern legal rights are resolved by lawyers in courts, and that the skills required for a successful legal career are effective advocacy and an extensive knowledge of the law. However, as Genn's research, *Paths to Justice* (Hart, Oxford 1999) indicates, that assumption is not entirely accurate. Many people and many disputes are excluded from litigation. Moreover, litigation does not necessarily benefit the client:

- It is a 'winner takes all' game
- It is stressful for the parties
- It is expensive
- Civil litigation may be particularly difficult for vulnerable people.

In addition, the provision of an effective and modern court system is very expensive and therefore government is keen to target court resources proportionately. The principle of proportionate dispute resolution underpinned the White Paper, 'Transforming Public Services: Complaints, Redress and Tribunals' published in July 2004. Mechanisms are in place to push disputants towards alternative dispute resolution (ADR). The Civil Procedure Rules which govern the procedures of litigation require consideration of the use of ADR. Pre-action protocols, which are requirements placed upon parties prior to litigation being initiated, require the consideration of ADR before proceedings are begun. Moreover, legal funding for representation may be refused if ADR is available and not used. Increasingly parties can expect there to be costs penalties if they fail to use ADR before going to court.

» abbreviation

The substantive consequences of these moves will no doubt be considered in your legal systems/legal process modules. However, it also has consequences for lawyers who need additional skills in order to provide an effective and complete service for their clients. You will study these skills in depth during the professional stage of your legal education, and whilst you are being trained as a lawyer. This chapter is going to introduce you to those skills, in particular the skills of negotiation and mediation. However, we begin with a brief description of the different processes involved in ADR.

» glossary

This chapter has been devised to introduce you to:

- The range of processes encompassed by ADR
- The skills involved in mediation
- The distinction between traditional lawyers' skills and those required of a mediator
- The role of negotiation in resolving disputes
- The principles underpinning effective negotiation techniques.

What is alternative dispute resolution (ADR)?

ADR is an umbrella term for a number of different approaches to the resolution of disputes. These vary in the extent to which they are distinct from court procedures, but share the objective of resolving disputes without the necessity of judicial intervention. The Ministry of Justice on its website defines ADR as:

> The collective term for the ways that parties can settle civil disputes with the help of an independent third party and without the need for a formal court hearing. (http://www.dca.gov.uk/civil/adr/index.htm)

Key Point

» glossary

There are three main forms of ADR: arbitration; conciliation; and mediation.

Arbitration

In arbitration an independent third party hears both sides in a dispute and makes a decision to resolve it. The arbitrator is impartial; this means he or she does not take sides. In most cases the arbitrator's decision is legally binding on both sides, so it is not possible to go to court if you are unhappy with the decision.

Most types of arbitration have the following in common:

- Parties both agree to use the process
- It is private
- The decision is made by a third party, not the people involved
- The process is final and legally binding
- There are limited grounds for challenging the decision
- Hearings are often less formal than court hearings. (Note, however, that some forms of arbitration do not involve hearings but are decided on the basis of documents only.)

Conciliation

Conciliation involves a third party helping the people in dispute to resolve their problem. The conciliator should be impartial and should not take one party's side.

All conciliation has the following elements in common:

- It is voluntary – the parties choose to conciliate or not
- It is private and confidential
- The parties are free to agree to the resolution or not
- Conciliated agreements are usually non-binding, although they can be made into binding contracts. In employment disputes, however, a signed conciliated agreement is binding.

Mediation

Mediation involves an independent third party helping disputing parties to resolve their dispute. The disputants, not the mediator, decide the terms of the agreement. The mediator has an important role, however, in 'reality testing' any agreement – that is, in checking carefully that the parties are able to do what they agree to do.

All types of mediation have the following in common:

- It is voluntary – the parties choose to mediate or not
- It is private and confidential
- The parties make the final decision on how to resolve the dispute
- The mediator is impartial – he or she does not take sides or say who is right and who is wrong
- The mediator is independent.

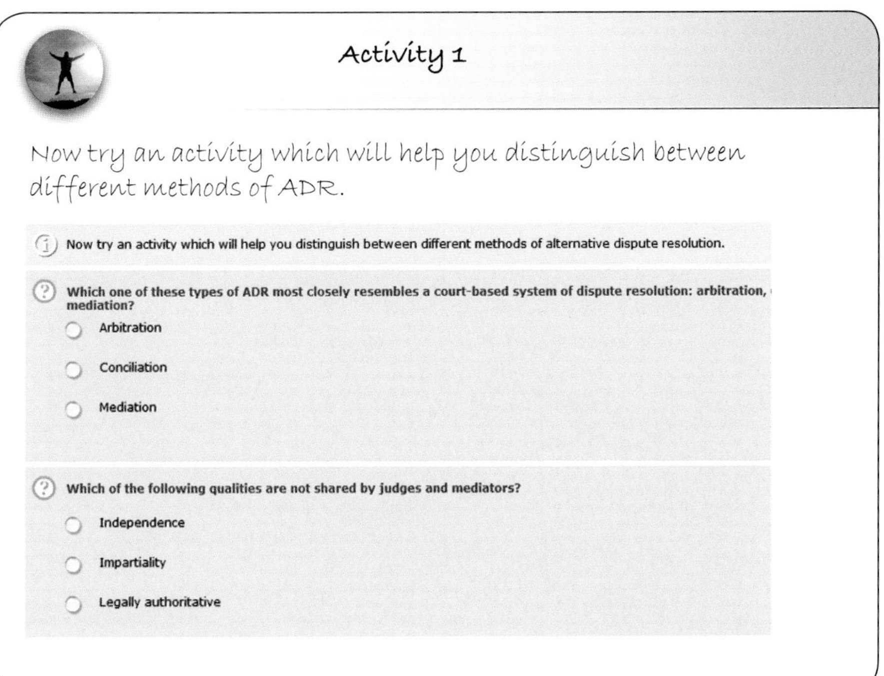

Activity 1

Now try an activity which will help you distinguish between different methods of ADR.

Now try an activity which will help you distinguish between different methods of alternative dispute resolution.

Which one of these types of ADR most closely resembles a court-based system of dispute resolution: arbitration, mediation?

- Arbitration
- Conciliation
- Mediation

Which of the following qualities are not shared by judges and mediators?

- Independence
- Impartiality
- Legally authoritative

The crucial quality of mediation is that the parties to the dispute decide for themselves how to resolve it. The mediator facilitates the parties in reaching that decision. He or she helps the parties consider what is important to them and to exchange that information. The concerns go beyond what is legally relevant and can address other issues including emotional and financial issues.

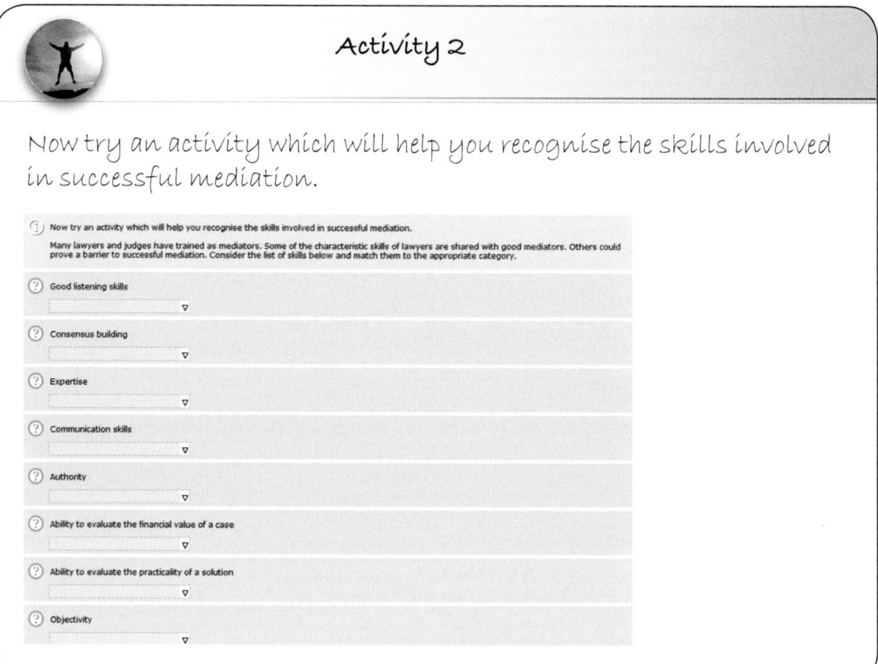

Activity 2

Now try an activity which will help you recognise the skills involved in successful mediation.

Now try an activity which will help you recognise the skills involved in successful mediation.

Many lawyers and judges have trained as mediators. Some of the characteristic skills of lawyers are shared with good mediators. Others could prove a barrier to successful mediation. Consider the list of skills below and match them to the appropriate category.

- Good listening skills
- Consensus building
- Expertise
- Communication skills
- Authority
- Ability to evaluate the financial value of a case
- Ability to evaluate the practicality of a solution
- Objectivity

There is no doubt that lawyers can be effective mediators; however it requires a different mindset, a move from focusing on winning cases, to one which views the best interests of the parties in a holistic way, not concerned only with financial outcomes.

Activity 3

Now try an activity which asks you to think about the mindset needed to be an effective mediator.

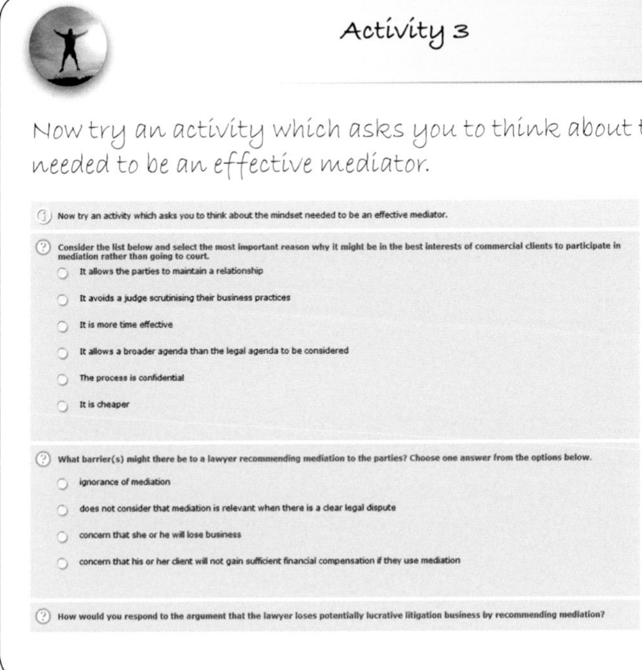

Now try an activity which asks you to think about the mindset needed to be an effective mediator.

Consider the list below and select the most important reason why it might be in the best interests of commercial clients to participate in mediation rather than going to court.

- It allows the parties to maintain a relationship
- It avoids a judge scrutinising their business practices
- It is more time effective
- It allows a broader agenda than the legal agenda to be considered
- The process is confidential
- It is cheaper

What barrier(s) might there be to a lawyer recommending mediation to the parties? Choose one answer from the options below.

- ignorance of mediation
- does not consider that mediation is relevant when there is a clear legal dispute
- concern that she or he will lose business
- concern that his or her client will not gain sufficient financial compensation if they use mediation

How would you respond to the argument that the lawyer loses potentially lucrative litigation business by recommending mediation?

The skill of negotiation is more closely identified with the work of lawyers than mediation. Over 90 per cent of court cases settle before the hearing, mostly following the negotiation of settlements by lawyers. However, successful negotiation techniques have more in common with mediation than might first appear, because the good negotiator takes into account a wider range of concerns than the legal strengths and weaknesses of the case. Moreover, negotiation is not solely the province of lawyers. All of us negotiate just about every day. Think for a minute about negotiations you have been involved in. Have you asked a supervisor for an extension to an essay deadline? Have you arranged childcare with a friend, or organised a venue for a group of your friends? All of these activities will have involved negotiating.

» glossary

» glossary

Note

What is negotiating?

G. Richard Shell, in Bargaining for Advantage (Penguin 1999) defines negotiation as:

> An interactive communication process that may take place whenever we want something from someone else or another person wants something from us.

Just because we negotiate all the time does not necessarily mean that we are competent negotiators. In the context of meeting our friends we can just shrug our shoulders and say, maybe next time we will go to see a film I want to see. However, for lawyers the stakes are much higher. This is why you will receive extensive professional training on negotiating skills if you decide to pursue a career in law. At this stage all we want to do is to introduce you to some of the concepts which underpin effective negotiation. The notes below are drawn from two leading works on effective negotiation: *Getting to Yes* by Roger Fisher and William Ury (Arrow Business Books, London 1987) and *Bargaining for Advantage* by G. Richard Shell (Penguin, London 1999) are readable and informative guides to effective and confident negotiation. We would recommend them highly.

Negotiation styles

The starting point for improving your negotiation skills is to understand your own personality – what it is that you bring to the negotiating table. For instance, if you are in general a pretty co-operative sort of person, no training course in the world is going to transform you into a hard, competitive negotiator.

Activity 4

Now try an activity which will help you reflect upon your likely negotiating style.

You should think about the various styles of negotiating and consider which most closely reflects your behaviour. Most of us are compromisers when we negotiate.

We split the difference or find an intermediate point according to some principle which we decide is satisfactory. Very few of us have the skills to be good problem-solvers when we are under pressure. However, it is possible to improve your problem-solving skills by thorough preparation for the negotiation. This can enable you to understand the different interests of the parties and perhaps change the focus of the negotiation – to expand the pie. We discuss this below. Note that underpinning these negotiating styles are two basic types of personality: the competitive personality and the co-operative one.

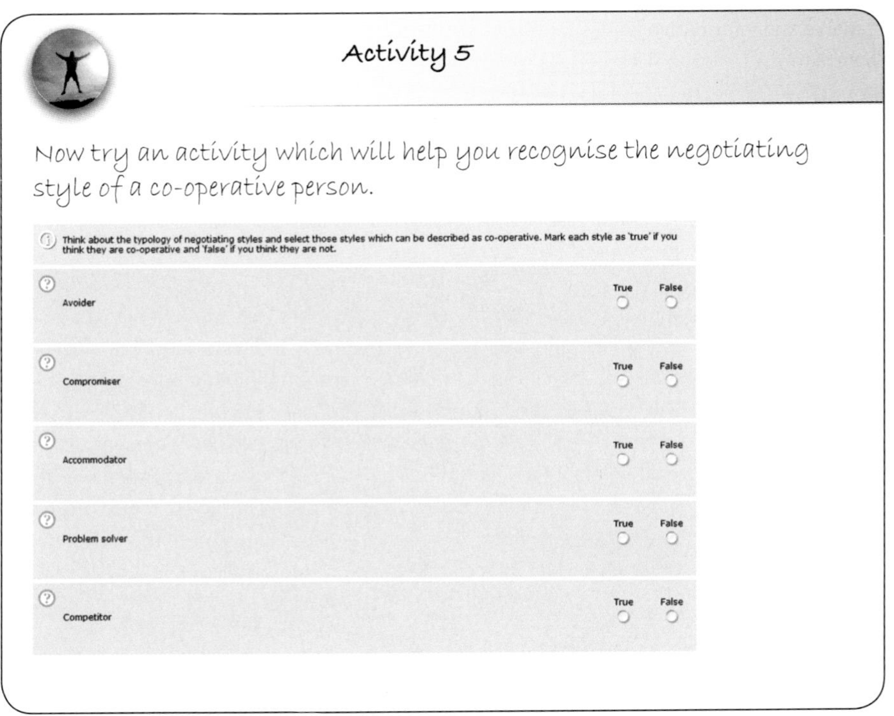

Activity 5

Now try an activity which will help you recognise the negotiating style of a co-operative person.

Think about the typology of negotiating styles and select those styles which can be described as co-operative. Mark each style as 'true' if you think they are co-operative and 'false' if you think they are not.

	True	False
Avoider	○	○
Compromiser	○	○
Accommodator	○	○
Problem solver	○	○
Competitor	○	○

Of course there are two parties to negotiation and when you are involved in a negotiation you should also take some time to work out which is the preferred style of your opponent. You will have to adapt your own strategies to their style – it is not necessarily productive, for instance, to co-operate with a competitive person. However, it is important to understand that a successful negotiation is not about 'winning', it is about being effective. Effective negotiation primarily depends upon preparation.

Preparation

You prepare for a negotiation by gathering information, both about your own interests, resources, and alternatives, and about the other party. You must find out as many facts as you can about the subject matter of the negotiation. So, for instance, if you are trying to negotiate about the level of rent you are paying, you must research rent levels of similar properties. It is not enough to

» glossary

» glossary

guess, and it can be fatal to lie. One crucial element of preparation is to understand the significance of the concept of Best Alternative to a Negotiated Agreement (BATNA). You have to focus on the consequences of not negotiating – what would happen if you walked away from the negotiation, rather than what you think you 'ought' to get from the negotiation. Imagine that you are representing someone who has been dismissed, and negotiating with the employer to settle the case. Your client's BATNA would be going to the employment tribunal, which would involve your fees, time and anxiety and no certainty of winning the case. The purpose of the negotiation is to do better than the BATNA, and not to reach some level of payment that you might consider fair.

You should not go into a negotiation without knowing the BATNA. You should also try to work out what the other party's BATNA is likely to be. In the context of an employment dispute, the employer's BATNA is likely to be similar to the former employee's – going to the employment tribunal to resolve the dispute. However, his or her legal advice is probably more expensive than the employee's and the employer is also likely to have greater concerns about bad publicity, and the costs to the organisation of providing witnesses. What matters is the relative strengths of the BATNAs. The stronger your BATNA the more powerful your negotiation position is.

Next you should prepare a list of possible areas for negotiation. List the most obvious issues, but don't stop there, try to think beyond the obvious. What other interests might the other party have? Work out how important each issue is, and how important the issue is likely to be to the other party. Look at where your interests coincide and where there may be possibilities for compromise. In employment cases your prime concern will be to negotiate about compensation for the dismissal, but you should also think about the importance of a reference, holiday pay and notice pay. The employer may place a high value on confidentiality of the outcome. This might not be significant to the employee, so may provide a useful area for compromise – you give us what we want in compensation and we will guarantee you confidentiality, for instance.

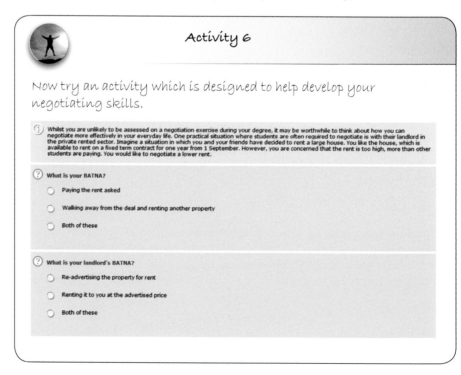

Activity 6

Now try an activity which is designed to help develop your negotiating skills.

Whilst you are unlikely to be assessed on a negotiation exercise during your degree, it may be worthwhile to think about how you can negotiate more effectively in your everyday life. One practical situation where students are often required to negotiate is with their landlord in the private rented sector. Imagine a situation in which you and your friends have decided to rent a large house. You like the house, which is available to rent on a fixed term contract for one year from 1 September. However, you are concerned that the rent is too high, more than other students are paying. You would like to negotiate a lower rent.

What is your BATNA?

- Paying the rent asked
- Walking away from the deal and renting another property
- Both of these

What is your landlord's BATNA?

- Re-advertising the property for rent
- Renting it to you at the advertised price
- Both of these

One other essential feature in preparing for negotiation is to disentangle positions from interests. If you argue about positions one party wins and one party loses. If you argue about interests then it is likely that to a greater or lesser extent both parties can have their interests met. So a landlord who decides that she is not going to accept a penny less than the advertised rent for the property is taking a position rather than considering her interests in maximising her revenue. Similarly, students who say they are not going to pay one penny more than their friends in rent are taking a position and not considering their interests.

There are other skills involved in effective negotiation. Two skills which are particularly worth mentioning are discussed below.

Listening

Whilst preparation is important you must listen carefully during the negotiations to see if the other party reveals needs and interests that you have not previously taken into account. The information may not be revealed directly to you, but may be in asides. For instance, in our example above the landlord may say that she prefers to let to female students because they look after the property better, and you are a group of young women. You have learned information which strengthens your position. You can also ask questions, summarise the discussion to date, and test that you have understood what is of importance to the other party by asking them. Remember that quite often the other party cannot say something explicitly because they do not have authority to say it, but they do try to signal possibilities to you and are expecting a response. Here is an example of a typical dialogue:

> *You say* – this offer is not good enough
>
> *They say* – it's the only one on the table. It's the deal we want, though clearly you want something as far away as possible from this.

On the face of it the other party is saying 'we're not moving', but in reality by adding the extra sentence – even though it is not couched in positive terms – they are offering you an opportunity. They are possibly saying that they want **you** to come back with a new version of their offer which might be more palatable to you, and which would get negotiations fruitfully under way.

If we put this in the context of negotiating about the rent level for the house, there may be an opportunity for you to come back with an offer to move into the property one month earlier for a lower rent, which will actually give the landlord a higher income over the period of the letting.

Snell puts the point succinctly:

> You often get more by finding out what the other person wants than you do by clever arguments supporting what you need.

It can be difficult to listen! We would recommend that you always take someone with you when you negotiate, whose role is to listen and take full notes if possible. Read the notes later and work out where you have been given opportunities to expand the offer the other party has made.

Using language to defuse situations

Effective negotiators avoid confrontation and build possibilities for compromise by a careful use of language. For instance, they do not contradict the other party, but use phrases such as 'please correct me if I am wrong' or 'we appreciate what you have done for us'. So in the example of wishing to negotiate a lower rent for a property, our students could say 'Please correct us if we are wrong, but we understand that the house next door is on the market for £200 less per calendar month than the rent you want us to pay'. Or they could say, 'We appreciate what you have done for us, in agreeing to rent the house to us from September, however we have some concerns about the rent level'. This demonstrates some empathy with the position of the landlord, and allows negotiations to continue.

Key Point

Effective negotiation requires:

- that you understand your particular negotiating style
- that you understand the negotiating style of the other party
- excellent preparation
- a firm grasp of your BATNA and that of the other party
- effective listening skills
- skilled use of language.

Conclusion

It is not appropriate during the undergraduate stage of your education to provide you with more detailed examples of the skills used in ADR. However, we hope that this has been a useful introduction, and that you can think about applying the principles we have outlined in your everyday life. There are times even during the academic stage of study when it is useful to understand that insisting on legal rights is counter-productive. So, for instance, the complexity of imposing a positive covenant on land might not be proportionate to the desired outcome, or the expense and stress involved in suing for contractual damages for illegal eviction may make the legal right unattractive to the victim. Such points, however, while demonstrating insight, are always likely to be marginal to the main focus of academic tests of legal understanding. Nonetheless, appreciating something about these skills at this point in your career should stand you in good stead for the future. Don't forget negotiating skills will be useful whatever career you decide to pursue.

Links

The Ministry of Justice provides extensive information on ADR
http://www.justice.gov.uk/whatwedo/alternativedisputeresolution.htm

The Advice Services Alliance runs a website dedicated to ADR
http://www.adrnow.co.uk/

For examples of ADR in practice you can look at Nominet UK which runs a dispute resolution service in connection with domain names
http://www.nominet.org.uk/

» Glossary

Academic articles [also 'scholarly articles'] Work (e.g. an essay) written by an academic expert in a particular field, interpreting or designed to explore an area of law, particularly contentious areas. These are extremely useful as reference sources for a deeper understanding of the law and for explorations and critique of the concepts and arguments within your own work.

Act of Parliament [also 'Statute'] A document setting out legal rules and which has (usually) passed through both Houses of Parliament in the form of a **bill** before receiving **Royal Assent** from the **Crown**.

Actus reus [Latin: a guilty act] One of the essential elements of a crime that must be proved to secure a conviction.

Advocacy The skill of arguing a case in a court setting.

Alternative dispute resolution (ADR) Any of a number of different techniques used to resolve **civil disputes** without the need for **litigation**. Examples are **arbitration**, **mediation**, **conciliation**.

Arbitration A type of alternative dispute resolution (ADR) in which an independent third party hears both sides in a dispute and makes a decision to resolve it. The arbitrator is impartial and in most cases the arbitrator's decision is legally binding on both sides.

Amendment The alteration of an existing law, either by passage of a new law (**statute**) inserting a new provision into an existing law, or by a piece of **delegated legislation**, where the statute being amended permits this.

Appellate courts Any courts which hear appeals from judgments and rulings of trial courts or lower appeals courts.

Assessments The main way, other than by examination, that you are likely to be tested at university. Assessments can take the form of writing essays, answers to problem questions, compiling case notes, multiple choice questions etc.

AustLII Australian Legal Information Institute. A pioneering service offering databases of freely available Australian federal and state law and other legal materials (http://www.austlii.edu.au/).

BAILII See **British and Irish Legal Information Institute**.

Bar The collective term for all barristers. To be 'called to the bar' means to be formally admitted to the profession by one of the **Inns of Court.**

Bar Council The organisation charged with furthering the interests of and of supporting barristers.

Barrister A legal practitioner (lawyer) able to plead at the **Bar**, meaning **advocating** for parties in court or at **tribunals**. A barrister must be a member of one of the four **Inns of Court**, which will have 'called him/her to the Bar' when admitted to the profession, following professional training.

BATNA The Best Alternative to a Negotiated Agreement – the best outcome that could be expected if parties walked away from **negotiation**. Negotiators should have this in mind when trying to negotiate a settlement for the parties they represent.

Bibliography A bibliography is a list of works used when researching a topic, e.g. for an essay. The listings in a bibliography should include author, title, date of publication, place of publication, publisher, page references (if relevant, e.g. for a chapter in a book or an **academic article** in a **journal** or **periodical**. Using a bibliography accurately to reference everything quoted or otherwise referred to in your work helps to avoid **plagiarism** – although there must be correct referencing throughout the work as well as merely listing books, articles etc. at the end of an essay is not enough.

Bills A draft of a proposed **Act of Parliament**. This normally needs to be passed by both Houses of Parliament before being given **Royal Assent** and signed into law. Bills can be public or private and their passage through Parliament will differ depending on their type.

Boolean searching A method of electronic database searching which involves linking terms with AND, OR, etc. to increase relevance.

British and Irish Legal Information Institute (BAILII) Access to databases of freely available legislation, case law and other legal materials from the UK and Ireland (http://www.bailii.org/).

Broadsheet Broadsheet newspapers are sometimes referred to as 'quality' or 'serious' newspapers, as opposed to tabloids. The term originated with their large paper format, although many have now moved to a smaller format.

Bundle of authorities A collection of previous decisions by appellate courts which provide legal guidance to a court (including **moot** courts) on questions in a current **civil dispute** (i.e. the **precedents** being relied upon); lawyers cite the previously decided cases as 'authorities' for his/her legal positions and contentions. A 'bundle' may also contain relevant **statute** law and, on occasion, academic or technical legal writing on a legal point.

CanLII Canadian Legal Information Institute. Databases of freely available Canadian federal and state law and other legal materials, in French and English (http://www.canlii.org/).

Cardiff Index to Legal Abbreviations The authoritative source for abbreviation of legal publications, developed at Cardiff Law School. The Cardiff Index covers legal publications from the British Isles, the Commonwealth and the United States, including those covering international and comparative law. A wide selection of major foreign language law publications is also included.

Casebooks Books containing extracts of the main cases you will need to know, as well as 'commentary' on them, included all together and organised by topic. They are often used in conjunction with **textbooks**. You can also see '**cases and materials**' books. These are like extended versions of casebooks, including not only cases and commentary on these, but other materials as well, such as extracts of articles or statutes, with commentary.

Cases Used here to mean the arguments put forward by both sides of a court action, as well as the report of the judicial decision.

Case note A written report and comment on a decided case, usually written by an academic with an interest in the area the case falls into.

Catchphrases See **Catchwords**.

Catchwords Keywords or phrases at the start of a law report, which define the legal issues of the case.

Caveat emptor [Latin: Let the buyer beware] The principle that a purchaser in a private sale takes responsibility for any defects in the wares bought.

Chapter number The number given to each **Act of Parliament** in a parliamentary session.

Citations The quoting of or reference for a legal **case** or authority.

Civil dispute A dispute arising in civil law (as opposed to criminal) between one person or entity against another person or entity, to be decided in a court of law, sometimes just called a 'lawsuit' or 'suit' (particularly in the US). The legal claims within a civil dispute are called 'causes of action' and the object of the court case is to resolve the dispute – usually by providing a remedy which, in most cases, will be damages (compensation), although other remedies are available in some instances.

Civil law The term 'civil law' has a number of meanings, the most common being either: (i) private law, as opposed to public or administrative law; (ii) a legal system based on Roman law, as opposed to **common law**.

Civil Procedure Rules Rules governing the procedures of **litigation**.

Claimant A party to a **case** seeking a remedy or demanding a right from the defendant.

Command Papers Documents prepared by the Government on 'Royal Command' – i.e. on behalf of the Queen – and presented to Parliament for consideration. Command Papers is the umbrella term for both White and Green Papers.

Common law The law based on rules developed by the 'common' (Royal) courts, as opposed to regional variations that existed before the time of the Norman conquest. Often used as another term interchangeable with 'case law'.

Conciliation A type of alternative dispute resolution (ADR) in which a third party helps the people in dispute to resolve their problem. The conciliator should be impartial and should not take one party's side.

Convenor A course convenor is the academic in charge of and responsible for the day-to-day running and usually teaching of a course or module.

Counsel Used singularly or as a plural to mean a barrister or barristers, e.g. 'counsel for the defence'.

Court of Appeal The Court of Appeal, which sits in London at the Royal Courts of Justice, consists of two divisions, Civil and Criminal. The Civil Division, which hears appeals from the three divisions of the High Court (Chancery, Queen's Bench and Family Division), the County Courts across England and Wales, and from certain Tribunals such as the Employment Appeal Tribunal, the Immigration Appeal Tribunal, the Lands Tribunal and the Social Security Commissioners. The Criminal Division hears appeals from the Crown Court. The Court of Appeal is the highest court within the Supreme Court of Judicature, which also includes the High Court and Crown Court.

Appeals from a Court of Appeal decision go to the **House of Lords**.

Crown The Queen (or King), as a representative of the state.

Deadlines The dates by which a formal piece of work must be completed and/or submitted to be marked.

Decision (EU) One of the forms of secondary legislation of the **European Union**. Decisions may be addressed to member states or to persons, and are binding upon them in their entirety.

Defendant A party against whom court proceedings (a **case**) is brought, by the **claimant**.

Devolution The statutory granting of powers from the central government of a state to government at national, regional or local level. It differs from federalism in that the powers devolved may be temporary and ultimately reside in central government, thus the state remains, de jure, unitary. Any devolved parliaments or assemblies can be repealed by central government in the same way as an ordinary statute can be. Federal systems, or federacies, differ in that sub-state government is guaranteed in the constitution. Devolution can be mainly financial, e.g. giving areas a budget which was formerly administered by central government. However, the power to make legislation relevant to the area may also be granted. In the UK, devolved government was created following simple majority referenda in Wales and Scotland in September 1997. In 1999, the Scottish Parliament, National Assembly for Wales and Northern Ireland Assembly were established.

Directive (EU) One of the forms of secondary legislation of the **European Union**. Directives are not directly applicable, but need to be brought into effect in member states by bringing in new legislative measures, or amending domestic legislation.

Distinguish To distinguish a case means to argue that the rule or precedent set in one court decision does not apply to a new case although there is an apparent similarity (i.e. it is 'distinguished').

EISIL Electronic Information System for International Law. This service gives access to authentic texts of international legal materials. It is an essential resource for the study of international law (www.eisil.org/).

Eiusdem generis [Latin: Of the same kind] The rule of **statutory interpretation** that says that when a list of specific items in a **statute** that belong to the same kind or class is followed by general words it is to be interpreted as confined to other items of the same class by a judge, when determining the true meaning of an **Act of Parliament**.

English Reports The leading collection of early law reports, from 1220 to 1865. English Reports was published in 178 volumes, and contains over 250 different series of reports. It is available in law libraries, and also on **Justis** and **Hein Online**.

ePolitix An internet service whose aim is to improve communication between politicians and the public. ePolitix contains a large amount of current information and commentary and is a valuable resource for keeping track of new legal and political developments (http://www.epolitix.com/).

Essay A written piece of work on any subject, usually fairly short in length, often undertaken for assessment or in an exam. Longer, more detailed essays are usually called dissertations.

Eur-Lex The **European Union**'s legal portal, containing the primary and secondary legislation and other legal resources of the EU (http://eur-lex.europa.eu/en/).

Europa The **European Union**'s web portal (http://europa.eu/). It is published in all 23 EU languages simultaneously – a remarkable publishing project.

European Court of Human Rights A court established by the 1950 European Convention on Human Rights, based in Strasbourg, France. Individuals can take cases against countries which are signatory to the Convention, claiming that the action of the state has somehow encroached upon the human rights and freedoms guaranteed by the Convention.

European Union A union of mainly Western European countries committed to European economic and political integration (known as the European Community, based originally on signatories to the 1957 Treaty of Rome), as well as, since 1 November 1993 (when the term 'Union' began to be used), two intergovernmental 'pillars' created by the Maastricht Treaty to deal with foreign affairs and with immigration and justice.

Explanatory notes Notes on a **statute** explaining the ambit of the **legislation** and how it may (or may not) be applied.

Expressio unius ext exculsio alterius [Latin: the inclusion of the one is the exclusion of the other] The rule of **statutory interpretation** that says that when a list of specific items in a **statute** is not followed by general words it is to be interpreted as exhaustive by a judge, when determining the true meaning of an **Act of Parliament**.

Formative assessment A formative assessment is one in which undertaking the assessment constitutes a learning experience in its own right. Writing an essay or undertaking a class presentation, for example, can be valuable formative activities as a means of enhancing substantive knowledge as well as for developing research, communication, intellectual and organisational skills. Therefore, formative assessments are not assessed in the sense that they are included in the formal grading of work. See http://www.ukcle.ac.uk/resources/assessment/formative.html for more information.

Gazette A term usually applied to a journal publishing official notices and news, such as government appointments, e.g. the *London Gazette,* but also adopted by some organisations, e.g. the *Law Society's Gazette*.

Golden rule The rule of **statutory interpretation** that says that ordinary words in a **statute** must be given their ordinary meaning and technical words their technical meanings by a judge, when determining the true meaning of an **Act of Parliament**, unless absurdity would result.

Government The body of ministers (Members of Parliament) charged with the running of the state.

Green Paper A type of **Command Paper**, generally in the form of a discussion document.

Halsbury's Halsbury's Laws of England and Halsbury's Statutes are two old established and authoritative publications, providing commentary on the law. Halsbury's Laws is a multi-volume legal encyclopaedia, and

Halsbury's Statutes is the standard source for tracing legislation in its paper form. They are both available in modified form on **LexisNexis Butterworths**.

Hansard Officially known as The Official Report of Parliamentary Debates – a verbatim record of debates and all other proceedings in Parliament.

Headnote A summary of a case, giving an outline of the facts and the principle decision, prefixed to the beginning of the report of decided cases.

Hein Online A commercial legal service offering access to back issues of a large range of legal journals, as well as other materials.

House of Commons The representative (lower) chamber of Parliament composed of Members of Parliament (MPs), one elected by the populace of each constituency of the United Kingdom.

House of Lords The term has two meanings: (i) the non-representative (upper) chamber of Parliament, composed of the remaining hereditary peers and appointed peers, and (ii) the more properly termed Lords of Appeal in Ordinary (**Law Lords**), the members of the House who have judicial function as the highest and final court of appeal for both civil and criminal cases in the UK.

Hybrid bill A **public bill** that affects the interests of individuals, organisations or local authorities, and which therefore has the characteristics of both public and **private bills**. See http://www.parliament.uk/documents/upload/L05.pdf for detailed information.

Incorporated Council of Law Reporting (ICLR) The organisation set up in 1865 to reform the publication of law reports. It publishes the series collectively known as the *Law Reports*, and also the Weekly Law Reports and several other series (http://www.lawreports.co.uk/).

Inns of Court The ancient legal societies, all situated in central London, now charged with part of a barrister's professional legal training. Everyone who becomes a **barrister** must become a member of one of the four remaining Inns: Gray's Inn, Inner Temple, Middle Temple and Lincoln's Inn.

Intute A UK service providing access to quality web resources in all subjects, divided by type and topic. The primary division is into broad subject areas, with law being a sub category of Social Sciences (http://www.intute.ac.uk/socialsciences/law/).

Journal indexes Indexes to the articles published in a range of journals, and the most efficient way of finding articles. The main legal journal indexes are *Legal Journals Index* (on **Westlaw**) and *Index to Legal Periodicals* (separate database).

Journals The authentic record of proceedings in both Houses of Parliament (as opposed to the verbatim record, Hansard).

Justis One of the major commercial legal services, containing separate databases of UK and EU case law and legislation, invaluable for students doing legal research.

Law Commission A body established by the Law Commissions Act 1965 to keep the law under review with a view to systematically developing and reforming it, including codifications, repeals of unnecessary and obsolete laws, and the elimination of inconsistencies (note: Scotland has its own Commission).

Lawlinks A gateway to legal information edited at the University of Kent (http://www.kent.ac.uk/lawlinks/).

Law Lords The Lords of Appeal in Ordinary, judicial members of the **House of Lords**.

Law Reports Reports of decisions handed down by the courts. Since 1865 these have mainly been handled by the Incorporated Council of Law Reporting, which publishes *The Law Reports* – reports of cases selected by the Council for their importance, written by lawyers and approved by the judges presiding. Further to the Council, there are other commercially published reports, e.g. the *All England Law Reports*.

Law Society The professional body for solicitors in England and Wales, incorporated by Royal Charter in 1831, which exists to further the professional interests and development of solicitors and to undertake statutory functions in relation to the admission to practice, conduct and disciplinary matters. It is also responsible for the examination of those intending to become solicitors and the organisation of educational and vocational training courses through the College of Law and recognised universities.

Lawtel A commercial legal service aimed at the UK market, associated with **Westlaw**.

Lectures (Usually) a one-way discourse giving key information on a subject to a class of students or another audience.

Legal aid Money paid from a scheme using public money to fund the legal costs of those unable to afford the costs themselves, administered by the *Legal Aid Board*.

Legislation The whole or any part of a country's written law, usually used to mean **Acts of Parliament** or **Statutes**, but also including delegated or secondary legislation.

LexisNexis Butterworths (LNB) One of the major commercial legal services, containing a large number of separate databases of legal materials, including legislation, case law and journals, invaluable for students when doing legal research. LNB is a US service with a separate UK interface.

LII Legal Information Institute. A service for the provision of free access to US legal materials, including primary and secondary sources. LII is a unique and extensive resource (http://www.law.cornell.edu/).

Literal rule The rule of **statutory interpretation** that says that words in the **statute** that are reasonably capable of having only one meaning must be given that meaning by a judge, when determining the true meaning of an **Act of Parliament**, whatever the outcome.

Litigation The taking of legal action by a person party to a court action (litigant).

LNB See **LexisNexis Butterworths**.

Lord Chancellor A senior and important role in the government of the UK, the Lord Chancellor is appointed by the **Crown** on the advice of the Prime Minister and is, by convention, always a peer, although there is no legal impediment to the appointment of a commoner. The Lord Chancellor's original responsibility was to act as the custodian of the Great Seal. He is a member of the Cabinet and, by law, is responsible for the efficient functioning and independence of the courts. Formerly, the

Lord Chancellor was also the presiding officer of the **House of Lords**, and the head of the judiciary, but the Constitutional Reform Act 2005 transferred both of these roles to others.

Mediation A type of Alternative Dispute Resolution (ADR) in which an independent third party helps disputing parties to resolve their dispute. It differs from other forms of ADR in that the disputants, not the mediator, decide the terms of the agreement.

Mens rea [Latin: A guilty mind] The state of mind that the prosecution must prove, along with the ***actus reus*** in order to secure a criminal conviction.

Mischief rule The rule of **statutory interpretation** that says that when a statute aims to cure a defect in the law, any ambiguity is to be resolved in such a way as to favour that aim by a judge, when determining the true meaning of an **Act of Parliament**.

Moot A moot is a mock court **case**, where students act as **advocates** to research and argue the law in support of their supposed clients' claim or defence. Moots are usually set in the **Court of Appeal** or sometimes the **House of Lords**, as the case will be an appeal on **points of law**, rather than a trial of the facts.

Mooter Someone who participates in a **moot**.

Negotiation The process of discussion, outside of a court in which lawyers work and bargain to gain the desired outcome for their clients, without resorting to **litigation**.

Neutral citations A system for the citation of cases independent of any commercial law report series. This was introduced in a Practice Direction in 2001, and extended to all new judgments in 2002 (http://www.hmcourts-service.gov.uk/cms/816.htm).

Noscitur a Sociis [Latin: It is known from its associates.] In **statutory interpretation**, when a word is ambiguous, its meaning may be determined by reference to the rest of the statute.

NZLII New Zealand Legal Information Institute. Databases of freely available New Zealand law (http://www.nzlii.org/).

Office for Public Sector Information (OPSI) The government office which regulates the provision of public sector information, and hosts legislation online and other official publications (http://www.opsi.gov.uk/).

Official Journal of the European Union The daily publication in which EU legislation is published, as well as other information and notices. The OJ is available online on the **Eur-Lex** web service.

OSCOLA Oxford Standard for the Citation of Legal Authorities. This has been developed at Oxford Law Faculty, and is regarded as the most authoritative citation manual for law.

Parliament The legislature of the UK, made up of the Sovereign (Crown) and the two Houses of Parliament, charged with the enactment of **legislation**, the sanctioning of taxes and public expenditure, and the scrutiny and criticism of **Government** policy and administration.

Periodical Another name for a journal, covering publications which are published regularly.

Personal development plans/portfolio Personal development planning is a component of what is known as a Progress File. You may have started a Progress File at school, but it may be something you have yet to be involved in. All universities are beginning to introduce Progress Files, of which there are three main components: a transcript of academic grades and achievements; personal development records and reflections; and a personal development plan – the process that is undertaken by the individual to reflect upon their own learning and achievement and to plan for their own educational, academic and career development.

Plagiarism In law this means taking the writings or literary concepts (a plot, characters, words) of another and selling and/or publishing them as one's own product. Quotes which are brief or are acknowledged as quotes, with accurate referencing, do not constitute plagiarism. The actual author can bring a lawsuit for appropriation of his/her work and against the plagiarist, and recover the profits. Normally plagiarism is not a crime, but it can be used as the basis of a fraud charge or copyright infringement, if prior creation can be proved. In terms of studying, plagiarism is similar, in that it is using someone else's work (e.g. in an essay you submit) without accurately referencing it. This includes work from **textbooks**, **casebooks**, **academic articles**, newspapers etc. – and even fellow students.

Plaintiff Now known as the **claimant**, the party to a **case** seeking a remedy or demanding a right from the **defendant**.

Point of law An issue arising in a civil lawsuit or criminal prosecution which only relates to determination of what the law is, how it is applied to the facts in the case, and other purely legal points in contention. All 'points of law' arising before, during, and sometimes after a trial are to be determined solely by the judge and not by a jury. 'Points of law' are differentiated from 'points of fact', which are decided in trials of first instance by the jury and only by the judge if there is no jury.

Pre-action protocols Requirements placed upon parties prior to **litigation** being initiated.

Precedent The part of a judicial decision from either the High Court, Court of Appeal or **House of Lords** comprising the ***ratio decidendi***, which establishes the legal rule (authority) in the future on the same legal question decided in the prior judgment and therefore binds lower courts. The doctrine that a lower court must follow a precedent is called ***stare decisis***.

Presumptions A rule of law which permits a court to assume a fact is true until such time as there is evidence to disprove or outweigh it (known as 'rebutting' it). Presumptions are based upon a particular set of apparent facts paired with established laws, logic and reasoning. They are rebuttable in that they can be refuted by factual evidence, i.e. one can present facts to persuade the judge that the presumption is not true. Examples of operative presumptions are: a child born of a husband and wife living together is presumed to be the natural child of the husband unless there is conclusive proof he is not; a person who has disappeared and not heard from for seven years is presumed to be dead, but the presumption could be rebutted if he/she is found alive; an accused person is presumed innocent until proven guilty.

Private bill A bill which affects individuals or organisations, or a local authority, by whom it is presented. See http://www.parliament.uk/documents/upload/L04.pdf for detailed information.

Private Member's bill A bill introduced into Parliament by a private member (back-bench MP). See http://www.parliament.uk/documents/upload/L02.pdf for detailed information.

Public bill A bill relating to matters of public concern, introduced either by the Government or a private member.

Qualifying law subjects The seven subjects/modules that undergraduate law students in the UK need to take and pass in order to be eligible to later become a professional lawyer (**solicitor** or **barrister**). These are defined by the **Law Society** and **Bar Council** and are Constitutional Law, European Law, Contract Law, Criminal Law, Tort Law, Property Law and Equity.

Ratio decidendi [Latin: the reason for deciding] The principle(s) of law on which a court bases its decision of a **case**, and the part of a case that is binding on inferior courts by virtue of the doctrine of **precedent**.

Rebuttal Evidence or argument introduced to counter, disprove or contradict the opposition's evidence or a **presumption**, or a responsive legal argument (i.e. responding to points made in argument by the opposing **counsel** in a case).

Regulation (EU) One of the forms of secondary legislation of the **European Union**. Regulations are of general application and directly applicable without the need for domestic legislative measures.

Repeal The total or partial annulment or revocation of an existing law, by passage of a repealing **statute** (a new law).

Rights of audience A term generally applied to solicitors who can argue cases before a court on behalf of clients, a position normally reserved for barristers.

Royal Assent The conventional and formal agreement of the **Crown** which converts a **bill** into an **Act of Parliament**.

Scholarly articles See **Academic articles**.

Seminars [see also 'tutorials'] A small class at university for more detailed discussion of points raised in lectures and from reading, and issues that arise from them.

Serial A term meaning journal which you will sometimes encounter in libraries.

Skeleton argument The bare bones of the argument, including sources that will be relied upon in submissions, that one 'side' presents to the court, before the trial or appeal begins (also used in **moots**).

Solicitor A legal practitioner admitted to practise law under the provisions of the Solicitors Act 1974. Solicitors undertake more general tasks than **barristers**, including the giving of legal advice and the conduct of some legal proceedings. Some solicitors have 'rights of audience', which means that they can argue cases before a court on behalf of clients.

Standing Committee (Parliament) The former term for a committee of Parliament appointed to take the Committee Stage of public bills. Since 2006 these have been re-named Public Bill Committees, and form one of several types of committee under the umbrella term General Committee. See http://www.parliament.uk/documents/upload/L06.pdf for detailed information.

Stare decisis [Latin: to stand by a decision] *Stare decisis* is the doctrine that a trial court is bound by higher court decisions (**precedents**) on a **point of law** which is raised in the lower court. Reliance on such **precedents** is required of trial courts until such time as an appellate court changes the rule, for the trial court cannot ignore the **precedent** (even when the trial judge believes it is 'bad law').

Statute [also 'Act of Parliament'] A document setting out legal rules and which has (usually) passed through both Houses of Parliament in the form of a **bill** before receiving **Royal Assent** from the **Crown**.

Statute Book The term statute book has two meanings, either (i) the book or books containing a country's **statute** law, or (ii) a book collating any and all relevant **statutes** and other **legislation** for a module of study.

Statute Law Database The official revised edition of the primary legislation of the UK, launched in 2006 (http://www.statutelaw.gov.uk/).

Statutory Instruments A form of delegated or secondary **legislation**, including Regulations or Orders, which give a power to make or amend statutory rules within the meaning given to them by pre-existing **statutes** (primary legislation).

Statutory interpretation The process of a judge (or judges) determining, using certain rules and presumptions, the true meaning of **Acts of Parliament**.

Summative assessment A summative assessment is one that is usually undertaken at the end of a period of learning in order to generate a grade that reflects the student's performance. The traditional unseen end of module examination is a typical form of summative assessment, as are graded essays and problem questions, or even presentations set as pieces of coursework. See http://www.ukcle.ac.uk/resources/assessment/formative.html for more information.

Textbooks A text written by an author on a particular area or discipline of law (e.g. contract law, family law, European law etc.). Not all textbooks carry the same 'weight' – e.g. some are more properly classed as 'introductory' while others go deeper into the subject and are more comprehensive in their treatment of it.

Transcript The text of judgments, without the editorial material provided in law reports, available before a law report is prepared. Transcripts of new cases are widely available on **Westlaw** and **LexisNexis Butterworths**, but are replaced by **law reports** if and when these are published. The **House of Lords** issues transcripts of its judgments shortly after they are handed down. All publicly available transcripts are on **BAILII**, and a number of other transcript services exist, including Casetrack.

Travaux Preparatoires Preparatory works forming the background to the enactment of legislation, e.g. the recommendations of a Royal Commission or follow-up of a public consultation document.

Tribunals A panel or board appointed to adjudicate in some matter, though not in a court setting. This can take the form of an administrative tribunal (which decides claims and disputes arising in connection with the administration of legislation, e.g. employment or mental health tribunal), domestic tribunal (which exercises jurisdiction over the internal affairs of a particular profession or association, e.g. the disciplinary committee of the **Law Society**) or tribunal of inquiry (used to investigate a matter of public importance).

Tutorials [See also 'seminars'] Used here to mean a small class at university for more detailed discussion of points raised in lectures and from reading, and issues that arise from them.

Web of Science The Web of Science is a major cross-disciplinary index to journals literature available online.

Westlaw One of the major commercial legal services, containing a large number of separate databases of legal materials, including legislation, case law and journals, invaluable for students when doing legal research. Westlaw is a US service with a separate UK interface.

White paper A type of **Command Paper**, containing statements of policy or explanations of proposed legislation.

WorldLII World Legal Information Institute. WorldLII has free access to law worldwide and has links to growing number Legal Information Institutes throughout the world as well as to other free resources (http://www.worldlii.org/).

Writing in the first person Writing as the person speaking, and referring to him or herself, by e.g. using the pronoun 'I'. For example, when putting forward an opinion or argument in an **essay**, using 'I think...'

» Common abbreviations

This list omits abbreviations to law journals and law reports, apart from a very few, as these can be found on the Cardiff Index to Legal Abbreviations http://www.legalabbrevs.cardiff.ac.uk/

AC	Law Reports: Appeal Cases
ADR	Alternative dispute resolution
AIT	Asylum and Immigration Tribunal
All ER	All England Law Reports
ASBO	Anti social behaviour order
AST	Asylum Support Trinunal
BAILII	British & Irish Legal Information Institute
BATNA	Best alternative to a negotiated agreement
BVC	Bar Vocational Course
CA	Court of Appeal
CAB	Citizens' Advice Bureau
CCJ	County Court Judgment
Cd	Command Papers (1900–1918)
CE	Council of Europe
Ch	Law Reports: Chancery Division
CICAP	Criminal Injuries Compensation Appeals Panel
CJ	Lord Chief Justice (when after a name)
CLS	Community Legal Service
Cm	Command Papers (1986 to present)
Cmd	Command Papers (1919–1956)
CML Rev	Common Market Law Review
CMLR	Common Market Law Reports
Cmnd	Command Papers (1957–1986)
CoE	Council of Europe
CPR	Civil Procedure Rules
CPS	Crown Prosecution Service
Cr App R	Criminal Appeal Reports
CRE	Commission for Racial Equality
Crim LR	Criminal Law Review
CST	Care Standards Tribunal
DBERR	Department for Business, Enterprise and Regulatory Reform
DCA	Department of Constitutional Affairs
DCMS	Department for Culture Media and Sport

DCSF	Department for Children, Schools and Families
DEFRA	Department for Environment, Food and Rural Affairs
DfT	Department for Transport
DH	Department of Health
DIUS	Department for Innovation, Universities and Skills
DPP	Director of Public Prosecutions
DTI	Department of Trade and Industry (now replaced by DBERR)
DWP	Department for Work and Pensions
EAT	Employment Appeal Tribunal
ECHR	European Convention of Human Rights
ECHR	European Court of Human Rights
ECJ	European Court of Justice
ECR	European Court Reports
EG	Estates Gazette
EISIL	Electronic Information System for International Law
EOC	Equal Opportunities Commission
EP	European Parliament
ER	English Reports
EU	European Union
EWCA Civ	Court of Appeal, Civil Division (England & Wales) in neutral citations
EWCA Crim	Court of Appeal, Criminal Division (England & Wales) in neutral citations
EWHC (TCC)	High Court (Technology & Construction Court) in neutral citations
EWHC (Admlty)	High Court (Admiralty) in neutral citations
EWHC (Ch)	High Court (Chancery Division) in neutral citations
EWHC (Comm)	High Court (Commercial Court) in neutral citations
EWHC (Pat)	High Court (Patents Court) in neutral citations
EWHC (QB)	High Court (Queen's Bench Division) in neutral citations
EWHC Admin	High Court, Administrative Court (England & Wales) in neutral citations
Fam	Law Reports: Family Division
FOI	Freedom of Information
FSA	Financial Services Authority
FSA	Food Standards Authority
FTT	Finance and Tax Tribunal
GCHQ	Government Communications Headquarters
GDL	Graduate Diploma in Law
GRP	Gender Recognition Panel
HC	House of Commons
HC	House of Commons Papers
HC	High Court
HCP	House of Commons Papers
HFEA	Human Fertilisation and Embryology Act
HFEA	Human Fertilisation and Embryology Authority
HL	House of Lords

HL	House of Lords Papers and Bills
HMCS	Her Majesty's Court Service
HO	Home Office
HRA	Human Rights Act
ICC	International Criminal Court
ICCPR	International Covenant on Civil and Political Rights
ICJ	International Court of Justice
ICLR	Incorporated Council of Law Reporting
ICR	Industrial Cases Reports
IFLP	Index to Foreign Legal Periodicals
ILP	Index to Legal Periodicals
IND	Immigration and Nationality Directorate
IPCC	Independent Police Complaints Commission
IPS	Identity and Passport Service
J	Justice (after the name of a judge)
JP	Justice of the Peace/Justice of the Peace Reports
LAG	Legal Action Group
Law Com	Law Commission
LBC	London Borough Council
LC	Law Commission
LC	Lord Chancellor
LCF	Law Centres Federation
LCJ	Lord Chief Justice
LJ	Lord Justice, Lady Justice (after the name of a judge)
LJI	Legal Journals Index
LNB	LexisNexis Butterworths
LPC	Legal Practice Course
LQR	Law Quarterly Review
LS	Legal Studies
LSG	Law Society's Gazette
MEP	Member of the European Parliament
MHRT	Mental Health Review Tribunal
MLR	Modern Law Review
MoD	Ministry of Defence
MoJ	Ministry of Justice
MP	Member of Parliament
MR	Master of the Rolls
NACRO	National Association for the Care & Resettlement of Offenders
NHS	National Health Service
NIO	Northern Ireland Office
NPS	National Probation Service

OFSTED	Office for Standards in Education
OJ	Official Journal of the European Union
ONS	Office for National Statistics
OPSI	Office for Public Sector Information
OSCOLA	Oxford Standard for the Citation of Legal Authorities
PACE	Police and Criminal Evidence Act
PC	Judicial Committee of the Privy Council
PCIJ	Permanent Court of International Justice
PD	Practice Direction
PGDL	Post Graduate Diploma in Law
POAC	Proscribed Organisations Appeal Commission
QB	Law Reports: Queen's Bench Division
QC	Queen's Counsel
R	*Regina, Rex*: the Queen, the King, the Crown
Reg	Regulation
Sch	Schedule
SFA	Serious Fraud Office
SI	Statutory Instrument
SIAC	Special Immigration Appeals Commission
SLD	Statute Law Database
SMP	Scottish Member of Parliament
SOCA	Serious Organised Crime Agency
SSCSA	Social Security and Child Support Appeals
Sub nom	*Sub nominee*; under the name of
Supp	Supplement
TLR	Times Law Reports
TSOL	Treasury Solicitor's Department
UCTA	Unfair Contract Terms Act
UKHL	House of Lords (United Kingdom) in neutral citations
UKPC	Privy Council (United Kingdom) in neutral citations
UKTS	United Kingdom Treaty Series
v	*Versus*, against
VAT	Value Added Tax
VTS	Valuation Tribunal Service
WEU	Women and Equality Unit
WLR	Weekly Law Reports
YJB	Youth Justice Board

» Index